A NEW MISCELLANY-AT-LAW

A New Miscellany-at-Law

∿

Yet Another Diversion for Lawyers and Others

by
The Rt. Hon. Sir Robert Megarry

Edited by Bryan A. Garner

·HART·
PUBLISHING

OXFORD AND PORTLAND, OREGON
2005

THE LAWBOOK EXCHANGE, LTD.
CLARK, NEW JERSEY
2005

Hart Publishing, Salters Boatyard, Folly Bridge, Abingdon Rd, Oxford, OX1 4LB
Telephone: +44 (0)1865 245533 Fax: +44 (0) 1865 794882
E-mail: mail@hartpub.co.uk
Website: http//:www.hartpub.co.uk

British Library Cataloguing in Publication Data Available

ISBN 13: 978-1-84113-554-0 (hardback)
ISBN 10: 1-84113-554-2 (hardback)

Published and distributed in North America (US and Canada) and South America by

The Lawbook Exchange, Ltd.
33 Terminal Avenue
Clark, New Jersey 07066-1321
USA
www.lawbookexchange.com

ISBN 13: 978-1-58477-631-4 The Lawbook Exchange, Ltd.
ISBN 10: 1-58477-631-5 The Lawbook Exchange, Ltd.

Library of Congress Cataloging-in-Publication Data

Megarry, Robert Edgar, Sir, 1910–
    A miscellany-at-law : still another diversion for lawyers and others
/by Sir Robert Megarry ; edited by Bryan A. Garner.
        p. cm.
Clark: The Lawbook Exchange, Ltd and Oxford: Hart Publishing, 2005.
Includes bibliographical references and index.
    ISBN 1-58477-631-5 (cloth : alk. paper)
    1. Law – – Anecdotes. 2. Law – – Humor. 3. Law – – England – – Anecdotes.
    4. Law – – England – – Humor. I. Garner, Bryan A. II. Title.
K183.M44 2005
340 – – dc22
                                                                2005049415

Typeset by Forewords, Oxford in Minion

Printed and bound in Great Britain by TJ International, Padstow, Cornwall

CONTENTS

SUBJECTS

Preface

~

All three volumes of *Miscellany-at-Law* had their fragmentary origin in my second year in reading law at Cambridge in 1930. The first year had been tediously full of history (of the Constitution, and of International Relations) and Roman law. But the second year brought English law, with its vitality and living presence. Every now and then there were phrases and sentences in judgments that were striking and noteworthy, there was wit, and there were remarkable events and curiosities. Some of these soon lost their appeal; but many survived in the notes that I began to make and keep. A quarter of a century later, the survivors, with many after-acquired companions, followed me through my apprenticeship, and into the first *Miscellany-at-Law* (1955).

After eleven years in silk and six on the Bench, there came the *Second Miscellany-at-Law* (1973); and in due time this should have been followed by a *Third*. But instead there came delay. The kindness of many friends as well as my own endeavours had led to a large accumulation of additional quotations, so many of which demanded inclusion. And then age and health gradually intervened, first to slow down and then to halt progress in dealing with what had become an *embarras de richesse.*

Over thirty years after the *Second Miscellany* appeared, there came an unexpected visit by my old friend Bryan Garner, shortly after my 94th birthday. In a trice, all was changed. As soon as he saw the incomplete typescript of this book, and learned of my inertia, he very generously offered to edit it and see it through to publication. He could not be gainsaid; and after I had spent a month's hard labour on revision, division, excision and completion, that is what he has done. My gratitude to him is inexpressible.

There were communication problems in editing in Dallas a book written by an opinionated author in London, but these were greatly lessened by my three daughters, each with the email facility that I lack.

The eldest, Lindsay Merriman, formerly at the Chancery Bar, played a large part in editing the book, as she did for the second *Miscellany*; and Susanna Sale and Jacquetta Megarry did much more than merely maintain the complex communications between London and Dallas.

It is slightly mysterious how the book came to be called *A New Miscellany-at-Law*, rather than *A Third Miscellany-at-Law*. Perhaps it is because the book has become even more miscellaneous than its predecessors. After being given the pleasure of attending many legal conventions and meetings of Bar Associations throughout the common law world, it could hardly be otherwise; and the American input has been considerable.

In common with so many, I owe a deep debt of gratitude to all who have played a part in law reporting over the years. Without their accurate and comprehensive volumes this book could not exist. Each citation from their works is intended as an expression of that gratitude. An equally deep debt is due to all who from time to time have given me suggestions for inclusion in *Miscellanies*. Most unhappily, time has made it impossible to produce an adequate list of Acknowledgements such as appeared in previous volumes. All that I can do is express here my deep gratitude to all those who have so kindly helped me in this way over many years. *Floreant.*

Lincoln's Inn
Feast of St. Bartholomew, 2005   R. E. M.

EDITOR'S NOTE

~

When visiting Lincoln's Inn in July 2004, I learned that my friend Sir Robert Megarry — whom I've known since Charles Alan Wright introduced us in 1988 — had completed most of the manuscript of his third *Miscellany-at-Law* but might not be able to see it through to publication. I immediately volunteered to help in that endeavour.

Many people in many places have helped bring this book to fruition. Richard Hart of Oxford immediately offered to publish it. Professor David Walker of Glasgow and Sir David Williams, Vice-Chancellor Emeritus of Cambridge University, both generously read and commented on the manuscript. Dean Darby Dickerson of Stetson University College of Law in Florida appropriated funds for a thorough check of the book's wide-ranging citations — this as a public service — and the work was ably overseen by Professor Brooke Joelle Bowman of Stetson. At LawProse, Inc., in Dallas, Texas, Tiger Jackson and Jeff Newman each read the manuscript for accuracy and consistency. Ms. Jackson also compiled the index and served as the canvasser of edits coming from all directions. My two LawProse interns, Rob Harris and Tim Taliaferro, proof-read the index and verified its accuracy.

The author's three daughters played crucial roles. Lindsay Merriman, formerly at the Bar and later a law teacher, thoroughly read the manuscript and proofs (as she had for the second *Miscellany*), offering insightful improvements throughout. During Lindsay's brief absences, Jacquetta Megarry of Dunblane, the guidebook publisher, helped with the distant editorial communications. And Susanna Sale of London, being near Lincoln's Inn, kindly shuttled voluminous messages between her father and me.

As a longtime enthusiast for the first two *Miscellanies*, I consider it a great honor that Sir Robert entrusted me with my role in the project. As David Walker put it in one of his touching notes from Glasgow, "We shall be doing legal literature a service if we can bring the third volume to publication." That is certainly how I view it.

How remarkable that the third volume in this trilogy appears precisely half a century after the first volume. The author's voluminous reading has yielded the most humorous imaginable materials from law-books. No one else has Sir Robert's deft touch for weaving together this type of amusing narrative. That touch has become even more refined over the years. Here it finds its apotheosis.

Dallas, Texas
August 2005   Bryan A. Garner

GLOSSARY AND ABBREVIATIONS

Glossary

ex parte	(from one side only); an application to the court made by only one party in the absence of others
master	A judicial officer of the court, below the rank of a judge
oratio obliqua	Speech as reported, not as spoken
puisne (judge)	A High Court judge below the rank of a presiding judge
quaere	Query; it is a question; it is doubtful
quare clausum fregit	"Why he broke the close": the old action for trespass to land
quo warranto	"By what authority": a writ for inquiring by what authority a person holds office
ratio (decidendi)	The reasoning on which a decision is based
secus	It is otherwise
stare decisis	"To stand by the decisions": the doctrine that decisions of the courts establish binding precedents

Abbreviations

A.B.A.J.	*American Bar Association Journal*
Atlay	J.B. Atlay, *The Victorian Chancellors* (1906)
B.	Baron (a judge of the former Court of Exchequer)
Bl.Comm.	*Blackstone's Commentaries* (15th ed., 1809)
Boswell's *Johnson*	James Boswell, *The Life of Samuel Johnson, LL.D.* (P. Fitzgerald ed., 2nd ed., 1888: in three volumes, including Boswell's *Hebrides*)
Calamandrei	Piero Calamandrei, *Eulogy of Judges* (J.C. Adams & C.A. Phillips Jr. trs., 1942)
Camp. C.JJ.	John, Lord Campbell, *Lives of the Chief Justices of England* (2nd ed., 1858) (in three volumes)
Camp. L. & B.	John, Lord Campbell, *Lives of Lord Lyndhurst and Lord Brougham* (1869)
Camp. L.CC.	John, Lord Campbell, *Lives of the Lord Chancellors and Keepers of the Great Seal* (5th ed., 1868) (in ten volumes)
Can. B.R.	*Canadian Bar Review*

C.B.	Chief Baron (head of the former Court of Exchequer)
C.J.	Chief Justice (plural, C.JJ.)
C.J.C.P.	Chief Justice of the former Court of Common Pleas
C.J.K.B.	Chief Justice of the former Court of King's Bench
Co.Litt.	*Coke upon Littleton*
D.N.B	*Dictionary of National Biography* (1885–1901, and later volumes)
Foss's *Biog. Dict.*	E. Foss, *A Biographical Dictionary of the Judges of England* (1870)
Foss's *Judges*	E. Foss, *The Judges of England* (1848–64) (in nine volumes)
Greville Diary	*The Greville Diary* (P.W. Wilson ed., 1927) (in two volumes)
Halsb. Laws	The Earl of Halsbury, *The Laws of England*
H.E.L.	Sir William Holdsworth, *A History of English Law* (1922–66) (in 16 volumes). For details of the various editions, see (1945) 61 L.Q.R. 346
Holmes–Laski Letters	*Holmes–Laski Letters* (M.DeW. Howe ed., 1953) (in two volumes)
Holmes–Pollock Letters	*Holmes-Pollock Letters* (M. DeW. Howe ed., 1941) (in two volumes). The English edition is titled *Pollock–Holmes Letters*
J.	Mr. (Mrs., Miss) Justice (plural, JJ.)
L.C.	Lord Chancellor (plural, L.CC.)
Lds. Jnl.	*Journals of the House of Lords 1509–*
L.J.	Lord (Lady) Justice (plural, L.JJ.)
L.K.	Lord Keeper (of the Great Seal); the Lord Chancellor in all save name and rank. The last was Lord Henley, in 1760
Manson	E. Manson, *Builders of Our Law During the Reign of Queen Victoria* (2nd ed., 1904)
1 Misc.	R.E. Megarry, *Miscellany-at-Law* (1955)
2 Misc.	R.E. Megarry, *A Second Miscellany-at-Law* (1973)
M.R.	Master of the Rolls. Formerly the head of the Court of Chancery under the Lord Chancellor; latterly the virtual head of the Court of Appeal
O.E.D.	*The Oxford English Dictionary* (2d ed. 1989)

P.	President (of the Probate, Divorce, and Admiralty Division, now the Family Division). Also law reports: Probate (England); Pacific (USA)
Parl. Hist.	J. Debrett, *Parliamentary Register, or, History of the Proceedings and Debates of the House of Commons* (in seventy-six volumes)
Pie-Powder	A Circuit Tramp [J.A. Foote], *Pie-Powder* (1911)
P.J.	Presiding Judge
Pull.	Serjeant Alexander Pulling, *The Order of the Coif* (1884)
Pulton	Ferdinando Pulton, *Collection of Sundrie Statutes, Frequent in Use* (1618)
Rastell	*Statutes at Large* (1618) (in two volumes)
Ruffhead	Owen Ruffhead, *Statutes at Large* (1769) (in eighteen volumes)
Rush. Coll.	J. Rushworth, *Historical Collection* (1721) (in eight volumes)
S.A.L.J.	South African Law Journal
Selden, *Table Talk*	*Table Talk of John Selden* (Sir Frederick Pollock ed., 1927)
S.-G.	Solicitor-General: the deputy chief advocate for the Crown (until recently, always a barrister)
S.S.	Selden Society
Sugden's *Property*	Sir Edward Sugden, *A Treatise of the Law of Property as Administered by the House of Lords* (1849)
Twiss, *Eldon*	H. Twiss Q.C., *The Public and Private Life of Lord Chancellor Eldon* (3rd ed. 1846) (in two volumes)
V.-C.	Vice-Chancellor: one of the judges of the old Court of Chancery; the present administrative head of the Chancery Division

1

~

LEX LOQUENS

A BOOK about the law may properly begin with the judges: "The law is the rule, but it is mute. The king judgeth by his judges, and they are the speaking law, *lex loquens*."[1]

At the summit, in his day, is the Lord Chancellor. On high authority, it has been said: "It is not generally realized that the Lord Chancellor need not be a Peer or have a seat in the House of Lords. The last example was the sainted Sir Thomas More."[2] But the accuracy of the example does not match that of the principle, since More, who resigned as Lord Chancellor in 1532, in fact had various successors in office who were not peers and had no seat in the House of Lords. More's immediate successor was Sir Thomas Audley, who, after less than a year as Lord Keeper, was Lord Chancellor for well over five years before being ennobled. (He was unrelated to the notorious Lord Audley who was beheaded for the rape of his wife.[3]) Again, there was Sir Christopher Hatton, who after less than a year as Lord Keeper, and never ennobled, held office for over four years before his death in 1591. A century later, Sir John Somers, who had been Lord Keeper since March 23, 1693, became Lord Chancellor on April 22, 1697, though he remained a commoner until December 2 of that year. He was the last Lord Chancellor to hold office for any substantial period without a peerage.[4]

---

[1] Co. Litt. 130a.

[2] Earl of Kilmuir, *Political Adventure* (1964), p. 234.

[3] *R. v. Lord Audley* (1631) 3 St.Tr. 401.

[4] Sir Robert Henley held the Great Seal as a commoner for nearly three years (1757–1760), but this was as Lord Keeper and not Lord Chancellor. He was made Chancellor in 1761 and held the post till 1766.

The last reign in which there was no Lord Chancellor but only Commissioners or Lords Keeper (some peers and some not) was that of William IV, when the seal was in commission from April 1835 to January 1836.

Since 1850 the Great Seal has always been held by the Lord Chancellor. In that year, the short interval of less than a month between Lord Cottenham L.C. and Lord Truro L.C. was filled by Lord Langdale M.R., Shadwell V.-C., and Rolfe B., who held the Great Seal as Lords Commissioners. Since then, apart from temporary absences of the Lord Chancellor from the realm and the like, the Great Seal has not been in commission. The last Lord Keeper was Sir Robert Henley, appointed on June 30, 1757, ennobled on March 27, 1760, and promoted Lord Chancellor on January 16, 1761. Since 1562 it has been clear that a Lord Keeper has always had authority, jurisdiction, and other rights equal to those of a Lord Chancellor;[5] the difference is merely one of honour. The two offices are alternatives, and normally did not exist concurrently.[6]

Often there is an appreciable gap between a commoner receiving the Great Seal and his patent of peerage passing the seal. Thus Sir Frederick Smith became L.C. on January 14, 1919, and Baron Birkenhead L.C. on February 3, 1919.[7] In the interval he delivered at least two judgments in the House of Lords,[8] though as he was not at the time a member of the House of Lords it does not at first appear how he managed to speak in it. The Woolsack is, of course, technically outside the House, so that he could have presided, in the same way that, for example, Sir Frederick Thesiger, when appointed Lord Chancellor, "sat Speaker" on March 1, 1858,[9] before he had become Lord Chelmsford. But it may be questioned how Sir Frederick Smith was able to take the requisite three or four paces to the left[10] so as to step within the House and speak as a member of it,

---

[5] 5 Eliz. 1, c. 18, 1562.

[6] *Pace* Henry Cecil, *Tipping the Scales* (1964), p. 82.

[7] See [1919] A.C. at p. v.

[8] *Krupp Aktiengesellschaft* v. *Orconera Iron Ore Co. Ltd.* (1919) 120 L.T. 386; *Fried. Krupp Aktiengesellschaft* v. *Public Trustee* (1919) Burrows' *Judgments Delivered by Lord Chancellor Birkenhead* (1923), p. 6. Both speeches seem to have been extempore.

[9] See (1858) 90 Lds. Jnl. 58; and see the curious arrangement in 1827: 2 Misc. 58.

[10] See Viscount Hailsham, *The Duties of a Lord Chancellor* (1936), p. 11; Lord Cross of Chelsea, *The Lawyer and Justice* (ed. B.W. Harvey) (1978), p. 197; Viscount Simon, *Retrospect* (1952), p. 255; Viscount Maugham, *At the End of the Day* (1954), p. 346; House of Lords Precedence Act, 1539, s. 8.

or to vote. Indeed, it has been said that his judgment "would . . . appear to be a breach of the convention . . . which prohibits the unennobled from utterance."[11] Yet whatever Sir Frederick may be thought to have been capable of, it is difficult to envisage Lord Buckmaster, Lord Finlay, Lord Dunedin, Lord Atkinson, and Lord Shaw all sitting meekly by while a new Lord Chancellor flouted the convention; and there is a simple explanation. As the Journals of the House of Lords show,[12] Parliament had been dissolved, so that there could be no sitting of the House of Lords as such. Instead, acting by virtue of a writing under the Royal Sign Manual dated November 25, 1918, the Lords of Appeal (a term defined as including the Lord Chancellor) were exercising their statutory power[13] to sit in the House of Lords and hear and determine appeals in the name of the House of Lords.

But there was no such statute to aid Sir Robert Henley L.K. in the eighteenth century. It was his inability to speak in support of his decisions below that caused him to be "frequently much out of Temper";[14] for he suffered the indignity of being obliged to move the reversal of some of his judgments, upon the opinions of Lord Hardwicke and Lord Mansfield, without being able to speak in defence of his own views.[15]

The office of Lord Chancellor or Lord Keeper has its full share of curiosities. There are those who do not know who was the first saint to hold it, or the first layman, nor when a lawyer was first appointed, or the last bishop. A person in his twenties has been appointed, and so has a lady; and for some eight months a Speaker of the House of Commons also presided over the House of Lords as Lord Keeper. There has even been a Lord Chancellor in the last century who had no seat in the Cabinet.

Further and better particulars should plainly be given. St. Swithin was

---

11 R.F.V. Heuston, *Lives of the Lord Chancellors 1885–1940* (1964), p. 400.

12 (1919), vol. 151, pp. 13, 14. For another instance, see (1950) 182 Lds. Jnl. 1.

13 Appellate Jurisdiction Act, 1876, ss. 5, 9. The reports sometimes state that a sitting was during a dissolution: see, e.g., *Fox* v. *Lawson* [1974] A.C. 803; *A. Schroeder Music Publishing Co. Ltd.* v. *Macaulay* [1974] 1 W.L.R. 1308.

14 Lord Eldon's *Anecdote Book* (1960), p. 154.

15 See Sugden's *Property*, p. 38.

appointed in 827 and held office for at least nine years,[16] although it may be doubted whether the office in those days was truly that of Lord Chancellor. For centuries the office remained in ecclesiastical hands, but at last, on December 14, 1340, the first layman was appointed.[17] He was Sir Robert Bourchier, a soldier; and within a year, on October 29, 1341, he was succeeded by the first lawyer, Sir Robert Parnynge (or Parning), the Chief Justice of the King's Bench.[18] But not until July 10, 1621, was there the last appointment of a cleric, John Williams, Bishop of Lincoln, who remained in office for more than four years. He was the only Protestant divine to have held the Great Seal.[19] After that, for over 370 years, only those who had been called to the English Bar were appointed.[20] But that ended when Lord Mackay of Clashfern, who had been an advocate at the Scottish Bar, a judge of the Court of Session, and from 1985 a Lord of Appeal in Ordinary, was appointed Lord Chancellor on October 27, 1987.[21] The office, indeed, has for nearly three centuries been that of the Lord High Chancellor of Great Britain, and not of England alone.

George Neville, Bishop of Exeter, was barely 28 years old when he was appointed by Henry VI on July 25, 1460; and soon afterwards, on March 10, 1461, he began some six years as Edward IV's Lord Chancellor, with a brief restoration under Henry VI for some four months on October 8, 1470. He was Archbishop of York from 1465 to 1476 and was a brother of the Earl of Warwick ("Warwick the King-Maker").[22] The lady was Queen Eleanor, the consort of Henry III. She was appointed Lady Keeper on August 6, 1253, and held office for nearly a year, giving birth to a daughter on November 25, 1253. After her son Edward I had been on the

---

[16] 1 Camp. L.CC. 30; 10 *ibid.* 317.

[17] 1 Camp. L.CC. 204.

[18] 1 Camp. L.CC. 211; 10 *ibid.* 321.

[19] 10 Camp. L.CC. 312, at 325. He was Archbishop of York (1641–1650).

[20] Alexander Wedderburn, Lord Loughborough and later Earl of Rosslyn (1793–1801), was of the Scottish Bar (1753) before moving to England in 1763. Henry Brougham, Lord Brougham and Vaux (1830–1834), was of the Scottish Bar (1800) and called in England in 1808.

[21] [1987] A.C. v.

[22] 1 Camp. L.CC. 315, 317, 333; 10 *ibid.* 323; T.D. Hardy, *A Catalogue of Lords Chancellors etc.* (1843), p. 51; Foss's *Biog. Dict.* 477.

throne for nearly 12 years she took the veil. But although she exercised her judicial and other functions in person while in office, her use of the Great Seal was heavily circumscribed. Although it was in her temporary custody, it was "sealed up under the King's Privy Seal, and under the seals of the Earl of Cornwall and others of the Council; and the Exchequer Seal was delivered to William de Kilkenny to use in England, instead of the Great Seal, during the King's absence in Gascony."[23]

The Speaker of the House of Commons who was made Lord Keeper and not Lord Chancellor so that he could continue to sit in the House of Commons was Sir Thomas Audley, on May 20, 1532. But his duality of office ended some eight months later when he became Lord Chancellor.[24] The Lord Chancellor without a seat in the Cabinet was Viscount Simon, from May 25 until July 6, 1945; for those were the days of the "Caretaker Government,"[25] and he was no Tory.

There is a pleasant appeal in the spectacle of a Lord Keeper and an Attorney-General and future Chief Justice seeking to escape a penalty by pleading ignorance of law. In 1598, when Coke was Attorney-General and a widower, he made his ill-fated marriage with Lady Hatton. The ceremony took place without banns or licence, and in a private house instead of the parish church. When this came to the ears of the ecclesiastical authorities, Coke, his wife, her father (Lord Burghley, son of the great Elizabethan statesman), Sir Thomas Egerton L.K. (soon to become Lord Ellesmere L.C.), the rector, and others of those present were prosecuted in the Archbishop's Court. In the words of counsel many years later, "they all, by their proctor, submitted to the censure of the archbishop, who granted them an absolution from the excommunication they had incurred. The Act of Absolution set forth,

---

[23] 1 Camp. L.CC. 126–28; 10 *ibid.* 319; Hardy, *supra* note 22, p. 8. Her tenure is not recorded in E.B. Fryde et al. (eds.), *Handbook of British Chronology* (3d ed. 1986), at p. 85.

[24] 2 Camp. L.CC. 80–84.

[25] *Annual Register* 1945, p. xiii. After Prime Minister Winston Churchill called a general election and resigned on May 23, 1945, an interim "Caretaker Government" was formed to carry out necessary government operations until the election was held on July 5. Members of the Conservative party predominated in the Caretaker Government, and all the Cabinet members were Conservatives.

that it was granted by reason of penitence, and the fact seeming to have been done through ignorance of the law."[26] Lord Hardwicke C.J. appears to have accepted this account of events.[27]

The appointment of Bishop Williams in 1621,[28] when for over 60 years no bishop had held the Great Seal, came as a surprise to the nation; and the Bar showed little enthusiasm. The new Lord Keeper, however, acquitted himself bravely:

The Terms of the Common Law, as in all other Professions and Sciences, seem Barbarous to the Vulgar Ear, and had need to be familiariz'd with pre-acquaintance; which, being the Primar of that Rational Learning, he had inur'd himself to it long before, and was nothing to seek in it. Yet one of the Bar thought to put a Trick upon his Fresh-man-ship, and trouled out a Motion Crammed like a Granada with obsolete Words, Coins of far fetch'd Antiquity, which had been long disus'd, worse then Sir Thomas Mores Averia de Withernam among the Masters of Paris. In these misty and recondit Phrases, he thought to leave the New Judge feeling after him in the Dark, and to make him blush, that he could not Answer to such mystical Terms, as he had Conjur'd up. But he dealt with a Wit that was never entangl'd in a Bramble Bush; for with a serious Face he Answer'd him in a cluster of most crabbed Notions, pick'd up out of Metaphysics and Logic, as Categorematical, and Syncategorematical, and a deal of such drumming stuff, that the Motioner being Foil'd at his own Weapon, and well Laugh'd at in the Court, went home with this New Lesson, That he that Tempts a Wise man in Jest, shall make himself a Fool in Earnest.[29]

Three centuries later "syncategorematical" was to be given a distant cousin-in-law when Diplock L.J. spoke of "every synallagmatic contract";[30] and as he afterwards observed, his use of this adjective "was

---

[26] *Middleton* v. *Croft* (1734) Cun. 55 at 61; and see H.W. Woolrych, *Life of Sir Edward Coke* (1826), pp. 41, 42.

[27] *Middleton* v. *Croft* (1736) Cun. 114 at 125; but as reported *sub nom. Middleton* v. *Crofts* (1736) 2 Atk. 650 at 670, this passage is omitted.

[28] See *ante* p. 4.

[29] J. Hacket, *Memorial of John Williams* (1692), vol. 1, p. 75.

[30] *Hongkong Fir Shipping Co. Ltd.* v. *Kawasaki Kisen Kaisha Ltd.* [1962] 2 Q.B. 26 at 65; and see *United Scientific Holdings Ltd.* v. *Burnley Borough Council* [1978] A.C. 904 at 928–30. The adjective and its origin are examined at (1986) 103 S.A.L.J. 488, 703.

widely thought to be a typical example of gratuitous philological exhibitionism."[31]

The reference to More is, of course, to the celebrated occasion in Bruges when More, still a student, was touring Europe:

> [More] being once at Burgesse in Flanders, an arrogant fellow had set up a Thesis, that he would answer any question could be propounded unto him in what Art soever: Sir Thomas made this question to be put up for him to answer, whether *Averia capta in Withernamia sunt irreplegebilia*; adding that there was one of the English Embassadors retinue, that would dispute with him thereof: This Thraso, or Braggadochio not so much as understanding those terms of our common Law, knew not what to answer to it, and so he became ridiculous to the whole city for his presumptuous bragging.[32]

The correct answer to the question whether beasts of the plough, taken in withernam, are capable of being replevied, seems to be "Yes, on restoration of the original distress."[33] The writ of *capias in withernam, in repetito namio*,[34] lay where a person had levied a distress, and the goods had then been wrongfully eloigned, i.e., carried out of the district to places unknown. The writ authorised the distraint of other goods in lieu of those eloigned, and the goods taken on this second distress could not be replevied by the owner (i.e., recovered by giving security for payment of the sum distrained for) unless he produced the goods originally distrained.[35]

Even when that is understood, there was still much scope for disputation, such as to the ambit of the term *averia*. A century later such points were still being argued:

[31] *United Dominions Trust (Commercial) Ltd.* v. *Eagle Aircraft Services* [1968] 1 W.L.R. 74 at 82.

[32] J. Hoddesdon, *History of Sir Thomas More* (1652), p. 26.

[33] See 3 Bl.Comm. 149 n. But the authority cited ("Raym. 475") does not seem very satisfactory: see *Designy's Case* (1682) T. Raym. 474 at 475, a case in which the defendant had "spirited away" to Jamaica "the eldest son of one Turbet, who was a scholar at Merchant-Taylors School, and a hopeful youth": see T. Raym. 474; 2 Show.K.B. 221. Halsbury's *Laws of England*, vol. 37 (4th ed. 1982), p. 78 cites "YB 7 Hen. 4, 27" for this: more fully, this is Y.B. 7 Hen. 4, Mich., fo. 27, pl. 5 (1405).

[34] "That you take in reprisal, in a second distress."

[35] See 3 Bl.Comm. 149.

Trespasse. Plaintiff declared that the Defendant did break his close and eat his grasse, &c. Cum *averiis suis, scilicet,* oxen, sheep, hoggs, *avibus, anglice* turkies, and the Judge in this Case[36] did hold that turkies are not comprised within the generall word *averia,* which is an old Law word, and these fowls came but lately into England, and upon this it was directed to sever the dammages, for otherwise if the dammages shall be joyntly given, and it be ill for this of the turkies, for the reason abovesaid, it will overthrow all the verdict.[37]

In 1810 an objection was taken to a modus[38] on turkeys on the ground that they had been first introduced into England in about 1555, which was within the time of legal memory; but the court managed to decide the case on another ground.[39]

It was Lord Hardwicke's son, Charles Yorke, who was appointed Lord Chancellor in 1770 but was found dead three days later "in circumstances suggesting suicide induced by the scorn of his fellows for a self-seeking political betrayal."[40] Some twenty-five years later, Francis Hargrave, the distinguished author and editor, wrote of Yorke in terms so euphuistic as almost to defy comprehension. Yorke was described thus:

That modern constellation of English jurisprudence, that elegant and accomplished ornament of Westminster Hall in the present century, the Honorable Charles Yorke Esquire: — whose ordinary speeches as an advocate were profound lectures; — whose digressions from the exuberance of the best juridical knowledge were illuminations; — whose energies were oracles; — whose constancy of mind was won into the pinnacle of our English forum at an inauspicious moment; — whose exquisiteness of sensibility at almost the next moment from the impressions of imputed error stormed the fort of even his highly cultivated reason, and so made elevation and extinction contemporaneous; — and whose prematureness of fate, notwithstanding the great contributions, from the manly energies of a

---

[36] Barkley J.

[37] *Usleys Case* (1637) Clayton 50.

[38] I.e., a composition for tithes.

[39] *Roberts* v. *Williams* (1810) 12 East 33. For an arbitration by a turkey, see *post* pp. 77–78.

[40] See 1 Misc. 11.

Northington and the vast splendor of a Camden, and notwithstanding also the accessions from the two rival luminaries[41] which have more latterly adorned our equitable hemisphere, caused an almost unsuppliable interstice in the science of English equity.[42]

At times, remarked Butler, Lord Thurlow L.C. "was superlatively great." Butler was in the House of Lords when Thurlow replied to the Duke of Grafton's reproach of Thurlow's plebeian extraction and his recent elevation to the peerage. Butler recounted:

[Thurlow] rose from the woolsack, and advanced slowly to the place, from which the chancellor generally addresses the house; then, fixing on the duke the look of Jove, when he has grasped the thunder; — "I am amazed," he said, in a level tone of voice, "at the attack which the noble duke has made on me. Yes, my lords," considerably raising his voice, "I am amazed at his grace's speech. The noble duke cannot look before him, behind him, or on either side of him, without seeing some noble peer, who owes his seat in this house to his successful exertions in the profession to which I belong. Does he not feel that it is as honourable to owe it to these, as to being the accident of an accident? — To all these noble lords, the language of the noble duke is as applicable and as insulting as it is to myself. But I don't fear to meet it single and alone. No one venerates the peerage more than I do, — but, my lords, I must say that the peerage solicited me, — not I the peerage. Nay more, — I can say and will say, that, as a peer of parliament, — as speaker of this right honourable house, as keeper of the great seal, — as guardian of his majesty's conscience, — as lord high chancellor of England,[43] — nay, even in that character also, in which the noble duke would think it an affront to be considered, — but which character none can deny *me*, — as a MAN, I am at this moment as respectable; — I beg to add, — I am at this time, as much respected, as the proudest peer I now look down upon." The effect of this speech, both within the walls of parliament and out of them, was prodigious.[44]

---

[41] *Semble* Lord Thurlow L.C. and Lord Loughborough L.C.

[42] Francis Hargrave, Preface to Sir Matthew Hale's *Jurisdiction of the Lords House, or Parliament* (1796), p. clxxxi. For other instances of such language, see *post* pp. 203–05.

[43] He was Lord Chancellor of Great Britain, and not of England alone: see Treaty of Union with Scotland 1706, Art. XXIV, ratified by Acts of Scottish and English parliaments (*Acts of the Parliaments of Scotland*, XI, 406, c. 7, and 6 Anne, c. 11).

[44] C. Butler, *Reminiscences* (4th ed. 1824), vol. 1, p. 188.

Dr. Johnson was one of Thurlow's admirers. In criticising Sir Joshua Reynolds as a companion, Johnson said, "Depend upon it, Sir, it is when you come close to a man in conversation, that you discover what his real abilities are; to make a speech in a public assembly is a knack. Now I honour Thurlow, Sir; Thurlow is a fine fellow; he fairly puts his mind to yours."[45] Later he said, "I would prepare myself for no man in England but Lord Thurlow. When I am to meet with him I should wish to know a day before."[46] By the end of the eighteenth century it had become an established convention that on elevation to the Bench a man who had a mistress must either marry her or put her away.[47] In this, as in many other matters, Lord Thurlow (of whom Fox said, "No man could *be* so wise as Thurlow *looked*"[48]) exhibited his customary independence of thought: for even while he was Lord Chancellor,[49] he openly lived with a mistress, by whom he had a considerable family.[50] But not long after, in 1806, Sir James Mansfield C.J. refused the Great Seal on the ground that all his children were illegitimate, and although he had married their mother after their birth, "he would not have their illegitimacy constantly proclaimed by accepting a peerage."[51]

Sugden did not take the same view. After having two or three children by his kitchen-maid, "he married her, and begot divers others." She was "an excellent woman, charitable and kind-hearted," but when Sugden became Lord Chancellor of Ireland in December 1834, she was not received at Court, and it was said that for this reason he resigned within a few months of being appointed.[52] In all, he had seven sons and seven

---

[45] Boswell's *Johnson*, vol. 3, p. 3.

[46] *Ibid.*, at p. 102.

[47] 7 Camp. L.CC. 314.

[48] 7 Camp. L.CC. 318; and see *ibid.*, at p. 220; Twiss, *Eldon*, vol. 1, p. 357; Lord Eldon's *Anecdote Book* (1960), p. 94, attributing a variant form to Fox or Burke.

[49] 1778–1793.

[50] 7 Camp. L.CC. 314; R. Gore-Browne, *Chancellor Thurlow* (1953), pp. 59, 133 (three daughters, at least one of whom was born after he had become Lord Chancellor).

[51] 3 Camp. C.JJ. 184.

[52] 1 *Greville Diary* 486, recording this under March 20, 1835. Yet he sat as late as April 22, 1835 (see Ll. & G. *t.* Sugd. 371), and does not seem to have formally resigned until the government fell.

daughters by her.[53] Yet when in 1852 he became Lord Chancellor of Great Britain, he accepted a peerage and became Lord St. Leonards, despite the state of his family.

Even the great Lord Eldon, so careful and ponderous in his utterances, was not immune from occasional lapses from accuracy. In a debate in the House of Lords in 1822 on the Roman Catholic Peers Bill, the Earl of Eldon L.C. said, "In the 5th of Elizabeth, by a strange anomaly, the House of Commons was at liberty to have Roman Catholic members, while the House of Lords was prohibited."[54] It would indeed have been strange if Elizabeth I, while requiring the exclusion of Roman Catholics from the finite body of peers in the House of Lords, had determined to open the House of Commons to an indefinite and possibly dominant body of Roman Catholics. In fact, the statute in question, 5 Eliz. I, c. 1,[55] did just the opposite. Section 16 imposed a general obligation on all elected to Parliament to take the statutory oath of supremacy[56] "before he shall enter into the Parliament-house, or have any Voice there." Section 17 then provided that "forasmuch as the Queen's Majesty is otherwise sufficiently assured of the Faith and Loyalty of the Temporal Lords of her High Court of Parliament; therefore this Act, nor any Thing therein contained, shall not extend to compel any Temporal Person, of or above the Degree of a Baron of this Realm, to take or pronounce the Oath abovesaid . . . ."[57]

Brougham had been an advocate at the Scottish Bar for some eight years before, at the age of 30, Lincoln's Inn called him to the English Bar; and 22 years later, to the very day, he took his seat on the Woolsack.[58] When he was 21, he had contemplated the English Bar with scant

[53] 55 *D.N.B.* 154. 2 Atlay 6 says that the union was blessed with "no fewer than ten children": this may have been the postnuptial score.

[54] (1822) 7 Hansard (N.S.) 1233.

[55] Twiss, *Eldon*, vol. 2, p. 67, says it was 5 Eliz. c. 7, s. 17; but 5 Eliz. c. 7, is "An Act avoiding divers foreign Wares made by Handicraftsmen beyond the Seas," and it has no s. 17.

[56] Under the Act of Supremacy, 1558, 1 Eliz. 1, c. 1.

[57] The next speaker in the debate was Earl Grey, and he got it right: see (1822) 7 Hansard (N.S.) 1238.

[58] Born September 19, 1778; call in Scotland, June 10, 1800; call in England, November 22, 1808; Woolsack, November 22, 1830.

enthusiasm: "The English Bar is in a very great degree tedious, and, to say the least of it, somewhat uncertain: I look forward with no small horror to five years' dull, unvaried drudgery, which must be undergone to obtain the privilege of drudging still harder, among a set of disagreeable people of brutal manners and confined talents."[59] In his career in England, he was unhampered by conventional restraints. Thus in 1822 he defended one Williams, a newspaper proprietor, for having criticised the clergy of Durham for ignoring the death of Queen Caroline. In his speech, Brougham strongly attacked the clergy, saying: "The insect brought into life by corruption, and nestled in filth, though its flight be lowly and its sting puny, can swarm and buzz, and irritate the skin and offend the nostril, and altogether give nearly as much annoyance as the wasp, whose nobler nature it aspires to emulate."[60]

Although eight years later Brougham took the Woolsack, elevation of place brought no elevation of tone. In the House of Commons, Sir Edward Sugden, a former Solicitor-General, drew attention to certain Chancery sinecures, having first given due notice to the Solicitor-General. In particular, he referred to the recent appointment (of Mr. Brougham, a brother of the Lord Chancellor) to the sinecure office of Registrar of the Court of Chancery, an office that Brougham had promised to abolish.[61] There was some debate on this. The next day, while Sugden was appearing as counsel in the Court of Chancery before Brougham, the Chancellor suddenly rose and left Sugden standing in the middle of a sentence.[62] He then went to the House of Lords, and proceeded to present "a Petition from the Merchants, Bankers, and Traders of the City of Leicester, complaining of the existing state of the law between Debtor and Creditor, and praying that their Lordships

---

[59] T.H. Ford (1984) 5 Jnl.Leg.Hist. (No. 3) at p. 109, citing R.H.M.B. Atkinson and G.A. Jackson (ed.), *Brougham and his Early Friends: Letters to James Loch 1798–1809*, vol. 1, pp. 151, 152, letter of June 24, 1800.

[60] Camp. L. & B. 335; see *R. v. Williams* (1823) 5 B. & Ald. 595. See also 2 *D.N.B.* 1364 (1917) (s.v. Brougham) ("His words came readily, he had great powers of sarcasm, and an unfailing store of humour").

[61] 14 Hansard (3d ser. 1832) 721.

[62] St. Leonards, *Misrepresentations in Campbell's Lives of Lyndhurst & Brougham* (1869), p. 17.

would support the Bill on that subject, which had been introduced by him (the Lord Chancellor)."[63]

Brougham then made this somewhat unpromising subject the occasion of what seems to have been an impassioned speech on the Chancery sinecures. In this, he referred to Sugden's enquiries on the previous day and again delved into entomology:

> Yes, I am bound to believe — nay, cannot for a moment doubt — that the learned Gentleman was wholly influenced by this most praiseworthy desire of information. How could I think otherwise, knowing as I do, in common with all your Lordships, that philosophers have long since eulogized this laudable thirst of knowledge as the most distinguished attribute of humanity, and as the most distinguished feature of an ingenious and lofty intellect? Yes, my Lords, we have all read, that it is this Heaven-born thirst of information, and its invariable concomitant a self-disregarding and candid mind, that most distinguishes man from the lower animals, from the crawling reptile, from the wasp that stings, and from the wasp that fain would, but cannot sting; distinguishes us, my Lords, not only from the insect that crawls and stings, but from the more powerful, because more offensive creature, the bug, which, powerful and offensive as it is, is, after all, but vermin. Yes, I say, it is this laudable propensity, upon which humanity justly prides itself, which I have no doubt solely influenced the learned Gentleman to whom I allude, to seek for information which it would be cruel to stingily gratify.[64]

Later that day in the House of Commons, Sugden made a restrained reference to these remarks, saying that he would take no further notice of them until he had them from a more authentic source.[65] The next day Sugden made a strong but dignified reply to Brougham's "use of offensive epithets from a vulgar vocabulary in language, which no private gentleman should utter on the one hand, or submit to on the other."[66] In what must have been an animated debate,[67] government supporters

---

[63] 14 Hansard (3d ser. 1832) 738.

[64] *Ibid.*, at p. 742.

[65] *Ibid.*, at p. 816.

[66] *Ibid.*, at pp. 827, 830. See also A.W.B. Simpson, *Biographical Dictionary of the Common Law* (1984), p. 496 (noting that Sugden "constantly clashed" with Brougham).

[67] 14 Hansard (3d ser. 1832), at pp. 827–49.

turned on Sugden for having attacked Brougham without proper notice; but nothing could palliate the Chancellor's language, and the debate leaves little doubt who had the best — or worst — of it.[68]

Brougham enjoyed four years as Lord Chancellor. But on a change of government in 1834 he lost office. After a few months, and an indecisive election, Lord Melbourne was back as Prime Minister; yet Brougham was left without office. He wrote furiously to Melbourne. The reply was crushing:

> You ask for specific charges. Allow me to observe that there may be a course and series of very objectionable conduct, there may be a succession of acts which destroy confidence and add offence to offence, and yet it would be difficult to point to any marked delinquency. I will, however, tell you fairly, that, in my opinion, you domineered too much, you interfered too much with other departments, you encroached upon the provinces of the Prime Minister, you worked, as I believe, with the Press in a manner unbecoming to the dignity of your station, and you formed political views of your own and pursued them by means which were unfair towards your colleagues. . . . Nobody knows and appreciates your natural vigour better than I do. I know also that those who are weak for good are strong for mischief. You are strong for both, and I should both dread and lament to see those gigantic powers which should be directed to the support of the State exerted in the contrary and opposite direction.[69]

That was the end. After some 34 years of brilliance, some 34 less than glorious years remained. Brougham often attended the House of Lords, both for legislative and political purposes, and also judicially. But the spark was rare, and all was subfusc, and for over a century *Punch* kept his nose in the mire.[70]

As is well known, there are many inaccuracies in Lord Campbell's *Lives of the Lord Chancellors* and *Lives of the Chief Justices*, and not least in the volume on Lord Lyndhurst and Lord Brougham, the publication of which was deferred until both were dead. Some of these errors,

---

[68] In a similar vein, the *D.N.B.* (1917) reports that while at school, Brougham "often indulged in riotous sports, and took part in twisting off knickers as eagerly as in philosophical discussions." Vol. 2, p. 1357.

[69] David Cecil, *Melbourne* (1955), p. 235.

[70] See 2 Misc. 12.

indeed, drove an ex-Lord Chancellor, Lord St. Leonards, to defend himself and others in a book entitled *Misrepresentations in Campbell's Lives of Lyndhurst and Brougham, corrected by St. Leonards.*[71] In this book Lord St. Leonards recorded that it was at a social dinner, at which he was present, that Sir Charles Wetherell thus addressed Lord Campbell: "Then there is my noble and biographical friend who has added a new terror to death."[72] Lord St. Leonards added: "I have lived to find that he has left behind him a new terror to life."[73]

Pollock C.B. felt no hesitation in expressing his views on the volume on Lyndhurst and Brougham:

> The Biography collects almost every story that malice had invented or scandal propagated of both the victims, but especially of Lyndhurst. The notoriously avowedly false ones are sometimes (not always) coupled with a doubt, but whatever filth and dirt could be collected to throw on the memory of either, Copley or Brougham, Campbell has diligently got together and left behind him as a tribute to their memory. . . . [A book reviewer] says *Campbell was an honorable man,* and in a few lines gives an example of trickiness in narrative which in a Biographer is absolutely *base and contemptible.* The truth is Campbell was neither *honorable* nor even *honest.* I forget the name of the Lady[74] who wrote a history of some Chancellor, I think Hardwicke, with great trouble and pains, and much research. When Campbell came to that Chancellor he borrowed literally *wholesale* (without permission or acknowledgment) from the pages of the Lady — as if he had made himself the researches which were entirely hers. *This* was not honest.[75]

There are many instances of lay peers sitting, speaking, and voting in appeals to the House of Lords before the practice ended in 1844.[76] One

---

[71] London, 1869.

[72] St. Leonard's *Misrepresentations, supra* note 62, at p. 2. Compare Camp. L. & B. 163, which puts into Lord Brougham's mouth the reference to a new terror to death. See also 1 Atlay 155, and compare 2 Atlay 48 n.2. The phrase seems to have been John Arbuthnot's (1667–1735): see the *Oxford Dictionary of Quotations* (2d ed. 1953), p. 14.

[73] St. Leonard's *Misrepresentations, supra* note 62, at p. 2

[74] Miss Agnes Strickland. She wrote to *The Times* to complain of Campbell's plagiarism. (See *D.N.B.* vol. iv, p. 50.)

[75] Lord Hanworth, *Lord Chief Baron Pollock* (1929), p. 203.

[76] See 1 Misc. 11.

of the most controversial was *Bishop of London* v. *Fffytche*, in which the Church routed the lawyers. What was in issue was the validity of a bond given by a clerk in holy orders before being presented to a living, whereby he was obliged to resign it at any time on the request of the patron; and there was a point of pleading as well. The bond had been held valid in the courts below, in accordance with a long line of authority. Lord Mansfield C.J. laid the writ of error before the House on February 3, 1783,[77] and when the hearing began some months later, the judges were ordered to attend;[78] and the next day the House put elaborate questions to them.[79] Soon afterwards the judges answered these,[80] and then, "after long Debate"[81] (so fierce, it seems, as to induce the Lords' Journal to reduce the defendant's name from a triple initial letter to a mere double,[82] and to lead one reporter to state the result of the case in his head-note as being the opposite of what in fact it was[83]), the House reached its decision.[84] This was to reverse the decision of the Court of King's Bench,[85] which had affirmed the decision of the Court of Common Pleas, and had been supported by seven out of the eight judges summoned to advise the House. The remaining judge, Eyre B., took the opposite view on the substantive point, though he too was in favour of dismissing the appeal, by reason of the point of pleading.

The voting in the House was close. The Bishop of London, who had lost in the courts below, carried the day by nineteen votes to eighteen. Thirteen of those voting were bishops, and to a man they supported the Bishop. Of the two law lords present, Lord Mansfield was against the Bishop and Lord Thurlow was in his favour. Thurlow, indeed, had interrupted Buller J. while he was advising the House, but after some

[77] 36 Lds. Jnl. 587.
[78] *Ibid.*, at p. 671 (May 8, 1783).
[79] *Ibid.*, at p. 672 (May 9, 1783).
[80] *Ibid.*, at pp. 683–85 (May 26, 28, 1783).
[81] *Ibid.*, at p. 687 (May 30, 1783).
[82] It had been a single in earlier proceedings: *Robert Lord Bishop of London* v. *Fytche* (1781) 1 Bro.C.C. 96.
[83] See 2 Bro.P.C. 211.
[84] *Bishop of London* v. *Ffytche* (1783) 2 Bro. P.C. 211; and see 11 Cl. & F. 426 n.
[85] *Bishop of London* v. *Ffytche* (1782) 1 East 488.

discussion between Thurlow and Mansfield, Buller had been able to resume.[86] In terms of speeches, the winning team consisted of the Bishops of Salisbury, Bangor, Llandaff, and Gloucester, and Lord Thurlow,[87] while only Lord Mansfield and the Duke of Richmond spoke against the Bishop.[88]

In later cases this decision was treated with scant respect. The courts took the view that while they were bound to follow it where the circumstances were the same, they need not adopt the principle of the decision.[89] Where the cases were not "precisely similar," they regarded themselves as still being bound by the previous line of decisions.[90] Finally, another case went to the House of Lords, and Lord Eldon L.C., who seems to have been the only law lord sitting, advised the House that it was bound by its former decision, and that the case on appeal fell within it;[91] and the House decided accordingly. In the end, as fore-shadowed by Lord Eldon in his speech,[92] legislation provided relief and validated such bonds in specified cases.[93]

In some cases, indeed, the law lords were content to concur in a leading speech delivered by a lay peer.[94] Thus in 1828, in a case that Lord Eldon said was "one of the most important cases that has ever occurred,"[95] Earl Lauderdale delivered a leading speech of some 33 pages, saying (very much *inter alia*) that "a more scandalous case never was brought before any court of justice."[96] Lord Eldon's concurrence took 24 pages (with a postscript of over two pages more), but Lord Lyndhurst L.C. was content with half a page of agreement.[97] The result

---

[86] T. Cunningham, *Law of Simony* (1784), pp. 79–81.

[87] *Ibid.*, at pp. 123–67.

[88] *Ibid.*, at pp. 167–75. See also R. Stevens, *Law and Politics* (1979), pp. 11–12.

[89] Sugden's *Property*, p. 23.

[90] *Partridge* v. *Whiston* (1791) 4 T.R. 359 at 360; and see *Bagshaw* v. *Bossley* (1790) 4 T.R. 78; *Newman* v. *Newman* (1815) 4 M. & S. 66.

[91] *Fletcher* v. *Lord Sondes* (1827) 1 Bli.N.S. 144.

[92] See *ibid.* at pp. 247, 252.

[93] 7 & 8 Geo. 4, c. 25, 1827; 9 Geo. 4, c. 94, 1828.

[94] See also 1 Misc. 11–12.

[95] *Macneill* v. *Macgregor* (1828) 2 Bli.N.S. 393 at 486.

[96] *Ibid.*, at p. 458.

[97] S.C., as reported in 1 Dow & Cl. at p. 264.

was that the House set aside a declarator of marriage granted by the Court of Session to a pursuer who was, said Earl Lauderdale, "a man of very low birth, and of distinguished immorality of character."[98] The House was thus able to "do away the chance of this immoral man getting the fruits of the fraud that he has attempted to commit."[99]

A few years earlier, in a Scottish case based on an Act of 1701 against "wrongous imprisonment,"[100] Lord Holland spoke in support of the speech delivered by Lord Eldon L.C. Lord Holland deplored the absence of any bias in the Scottish courts in favour of liberty:

> A disposition is manifested to dwell on every argument, to catch at every twig, by which the Court can be spared the dreadful mortification of granting a helpless and injured individual the redress to which he is entitled against the arm of power exercised with oppression. One Judge is represented as saying, (and if the report is false, a grosser libel was never propagated against the character of a Judge than this authenticated book of Reports,) that the act of 1701 had been compared to the English *Habeas Corpus*, had been called the *Magna Charta* of Scotland, the palladium of civil liberty; but that he, ever since he sat on the bench, and long before, had considered it as a galimatias[101] of nonsense! as an act framed with an intention of being so; that he did not care what the Act of Parliament said, but always decided according to right reason, which was paramount to all Acts of Parliament. I do not, my Lords, pretend to quote the exact words in the book, for it has been mislaid; but such I am sure was nearly the substance of what is put into the mouth of a Scotch Judge.[102]

A marginal reference in the report indicates that Lord Holland was referring to the judgment of Lord Hermand in the court below.[103] The report does not, indeed, attribute to Lord Hermand the word "galimatias" nor, of course, its somewhat pleonastic use by Lord Holland, though Lord Hermand does appear to have observed of the Act of 1701

---

[98] S.C., 2 Bli.N.S. at p. 453.

[99] *Ibid.*, at p. 458 (*per* Earl Lauderdale).

[100] *Acts of the Parliaments of Scotland*, X, 272, c. 6.

[101] These were days in which this word had some currency: see, e.g., 1 *Greville Diary* 339, 519; and see Megarry, *Arabinesque-at-Law* (1969), p. xii.

[102] *Andrew v. Murdoch* (1814) 2 Dow 401 at 430–31.

[103] *Andrew v. Murdoch* (1806) Buch. Rep. 1 at 51.

that he has "considered it for thirty years of my life, as the most absurd provision that ever was put upon paper," and that a very learned friend of his had said that "the framers of the act of 1701 did not wish that it should be understood."[104] He is also reported as saying "I do not care what the act of Parliament says on this subject, because I hold that there is a power paramount to acts of Parliament, and that is the power of right reason, to which Kings and Parliaments themselves must be subject."[105] After giving his opinion on the main point at issue, he said: "That is my opinion. It is founded upon reason, and plain sense; and all the acts of Parliament in the world will never convince me that it is wrong."[106]

It was this case that once brought to the fore Lord Hermand's low opinion of one of his brethren, Lord Meadowbank. After Lord Holland's speech in the House of Lords, "Lord Gillies could not resist the pleasure of reading Holland's remark to Hermand, who was generally too impetuous to remember his own words. He entirely agreed with Lord Holland, and was indignant at the Court suffering 'from the rashness of fools.' 'Well, my Lord, but who could Lord Holland be alluding to?' 'Alluding to? who *can* it be but that creature Meadowbank?'"[107]

Even after 1844, the lay peers were not unanimous in accepting exclusion from things judicial. On June 30, 1873, the great conveyancing case of *Bain* v. *Fothergill*[108] was argued before the House of Lords, with the judges in attendance. One of the law lords, Lord Colonsay, who was "the first Scottish lawyer raised to the peerage for the purpose of being constituted a member of the court of ultimate appeal,"[109] died early in the following year, and only Lord Chelmsford and Lord Hatherley seem to have been left to hear the advice of the judges and give judgment.[110]

---

[104] *Ibid.*

[105] *Ibid.*, at p. 52.

[106] *Ibid.*

[107] Lord Cockburn, *Memorials of His Time* (1909), p. 126.

[108] (1874) L.R. 7 H.L. 158.

[109] 35 *D.N.B.* 248.

[110] See L.R. 7 H.L. 162 n.; but see the larger attendance recorded in (1874) 106 Lds. Jnl. 141, 281. Martin B., who on behalf of the judges had requested time to consider the questions put by the House, retired from the Bench before the advice was given.

But not long afterwards, the second Lord Denman, a son of the Chief Justice, said in the House of Lords that on the hearing of an appeal "there was no danger of any lay Peer being allowed to vote"; and "he mentioned having been on a Committee of the whole House, and having tried to vote on a case of Bain against Fothergill."[111] This certainly indicates that the House had not fallen below its quorum of three. It also shows Lord Denman as underrating his own tenacity and overrating the resistance of the House; for some seven years later he succeeded in both speaking and voting on an appeal.[112]

At one time the Irish House of Lords attempted to assert a judicial jurisdiction. In 1719 the House directed the Gentleman Usher of the Black Rod to take Gilbert C.B. and Pocklington and St. Leger BB. into custody; it does not appear how long their detention lasted.[113] Their offence was obedience to an order of the House of Lords of Great Britain in a case called *Annesley* v. *Sherlock*. Parliament promptly passed an Act that, after reciting that "the House of Lords of Ireland have of late, against Law, assumed to themselves a Power and Jurisdiction to examine, correct and amend the Judgments and Decrees of the Courts of Justice in the Kingdom of Ireland," enacted that the House of Lords of Ireland had no judicial authority.[114] This Act, however, was repealed in 1782,[115] and when an Act of 1783[116] provided that all actions in Ireland were to be decided there finally, and without appeal to the courts in England, the judicial authority of the Irish House of Lords seems to have been restored. But the end came with the Act of Union 1800,[117] which enacted that all appeals that "might now be finally decided by the House of Lords of either Kingdom" should thenceforth be finally decided by the House of Lords of the United Kingdom.

---

[111] 227 Hansard (3d ser.) col. 918 (25 Feb. 1876).

[112] See 1 Misc. 13.

[113] *Re Gilbert* (1719) 15 St.Tr. 1301; 8 Foss's *Judges* 31.

[114] 6 Geo. 1, c. 5, 1719.

[115] 22 Geo. 3, c. 53, 1782.

[116] 23 Geo. 3, c. 28, 1783.

[117] 39 & 40 Geo. 3, 1800, art. 8.

2

~

JUDEX NON JURIDICUS

FOR CENTURIES England has been fortunate in the judges that it has produced. Imperfections there have been aplenty. But instances of members of the Bar who, on appointment to the Bench, have demonstrated that they wholly lack the judicial quality have been exceedingly few. Much has been due to previous part-time experience as a recorder, chairman of Quarter Sessions, or Commissioner of Assize; for this proves wonderfully revealing. Yet this was experience in crime, and not in Chancery or the county courts. The change came not long after the Courts Act 1971 had greatly widened and improved the scope for temporary and part-time judicial appointments. The policy was adopted of not appointing to the Bench anyone who had had no previous judicial experience. This virtually ended the risk of making appointments that never should have been; and such appointments have long dropped out of sight. Yet two examples from the nineteenth century may be given, one at home and the other abroad.

William Ramshay was appointed judge of the County Court of Lancashire at Liverpool in April 1850.[1] The appointment was made by the Chancellor of the Duchy of Lancashire, the Earl of Carlisle; the new judge's father and grandfather had both been land agents for the earl. Many complaints about the judge's conduct soon arose, and in June 1851, the Chancellor held an inquiry in the Duchy Court at Waterloo

---

[1] This account is based on *Ex parte Ramshay* (1852) 18 Q.B. 173, esp. at pp. 175, 176; *The Law Times* (1850–1853), vol. 15, p. 75; vol. 17, pp. 101, 109, 213, 215; vol. 18, pp. 15, 16, 26, 27, 38, 72, 73, 85, 86, 97, 100, 176; vol. 20, p. 151.

Bridge, London. Whateley Q.C. appeared for the promoters of the inquiry, the Liverpool Guardian Society; Serjeant Wilkins appeared for the judge. One of the main complaints was that the judge used offensive language and applied opprobrious names to the suitors in his court; and there was evidence that he called witnesses "fools" and "blockheads." At the end of the first day of the hearing, the Chancellor, who had a statutory power of removal "for Inability or Misbehaviour,"[2] in effect prohibited the judge from sitting until the inquiry had concluded; and after an adjournment of a fortnight, the hearing was resumed. In August 1851, some 11 weeks after the inquiry had begun, the Chancellor held that he did not feel himself to be called upon to remove the judge from office.

Five days later the judge took his seat in court again. Some 150 cases had been fixed for hearing at 9 a.m., but not until a little before 1 p.m. did the judge appear. He began by referring to the attempts to remove him from office while he was labouring under "the distressing and dangerous illness" by which he had "been so long afflicted." He then commented on the defeat of "the machinations of certain ill-disposed and unscrupulous persons who had endeavoured to cover him with disgrace and dishonour," and continued, though often not very audibly, with many more comments in that vein.

That was not all. The judge then proceeded to issue invitations to a banquet to be held in his court "in honour of the great principle of judicial independence, so long and so recklessly assailed in this town." He failed to persuade the Mayor to attend the banquet; but both the Liverpool Stipendiary Magistrate and the judge of the Cheshire County Court were guilty of what *The Times* was to describe as the "glaring impropriety" of being present at "this most unseemly festival." The judge's "long rambling speech" insinuated that the death of his predecessor (who had been drowned) was attributable to persecution by the Liverpool press. He said that he was determined to teach the press of Liverpool to behave better, and he assured them that "the greater their insubordination the greater would be their punishment." Later he

---

[2] County Courts Act, 1846, s. 18.

toasted a Hungarian who was present, and recited some doggerel verses expressing the hope that England, France, and Hungary would fight again the battle of freedom on the plains of Hungary.

There was a prompt response from the press. On September 27, 1851, the *Liverpool Journal* exhibited a number of placards containing a line in large type that read: "Mr. Ramshay's Opinion of the People of Liverpool"; and some of these placards were within 10 or 12 yards of the court. The judge directed bailiffs of the court to bring the editor before him; but the editor, on legal advice, refused to go unless a warrant was produced. At one stage he produced a knife in his defence, and there was a scuffle; but the bailiffs left without the editor. The judge then issued a summons, and in obedience to this the editor, for whom Sir George Stephen appeared, duly attended the court on September 29, 1851. Under cross-examination, one of the bailiffs admitted having not been quite sober at the time, as he had had "two twopennyworths of whiskey." When asked who had ordered him to arrest the editor, the bailiff was silent, and the judge then said: "I did. I gave him the order. By the word 'bring' I meant to use force if necessary; and even if it required ten thousand men I should get them. I care for no man living who opposes me."

In addressing the judge, Sir George Stephen said that if officers had entered his house without legal authority and had attempted to take him into legal custody, he, instead of merely threatening them with a knife, would have shot them. This statement evoked "a perfect burst of applause" from the "very respectable audience" in court; and the judge thereupon called on the bailiffs to do their duty and bring before him any of the persons who had been "engaged in that outrage." This produced no response; but after the judge had threatened to fine the bailiff at the door £5 unless he pointed out the guilty persons, the bailiff said that he could not point out any one in particular, as he believed that the noise was general. After further exchanges, the case proceeded. In the end the judge fined the editor "£5 each on 3 cases of assault," and imposed (apparently in default of payment) "seven days' imprisonment each for two cases of alleged assault on the officers of the court." The editor went to prison, but later was "released by subscriptions of his friends under protest."

A memorial to the Earl of Carlisle as Chancellor of the Duchy was promptly presented, seeking the removal of the judge and the appointment of another judge, "of learning, temper, and moderation, in his stead"; and many thousands signed it. On November 5, 1851, less than three months after his previous decision, the Chancellor began another inquiry, sitting at Preston, with Ellis Q.C., the Attorney-General of the Duchy, as an assessor.

Monk and Tindal Atkinson appeared in support of the petition, and Serjeant Wickens, Sowler, Ovens, and Thorburn appeared for the judge. It seems that in fining the editor, the judge had said that he "looked like a man in whose eyes and face the worst passions and the worst feelings of human nature were depicted." The judge had also fined a man ten shillings for putting his hat on in an outer room that adjoined the court in which the judge was sitting. The fine was later reduced to five shillings, but the poor man, being unable to pay, was committed for two days to Lancaster Castle.

The speech of Serjeant Wickens in reply to these and other allegations "extended over two days," though to no avail. On November 24, 1851, the Chancellor of the Duchy removed the judge on the grounds of his being "unable duly and properly to execute" his office, and of his misbehaviour in office. He appointed Mr. Joseph Pollock in his place. Ramshay then sent the clerk of the court a letter, purporting to adjourn the next sitting of the court, which was due to take place on December 29. Judge Pollock nevertheless took his seat on that date; and a further purported adjournment by Ramshay was also ignored. In January 1852, Ramshay initiated *quo warranto* proceedings in the Queen's Bench against Judge Pollock. But on February 10 Lord Campbell C.J., delivering the judgment of the court, held that there were no grounds for interfering with the decision of the Chancellor. That seems to have been the end for Ramshay. His name appeared in the *Law List* for 1853 as counsel but was omitted from the *Law List* for 1854. It does not appear whether the disappearance was due to death, retirement, or some other cause. All that need be added is that ultimately the Treasury paid all the costs of the inquiry at Preston.

Ramshay's judicial career was shorter and less remarkable than that of John Walpole Willis.[3] He was born on January 4, 1793, and after Rugby, Charterhouse, and Trinity Hall, Cambridge, Gray's Inn called him to the Bar in 1816. For some years he practised successfully at the Chancery Bar, with chambers at 8 Stone Buildings, Lincoln's Inn. His *Pleadings in Equity* appeared in 1820, and his treatise on the *Duties and Responsibilities of Trustees* was published in 1827. In that year he was appointed to the Court of King's Bench in Upper Canada, later to be Ontario. The expectation was that a Court of Chancery would be established in the Province, and that he would be the judge. But soon after he arrived in York (as Toronto was then called), he came into collision with many Canadians, not least the Attorney-General of the Province, the future Sir John Robinson C.J., whom he regarded as being his rival. Willis asserted that it was for him to state to the Crown officers what their duties were, and that it was for them to perform those duties according to his directions. In open court he charged Robinson with neglect of duty in failing to launch prosecutions in various cases, one of them relating to a duel that had been fought over ten years earlier.

This seems to have been the case of H.J. Boulton, who had become the Solicitor-General. He had been the second for S.P. Jarvis in a duel for which the somewhat surprising venue had been the barn of Elmsley C.J.; and Jarvis had killed his opponent, J. Ridout. In 1817 Jarvis had been tried for murder; but he had been acquitted, and this had put an end to the charge against Boulton of being an accessory. Despite this, the outburst by Willis in 1828 seems to have been at least partly responsible for Boulton being indicted for the murder of Ridout; but at the trial, before Willis J. himself, there was a not unexpected acquittal.[4] Apart from this and other incidents, concern was felt at the manner in which

---

[3] See generally W. Kingsford, *History of Canada*, vol. 10 (Toronto & London, 1898), pp. 258–80, and H.F. Behan, *Mr. Justice J.W. Willis* (Glen Iris, Victoria, 1979), which quoted extensively from contemporary newspaper reports.

[4] W.R. Riddell, *Upper Canada Sketches* (1922), pp. 24–31.

Willis proclaimed his zeal for law reform. Through the newspapers he announced that he was preparing for publication a work on the jurisprudence of Upper Canada, with a hint that the motto "Meliora sperans"[5] would appear on it.

In 1828, the year after his appointment, the decisive event occurred. Campbell C.J. went on six months' sick leave preparatory to retiring, and Willis unsuccessfully sought appointment in his place. He then announced that in the absence of the Chief Justice, he and the other judge, Sherwood J., could not properly constitute the Court of King's Bench. Sherwood J. took the opposite view, but Willis refused to sit in the court. This was seen as an attempt to procure appointment as at least acting Chief Justice. In the end, this, coupled with other unhappy events, led the Executive Council to recommend the Lieutenant-Governor to revoke the commission of Willis as a judge. This was done under the Colonial Leave of Absence Act 1782,[6] sometimes miscalled Burke's Act.[7] In the case of misbehaviour of any person in office, the Act authorised the Governor and Council, subject to appeal to the Privy Council, "to amove such person" from his office. The patent of amotion for Willis was dated June 27, 1828.[8] He had been in Canada for less than ten months.

Willis at once went to England to contest his amoval. Ultimately various charges and counter-charges were investigated by the Privy Council, the government bearing the expense.[9] Willis received strong support from the House of Assembly of Upper Canada, which presented an address to the King, signed by the Speaker, dated March 14, 1829. The address took a view adverse to the Executive. It stated that the removal of Willis was "violent, precipitate and unjustifiable," and that he had been

---

5 "In hope of better things."

6 Sect. 2; and see *Willis* v. *Gipps* (1846) 5 Moo. P.C. 379 at 388, 390. The Act, 22 Geo. 3, c. 75, was repealed by the Statute Law Revision Act 1964.

7 It is a near miss, by only seven chapters; for Burke's Act is 22 Geo. 3, c. 82, 1782 (the Civil List and Secret Service Money Act 1782, now mostly repealed). See Sir Kenneth Roberts-Wray, *Commonwealth and Colonial Law* (1966), p. 492, n. 53.

8 See (1830) 24 Hansard (2d ser.) cols. 552, 554.

9 *Ibid.*, at col. 554.

"a victim of Provincial persecution."[10] The upshot was that in 1829, the Privy Council held that Willis had been wrong in refusing to sit *in banco* with Sherwood J. during the absence of Campbell C.J., but that the summary amotion, effected without giving Willis any opportunity of meeting specific charges, could not be sustained.

Willis did not return to Canada. In March 1831, he was appointed Vice-President of the Court of Civil and Criminal Justice of British Guiana.[11] Although it has been said that he later became Chief Justice there,[12] in 1835 he seems to have been passed over in favour of a judge junior to him. This made him very bitter, and within three months he returned to England on sick leave;[13] he seems to have had chronic liver trouble.[14] Scant material about this period of his life is available, and it has been said that in British Guiana Willis "quarrelled with everybody and was again removed";[15] but although the quarrels seem likely enough, the removal appears to have been more complex. While Willis was in England, the Governor seems to have been trying to persuade a reluctant Colonial Office not to allow Willis to return. At the last minute, on the eve of his return, resistance crumbled, and Willis was persuaded to prefer Australia to British Guiana.[16] So in 1837[17] he received his third judicial appointment. This time it was as a judge of the Supreme Court of New South Wales. In November he arrived in Sydney, and in February 1838 he took his seat in court there.

A peaceful start was all too soon followed by many quarrels. In 1841 Willis was appointed resident judge for the district of Port Phillip, later

---

10 *Parliamentary Accounts and Papers*, 1831–1832, vol. 32, No. 740, pp. 4, 5.

11 B.A. Keon-Cohen (1972) 8 Melb. L.R. 703 at 704.

12 (1877) 21 S.J. 874.

13 Behan, *supra* note 3, pp. 39, 40; Keon-Cohen, *supra* note 11, at p. 704. See also the obituaries at (1877) 12 L.J. News. 553 and (1877) 21 S.J. 874, stating that his return in 1836 was due to ill-health, and asserting that he twice refused a knighthood.

14 See Keon-Cohen, *supra* note 11, at pp. 707, 708.

15 Sir Arthur Dean, *A Multitude of Counsellors* (1968), p. 11; and see D.B. Read, *Lives of the Judges of Upper Canada* (1888), p. 117.

16 Behan, *supra* note 3, pp. 40, 41.

17 It was in this year that a Court of Chancery was at last constituted in Upper Canada under the Provincial Act 7 Will. 4, c. 2, 1837, after many other proposals had come to nothing: Riddell, *supra* note 4, p. 30.

to become the State of Victoria. Doubtless it was thought that distance might lend him enchantment in the eyes of his brother judges and others. On March 9, 1841, he arrived in Melbourne with over 43 tons of luggage.[18] Yet the move brought no improvement: there were still many troubles,[19] and on December 21, 1842, the Governor brought various complaints of misbehaviour in office by Willis before the Executive Council. Without notifying Willis, the Council then proceeded to consider the complaints, and further considered them on January 16, 17, and 20, 1843. By May 1843, Willis had "quarrelled with the Governor, the Executive Council, and the Judges of New South Wales, the Super-intendent of Port Phillip, the magistracy, the legal profession, the press, and was distasteful to more than one half the community."[20] Finally, by a writ dated June 17, 1843, based on misbehaviour in office, Willis was amoved under the Act of 1782 from his office as a judge of the Supreme Court of New South Wales, and his appointment as Resident Judge at Port Phillip was revoked.[21] Another writ of the same date superseded and inhibited Willis from the exercise of all power and authority as a judge.[22] These operated not as a mere suspension,[23] but as removal from office or dismissal.[24] The writs were delivered to Willis on June 24, 1843, while he was sitting *in banco*; the deputy registrar came into court and spoke to Willis, who retired to his chambers, and the deputy registrar then delivered the writs to him.[25]

Again there was an appeal to the Privy Council, and after some procedural delays, this was heard in 1846. During the argument, Lord Lyndhurst L.C. referred to the amotion of Willis in 1829 as being the only previous case of the amotion of a judge under the Act.[26] As was the

[18] Keon-Cohen, *supra* note 11, at p. 708.

[19] *Ibid.*, at pp. 709–11.

[20] Read, *supra* note 15, at p. 120.

[21] See *Willis* v. *Gipps* (1846) 5 Moo. P.C. 379 at 383.

[22] *Ibid.*

[23] *Pace* Dean, *supra* note 15, at pp. 12, 13.

[24] See *Willis* v. *Gipps, supra* (S.C. 5 St.Tr. (N.S.) 311), and the *Memorandum* (1870) 6 Moo. P.C. (N.S.) App. 9 at 10.

[25] Keon-Cohen, *supra* note 11, at p. 712.

[26] *Willis* v. *Gipps, supra* note 21, at p. 388.

practice,[27] no formal judgment was delivered. The report of the Judicial Committee was that "there were sufficient grounds for the amotion of Mr. Willis," but that as the Governor and Council ought to have given him some opportunity of being heard, the order of June 17, 1843, should be reversed; and the Queen ordered accordingly.[28] That was the end of Willis as a judge, for the Secretary of State then revoked both of the judicial appointments that Willis had held. But the decision of the Judicial Committee, reversing the earlier removal, was not without value to Willis, for it brought him arrears of salary of over £4,800. Willis lived on for over 30 years more, and died on September 10, 1877, in his 85th year.

One verdict on Willis was that he was "quite unfitted for judicial office. . . . He was vain and conceited, quick-tempered and quarrelsome, vindictive in action and violent in language. He quarrelled with all those with whom he had to do: the Bar, the attorneys, parties, witnesses and the press. Well-known and respected citizens . . . were committed for contempt of Court."[29] Another verdict was that he was "impotent to control a bad temper, lacking in dignity, and capable of being easily prejudiced — in politics he was a partizan, an intermeddler in other people's affairs, and always eager to over-step the bounds of judicial propriety and dabble in matters not regularly before him."[30] A third view was that Willis "had an overweening confidence in his own merits and judgment, and a perfect contempt for all Colonials and Colonial officials from the Lieutenant-Governor and Chief Justice down."[31] Sir Victor Windeyer's phrase "irascible and tempestuous"[32] seems both economical and expressive.

Yet Willis was not without his merits. It has been said that he "possessed a brilliant, scholarly mind, sound legal knowledge and was imbibed [*sic*] with the highest ideals of a judge's role. He had a highly

---

[27] See *Montagu* v. *Van Dieman's Land* (1849) 6 Moo. P.C. 489 at 499.

[28] *Willis* v. *Gipps*, *supra* note 21, at p. 392.

[29] Dean, *supra* note 15, at p. 12.

[30] Read, *supra* note 15, at p. 119.

[31] Riddell, *supra* note 4, at p. 30.

[32] In *A History of the New South Wales Bar*, ed. J.M. Bennett (1969), p. 53.

developed sense of justice and unquestionable professional integrity. He
was impartial, hardworking, a stickler for punctuality and court
procedure; and he was lauded for "fearless independence" and "wisdom
and integrity of judicial decisions . . . unwearied assiduity, unflinching
firmness, and unbending independence in effecting substantial justice."[33]
Yet even if he had these qualities to the full, they could unhappily be laid
waste by an arrogant and intemperate nature and the consequent
injudicious and unjudicial behaviour.

A precipitating cause of the Australian amotion seems to have been
the conduct of Willis when he received a judgment of the Full Court
reversing a decision of his to strike a solicitor off the rolls. He read out
the judgment in court, making gibes and caustic comments about the
judgment and the judges, and ridiculing the solicitor; and for months he
refused to reinstate the solicitor on the ground that he (Willis) wished
to appeal to the Privy Council and could not get the papers needed
for this.[34] Whatever his good qualities, he cannot have thought this to be
proper judicial conduct. There was also his attitude to the requirement
that a person should be given an opportunity of being heard before he
was condemned. As a litigant, he twice relied on this for success in the
Privy Council; yet as a judge he repeatedly denied it to others. He refused
to hear witnesses and members of the public in their defence before he
committed them to prison; and in 1843 Willis peremptorily ordered that
the Honourable James Murray, a barrister who was out of the country,
should have his name struck off the roll of the court "with every mark of
ignominy and disgrace."[35] Willis did this on the strength of an allegation
made by a builder in insolvency proceedings that his insolvency was
attributable to Murray not having proceeded with a building contract
with him but selling the unfinished premises instead.

Quite simply, Willis was a judicial disaster. It would be interesting to

[33] Keon-Cohen, *supra* note 11, at p. 703, quoting in part from an Address presented to Willis
by some inhabitants of Melbourne after his amotion.

[34] Dean, *supra* note 15, at p. 12; Behan, *supra* note 3, at pp. 188–91. For Willis, such comments
were normal: Behan, *supra* note 3, pp. 49, 74.

[35] Behan, *supra* note 3, p. 82. Murray died in Borneo soon afterwards, and probably never
heard of the striking off.

see a likeness of the judge who, on three continents, was thrice appointed and thrice removed. But what is said to be a photograph of him[36] appears in fact to be a portrait of James Shaw Willes, who graced the Court of Common Pleas from 1855 to 1872.[37]

[36] *Ibid.* Frontispiece; from the La Probe Library, Victoria.

[37] See A.W.B. Simpson, *Biographical Dictionary of the Common Law* (1984), pp. 278–79, an enlargement of an almost identical photograph of Willes given to R.F.V. Heuston by a great-niece of the judge; and see the etching in *The Green Bag* (1901), p. 363.

3

~

BEGGAR OR FOOL

TO ERR is human — and judges are famously human: "Judges at last are but men subject to the imperfections and frailties of other men, encompassed by error, seasoned with sin, and fettered by fallibility."[1] This includes the United States Supreme Court, even in the eyes of a nineteenth-century justice: "We pretend not to more infallibility than other courts composed of the same frail materials which compose this."[2] Jackson J. carried this view forward to the twentieth century: "Reversal by a higher court is not proof that justice is thereby better done. There is no doubt that if there were a super-Supreme Court, a substantial proportion of our reversals of state courts would also be reversed. We are not final because we are infallible, but we are infallible only because we are final."[3] So too Atkin L.J.: "The number of successful appeals from the Court of Appeal to the House of Lords is about 33 per cent. There is no reason for believing that if there was a higher tribunal still the proportion of successful appeals to it would not reach at least that figure."[4]

In more recent years the odds against success on appeal seem to have shortened from 2 to 1 against to evens. In a case about a shipment of soya beans, Lord Denning M.R. said that in certain cases some three years earlier "the trade set us an examination paper with many questions

[1] *State ex rel. Boone* v. *Metts*, 88 So. 525, 531 (Miss. 1921) (Ethridge J., dissenting).
[2] *Martin* v. *Hunter's Lessee*, 14 U.S. (1 Wheat.) 304, 364 (1816) (Johnson J., concurring).
[3] *Brown* v. *Allen*, 344 U.S. 443, 540 (1953) (Jackson J., concurring).
[4] (1927) 3 Camb. L.J. 1 at 9.

to answer. We did our best, but recently our papers were marked by the House of Lords . . . .[5] They only gave us about 50 per cent. The House of Lords are fortunate in that there is no one to examine them or mark their papers.[6] If there were, I do not suppose they would get any higher marks than we."[7] A modern examination of the transcripts of judgments in all civil cases decided by the Court of Appeal during five sample years (1955, 1965, 1972, 1973, and 1974) shows that the percentage of successful appeals was a remarkably consistent 40; and if transcripts of fewer than ten pages were excluded, thereby omitting peremptory judgments dismissing hopeless appeals, the percentage was not far short of 50.[8] Idiosyncrasies in the appellate process are many: "It is a characteristic of our system that the higher court often seems partial towards thinking that the important point is the one which was not taken in the lower court."[9]

From the fundamental recognition of fallibility flows one of the fundamental rules for deciding appeals:

Beyond question . . . it is generally the duty of an appellate Judge to leave undisturbed a decision of which he does not clearly disapprove. I conceive that, in our court, as in the civil law, it is the rule that "gravely to doubt is to affirm." Considering that the Judge appealed from is frequently as qualified to form an opinion as he that is appealed to, and remembering in how many cases the opinions both of original and appellate Courts are, upon a fresh consideration, found to be mistaken, I hold that a reversal cannot proceed from a Judge fit for his office, without a full conviction of the error of the judgment which he is reviewing.[10]

---

[5] Citing *Bremer Handelsgesellschaft m.b.H.* v. *Vanden (Avenne-)Izegem P.V.B.A.* [1978] 2 Ll.Rep. 109.

[6] Few academic lawyers would agree; and the comment ignores the European Court of Justice.

[7] *Bremer Handelsgesellschaft m.b.H.* v. *C. Mackprang Jr.* [1979] 1 Ll. Rep. 221 at 222.

[8] See K.J. Eddey, *The Law Reporting of the Court of Appeal (Civil Division)* (1977) unpublished Oxford University thesis, pp. 300, 301. The range was from 43% for 1973 to 52% for 1972.

[9] *Re Citro* [1991] Ch. 142 at 159 (*per* Nourse L.J.).

[10] *Attorney-General* v. *Corporation of Beverley* (1855) 24 L.J.Ch. 374 at 376 (*per* Knight Bruce L.J.)

Lord Goddard C.J. put the point succinctly: "The function of a court of appeal is to exercise its powers where it is satisfied that the judgment below is wrong, not merely because it is not satisfied that the judgment was right."[11]

This may be an explanation of the course taken by *Dawson* v. *Clarke*,[12] an appeal from the decision of Grant M.R.[13] Lord Eldon L.C. at first, on April 2, 1810, expressed doubt about the decision below, but decided nothing. Over a year later, on August 5, 1811, he spoke again, referring to difficulties that he felt, but still decided nothing. Finally, on August 23, 1811, he delivered judgment in a single sentence, affirming the decision on different grounds that, however, left Grant M.R. unrepentant.[14] One of the counsel in the case later became Richards C.B., and as such he observed in a later case[15] that "I certainly never saw the Lord Chancellor so perplexed in any case, in the whole course of my experience in his Court, as he was in that of *Dawson* v. *Clarke*; and I know that he had very great difficulty in coming to a conclusion upon it."

Reversals take many forms. Often they are softened by words of compliment to the judge. In reversing a decision of Judge Carr in a factory accident case, Sellers L.J. delivered a reasoned judgment with which Davies L.J. briefly concurred. Russell L.J. was even more brief. All that he said was: "I agree. In this case a very experienced workman (in a sense) slipped, as sometimes happens. So also, it may be said, did a very experienced judge."[16] Some judges seek to make their judgments appeal-proof, though few emulate the formula ascribed to an Ontario county court judge in the 1970s: "I find all the facts that are consistent with this judgment and reject all those facts that are inconsistent therewith."[17]

---

11 *Stepney Borough Council* v. *Joffe* [1949] 1 K.B. 599 at 603.
12 (1811) 18 Ves. Jun. 247.
13 *Dawson* v. *Clark* (1809) 15 Ves. Jun. 409.
14 *Southouse* v. *Bate* (1814) 2 V. & B. 396 at 399.
15 *Parsons* v. *Saffery* (1821) 9 Price 578 at 587.
16 *Eaves* v. *Carringtons Ltd.* [1964] C.A. Trans. 98, at p. 5.
17 Collected in Toronto in 1990.

By contrast, sometimes a judge expresses the hope to be reversed:

> In entering the order here appealed from vacating the probate court order allowing the mentioned fees, the circuit judge[18] made it plain that he did so reluctantly, feeling that he was impelled by precedent to effect what he considered an unjust result. In his written opinion he said: "The Court fervently hopes the petitioners . . . in this case will appeal his decision and that it will be promptly and definitely reversed by the Supreme Court in which event the Court will join a host of others in dancing in the streets." Let him prepare to dance. The order of the circuit court is reversed, with costs to defendants.[19]

Hopes such as these tend to be concealed by mere statistics. One of the entries in *The Sporting Annual (Illustrated) 1903*[20] is a table[21] of the "glorious uncertainties of the law." This sets out the number of appeals from 26 High Court judges from October 1901 until the beginning of the long vacation in 1902, and the results. The list was headed by Kekewich J.,[22] with 50 appeals, 25 upheld and 25 reversed. There were four other draws (Bucknill J. (11-11), Phillimore J. (7-7), Kennedy J. (5-5) and Bruce J. (1-1)), and two losses, Lord Alverstone C.J. (3-4), and Swinfen Eady J. (1-3). After adding some appeals from other courts, the result was that out of 475 appeals, 299 were dismissed and 176 (or 37%) were allowed. Apart from Buckley J., with 31 appeals and a score of 19-12, Kekewich J. suffered at least twice as many appeals as any other judge; yet he could also justly claim that he had been upheld half a dozen times more than any other judge.

That of itself would do much to dispose of the old story of the children in the Kekewich nursery being told by their nurse: "Jam for tea today, children! Your father has been *upheld* by the Court of Appeal!"[23]

---

[18] Toms J.

[19] *Detroit Edison Co.* v. *Janosz*, 87 N.W.2d 126, 130 (Mich. 1957) (*per* Dethmers C.J.).

[20] Anthony Treherne & Co. Ltd. (1903), p. 337.

[21] Compiled from (1902) 113 L.T. News. 387.

[22] R.F.V. Heuston, *Lives of the Lord Chancellors 1885–1940* (1964), at p. 43.

[23] For one version, see (1985) 129 S.J. 857. There were children enough (two sons and five daughters), but all had probably left the nursery when he attained the Bench 28 years after his marriage.

Another old story is of an appeal in which counsel for the appellant began with the words: "If your Lordships please, this is an appeal from a decision by Mr. Justice Kekewich; but there are also other grounds for the appeal." That story, too, is almost certainly apocryphal; yet there is at least one report that gives some colour to it. This begins as follows.

"APPEAL from Kekewich J.
"*Warrington*, Q.C., and *John Dixon*, for the appellant, a son of John Birks Piggott, were stopped by the Court.
"*S. Dickinson*, for the respondent, a grandchild of John Birks Piggott. I submit that the decision of the learned judge below is right, and that . . . ."[24]

Though a master of Chancery procedure, Kekewich J. tended to justify the caption in his Vanity Fair cartoon ("A Hasty Judge") by jumping too soon and delivering judgments that, if not right, were plainly wrong.

For some disappointed litigants, a mere right of appeal is inadequate. The perils of judicial office are such that Lord Stair[25] once said, "No man but a beggar, or a fool, would be a Judge."[26] A memorandum in the Kentucky Reports for 1878 and 1879 concerns Elliott J., one of the judges of the State Court of Appeals. "On his way from the court-room to his hotel immediately after the court had adjourned, at about one o'clock P.M., March 26, 1879, he was interrupted at the steps of the Capital Hotel, and without any warning whatever was shot and instantly killed by Thomas Buford, a disappointed litigant, who, as administrator of his sister, was appellant in the case of Buford &c. v. Guthrie, and Buford &c. v. Guthrie, &c., reported in this volume on pages 677 and 690. The news of the death of Judge Elliott created a profound sensation in the state and throughout the civilized world. It is believed that history records but one similar occurrence, which was the killing of Sir George Lockhart, President of the Court of Sessions [*sic*] in Edinburgh in

24 *Re Birks* [1900] 1 Ch. 417 (appeal allowed).

25 Stair, *Institutions of the Law of Scotland* (2d ed. 1693), Book IV, tit. 1, s. 5. In *Maharaj* v. *Attorney-General (No. 2)* (1977) 29 W.I.R. 325 at 334, Hyatali C.J. referred to the dictum as being a "memorable quip of Lord Gifford": but there is no trace of it in Lord Gifford's speech.

26 *Miller* v. *Hope* (1824) 2 Sh.Sc.App. 125 at 134 (*per* Lord Craigie, citing no authority, and not classifying his brethren).

1689."[27] Buford was duly convicted and sentenced to imprisonment for life.[28] On the other hand, Lockhart's assailant, one John Chiesley, was promptly tortured and executed. He had shot Lockhart in the High Street in Edinburgh on Sunday, 31 March 1689, in revenge for a decision given against him in proceedings by his wife.[29]

Another dramatic case[30] arose out of an assault on Field J. when he had been a member of the United States Supreme Court for over a quarter of a century.[31] A Mr. and Mrs. Terry had been concerned in litigation before him while sitting with other judges in the Circuit Court, and while he was delivering judgment there was a scene of great violence in which Mrs. Terry interrupted the judgment with allegations that the judge had been bribed. The judge directed her to be removed from Court, the marshal attempted to do so, Mr. Terry defended her, drawing a knife in the process, and ultimately both were removed from court. Both were committed for contempt. After their release, they openly proceeded to plan to kill the judge, so openly, indeed, that the newspapers published conjectures about the attack.

In consequence, a marshal was deputed to travel with the judge and protect him. While the judge was in the train on circuit in California, the Terrys joined it. They found the judge in the dining car, and Terry struck him twice on the face; as he was about to deliver a third blow, the marshal called on him to stop, saying that he was an officer. Terry put his hand into his bosom where he kept his knife, and the marshal at once fired two shots at Terry, who died in a few minutes.

A local justice of the peace promptly issued a warrant for the arrest of

---

[27] 77 Ky. (14 Bush) p. xiv.

[28] *Ibid.*, at p. xv.

[29] 34 *D.N.B.* 45. On Chiesley's trial, see H. Arnot, *Collection of Celebrated Criminal Trials in Scotland from AD 1536 to 1784* (1812), pp. 168–74. Arnot at pp. 173–74 narrates that two other supreme court judges in Scotland have been murdered, all of them on account of cases to which they were either party or judge: Robert Galbraith, in February 1543, and John Graham, in February 1592. By the Treason Act 1708, to kill any of the Lords of Session or Justiciary, when in the exercise of their office, was declared high treason. See also G. Brunton & D. Haig, *Senators of the College of Justice from 1532* (1832), pp. 419–26, at 425–26.

[30] *In re Neagle*, 135 U.S. 1 (1890). See the full account by Walker Lewis, *The Supreme Court and a Six-Gun: The Extraordinary Story of* In re Neagle, 43 A.B.A. J. 415 (May 1957).

[31] *In re Neagle*, 135 U.S. at 54.

both marshal and judge. The Governor of California forthwith procured the State Attorney General to obtain the dismissal of the charge against the judge, but the marshal was arrested. In proceedings for habeas corpus the Circuit Court then released the marshal, and it was an appeal against this decision that brought the matter before the Supreme Court. Field J. naturally took no part in the case, but the court (with Fuller C.J. and Lamar J. dissenting) affirmed the decision that in doing his duty the marshal had done no murder.[32]

County courts are more dangerous places for the judiciary than is often realised. In 1889, a maker of artificial teeth had brought an action in Nottingham County Court before Judge Bristowe Q.C.; and he failed. After writing a letter to his mistress, referring to his intention to shoot the judge, the litigant went to the railway station used by the judge and shot him from behind, narrowly missing his heart. For this he was duly convicted of shooting with intent to kill, and sentenced by Pollock B. to twenty years penal servitude.[33]

Nine years later a county court became the locus in quo. In Manchester County Court Judge Parry delivered judgment depriving a bailiff of his certificate on the ground of misconduct; and shortly afterwards the bailiff shot him on the bench. The assailant seems to have been as poor a marksman as he was unsatisfactory as a bailiff, for although he fired three shots at short range, the judge suffered no more than a facial wound, severe shock, and partial deafness in one ear; and he continued on the Bench for nearly twenty-nine years more.[34]

It was left for the United States to demonstrate the fraternal perils of the Bench from within. In 1955 Joseph A. Peel was the municipal judge of West Palm Beach, Florida. This seems to have been a part-time appointment, with a salary of $3,100 a year to supplement his earnings in private practice as a lawyer. On July 6, 1953, he had been charged with having represented both parties in a divorce action. This charge had

32 *Ibid.*, at p. 99.

33 *R.* v. *Arnemann* [1890] *The Times*, Mar. 10, p. 10; and see (1889) 88 L.T.News. 65. For the welcome to the judge when he took his seat again over six months later, see (1890) 89 L.T.News. 141.

34 Sir Edward Parry, *My Own Way* (1932), pp. 216, 302.

been referred to Judge Curtis Chillingworth, the senior judge of the Fifteenth Judicial District of Florida. After hearing the evidence he decided that it sufficed to administer a public reprimand to Judge Peel, then some 29 years old, because of his "youth and inexperience."

That was the background when, nearly two years later, another complaint was made against Judge Peel. This came before Judge White, the other circuit judge in Palm Beach County. Under the Florida procedure, if he found that there were sufficient grounds for the complaint, he was required to refer it to Judge Chillingworth. This time the complaint was that Judge Peel had told a client of his, a Mrs. Shupe, that she had become validly divorced, that Mrs. Shupe had thereupon remarried and had had a baby, and that in fact there had been no divorce. On June 1, 1955, Judge Peel's lawyer sought an adjournment in order to find a witness; and Judge White adjourned the case for two weeks.

On the adjourned hearing, neither Judge Peel nor his lawyer appeared; but the judge had not been idle. At about midnight the previous day, two men employed by him had called at Judge Chillingworth's house, and at gunpoint had taken Judge Chillingworth and his wife out to sea and had killed them, dropping their weighted bodies overboard. All that the authorities knew at the time was that Judge Chillingworth and his wife had mysteriously disappeared. A month later the Governor of Florida asked the Supreme Court of Florida whether he could declare the office vacant and appoint a successor; but to this question the court answered No.[35] Nearly a year later, after exhaustive investigations had yielded no trace of the judge, the Governor repeated his question to the Supreme Court; and this time the answer was Yes, subject to the missing judge's right to recover his office by *quo warranto* if he was living but had been forcibly detained, and later returned.[36]

In the meantime, about three months after the murder, Judge Peel had been suspended for ninety days by Judge Lamar Warren on the grounds of misconduct and dishonesty in telling Mrs. Shupe that she was

[35] *In re Advisory Opinion to the Governor*, 81 So. 2d 778 (Fla. 1955).
[36] *Advisory Opinion to the Governor*, 88 So. 2d 756 (Fla. 1956).

divorced; and at some stage Judge Peel resigned from the bench. For over five years Judge Chillingworth's fate remained a mystery. During that time, there was another incident. About two years after the murder, Judge Peel had insured the life of a young attorney who had been in his office for $50,000, or double that sum if he died a violent death. An attempt to murder the attorney failed. He was seriously injured, but lived, and Judge Peel was arrested on a charge of second-degree assault. But the alleged assailant was acquitted of first-degree assault, and the charge against Judge Peel was dropped.

In 1960 the mystery of Judge Chillingworth's death was solved by the confession of the two men who had killed him and his wife. They said that they had committed the murders on the order of Judge Peel, who feared that he would be disbarred by Judge Chillingworth.[37] On October 4, 1960, Judge Peel was arrested, and on March 7, 1961, his trial for murdering the judge began. There were other charges, too, including the murder of Mrs. Chillingworth, and a conspiracy to murder one of the two assassins. (Judge Peel had at first offered a fee of $2,000, but by stages it had been increased up to $5,300. Judge Peel was later tried and acquitted on a charge of attempting to murder him.) There were also some 160 counts of fraud in respect of a company. The jury convicted the judge of being an accessory before the fact to murder; but a majority recommended him to mercy, and so instead of being sentenced to death he was ordered to be imprisoned for life.

Both murderers gave evidence against Judge Peel, though one did so only in return for immunity from prosecution. The other pleaded guilty and was sentenced to death,[38] but ultimately had his sentence commuted to life imprisonment; he died in prison in 1996.[39] Judge Peel served 21 years of his life sentence and then died of cancer one week after his release from prison in 1982.[40] The murderer who was granted immunity

[37] See *San Francisco Examiner*, Nov. 23, 1960.

[38] See generally the full account, through the early 1960s, in Jim Bishop, *The Murder Trial of Judge Peel* (N.Y.: Simon & Schuster, 1962). In the United States, it is common for a judge to continue to bear the title "Judge" after ceasing to hold office.

[39] Rick Stone, "Evil Under the Sun," *Sun-Sentinel* (Ft. Lauderdale, Fla.), 31 Oct. 2004, at p. 12.

[40] *Ibid.*

spent the rest of his life in Florida and died there, a free man, in May 2004.[41]

Some holders of judicial office have been unorthodox in less violent ways. There must be some who could not readily lay their hands upon a reported judgment of Prince Albert, Queen Victoria's consort, on the circumstances in which a petition lay in equity for taking an account of the mesne profits of a mine, and whether a petition in equity for delivery up of the mine would be held bad on demurrer if no impediment to an action for possession at law was alleged. The case is entitled *Vice* v. *Thomas.*[42] It was decided in 1842 in the Court of the Stannaries of Cornwall, on appeal against an order of the Vice-Warden of the Stannaries of Cornwall.

It was a strong court. Prince Albert, the Lord Warden, presided, "with the aid and assistance"[43] of Lord Lyndhurst L.C., Lord Brougham, Lord Langdale M.R., Wigram V.-C., and Parke B. The appeal was argued on May 21, 1842, by Sir William Follett S.-G. and Mr. Sutton Sharpe for the appellants, and by Mr. Erle and Mr. Barlow for the respondents. On May 30, 1842, Prince Albert L.W. delivered the reserved judgment of the court, allowing the appeal. The judgment, some four pages long, cannot have much gratified Dampier V.-W.; for his decision on one point was said to be "clearly at variance with the first principles of equity as administered in the High Court of Chancery."[44] The appellate jurisdiction of the Lord Warden survived for over thirty years more until the Judicature Act 1873[45] transferred it to the Court of Appeal;[46] and the Vice-Warden's Court itself endured until it was abolished in 1896 and its jurisdiction was transferred to such county courts as the Lord Chancellor might direct.[47] The twentieth century cannot offer any Royal

[41] *Ibid.*

[42] 4 Y. & C. Ex. 538; 2 Coop.t.Cott. 122; and see the more ample report by E. Smirke, *The Case of Vice v. Thomas* (1843).

[43] Under 6 & 7 Will. 4, c. 106, 1836, s. 5.

[44] 4 Y. & C. Ex. at 559.

[45] Sect. 18(3); and see Judicature Act 1925, s. 26(2)(d).

[46] See, e.g., *Re West Devon Great Consols Mine* (1888) 38 Ch.D. 51 at 52.

[47] Stannaries Court (Abolition) Act 1896, s. 1(1).

judgment, though it has contributed instances of judgments delivered by a marquess,[48] by a Lord Chancellor sitting as a puisne judge in divorce cases,[49] by an ex-Lord Chancellor sitting as a puisne judge of the Chancery Division[50] and in divorce,[51] and by an Admiral of the Fleet.[52]

Then there are lesser judicial offices. Lord Buckmaster once happened to pick up a *Law List* for 1815:

> I was amazed when I found that the office of senior registrar in the Court of Chancery, a most august if somewhat dry official, was held by the Duke of St. Albans, and I marvelled greatly what the Duke of St. Albans would do as a senior registrar in the Court of Chancery until an inspiration came to me and I remembered that in one of the frolicsome days of Charles II he had made Miss Nell Gwyn Chief Registrar of the Court of Chancery, an appointment which did credit to his originality, and I undertake to say that if she attended to the duties of that office no more popular registrar could be conceived. I also remembered that the Duke of St. Albans was the lineal descendant of Miss Gwyn, and the truth is that this office in 1815 was being carried on as a sinecure office and given to the Duke of St. Albans, when the real purpose of the office was to enter and draw up judgments, enter the names of witnesses, and do that common, rather dreary official work that is connected with our Courts of Chancery.[53]

The records show that on September 9, 1676, Charles II granted the reversion of the office of Registrar of the Court of Chancery to the Duke of Monmouth and others, and on April 2, 1680, the grantees executed a deed declaring that they held the office in trust for "Ellen Gwinne." On July 9, 1687, she demised the office to Charles, Duke of St. Albans and the heirs of his body; and thereafter there were other grants.[54] The *Law*

[48] Marquess of Reading in *Re Transferred Civil Servants (Ireland) Compensation* [1929] A.C. 242, J.C.

[49] Lord Birkenhead in *Walter* v. *Walter* [1921] P. 302 (holding himself bound by the Court of Appeal: see p. 303); *C.* v. *C.* [1921] P. 399; *Gaskill* v. *Gaskill* [1921] P. 425; and *Wilkinson* v. *Wilkinson* (1921) 37 T.L.R. 835.

[50] Lord Buckmaster in *Re Clout & Frewer's Contract* [1924] 2 Ch. 230 and *Re St. Germans Settled Estates* [1924] 2 Ch. 236.

[51] Lord Buckmaster in *Powell* v. *Powell* [1922] P. 278.

[52] Admiral of the Fleet Sir George Callaghan in *The Feldmarschall* [1920] P. 289 at 304.

[53] (1925) 10 *Proceedings of the Canadian Bar Association* 87.

[54] T.D. Hardy, *A Catalogue of Lords Chancellors* etc. (1843), pp. 119, 121–23.

Lists for 1779 to 1829 all show the Duke of St. Albans as Principal Registrar; but reform was on the way. A statute of 1805[55] had validated all appointments of deputy registrars notwithstanding any vacancy in the office of Registrar, but with an Act of 1833 came the end, if, indeed, the Duke had not previously lost the office by omitting to get the patent renewed.[56] For the Act[57] constituted the four existing deputy registrars, with two others, as registrars; and His Grace was Principal Registrar no longer. Three centuries after the grant, proceedings concerning Nell Gwynne House in Chelsea aptly fell for determination in the Chancery Division.[58]

A note in *Coke upon Littleton* records another seventeenth century case. "The celebrated Ann countess of Pembroke, Dorset and Montgomery,[59] had the office of hereditary sheriff of Westmorland, and exercised it in person. At the assizes at Appleby, she sat with the judges on the bench."[60] A contemporary inscription records her office in 1651 as "High Sheriffesse by inheritance of the countie of Westmorland"; and in the nineteenth century Lord Campbell was content to adopt "Sheriffess" as the feminine of "Sheriff."[61] In the next century, Barton J. spoke of the Countess as "a masterful lady," and referred to her case in holding that a woman was disqualified by her sex from being clerk of Petty Sessions, though by statute and not at common law.[62] An appeal failed,[63] but then the Sex (Disqualification) Removal Act 1919 (at times misquoted as the Sex Removal (Disqualification) Act) was passed. A further appeal to the House of Lords was adjourned so as to enable Lord Birkenhead L.C. to communicate with the Lord Lieutenant of Ireland, and then it was withdrawn.[64] Statute thus seems to have brought a happy ending.

---

[55] 45 Geo. 3, c. 75, 1805.

[56] Hardy, *supra* note 54, p. 119. The Law List of 1829 includes the Duke; that of 1830 omits him.

[57] 3 & 4 Will. 4, c. 94, 1833, s. 2.

[58] *Royal Mutual Benefit Building Society* v. *Walker* (1968) 45 T.C. 171 at 186.

[59] Anne Clifford, 1590–1676: see 11 *D.N.B.* 56.

[60] Co.Litt. 326a, n.(2).

[61] Camp. L. & B. 216.

[62] *Frost* v. *R.* [1919] 1 I.R. 81 at 83.

[63] See 2 Misc. 55.

[64] See *Frost* v. *R.* [1920] W.N. 178; (1920) 152 Lds. Jnl. 126, 473.

From Scotland there have from time to time come complaints that Scottish appeals are decided by a predominantly English House of Lords; and for many years it was indeed customary for there to be only two Scottish Lords of Appeal in Ordinary. "The Scottish Lords could then never by themselves affect any doctrine of English law. But in Scottish appeals the English Lords could have their way every time if so minded."[65] This leaves out of account any other Scottish law lords that there might be, such as peers who have held high judicial office; and it assumes, perhaps, a singular solidarity among the English in resisting the reasoning of the Scots. It is certainly not unknown for two of the law lords to agree with all of the English judges below, but for the day to be carried by two Scottish voices and one English. Thus in one case in 1961,[66] Danckwerts J., Lord Evershed M.R., Willmer and Upjohn L.JJ., Lord Tucker and Lord Hodson were all of one mind; but Lord Reid and Lord Guest thought differently. Lord Birkett, who sat not as a Lord of Appeal in Ordinary but as a peer who had held high judicial office, agreed with Lord Reid and Lord Guest, so that it was Scotland that made his lone English voice prevail over his six brethren in unison.

Sometimes, too, appeals are heard by a House that includes three Scots. Thus in 1914 Lord Kinnear, who was not a Lord of Appeal in Ordinary but a Scottish judge who had been ennobled, sometimes sat with two other Scots (Lord Dunedin and Lord Shaw of Dunfermline), an Irishman (Lord Atkinson), and an Englishman (Lord Parmoor).[67] And in 1935 Lord Alness, whose status was the same as that of Lord Kinnear, sometimes joined Lord Thankerton and Lord Macmillan to make a Scottish majority.[68]

The golden age for Scotland, however, was in the early 1930s,[69] when for over two years Scotland had three Lords of Appeal in Ordinary instead

[65] D.M. Walker (1955) 18 Mod.L.R. 321 at 334 n.57, writing of a test scrutiny of appeals in [1951] A.C.

[66] *Winter* v. *Inland Revenue Commissioners* [1963] A.C. 235.

[67] See, e.g., *Smith* v. *Fife Coal Co. Ltd.* [1914] A.C. 723; *Brown* v. *John Watson Ltd.* 1914 S.C. (H.L.) 44.

[68] See, e.g., [1936] A.C. 32, 45.

[69] This point was considered in outline in 1 Misc. 310.

of the customary two.[70] The three, Viscount Dunedin, Lord Thankerton, and Lord Macmillan, often sat together and provided a solid Scottish majority. Sometimes they sat with one or two other law lords to decide Scottish appeals,[71] but there are many examples of the House so constituted deciding English appeals.[72] Thus in one case, such a House reversed a majority decision of the Court of Appeal reversing a unanimous decision of a Divisional Court of the King's Bench Division, which on a case stated by Quarter Sessions had held a decision of an Assessment Committee to be wrong.[73] Yet there seems to have been no outcry that for this reason England was visibly an oppressed majority. In 1986 something of a revival came, when Lord Fraser of Tullybelton, after retiring as a Lord of Appeal in Ordinary, sometimes sat with Lord Keith of Kinkel and Lord Mackay of Clashfern in English appeals.[74] When in October 1987 Lord Mackay became the first Lord Chancellor since the days of the Stuarts never to have been at the English bar, and soon afterwards Lord Jauncey of Tullichettle took his place as a law lord, Scotland had unquestionably outstripped the thirties.

In days when there is talk of training and examining judges for office, one may look at Scottish experience. For centuries anyone appointed a judge of the Court of Session was required to undergo a trial as a judge before he was admitted as a member of the court. Until he was admitted he was known as the "Lord Probationer." The process seems to have originated in days when the Crown sometimes appointed ill-qualified

---

[70] Lord Macmillan was appointed on February 3, 1930, in place of Lord Sumner; Lord Dunedin retired on April 5, 1932 (1932, 173 L.T.News. 232: [1932] A.C. omits this).

[71] See, e.g., [1930] A.C. 503, 588; [1931] A.C. 351 (two Scots in a House of three).

[72] See, e.g., [1930] A.C. 415, 527, 549; [1931] A.C. 726; (1931) 16 T.C. 570; [1932] A.C. 392, 624, 663; [1933] A.C. 1, 28; and see generally (1956) 19 Mod.L.R. 95, 425. Cf. R.M. Jackson, *The Machinery of Justice* (5th ed. 1967), p. 92: "It is arguable that we have gained greatly from having Scots lawyers in the House of Lords . . . . If the rabid nationalism that is afflicting the world should reach England, we may see a rebellion against a state of affairs in which two Scotsmen and a Welshman may lay down the law of England, but so far we have escaped such adolescent neuroticism."

[73] *Toogood & Sons Ltd.* v. *Green* [1932] A.C. 663.

[74] See, e.g., *Sevcon Ltd.* v. *Lucas CAV Ltd.* [1986] 1 W.L.R. 462; *President of India* v. *Lips Maritime Corporation* [1988] A.C. 395, reversing the Court of Appeal.

persons. An Act of James VI of 1579[75] recited (*inter alia*) that it was "heavilie murmured be divers Lieges of this Realme; that our Soveraine Lord electis and chusis zoung men, without gravitie, knawledge and experience, not havand sufficient living of their awin, upon the Session." The Act then provided that when there was a vacancy upon the Bench the King should "present and nominate theirto ane man that fearis GOD, of gude literature, practick, judgement, and understanding of the Lawes, of gude fame, havand sufficient living of his awin, and quha can make gude expedition and dispatch of matters, tuiching the Lieges of this Realme, Quha sall be first sufficientlie tryed and examinate, be ane number of the saidis ordinar Lordes. And in case that persone presented be the Kingis Majestie, be not founde sa qualified be them, as is befoir descrived, our Soveraine Lord, with advice of his saidis three Estates, declairis, that it sall be leasum to the saidis Lordes to refuse the persone presented to them." Thereupon the King was to present another person. A further statute of 1592[76] repeated the qualifications required for appointment, and recited that it is required "that his Hienes gude intention be mair specially expressed toward the complaint of cheising of zoung men, without gravity, knawledge, and experience, upon the said Session, not having sufficient living of their awin." The statute then required (*inter alia*) that the person appointed "be of the age of twenty five zeires at the least compleit."

The first form of trial was devised in 1590. It required the candidate to sit for three days as a reporting auditor of interlocutory matters, giving his opinion first, and then for three days as a reporting judge in actions and causes.[77] In subsequent cases, the six days were reduced to five or four,[78] and ultimately the process whereby the Lord Probationer was to be "tryed and examinate" was regulated by the Act of Sederunt of

---

[75] Sixth Parliament of James VI, 1579, Statute No. 93 (*The Laws and Acts of Parliament of King James I and His Successors* (1682), p. 435); *Acts of the Parliaments of Scotland*, III, 153, c. 38.

[76] Twelfth Parliament of James VI, 1592, Statute No. 134 (*ibid.*, at 630); *Acts of the Parliaments of Scotland*, III, 569, c. 50.

[77] R.K. Hannay, *The College of Justice* (1933), pp. 99, 100, 116–18.

[78] *Ibid.*, at pp. 119, 120.

July 31, 1674. The Lord Probationer was to sit for "three days with the Ordinary in the Outer House, and report cases to the Inner, and one day in the Inner House."[79] The passage of the years brought erosion, however, and by the latter part of the nineteenth century "the whole trials are now passed in a few hours of one day."[80] If the Lord Probationer did not perform satisfactorily, the Court could exercise its power of rejection; and although this was unlikely, in the reign of Charles II Sir William Bellenden was thus rejected.[81]

The case of Mr. Patrick Haldane was more complex. The Articles of Union with Scotland 1706 provided that none were to be named as Ordinary Lords of Session but such who had "served in the colledge of justice as advocates . . . for the space of five years."[82] Haldane had been a member of the Faculty of Advocates for a little under seven years when on December 12, 1721, he was nominated a Lord Ordinary of the Court. The Faculty of Advocates, however, objected before the Court of Session that Haldane had spent most of that period serving as an M.P., and but little of it in practice in the Court of Session. After considering the facts put forward by Haldane, the Court pronounced an interlocutor that these facts were "not sufficient to make it appear that he is qualified to be an ordinary Lord of Session."[83] The Lord Advocate thereupon exhibited a representation to the Court insisting that the Court had no power to reject the Crown's nomination; and Haldane petitioned to be admitted to trial in common form. The Court nevertheless adhered to its interlocutor and refused to admit Haldane to trial; and from this decision an appeal was taken to the House of Lords. There the decision was reversed, and it was ordered that Haldane "be forthwith put upon trial according to law."[84]

---

[79] *Acts of Sederunt, 1553–1790*, p. 115; A.J.G. Mackay, *The Practice of the Court of Session*, vol. 1 (1877), p. 94; and see Hannay, *supra* note 77, at pp. 127, 128.

[80] Mackay, *supra* note 79, at p. 94.

[81] *Ibid.* For earlier Bellenden troubles, see Hannay, *supra* note 77, at pp. 114, 117 (Sir Lewis Bellenden in 1578 and Thomas Bellenden in 1591).

[82] Art. XIX.

[83] *Haldane* v. *Dean & Faculty of Advocates* (1723) Robert.App. 422 at 424. And see *The Minute Book of the Faculty of Advocates*, vol. 2 (1713–1750) (The Stair Society, vol. 32) (1980), pp. 41–62.

[84] *Ibid.*, at p. 429; 22 Lds. Jnl. 77.

The matter did not end there. On January 21, 1724, a petition of complaint and appeal was presented to the House of Lords and duly read. It complained about the Lords of Session in respect of their proceedings pursuant to the decision of the House of Lords; and it was referred to a committee of the House.[85] What seems to have happened is that after the original decision of the House, further objections to Haldane had been put forward. The Ordinary Lords of Session had then voted 7–6 against admitting Haldane, but there had been two Extraordinary Lords of Session who had both voted for Haldane, despite a challenge to their right to vote made by the Ordinary Lords. This time there seems to have been no decision by the House of Lords, for in the end Haldane, under pressure, accepted a Commissionership of Excise in lieu of a seat on the Bench.[86] Many years later he made another attempt to become a member of the Court of Session; but this was in 1750, when he was 67 and in failing health, and the attempt failed.[87]

One result of the petition of complaint and appeal in 1724 was that within little more than a month, on February 25, 1724, Viscount Townshend introduced a Bill into the House, entitled "An Act for explaining the Law Concerning the Trial and Admission of the Ordinary Lords of Session."[88] This seems to have been the Bill that became law as the statute 10 Geo. 1, c. 19, and later became known as the Court of Session Act 1723.[89] Under section 1 of this Act, the qualifications of any person appointed an Ordinary Lord of the Court of Session "may be examined, and shall be tried by the Ordinary Lords of the Court of Session only."[90] If he was found to be duly qualified, the Lords of Session were forthwith to admit and receive him; but if the Lords of Session

---

[85] 22 Lds. Jnl. 243.

[86] See *The History of Parliament: The Commons 1715–1754. II: Members E–Y* (1970), p. 95.

[87] *Ibid.*, at p. 96.

[88] 22 Lds. Jnl. 267.

[89] This is the title conferred by the Short Titles Act 1896, though the Act seems to have been passed in 1724. The regnal year 10 Geo. 1 ran from August 1, 1723, to July 31, 1724, and the session in which the Act was passed began on January 9, 1724 (new style). The Royal Assent was given on April 24, 1724: 22 Lds. Jnl. 332.

[90] By s. 2, when any of the places of the four Extraordinary Lords of Session then in office became vacant, no successor was to be appointed.

believed that there was "just ground to object to the qualifications of the person nominated," they were to "transmit and certify the whole matter to His Majesty, His Heirs and Successors, in order that the Royal Pleasure may be finally had thereupon." The Crown could then require the person nominated to be received and admitted, despite the objection, or else nominate someone else, who would then be subject to the process of examination and determination. The Act thus put an end to the Court's power of rejection and substituted a mere power to require the Crown to reconsider the appointment.

The modern practice was for the Lord Probationer to sit with a Lord Ordinary in the Outer House and hear debate in at least two cases in his Roll, and to "make report thereon and suggest judgment therein in presence of the Lords of the First Division of the Inner House." He was then to hear debate in a cause before the First Division and to "resume" the same (i.e., summarise the argument) and give his opinion "thereanent" in the presence of the Lords of the First Division.[91] For this process short cases with a concise issue were obviously convenient, and were usually found. Such trials must have been anxious occasions for new judges. The English equivalent would have been for the new judge to sit with a puisne judge, hear at least two cases, and then repair to the Master of the Rolls' Court. There, in the presence of the members of that Division of the Court of Appeal, he would have to give an account of the cases that he had heard and suggest what judgments should be given. He would then have to hear an appeal, summarise the arguments, and express his conclusions, still in the presence of the Court of Appeal. In Scotland, there seem to have been no cases in which the Crown has been asked under the Act of 1723 to reconsider an appointment, though at least once in modern times the First Division disagreed with the new judge's report, but considerately treated the matter as if it were an appeal.[92] Finally, on July 28, 1933, Parliament swept away the whole process of trial and examination.[93]

---

[91] Codifying Act of Sederunt 1913, A i, 1.

[92] Private information.

[93] Administration of Justice (Scotland) Act, 1933, s. l.

A new judge appointed to the bench of the Court of Session in Scotland has long taken the judicial title of "Lord," prefixed by "Honourable." Some retain their surnames, while others — particularly if they have landed estates, or to avoid duplication of names — adopt territorial titles. Thus Mr. James McNeill might become either "Hon. Lord McNeill" or "Hon. Lord Gorbals", at his choice. Yet until the twentieth century, this practice had concomitants that sometimes led to matrimonial embarrassment, especially in ignorant foreign lands such as England; for the husband's appointment conferred no title upon his wife. Some fortitude was thus required to meet the gaze under eyebrows raised when a hotel register disclosed that "Lord Gorbals and Mrs. McNeill" were occupying the same bedroom. (Legend has it that the irrepressible Sir Frank Lockwood, impressed by a similar custom whereby Scottish landowners were known by the title of their estates, once registered as "26 Lennox Gardens and Mrs. Lockwood"[94]). Retirement from the Scottish bench brought with it a return to regularity, tempered by some inconvenience, because, it seems, "Hon. Lord Gorbals" became once again "Mr. McNeill". If a judge had been raised to the peerage, of course, he used his title as peer.

It is, perhaps, odd that Queen Victoria should have tolerated even the semblance of judicial sin for those who were overtly as virtuous on the bench as they had been before; but Edward VII had an eye for these affairs. A Royal Warrant dated 3 February 1905 not only authorised the husbands to retain their titles for life, but also gave each wife the right "to assume and use the title 'Lady' and to continue to use the same during the life of her husband, and after his death so long as she remains a widow."[95] Purists may question the wording of the Warrant: for what if (though perish the thought) the marriage ends in divorce? Could Lady Gorbals, marrying a Mr. Smith, properly call herself "Lady Smith" so long as her former husband lives? If so, presumably she would become Mrs. Smith when he died, unless, perhaps, Mr. Smith predeceased Lord Gorbals. For then, after the death of Lord Gorbals, she could say that her

[94] "Veritas," *The Bench, The Bar and the Bear Garden* (1935), p. 68.
[95] London Gazette, 1905, vol. 1, p. 1113 (Feb. 14, 1905).

title continues "after his death so long as she remains a widow": although not *his* widow, she is *a* widow. Let us hope that we shall never know.

Critics of the Bench will find a striking contribution to their armoury in an article entitled "The Second Division's Progress," which appeared in the *Juridical Review* in 1896.[96] After paying tribute to the First Division and the Outer House,[97] the author laments that "the remaining section of the Court presents a very different picture. Of the Second Division in their judicial character, no one speaks well." At that time, the Second Division consisted of Lord Kingsburgh, the Lord Justice-Clerk, who presided over it for 27 years,[98] Lord Young,[99] Lord Rutherfurd-Clark, and Lord Trayner. The writer then refers to an article written eight years earlier, in which it was said:

> There can be no doubt that the conduct of business in this Division has never before occasioned such lively dissatisfaction as during the last dozen years. We do not quote here any of the innumerable tales and gibes at the expense of that Division, which float about the mouths of practitioners. . . . The complaints against the Division are that little justice is done to the arguments, and that there is no confidence that a case will be disposed of in accordance with rules and principles which have generally commended themselves to lawyers, or which have hitherto been understood to obtain as the law of Scotland. To formulate the complaints a little more amply and precisely, they are: —
>
> 1. That by a system of constant interruption from and conversation upon the Bench, the arguments of counsel are torn to tatters; that it is frequently thereby rendered impossible to state an argument with intelligence or connection, and sometimes counsel who have a strong case are hunted to earth without any opportunity of stating it.
>
> 2. That as the judge will not listen with patience to statements which do not at the very outset make clear the nature of the dispute, or to the reading

[96] 8 Jurid. Rev. 268 *et seq.*

[97] The First and Second Divisions of the Inner House hear appeals; the Outer House is the trial court.

[98] 1888–1915. See his autobiography, *Life Jottings of an Old Edinburgh Citizen* (1915); 35 Jurid. Rev. 107.

[99] See G.W.T. Omond, *The Lord Advocates of Scotland* (2d ser. 1914), p. 260; 17 Jurid. Rev. 178, 209.

of any considerable portion of the evidence, they form hasty impressions, which dominate them throughout the hearing, and prevent their giving attention to arguments or evidence which tend in a contrary direction.

3. That in disregard of authority, such effect has been given to certain prepossessions in regard to the disposal of certain classes of cases, and to certain opinions as to the policy of the law, as to shake public confidence in the consistency and continuity of the law as interpreted by the decisions of the Court.

These are somewhat serious statements, but they are statements which, I venture to think, would be subscribed to by every counsel and agent practising in the Court of Session. Nobody who has any considerable practice, but has had some experience of one or other of these forms of complaint; and the result is that the most intense dissatisfaction is felt by every agent who holds a judgment when his case is "transferred to the Second Division," and that many even of the most experienced and painstaking counsel dislike exceedingly having to plead before that Division.

The writer of the 1896 article then added that these words had been written eight years before, but "Can it be doubted that these evils, which the writer touched with gentle hand, have since increased, are increasing, and ought to be diminished?" He said that "of law, Lord Kingsburgh never, at least when at the Bar, professed any knowledge." Of Lord Rutherfurd-Clark, it was said that had he chosen, he might have checked the downward progress of the Second Division. "Unfortunately, he did not choose. He yawned through the livelong day, and often contented himself with some such formula as 'I agree,' 'I doubt,' 'I don't see how the proposed judgment can be reconciled with the cases, but I don't differ.'" After a tribute to Lord Rutherfurd-Clark's great abilities, the writer adds "these talents he allowed to sleep while he took his pleasure in baiting counsel from a safe position, and attained in that form of pastime no inconsiderable skill. Still it was baiting and not 'savaging,' to use an expression which the English Bar invented."

The article then turned to Lord Young, who

might furnish with brains the Queen's Counsel of the three kingdoms, with the dependencies, and retain sufficient, if combined with a few common-place but useful virtues, to make a very good judge. One need not go to

history for examples that some qualities which make the success of the
advocate are often the spoiling of the judge. Sometimes quickness of
apprehension means only hastiness of conclusion. The evil lies in this: what
their lordships cannot see in the twinkling of an eye, is not worth seeing.
Why argue a case which has been seen through at a glance? If a case is dry, or
uninteresting, or full of details, it does not deserve attention. The arguments
of counsel are superfluous. Counsel in arguing against the pleasure of the
court, or attempting to change first impressions, are truly committing
contempt of Court. To listen to reason or precedents in such circumstances is
a "waste of public time." Apparently to rise at two o'clock or even eleven
o'clock is a judicious use of public time. . . . The Division have in one sense
earned the name of a Court of "Terminer *sans* Oyer."[100]

The article goes on to refer to the "unprecedented" recent succession
of reversals which the Division had suffered in the House of Lords:

As the public press has observed in commenting on these reversals, it is not
the fact but the manner of reversal which is significant. One would search in
vain the former judicial annals of the House of Lords for language of such
severe rebuke as the Lords of Appeal have felt it their duty to use in
characterising the judgments under review, especially those in which the
Division reversed Lord Kincairney and Lord Stormonth Darling. Is it
possible that the Second Division have never realised that they no longer
inspire public confidence or public trust, and that the legal profession in all
its branches is compelled to regard them with positive fear and dislike? . . .
The most experienced practitioner cannot form any confident opinion as to
how the Second Division will decide any case whatever. He cannot predict
what argument they will listen to, or whether they will listen at all. . . . How
can counsel perform their duty if argument is turned into dialogue in which
they play the part of targets or occasional interlocutors? If counsel is stating
the facts, the Court are instantly curious to put legal conundrums; if he is
citing precedents, nothing will serve them but the exact age of the most
unimportant witness. One often sees an unfortunate counsel trying to face
four questions at once, all on different points, like the early Christian
exposed in the arena to fight simultaneously with an elephant, a tiger, a
leopard, and a bear. But even when the Division has 'amiable intervals,' a
counsel is often reduced to the dilemma of either leaving important points

[100] The phrase seems to have been borrowed from England: see, e.g., 1 Misc. 245.

unstated and leading cases uncited, or of drawing down thunder and lightning on his devoted head.

Finally, the article reminds the court of various old and authoritative statements on the judicial virtues, and reaches the unhappy conclusion that no effective remedy exists:

> If judges are to care nothing for public opinion, to prefer the distrust of the whole legal profession to their confidence and esteem, and to disregard the unwritten but time-honoured standards of judicial duty, the hour for drastic reform will soon strike. . . . It is written in "The Mirror of Justices,"[101] a work of didactic excellence but doubtful accuracy, that Alfred, "England's darling," in one year hanged forty-four judges for having vexed the people by unrighteous decisions.[102] That method was effective, if barbaric; and some of us, in our more indignant moments, are inclined to cry, "Oh, for one hour of Alfred!"

The author of this "outspoken and detailed indictment" was Neil J.D. Kennedy, who boldly appended his initials to the article.[103] He had been admitted an advocate in 1877, and after being Professor of Law in the University of Aberdeen,[104] he was to become Lord Kennedy and Chairman of the Scottish Land Court.[105] Lord Macmillan, who four years later became editor of the *Juridical Review*,[106] later described the Second Division at this time as "a most unsatisfactory and unpopular Court" whose members "were incompatible in temperament and incapable of cooperation."[107] "To 'murmur' a judge[108] was in old Scots Law a punishable offence," and "there was much speculation whether the

---

[101] *Sic.* See *The Mirror of Justices*, Bk. 5, c. 1, para. 108; 7 S.S. 166; but see *ibid.*, at xxvi.

[102] See, e.g., *Bushell's Case* (1671) Vaugh. 135 at 139; S.C., T. Jo. 13 at 15, where Vaughan C.J. accepted this account.

[103] Lord Macmillan, *A Man of Law's Tale* (1952), p. 46.

[104] 1901–1906. See *Scottish Law List, 1906*.

[105] 1912–1918; Lord Macmillan, *supra* note 103.

[106] Lord Macmillan, *supra* note 103, at p. 42.

[107] *Ibid.*, at p. 46.

[108] To cast aspersions on a judge's integrity: Judges Act 1540 (*Acts of the Parliaments of Scotland*, II, 374, c. 22); see David Hume, *Commentaries on the Law of Scotland Respecting Crimes* (4th ed. 1844) I, pp. 405–06 (citing old cases).

arraigned judges would take any action against their assailant, but nothing happened, and until the retirement of Lord Trayner in 1904 and of Lord Young in 1905 things went on much the same."[109] As Lord Pitfour once said, "Some Judges are like the old Bishop, who, having begun to eat the asparagus at the wrong end, did not choose to alter."[110] The last conviction for murmuring a judge seems to have been in 1870, when a month in prison and a fine of £50 were imposed for making defamatory comments about a Sheriff-Substitute in letters to the Lord Chancellor and the Home Secretary.[111] In 1964 the statutory basis for the offence was removed.[112]

---

[109] Lord Macmillan, *supra* note 103, at p. 46.

[110] *Sinclair* v. *Sinclair*, 1768, Hailes Dec. 247 at 248, quoted in 1 Misc. 316.

[111] *H.M. Advocate* v. *Robertson* (1870) 1 Coup. 404.

[112] Statute Law Revision (Scotland) Act 1964 (repealing in part the Judges Act 1540).

4
~

INTO BATTEL

ONE well-known instance of reputed judicial conservatism and technicality had its roots in a provision in Magna Carta ordaining that
common pleas "*non sequantur curiam nostram*" but should be held "*in
aliquo certo loco.*"[1] For many centuries that "certain place" was in
Westminster Hall,

> next the hall-door,[2] that suitors and their train might readily pass in and out.
> But the air of the great door, when the wind is in the North, is very cold, and,
> if it might have been done, the court had moved a little into a warmer place.
> It was once proposed to let it in through the wall (to be carried upon arches)
> into a back room which they call the Treasury. But the Lord Chief Justice
> Bridgman[3] would not agree to it, as against magna charta, which says that
> the Common Pleas shall be held *in certo loco*, or in a certain place, with
> which the distance of an inch from that place is inconsistent; and all the
> pleas would be *coram non judice*.[4]

In fact, it is plain that the Crown had power to change the "certain
place" from time to time, and in fact occasionally did so, so that the
Court on many occasions sat at York, and sometimes elsewhere, such as
St. Albans or Hertford.[5] Indeed, Serjeant Pulling went so far as to

---

[1] Cap. 17. ("shall not follow Our court"; "in some certain place"); Magna Carta 1235,
cap. 11. See also W.S. McKechnie, *Magna Carta* (2d ed. 1914) 261–69.

[2] See the illustration in (1942) 8 Camb. L.J. 1, showing the court on the west of the great
northern entrance.

[3] He held this office from 1660 to 1668.

[4] R. North, *Lives of the Norths* (1826 ed.), vol. 1, p. 199.

[5] See 1 H.E.L. 197; Pull. 90, 91.

describe the story of the conservatism of Bridgman C.J. in this respect as "twattle,"[6] though Maitland uncharacteristically repeated it without comment.[7] Not for the last time, a jocular comment may well have been taken as a verity.

Before the Law Courts in the Strand were ready for occupation, the courts often had to sit in a variety of places. The Court of Appeal and Divisional Courts frequently sat in committee rooms in the House of Lords.[8] Once Martin B. was sitting with Bramwell B. "in the little room up many stairs, known as the second Vice-Chancellor's Court at Westminster, now happily among the courts abandoned, while a long-winded counsel was 'distinguishing' the case before them from a decision of the House of Lords. After painfully enduring the operation for some time, the baron said, 'You are very much mistaken, if you think that my brother Bramwell and I, sitting in this cock-loft, are going to overrule the House of Lords.'"[9] More recently, a case[10] appeared in the reports as an ordinary decision of the House of Lords on estate duty. In fact, it was a case (indeed, the only case, it is said) in which judgment was delivered not in the House of Lords but in Church House, Westminster:[11] for those were the days of flying bombs.

Some of the perils of argument are unforeseen. In a case of detinue in 1785, Mr. Wood was addressing the Court of King's Bench in Westminster Hall when

> the whole Court, which happened to be very much crowded, became an entire scene of confusion, every one rising at an instant, and looking upwards. Terror was strongly expressed in every man's countenance. Mr. Justice Willes got out by the private door on his side of the Court. Lord Mansfield, Mr. Justice Ashurst, and Mr. Justice Buller left the Court with great precipitation by the usual entrance, and retired into the Lord Chancellor's private room. The Bar, the bystanders, all present to the number

6 Pull. 91.

7 See (1942) 8 Camb. L.J. 8.

8 *A Generation of Judges* (1886), pp. 179, 215.

9 *Ibid.*, at p. 93.

10 *Barclays Bank Ltd.* v. *Attorney-General* [1944] A.C. 372.

11 (1949) 93 S.J. 434.

of near two hundred (except about eight or ten) rushed out of Court with the utmost precipitation. The barristers pressed towards the curtain, which being down very much impeded their escape. Entangled with this and their gowns, the greatest part of them fell, with those from other parts of the Court, one over another on the steps into the hall. Some thought the roof had given way, some that there was an earthquake — all ignorant of the real cause.

The panic, however, was as short as it was ridiculous: in a few minutes as many as could returned, and in about a quarter of an hour the Court was resumed, without any one having received material injury.

Lord Mansfield then addressing himself to Mr. Wood and the Bar in general, told them, if they had any wits left, they might go on.

A maid-servant belonging to an officer of the House of Commons accidentally threw a little dirty water on the skylight of the Court, and a few drops coming through an aperture and falling on the heads of two or three caused all this strange confusion.

An instance this not much to the honour of human abilities. That men possessing the strongest mental powers, accustomed to a quick application of them, and at the moment this happened in the very exercise of them, should be unable to apply the smallest degree of reflection, which in this case would have been fully sufficient to have prevented the consequences, is truly unaccountable.[12]

Yet this is not quite the whole story: the Scottish Bench (not for the first time, nor the last) came better out of the incident than any of the English. It seems that Lord Monboddo, of the Court of Session, was present at the time, "and being short-sighted and rather dull in his hearing, he sat still during the tumult, and did not move from his place. Afterwards, being questioned why he did not bestir himself to avoid the ruin, he coolly answered that he thought it was an annual ceremony with which, as an alien to our laws, he had nothing to do."[13]

Lord Eldon, however, may be permitted the last word, though it is perhaps not entirely clear whether he is speaking of the same Westminster Hall panic as that described above:

[12] *Land* v. *Lord North* (1785) 4 Doug.K.B. 266 at 273.
[13] W.F. Gray, *Some Old Scots Judges* (1914), p. 54, citing from an unnamed contemporary newspaper (some italics and punctuation have been removed).

During a solemn Argument in the Court of Kings Bench, the Servant of the Coffee House of the House of Commons, I think Waghorn's, was trundling her mop near the Sky Light of the Court of Kings Bench; it slipped out of her hand — fell upon the Sky Light, and came down into the Court, alarming Judges, Counsellors, Students, and Suitors most dreadfully. All moved from their Benches and seats in the utmost Consternation, and the Court was left without hardly an Individual in it. This being occasioned by the violence from above — a young Student observed — it is fine Talking, when you say Fiat Justitia, ruat Coelum[14] — A Girls Mop from the Ceiling alters the Thing entirely — then Ruit Justitia — the whole Court is off.[15]

A footnote to the account of the 1785 panic considerably adds an excuse. "It is not unlikely that the dreadful accident which occurred at Worcester in the year 1757, when the roof of the Court fell in during the trial of a cause before Mr. Justice Wilmot, might have caused the panic at Westminster. At Worcester several persons were killed."[16] The judge's account of this incident, in a letter to his wife written within two hours of the event, sets out how

between two and three, as we were trying causes, a stack of chimneys blew upon the top of that part of the hall where I was sitting, and beat the roof down upon us; but as I sat up close to the wall, I have escaped without the least hurt. When I saw it begin to yield and open, I despaired of my own life, and the lives of all within the compass of the roof. Mr. John Lawes [the judge's secretary[17]] is killed, and the attorney in the cause which was trying is killed, and I am afraid some others: there were many wounded and bruised. It was the most frightful scene I ever beheld. I was just beginning to sum up the evidence, in the cause which was trying, to the jury, and intending to go immediately after I had finished: most of the counsel were gone, and they who remained in court are very little hurt, though they seem to have been in the place of greatest danger. . . . Two of the jurymen, who were trying the cause, are killed; and they are carrying dead and wounded bodies out of the ruins still."[18]

[14] Let justice be done, though the heavens fall.

[15] Lord Eldon's *Anecdote Book* (1960), p. 164.

[16] *Land* v. *Lord North, supra* note 12, at 273 n.

[17] *Law and Lawyers* (1840), vol. 1, p. 339.

[18] *Memoirs of the Life of Sir John Eardley Wilmot* (1802), p. 10. For another panic but no serious injuries (apparently at Derby between 1834 and 1844), see R. Walton, *Random Recollections of the Midland Circuit* (1869), pp. 128–31.

Even the animal world has contributed to panic in Westminster Hall. In about 1670,

> there was so great an alarm in Westminster Hall that the gates were commanded to be shut. The King's Bench rose up in great disorder; but when they understood it was only a mad cow, they sat down again. But the fright in Westminster Hall hath furnished the whole town with discourse; for she, having tossed several persons in King's Street, and coming into the Palace Yard towards the Hall gate, several persons drew their swords; others endeavoured to seize upon the officers' staves at the door to defend themselves with. Those in the hall, who saw the bustle and swords drawn, were affrighted, and some cried out the fifth monarchy men were up and come to cut the throats of the lawyers who were the great plague of the land. Some flung away their swords that they might not seem to make any defence; others their periwigs, that they might appear to be meaner persons; the lawyers their gowns; and your friend Serjeant Scroggs,[19] who of late hath had a fit of the gout, was perfectly cured, stript himself of his gown and coif, and with great activity vaulted over the bar, and was presently followed by the rest of his brethren.[20]

Yet one way or another, the usual culprit was water. In the reports of Hutton J., a judge of the Common Pleas, sandwiched between a case on assumpsit and a case on the Statute of Limitation 1623, there appears the following "report" for 1629.

> A strange increase of water in Westminster-Hall:
> Memorand. That on Friday the twenty third day of October, by reason of the greatness of the spring-tide, and a great flood, the Hall of Westminster was so full of water, that neither the serjeants could come to the Bar, nor any stand in the hall, for there was a boat that rowed up and down there, and therefore all that was done, my brother Harvy[21] went to the stairs which came out of the Exchequer, and rode to the Treasury, and by this way went and set in the Court, and adjourned all the juries, for it was the fourth day del tres Mich. And after that we were in the Exchequer Chamber, and heard four or five motions of the prothonotaries there. This coming into Court was

---

[19] Later the infamous Scroggs J. and C.J.: and see 2 Misc. 24.
[20] 6 H.E.L. 505, citing Hatton Correspondence (C.S.) i, 60–61.
[21] Harvey J.

not of necessity, unless it had been the essoign day, or that the Court should be adjourned, crast. Animar.

The Chancery and Kings Bench sate, for they came by the Court of Wards.[22]

Essoigns, it may be mentioned, were excuses for non-appearance, and so the essoign day was the day on which applications for time or for an adjournment were made. "Crast. Animar." was November 3rd, crastinus Animarum being the morrow of All Souls' Day, November 2nd. Formerly[23] this was the day on which the judges and other great officers of State were required to sit in order to provide lists of three qualified persons for each county.[24] From these lists the Sovereign selected a sheriff for each county by the process known as "pricking the sheriffs," or "pricking for sheriffs." This supposedly originated with Elizabeth I touching the names that she chose with a knitting needle.

It is well known that trial by battle,[25] though long obsolete, remained a legal possibility until after *Ashford* v. *Thornton*[26] had brought the anachronism into unfavourable prominence in 1818. It fell to that strong Tory, Lord Eldon, L.C., to sponsor the Bill abolishing this mode of trial. He performed his task with an engaging discussion of some of the detail of what was to cease to be law.[27] Previous parliamentary attempts to secure this reform between 1620 and 1641, in 1770, and in 1774 had proved abortive.[28]

Curiously enough, *Ashford* v. *Thornton* seems to have had a contemporaneous Irish parallel. In *O'Reilly* v. *Clancy*,[29] Clancy had been acquitted of the murder of O'Reilly's brother at the Mullingar Summer Assizes in 1815 because the prosecution had brought no witnesses but

[22] Hut. 108.

[23] See 1 Bl. Comm. 340–42.

[24] *Ibid.*; and see *Memorandum* (1563) 2 Dy. 225b: plague.

[25] Or "battel," which may be technically more correct.

[26] 1 B. & Ald. 405; and see 1 Misc. 234.

[27] 40 Hansard (1819) col. 1203.

[28] E.A. Kendall, *Trial by Battle* (3d ed. 1818), pp. 135, 136, 235–38, 296–304; (1774) 7 Debrett *Parl. Hist.* 229–34.

[29] 2 *Notes and Queries* (2d ser., 1856), p. 241.

had relied on a confession; and this had been held inadmissible. O'Reilly then brought an appeal of murder within the allotted year and a day, and after much discussion and many adjournments, Clancy offered battle. In the end, on a compromise between counsel, Clancy pleaded guilty and was transported for life. The offer of battle horrified Downes C.J.:

> Can it be possible that this "wager of battle" is seriously insisted on? Am I to understand this monstrous proposition as being propounded by the bar — that we, the judges of the Court of King's Bench — the recognised conservators of the public peace, are to become not merely the spectators, but the abettors of a mortal combat? Is that what you require of us?[30]

The case in Ireland seems to have met the same fate as befell *Ashford* v. *Thornton* in England.[31]

It is difficult to ascertain when the last actual combat took place. Kendall, whose book Lord Eldon thought "learned and able,"[32] states flatly that "battles were fought in 1631 and 1638,"[33] but this seems at least doubtful.[34] The case in 1631 concerned a trial by duel awarded by the Court of Chivalry.[35] Lord Rea accused Ramsey of plotting against the King, and after many formalities and an examination of the issues (aided by the King's Advocate, one Dr. Duck), a day was fixed for the battle, which was to be held "in the fields called Tuttle-fields, in or near Westminster."[36] Both parties were admonished "to keep within the bounds assigned them, to wit, that the lord Rea should not go westward beyond Charing-cross, nor Mr. Ramsey beyond Whitehall eastward."[37]

[30] Phillips, *Curran and His Contemporaries* (1850), p. 412.

[31] The 1819 Act that abolished trial by battle showed no intention to exclude Ireland, and so applied to it. See 59 Geo. 3, c. 46.

[32] See 40 Hansard (1819) col. 1204.

[33] Kendall, *supra* note 28, p. 135; and see W. Herbert, *Antiquities of the Inns of Court and Chancery* (1804), p. 118; see also J.P. Gilchrist, *The Origin and History of Ordeals* (1821), p. 30; G. Neilson, *Trial by Combat* (1890), pp. 147, 322.

[34] As to 1631, see the text above: as to 1638, Holdsworth says "the fight did not take place," though he cites no authority: see 1 H.E.L. 310; see also (1885) 11 *Notes and Queries* 145.

[35] *Lord Rea* v. *Ramsey* (1631) 3 St. Tr. 483.

[36] *Ibid.*, at col. 507.

[37] *Ibid.*, at col. 509.

But Charles I then "revoked his letters patents, given to the said lords for the trial of this cause, not willing to have it decided by duel. And so there was nothing more done in it."[38]

The case of 1638 was *Claxton v. Lilburn.*[39] On 6 August 1638, before Barkley J. in the Durham Court of Pleas, gauntlets were cast down between the parties. There were various adjournments, and later that month Charles I was informed that the battle was due to take place on December 22. He ordered

> that the Judges of that Circuit, upon conference with their Brethren, should be thereby prayed and required to take the same Case into due and serious consideration; and if they could find any just way by Law how the said Combat might be put off, and the Cause put into another way of Trial; for his Majesty, out of his pious care of his Subjects, would have it so, rather than the admit of a Battel. . . . Afterwards both Parties brought their Champions into the Court of Durham, having Sand-bags and Battoons, and so tendered themselves in that fighting posture: But the Court upon the reading the Record, found an Error in it, committed by a mistake of the Clerk, (some thought wilfully done) whereupon the Court would not let them join Battel at that time. Thus did the Court several times order to avoid Battel by deferring the Matter, though Champions on both sides were ever present in Court at all Meetings to join Battel.[40]

"At the day to be performed, Berkley, Justice, there examined the champions of both parties, whether they were not hired for money?"[41] They confessed that they were, and the case was adjourned. "And by the king's direction all the Justices were required to deliver their opinions, whether this were cause to de-arraign the battail by these champions?"[42] But the judges held that this objection came too late. There is silence about what happened next, though if battle had been done one would have expected some record of it to have appeared.

---

38 *Ibid.*, at col. 513.
39 2 Rush. Coll. 788; Kendall, *supra* note 28, p. 292.
40 2 Rush. Coll. 789.
41 *Claxton v. Libourn* (1638) Cro. Car. 522.
42 *Ibid.*

In the sixteenth century, battle was nearly done in *Lowe* v. *Paramour*.[43] The report describes the procedure in some detail.[44] All was ready for battle at Tothill, Westminster, before Dyer C.J. and Weston and Harper JJ. of the Court of Common Pleas, with some 4,000 spectators.[45] The champions (Nailor for Lowe, and Thorne for Paramour) were in their places, but the plaintiff made default in appearance, and the defendant's serjeant claimed and was awarded a nonsuit. Nailor nevertheless "challenged the said Thorne to play with him halfe a score blows, to shew some pastime to the Lord Chiefe Justice, and the other there assembled; but Thorne answered, that he came to fight, and would not play. Then the Lord Chiefe Justice, commending Nailor for his valiant courage, commanded them both quietly to depart the field, &c."[46]

There is some authority for saying that the last actual trial by battle in England was held in 1446.[47] A servant "appeached" his master of treason, and on the day of battle at Smithfield, the master, "being welbeloved, was so cherished by his friends and plied so with wine, that being therwith overcome was also unluckely slaine by his servant"; the servant was later hanged for felony.[48] But there appears to have been another battle ten years later, at Winchester, in which the appellant lost, and after he had confessed that his accusation was false, he too was "hanggyd."[49] Yet although from the materials surviving it is far from easy to distinguish trial by battle from duels, there seem to have been battles even later than this. In May 1492, Sir James Parkar fought Hugh Vaughan at the King's manor of Sheen,[50] upon a controversy about the arms that Garter King-at-Arms had given Vaughan; and Parkar was slain at the first course.[51] In Ireland, on September 12, 1583, an O'Connor fought an O'Connor on a charge of treason, and the accused was

[43] (1571) Dy. 301a.

[44] See also *Reade* v. *Rochforth* (1555) Dy. 120a; S.C. (1556) Dy. 131a.

[45] For the weapons, shields, and clothing, see M.J. Russell (1983) 99 L.Q.R. 432. See also M.J. Russell (1980) 1 J. Leg. Hist. 111.

[46] Kendall, *supra* note 28, at 158; and see Stow's *Annales* (1615), pp. 668, 669.

[47] See (1885) 11 *Notes and Queries* (6th ser.) 145.

[48] Stow's *Annales, supra* note 46, at p. 385.

[49] *Whytehorne* (or *Whythorne*) v. *Fyscher* (1456) 17 Camden Soc. (N.S.) 199; see p. 202.

[50] "Within the Kinges Mannor of Shine, nowe called Richmond, in Southerie" (Surrey).

[51] Stow's *Annales, supra* note 46, at p. 475.

killed.[52] The last judicial combat in Britain seems to have been in Scotland, where on March 15, 1597, Adam Bruntfield accused James Carmichael of murder, and fought and slew him.[53]

One of the many curiosities of trial by battle was that if the defendant to an appeal of murder was killed in the battle, it was still necessary for the court to give judgment against him that he be hanged, so that his land would duly escheat to his lord.[54] The result of the trial by battle was, it seems, merely the equivalent of a verdict of guilty by a jury, requiring to be perfected by judgment of the court. In civil cases (e.g., under a writ of right) no such problem could arise, for as the death of the party would cause the action to abate, battle was done not in person but by champion.[55]

Although it is far from easy to discover the last actual trial by battle, there is no difficulty in acclaiming *Ashford v. Thornton*[56] as the last appeal of murder brought into court before the Act of 1819[57] swept away "all Appeals of Treason, Murder, Felony or other Offences," and also wager or trial "by Battel in any Writ of Right." Yet it seems that the passing of the Act was occasioned not directly by *Ashford v. Thornton*, which had been finally disposed of some fifteen months before, but by the entry of another appeal of the same kind. To meet this threat, a Bill was introduced within a day or two, and this passed its first, second, and third readings in one night.[58] Nor is it right to regard *Ashford v. Thornton* as the exhumation of a process thought dead for some two centuries; for the case had had its precursors. In 1729 and 1730 there were three appeals.[59] In one of them,[60] the Warden of the Fleet Prison

---

[52] G. Neilson, *Trial by Combat* (1890), pp. 205, 206; 6 Holinshed's *Chronicles* (1808 ed.), p. 455.

[53] Neilson, *supra* note 52, at p. 307.

[54] Co.Litt. 390b.

[55] 3 Bl.Comm. 339.

[56] *Supra* note 26.

[57] 59 Geo. 3, c. 46, 1819.

[58] (1885) 11 *Notes and Queries* (6th ser.) 463. The Bill was debated in the House of Lords on June 18, 1819 (see 40 Hansard 1203) and received the Royal Assent on June 22, 1819.

[59] See *Bigby* v. *Kennedy* (1770) 5 Burr. 2643 at 2644. See also *Armstrong* v. *Lisle* (1696) Kel. 93; and the case of the future Cowper J., *R.* v. *Cowper* (1699) 13 St. Tr. 1100.

[60] *Castell* v. *Bambridge* (1730) 2 Stra. 853 at 854.

had been prosecuted on the report of a committee of the House of Commons. The charge was of murdering one of his prisoners by the unusual method of knowingly imprisoning him with a man sick with small-pox, in consequence of which the prisoner caught the disease and died. The warden was acquitted, whereupon the prisoner's widow launched an appeal of murder; but again the jury acquitted him. After these cases, there seems to have been a lull for some forty years.[61]

Yet then there were two further cases. In the first of these,[62] in 1770, after much learning had been displayed, the appellant did not prosecute the appeal. Indeed, it was not unknown for an appeal to be compromised, as in one case[63] where the verdict was Guilty of manslaughter only, and the effect of a general pardon was argued. In the end the victim's widow accepted 40 marks for discontinuing the suit.[64] In the other case,[65] in 1771, the defendant successfully pleaded *autrefois convict* of manslaughter.[66]

Not every appeal of murder failed, however. Thus in an appeal in 1639, judgment was given that a widow should be burned to death for the murder of her husband by poisoning him.[67] After the case in 1771, there seems to have been another lull until *Ashford* v. *Thornton* in 1818 and the Act of 1819. A Scottish attempt in 1985 to claim trial by battle, made by two brothers charged with armed robbery, was abandoned when, it seems, it was realised that there was nothing that ousted the presumption that the Act of 1819 applied to the whole of the United Kingdom,[68] even though the statutory words of abolition are far from being all-embracing.

---

[61] See *Bigby* v. *Kennedy, supra* note 59, at 2645 ("almost half a century").

[62] *Bigby* v. *Kennedy* (1770) 5 Burr. 2643.

[63] *Shackborough* v. *Biggins* (1598) Cro.Eliz. 632.

[64] *Shuckborough* v. *Biggen* (1599) Cro.Eliz. 682; *Stroughborough* v. *Biggin* (1599) Moo.K.B. 571.

[65] *Smith* v. *Taylor* (1771) 5 Burr. 2793.

[66] See also *Siddens* v. *Johnson* (1684) 2 Show.K.B. 375, where the record in such a case is set out.

[67] *Pigot* v. *Pigot* (1639) Cro.Car. 531.

[68] *R.* v. *Burnside* [1985] *The Times,* Apr. 23; the *Guardian,* Apr. 20, 23; the *Daily Express,* Apr. 23.

As for *Ashford* v. *Thornton* itself, strange stories still go the rounds. One modern account may be taken:

> Trial by battel, on both the civil and criminal sides, was abolished by statute only as recently as 1819, as a result of a murder case the previous year. This was the famous case of Ashford v. Thornton, in which a young girl called Mary Ashford was murdered in circumstances of peculiar savagery. The evidence pointed overwhelmingly to the guilt of an Abraham Thornton, and the victim's brother instituted a prosecution for murder against him. Thornton, who was a powerful and dangerous brute, insisted on his right to wage a battel, and his accuser's advisers prevailed on him not to appear, but to allow the law to take its course in the courts. Thornton was accordingly indicted for murder at the next sessions when he successfully pleaded *autrefois acquit*, and a reluctant judge was compelled to discharge him. This flagrant miscarriage of justice spelled the end of battel as a mode of trial, and thereafter prisoners on serious charges must entrust their liberty to the, perhaps, equally hazardous, if more sedate, determination of their peers in the jury box.[69]

As thus recounted, *Ashford* v. *Thornton* was indeed a "flagrant miscarriage of justice." Despite evidence that "pointed overwhelmingly" to his guilt, the accused escaped trial by insisting on "his right to wage a battel" and when the victim's brother not surprisingly refused to do battle with "a powerful and dangerous brute," the brute defeated justice by a plea of *autrefois acquit* which, on those facts, was wholly without merit.

The main fact that this account fails to mention is that Thornton had previously been tried for the murder (the cause of death was drowning) and had been acquitted.[70] The trial had been at Warwick Summer Assizes on August 8, 1817, by a judge and jury in the usual way; trial by battle was not available to a defendant on a prosecution on indictment. The trial lasted for "upwards of twelve hours," and after hearing the evidence (which included eleven witnesses for the prisoner, establishing an alibi) Holroyd J. summed up for about two hours.[71] The judge

---

[69] Rex Mackey, *Windward of the Law* (1965), p. 72.

[70] John Cooper, *A Report of the Proceedings against Abraham Thornton* (1818), p. 141.

[71] *Ibid.*, at p. 56.

concluded with an observation that it was the duty of the jury "well to consider, whether it was possible for the pursuit to have taken place, and all the circumstances connected with it, and for the Prisoner to have reached Holden's house, a distance of nearly three miles and a half, in so short a time — a period of not more than 20 minutes."[72] The jury, after some six minutes of consideration, "returned, by their Foreman, without retiring, a Verdict of NOT GUILTY."[73] Serjeant Copley (the future Lord Lyndhurst L.C.), who was one of the team of three counsel prosecuting for the Crown, then offered no evidence on a charge of rape, and Thornton was discharged.[74]

The evidence that "pointed overwhelmingly to the guilt of the accused" seems to have appeared rather less than overwhelming to the judge and to a jury that acquitted the prisoner without leaving the jury box. The acquittal cannot have been due to any eloquence by defending counsel, for although prosecuting counsel made an opening speech, under the law as it then stood counsel for the defence could not address the jury at all.[75] The "powerful and dangerous brute" was described by an eye-witness as "a stout, well-looking young man, about five feet seven inches high, with a fresh complexion," about 25 or 26 years old.[76]

Two months after this verdict of Not Guilty, Thornton was again arrested and again charged with the murder of which the jury had acquitted him. This arrest was made on a warrant issued by the High Sheriff of Warwickshire dated October 9, 1817, as a result of a writ of appeal that Mary Ashford's eldest brother and heir-at-law, William Ashford, had caused to be issued on October 1, 1817."[77] He was "a plain, country young man, about twenty-two years of age, of short stature, sandy hair, and blue eyes."[78] The writ of appeal initiated the moribund process of an appeal of felony, the chief object of which "was to compel

---

[72] *Ibid.*
[73] *Ibid.*
[74] *Ibid.*
[75] *Ibid.*, at p. 45.
[76] *Ibid.*, at p. 57.
[77] *Ibid.*, at pp. 58, 67.
[78] *Ibid.*, at p. 66.

the Defendant to make pecuniary compensation. For when the verdict in
an Appeal was given in favour of the Appellant, he might insist upon
what terms he pleased, as the ransom of the Defendant's life, or a
commutation of the sentence."[79] Thornton's advisers met moribundity
with moribundity; and so the appellee waged his battle. The appellant,
being "of short stature," did not take up this wager against an appellee
who was "about five feet seven inches high." The brother was, it seems,
willing enough to attempt to put Thornton in jeopardy a second time,
perhaps with the intention of making money; but he was not willing to
put himself in jeopardy, whether for money or otherwise.

The account of the plea of *autrefois acquit* is also at some remove from
the facts. Thornton, it is said, was indicted for murder "at the next
sessions when he successfully pleaded *autrefois acquit*, and a reluctant
judge was compelled to discharge him." In fact, the indictment had
already been tried before the wager of battle was made; and it had been
terminated not by a plea of *autrefois acquit* but by a verdict of acquittal.
For the "reluctant judge" who was "compelled to discharge him" may be
substituted "a willing court" that "suggested a plea of autrefois acquit
and acted on it." What really happened was this.

The appeal of felony came on for hearing in the Court of King's
Bench on November 6, 1817, before Lord Ellenborough C.J., Bayley,
Abbott, and Holroyd JJ.[80] It was adjourned until November 17, when
Thornton waged his battle by pleading "Not Guilty; and I am ready to
defend the same with my body," and then throwing down a large
gauntlet.[81] There were then, on subsequent dates, a counterplea, a
replication, and a general demurrer, and on February 6 and 7 and April
16, 1818, the case was argued. At the end of the argument, after
remaining in consultation for about a quarter of an hour, the four judges
gave judgment seriatim, holding that Thornton was entitled to wage his
battle.[82]

---

[79] *Ibid.*, at p. 61.

[80] *Ibid.*, at p. 66.

[81] *Ibid.*, at p. 72.

[82] *Ibid.*, at pp. 74–124; and see *Ashford* v. *Thornton* (1818) 1 B. & Ald. 405.

Four days later, in the same court, counsel for the brother stated: "I have nothing further to pray."[83] Whereupon

> by consent of both parties, the court ordered that judgment be stayed on the appeal: and that the appellee be discharged. The proceedings were then handed over to the Crown side of the court, and Thornton was immediately arraigned by Mr. Barlow on the appeal, at the suit of the King, to which he pleaded instanter "autrefois acquit." The Attorney-General then, being present in court, confessed the plea to be true. Whereupon the court gave judgment that the appellee should go thereof without day. The appellee was immediately discharged.[84]

The suggestion of a plea of *autrefois acquit* came from the court. For as soon as the appellant had agreed that the appellee should be discharged, Bayley J. said to counsel for the appellee that his client "must now be arraigned at the suit of the Crown: so that you will plead the Trial and Acquittal which has already taken place, but of which, upon the present proceedings, the Crown must be supposed ignorant, although it is a fact well known to the parties." Lord Ellenborough C.J. then added: "This is a proceeding between individuals of which the Court knows nothing. He must be arraigned at the suit of the Crown, to which he may plead the Record of his former Acquittal. The Attorney-General must be present, and will, perhaps, give his assent to this Plea";[85] and this is what in fact occurred.

High judicial functions have been discharged in many places besides the courts. Shadwell V.-C. "was in the habit of bathing every day, whatever the weather, in one of the creeks of the Thames, near Barn Elms, and while thus engaged is said to have granted an injunction on one occasion in the long vacation."[86] Again, Lord Lyndhurst L.C. once heard an application for an injunction by W.H. Bennet, the law reporter, at the English Opera House. The Lord Chancellor moved from the front of his box to the back, heard the application, and granted the

---

83 Cooper, *supra* note 70, p. 140.
84 *Ashford* v. *Thornton* (1818) 1 B. & Ald. 405 at 460.
85 Cooper, *supra* note 70, at p. 140.
86 51 *D.N.B.* 340; and see 9 Foss's *Judges* 264.

injunction.[87] The process has not been confined to interlocutory applications. Once when Knight Bruce V.-C. had a decision of his reversed by
Lord Cottenham L.C., the reporter stated that "in consequence of the
state of his Lordship's health, the hearing took place at his private
residence, and no reporter was present."[88] But a shorthand-writer must
have been there, for one report sets out extracts from a shorthand note
of the judgment, and three other reports appear to give the judgment in
full.[89]

A more recent instance is that of Sir Samuel Evans P., who in 1916
held a sitting of the Prize Court in his dressing-gown in an armchair in
his bedroom, while recovering from an illness;[90] and it was Huddleston
B. who in 1890, being afflicted with gout, charged the grand jury at
Lewes from his bed.[91] It is also recounted that the elder Bucknill J. once
made an order while out shooting (counsel and a solicitor having shared
with a pheasant the perils of the judicial gun), that Pickford J. decided an
urgent matter while out riding, and that Hawkins J. once gave a decision
on Brighton pier.[92]

More recently, directions were given for the hearing of the evidence of
an 84-year-old witness in frail health in a village hall in Suffolk. The
judge relied on some of the foregoing precedents:

> I think it would be unduly burdensome to all concerned if they were
> required to be robed in the usual way merely for the purpose of hearing the
> evidence of one witness; and there may well be difficulties in such matters as
> the provision of suitable robing rooms. Accordingly, I shall not robe, and I
> direct that the registrar and counsel shall similarly not be robed. Robes are

---

[87] W.H. Bennet, *Select Biographical Sketches* (1867), p. 215.

[88] *Re The Vale of Neath and South Wales Brewery Co.: Morgan's Case* (1849) 1 De G. & Sm.
750 at 774. Two other reports are to the same effect, one explaining that this was why there
was no report of the argument ((1849) 1 H. & Tw. 320 at 329 n.(1)) and the other merely
saying that the case was heard at the Lord Chancellor's private house ((1849) 1 Mac. & G.
225 at 241 n.). The fourth report ((1849) 18 L.J.Ch. 265) is silent about the venue.

[89] See the last footnote: it was De Gex & Smale who abbreviated.

[90] *The Times*, Feb. 1, 1916, p. 5.

[91] (1890) 89 L.T.News. 269; 90 L.T.News. 99.

[92] F. Payler, *Law Courts, Lawyers and Litigants* (1926), p. 100. (They were later Lord
Sterndale M.R. and Lord Brampton.)

convenient in normal circumstances as an indication of the functions of those engaged in the proceedings, and as enhancing the formality and dignity of a grave occasion. In their appearance they also lessen visual differences of age, sex and clothing, and so aid concentration on the real issues without distraction. But robes are not essential, and the court may dispense with them where there is good reason. Jurisdiction is neither conferred nor excluded by mere matters of attire or locality, and I need not discuss the numberless occasions on which judges have exercised a variety of judicial functions in unusual places without the aid of robes for them or for counsel, from Lord Lyndhurst L.C. in a box at the opera to Sir Lancelot Shadwell V.-C. while bathing in the Thames and Sir Samuel Evans P. in a dressing-gown in his bedroom."[93]

Even the railways have provided curial accommodation. R.S. Wright J. is said to have made an order in a railway carriage,[94] and at one time justice in Wales seems to have been affected with a degree of sideradromophilia. Thus in Mold County Court in 1904, the judge and both counsel wished to catch a train, and so it was decided to continue the hearing there. Counsel (S. Moss M.P. and Ellis Griffiths M.P.) both addressed the judge in a railway carriage, and judgment was reserved.[95] A few years earlier, Bridgend County Court had gone even further; for in a case that, "when the hour arrived for the judge to leave by train," was still part-heard, the judge, the advocates, and the remaining witnesses travelled together by train to Llantrisant, evidence being heard en route. "On reaching Llantrisant, Judge Williams gave his decision in the stationmaster's office, finding for the plaintiff."[96] The rule that justice must be done in public has, it seems, many facets. But although a magistrate's court is a "place to which the public . . . have access," it is not a place of recreation or entertainment so as to support a conviction for being drunk in such a place.[97]

[93] *St. Edmundsbury and Ipswich Diocesan Board of Finance* v. *Clark* [1973] Ch. 323 at 330.

[94] F. Payler, *supra* note 92, p. 100.

[95] (1904) 39 L.J.News. 232.

[96] (1891) 92 L.T.News. 127.

[97] *S.* v. *Buthelezi*, 1979 (3) S.A. 1349 ("place of entertainment, café, eating house, race course or other premises or place to which the public are granted or have access": *ejusdem generis* rule applied).

In a case in the mid-1970s, there was an opposed application for the judge to hold a view of the land in dispute. An unusual feature was that the land was a small Pacific island almost on the equator (Ocean Island, now called Banaba); it had been extensively mined, and serious questions of time and money arose. The Rules of Court,[98] it was held, gave the judge a discretionary power to view land outside the jurisdiction. But the question was whether it was right to exercise the power:

> It is by no means easy to weigh the advantages of a view against the disadvantages. However, I have to do the best that I can. As a means of enabling me to understand and apply the evidence, the advantages seem to me to be more or less balanced by the disadvantages: and if that were all, I should not find it easy to reach a decision. One matter, I think, should be left wholly out of account, and that is inconvenience to the judge. A view of Ocean Island would, of course, be far removed from being a pleasant holiday trip to the South Seas. The journey would be long and exhausting, and a proper inspection of the rugged terrain of the island would in all probability involve a considerable degree of strenuous agility in a high temperature. Nevertheless, although there must be some limits to the degree of judicial wear and tear that can be expected, I do not think that I should give any real weight to what is involved in this case; for this seems to me (though by no great margin) to fall within the bounds of what a litigant is reasonably entitled to expect from the judge.[99]

There was also a further consideration. At one time it had been said that the function of a view was to enable the judge to follow the evidence. But that seemed too restricted an approach:

> What a judge perceives on a view is itself evidence, in the same way as what he sees and hears in the courtroom. Just as a portable object may be brought into court and, being made an exhibit, become real evidence, so if the judge duly views a place or object which cannot be brought into court that place or object provides real evidence through the medium of the judge's eyes, ears, touch, tongue or, as in one recent case before me, his nose.[100] On this footing

[98] Ord. 35, r. 8.

[99] *Tito v. Waddell (No. 1)* [1975] 1 W.L.R. 1303 at 1307.

[100] *Penn v. Wilkins* (1974) 236 E.G. 203. To "hold a smell" has yet to attain the legal vocabulary.

the tendering of real evidence no longer depends upon the res being portable.

One result of a view having this nature is that the present application must be regarded not as a mere application by the plaintiffs for me to view Ocean Island in order that I may better understand the evidence, but as an application by the plaintiffs to tender certain evidence. True, it is evidence the adduction of which is, by virtue of Ord. 35, r. 8, made a matter of judicial discretion; but still it is evidence. Quite properly, it has not been suggested that this evidence is irrelevant or inadmissible: the contention is merely that it is unnecessary and too expensive in terms of time and money. Nevertheless, I think that the court ought to exercise some caution in refusing an application for a view. In some cases it may be clear that to hold a view would achieve nothing save to waste both time and money. But except in reasonably plain cases of this kind I think the court ought to incline in favour of granting any such application. In short, in my judgment the proper approach is to consider not whether a sufficient case for holding a view has been made out, but whether there are sufficient grounds for rejecting the application to hold a view.[101]

No such grounds appeared, and so, between Day 74 and Day 75 of the hearing, this decision carried the judge, his clerk, counsel, and solicitors round the world in 15 punishing days.[102]

In another case,[103] the excursion was made under Order 39. The point emerged a little mysteriously. The Daily Cause List initially showed the trial as beginning in the Commercial Court in London before Staughton J. on October 15, 1984, and continuing daily, with Fridays off, in a wholly unremarkable way. But then, on Thursday, November 29, the case was not in its accustomed place in the List. An answer to those who were puzzled appeared in the List on Friday, though the answer raised further questions of its own; for the List showed that the case was continuing in Vancouver, British Columbia, Canada. Thursday had plainly been a travelling day in an unusually ample sense. Then on Monday, December 3, the List showed the case as continuing, but this time in Seattle, Washington, U.S.A.; and Tuesday and Wednesday were the same.

---

[101] *Tito* v. *Waddell (No. 1), supra* note 99, at p. 1308.

[102] *Tito* v. *Waddell (No. 2)* [1977] Ch. 106 at 124.

[103] *Bibby Bulk Carriers Line Ltd.* v. *Cobelfret NV (The Cambridgeshire)*, unrep.

Thursday, however, seems in a sense to have been a return day, for on Friday the judge was shown as sitting to hear other matters in the Commercial Court in London; and once the weekend had gone, the case resumed its Monday to Thursday life in that court. The excursion, it appears, had taken place under letters of request[104] addressed to the judicial authorities of British Columbia and the State of Washington. These had asked that the evidence of witnesses should be taken there, and that Staughton J. should be appointed as the person to take it; and when the requests had been granted, the judge, with five solicitors and ten barristers engaged in the case, had duly obtained the evidence.[105]

Even when judges do sit in the usual courts in the usual way, they have been known to forget what court they are constituting. Thus in one case in 1957 Lord Goddard C.J. and Devlin and Pearson JJ. each delivered a judgment in a case upholding a conviction. They were sitting in the Court of Criminal Appeal, and statute provided that unless the court directed to the contrary in cases where there was a question of law on which it would be convenient that separate judgments should be pronounced, only one judgment was to be delivered.[106] At the end of the judgment delivered by Pearson J., Lord Goddard C.J. said that the court had overlooked that they were in the Court of Criminal Appeal, and in considering a Divisional Court case that had been cited to them, they had thought themselves to be in a Divisional Court (where, of course, separate judgments are common). After referring to the statutory restriction on delivering separate judgments, he said that "the Court had better say in the present case that they considered it convenient so to do."[107] Not many who know of the career and interests of Lord Goddard would guess that one of his earliest reported appearances at the Bar (at the age of 22 and within a year of call) was in a case in the Chancery Division in 1899 on a "name and arms" clause in a will.[108]

---

[104] Issued under Order 39.

[105] Information from an authoritative source.

[106] Criminal Appeal Act 1907, s. 1(5). See, e.g., *R. v. Norman* [1924] 2 K.B. 315, where eight judges concurred in one judgment, four in a dissenting judgment, and one gave no judgment.

[107] *R. v. Ibrahim* [1957] *The Times*, Dec. 11.

[108] *Re Eversley* [1900] 1 Ch. 96; 69 L.J.Ch. 14.

The ultimate Court Celestial should also be remembered. It is recorded that while at the Bar the elder Henn Collins[109] dreamed that he was at the Day of Judgment. After several cases had been heard and quickly determined, the name of a member of the Bar noted for his prolixity of argument was called. Thereupon the Recording Angel, as Clerk of the Assize, arose with a sorrowful mien and called out: "No other case will be taken today!" Hawkins J., who was not lacking in self-esteem, had a different dream. He had become weary of waiting for his case to come on, and sent his card to the Tribunal, asking whether he "could be of any assistance to them by taking a few short undefended cases in a second Court."[110] Perhaps it was a recollection of his dream that once led Henn Collins J. to observe in the Railway and Canal Commission: "We are not a court of conciliation, or a tribunal of honour. We are not made judges of prudence or of generosity."[111]

Arbitrations, of course, take place in a wide variety of places and may exhibit a wide range of peculiarities. In some part of County Down in the nineteenth century a somewhat unusual form of arbitration was current. The parties agreed upon an impartial chairman, who sat at the head of a long table with the parties on either hand. Down the middle of the table a line was drawn, and grains of oats were placed along it at intervals of a few inches. A foot or so from the head of the table the line stopped, and two grains of corn were placed a few inches from the middle, one in front of each party. Then, with the chairman as umpire, a hen turkey was gently placed on the table at the far end. The turkey would then delicately peck her ladylike way all up the table until, when she reached the two grains of corn at the top, she delivered her award in favour of one party or the other by taking first the grain nearer to him.[112]

Once, however, the loser in such an arbitrament was a litigious

---

109 Afterwards J., L.J., M.R., and law lord.

110 Sir Edward Parry, *My Own Way* (1932), p. 244.

111 *Rickett, Smith & Co. Ltd.* v. *Midland Railway Co.* [1896] 1 Q.B. 260 at 264.

112 Compare ornithomancy, or divination by a cock's picking up grains: see *Roget's Thesaurus* (1936 ed.), p. 171, and cp. *O.E.D.* (2d ed. 1989), s.v.

creature who refused to accept the decision as just, and brought a civil bill in the county court against the winner. On the facts having been proved, the county court judge dismissed that action, whereupon the plaintiff exercised his right to appeal to the assize judge. This was that aged and learned equity lawyer, Lefroy C.J., who, unlike counsel for the defendant, knew little of local customs. During the cross-examination of the plaintiff, the following passage occurred.

> COUNSEL: "Tell me, wasn't the turkey for the defendant?" (*No answer*)
> COUNSEL: "Tell my Lord the truth, now. Wasn't the turkey for the defendant?"
> CHIEF JUSTICE: "What on earth has a turkey to do with this case?"
> COUNSEL: "It's a local form of arbitration, my Lord."
> CHIEF JUSTICE: "Do you mean to tell me that the plaintiff has brought this case in disregard of the award of an arbitrator?"
> COUNSEL: "That is so, my Lord."
> CHIEF JUSTICE: "Disgraceful! Appeal dismissed with costs here and below."
> COUNSEL (*sotto voce*):   "The Lord Chief Justice affirms the turkey."[113]

The test of a successful arbitration is traditional. "The very definition of a good award is, that it gives dissatisfaction to both parties."[114] But there are other considerations. One dispute was referred to arbitration, and was heard by two arbitrators and an umpire. At the end of the proceedings, but before any award had been made, both arbitrators and the umpire accepted the invitation of one of the parties, an innkeeper, to dine with him and his attorney at his inn. "Much wine was drunk, many allusions made to the reference, and the umpire, in consequence of excess, was obliged to sleep at the inn."[115] The umpire then made an award that was rather nearer the figure put forward by the innkeeper's arbitrator than the figure put forward by the other arbitrator, and in due

[113] Traditional (at secondhand from an Irish judicial source). Some confirmation of this account appears from a cartoon dated "Feb. 1815", entitled "An Arbitrator giving his award." This shows a human-headed turkey, wearing bands and a full-bottomed wattle, and raising a deliberative claw. The date, however, seems to exclude Lefroy C.J., since he did not become a judge until 1841. For problems about turkeys, see *ante* pp. 7–8.

[114] *Goodman* v. *Sayers* (1820) 2 Jac. & W. 249 at 259 (*per* Sir Thomas Plumer M.R.).

[115] *Re Hopper* (1867) L.R. 2 Q.B. 367 at 369.

course the other party applied to set aside the award on the ground (*inter alia*) of the umpire's misconduct. The Court of Queen's Bench, however, although subscribing to the doctrine that "a person who has to administer justice should be above suspicion,"[116] could find no evidence of any intention to corrupt the umpire or of his having been influenced by his evening's entertainment, and on these grounds upheld the award.[117]

It was otherwise with Dr. Titus Oates, of infamous memory. Some years after his conviction for perjury he was somewhat unexpectedly appointed an arbitrator in a dispute about a will. He seems to have got himself appointed by privately persuading the respondents that he would be in their favour. Once in the saddle, however, he decided against them and thus revenged himself on them for being instrumental, as he thought, in his having lost an appointment as a preacher, and for preventing him from preaching the funeral sermon for the testatrix. Yet he plainly had uttered far too many far from judicious words. One example may suffice. The respondents had proved the will at Doctors Commons; and Dr. Oates had declared that they "deserved to lose the cause, because they brought it into that cursed *Babylonish* Court of Doctors Commons, which, he said, was nothing but a damned relict of popery."[118] Sir Nathan Wright L.K. set aside Dr. Oates' award, saying that neither the reference nor the award had been fairly or indifferently obtained, and that the award appeared to have been made "revengefully and partially";[119] and an appeal to the House of Lords failed.[120]

---

[116] *Ibid.*, at p. 374 (*per* Cockburn C.J.).

[117] *Re Hopper* (1867) L.R. 2 Q.B. 367. Contrast 2 Misc. 13–19.

[118] *Parker* v. *Burroughs* (1702) Colles 257 at 261.

[119] *Ibid.*

[120] *Ibid.* (1703) at p. 262. See also *Korin* v. *McInnes* [1990] V.R. 723.

5

~

ARS BABLATIVA

TRADITIONALLY the Bar is never a bed of roses; it is "either all bed and no roses, or all roses and no bed."[1] A complementary comment is that anyone who gets into full practice at the Bar will either die before he is 50 or live to be over 80. Yet occasionally there is someone who prevents success from becoming servitude. Chaloner Chute, who was Treasurer of the Middle Temple in 1655, showed "a transcendent genius, superior to the slavery of a gainful profession." For he would do what "no eminent chancery practiser ever did, or will do the like." Namely "if he had a fancy not to have the fatigue of business, but to pass his time in pleasure after his own humour, he would say to his clerk, 'Tell the people I will not practice this term'; and was as good as his word: and then no one durst come near him with business. But when his clerks signified he would take business, he was in the same advanced post at the bar, fully redintegrated as before, and his practice nothing shrunk by the discontinuance."[2]

The demands of the profession are many. In Bacon's words: "I hold every man a debtor to his profession; from the which as men of course do seek to receive countenance and profit, so ought they of duty to endeavour themselves by way of amends to be a help and ornament thereunto."[3] Contributions come from many sources. Bacon again said:

---

[1] Attributed to many, but usually to Rufus Isaacs: see D. Judd, *Lord Reading* (1982), p. 24.

[2] R. North, *Lives of the Norths* (1826 ed.), vol. 1, p. 14.

[3] Bacon, *The Elements of the Common Law of England: Preface* (*Bacon's Law Tracts* (2d ed. 1741), p. 28).

"Reading maketh a full man, conference a ready man, and writing an exact man."[4] Yet "the law sharpens the mind by narrowing it,"[5] or, as it has also been put, "Whilst it sharpens the edge it narrows the blade."[6] Frankfurter J. put it more kindly: "if lawyers are good, if lawyers have range, if lawyers are true to their function, then they are what I venture to call experts in relevance."[7] They have learned to use Occam's razor, which "requires the elimination of all facts which are not essential to the subject to be examined,"[8] without forgetting the power of the seemingly remote to become proximate.

It has not always been clear whether a barrister who took silk was thereupon entitled to be made a bencher of his Inn. The first case was that of Francis North, the future Lord Guilford, L.K. He was made a K.C. in 1668[9] when he was not a Serjeant, Reader, or Bencher, and was but 31 years old. The Benchers of the Middle Temple refused to elect him a bencher, and so North

> waited upon the several chiefs, and with modesty enough acquainted them of the matter, and that, as to himself, he could submit to any thing; but as he had the honour to be his majesty's servant, he thought the slight was upon the king, and he esteemed it his duty to acquaint their lordships with it, and to receive their directions how he ought to behave himself, and that he should act as they were pleased to prescribe. They all wished him to go and mind his business, and leave this matter to them, or to that effect. The very next day in Westminster-hall, when any of the benchers appeared at the courts, they received reprimands from the judges for their insolence, as if a person whom his majesty had thought fit to make one of his counsel

---

[5] Bacon, *Of Studies: Essays, No. 50* (ed. R. Whately, 1867, p. 501).

[6] Holmes, J., cited in *Student Book Note,* 36 Temple L.Q. 257, 257 (1963). Francis Biddle, *A Casual Past* (1961), p. 336, ascribes the saying to Edmund Burke.

[7] A. Polson, *Law and Lawyers* (1858), p. 177, attributing the comment to "Coleridge," *semble* John Coleridge J.

[8] Frankfurter, *Personal Ambitions of Judges: Should a Judge "Think Beyond the Judicial"?,* 34 A.B.A.J. 656, 747 (Aug. 1948).

[8] *First Energy (U.K.) Ltd.* v. *Hungarian International Bank Ltd.* [1993] B.C.L.C. 1049 at 1411 (*per* Steyn L.J.). The dictum of Occam (1280–1349) known as his razor is "Entia non sunt multiplicanda praeter necessitatem" (Beings ought not to be multiplied except out of necessity).

[9] See 1 Sid. 365.

extraordinary, was not worthy to come into their company; and so dismissed them unheard, with declaration that until they had done their duty in calling Mr. North to their bench, they must not expect to be heard as counsel in his majesty's courts. This was English, and that evening they conformed, and so were reinstated.[10]

For nearly three centuries after this, silks were promptly elected benchers of their Inns, with few exceptions. One of those exceptions was a barrister of the Inner Temple named Howarth, in about 1765, and another was more recent.[11] Sometimes there were temporary delays, as where a barrister took silk after a call to the Bench had already been made in that term. Thus Alderson B. remembered Charles Wetherell and James Scarlett (later Lord Abinger C.B.) "sitting at the Bar table with silk gowns . . . and very indignant they both of them were. . . . The custom being for the whole Bar to rise when the Bench went out, both Sir Charles Wetherell and Lord Abinger sat in their silk gowns, and would not pay them that usual mark of respect."[12] Early in the nineteenth century, most benchers were still juniors. In the Inner Temple in 1827, there were only six K.C.s; but by 1846 there were twenty-four.[13]

The matter was authoritatively settled in 1846. Abraham Hayward took silk but was not elected to the Bench of the Inner Temple. He then petitioned the judges, as visitors of the Inn, to cause him to be received as a bencher. It seems that he had been duly proposed and seconded for election to the bench but had been blackballed by a bencher with whom he had had a dispute many years before. After a full and illuminating argument before eleven judges, it was unanimously held that the benchers had the right to determine whether to add to their number by any new election, and, if so, whom to elect; and so the petition failed.[14] But the judges also said that a mode of election whereby one black-ball

---

[10] R. North, *Lives of the Norths* (1826 ed.), vol. 1, p. 68.

[11] See *Re Hayward's Petition* (1846) *Report on the Proceedings before the Judges as Visitors of the Inns of Court on the Appeal of A. Hayward Esq. Q.C.* (1848), pp. 80, 81 (*per* Serjeant Talfourd).

[12] *Re Hayward's Petition, supra* note 11, at pp. 81, 82.

[13] *Ibid.*, at p. 135 (*per* Sir Frederick Thesiger).

[14] *Re Hayward's Petition, supra* note 11, at p. 158.

excluded was unreasonable. The next year the benchers changed the rules, requiring four black balls to exclude. Nevertheless, the last *Law List* in which Hayward's name appears, that for 1883, shows him as the third senior in the list of silks, but still not a bencher. Part of the explanation may lie in the fact, recorded in an obituary, that "his friend Lord Lyndhurst" had given him his silk gown, and that, with interests that were primarily literary (he edited the *Law Magazine* from 1828 to 1844), "he scarcely ever set himself seriously to practice."[15]

During the argument in Hayward's case, Sir Frederick Thesiger referred to the occasion when the judges berated the benchers for not making North a bencher, and the benchers had to sit silent. "In consequence of their silence it was called the 'dumb day' in Court." In this, however, he seems to have confused the "dumb day" with the "deaf day," and Alderson B. corrected him: "The 'dumb day' was when all the Serjeants refused to move at the side bar."[16] This no doubt refers to an occasion some seven or eight years after the judges had coerced the benchers into electing North. By this time, North had become Sir Francis North, C.J. C.P., and his younger brother Roger was newly called to the bar. Although the serjeants alone had audience in the Common Pleas, it had become the practice to hear attorneys and young counsel in matters of form and practice in the King's Bench at the side bar and in the Common Pleas in a back room called the Treasury. The serjeants began to resent and fear this competition, and in the end resolved to show their feelings by making no motions at all on one day, and take the opportunity that would then arise to explain how there was no business. They did this not long after North had been promoted to the bench in 1675: when called upon to move, each in turn rose, bowed, and sat down again. North then said: "Brothers, I think we must rise; here is no business."[17]

At this, an attorney stepped forward and said that he had instructed a serjeant to move, and desired him to do so. North sought and obtained

15 (1884) 76 L.T.News. 291.

16 *Re Hayward's Petition, supra* note 11, at p. 137.

17 North, *supra* note 2, p. 210; and see at p. 199.

an explanation, and then said that when the court sat the next day, it would hear the attorneys, or their clients, or barristers, or any person who thought fit to appear, rather than let justice fail. "This was like thunder to the serjeants", who, that afternoon in private and the next day in court, with great humility begged pardon; and North and the other judges then "gave them a formal chiding with acrimony enough; all which, with dejected countenances, they were bound to hear. When this discipline was over, the chief pointed to one to move; which he did (as they said) more like one crying than speaking: and so ended the comedy, as it was acted in Westminster-hall, called the Dumb day."[18] The "dumb day" was thus the day when the serjeants stood silent, while the "deaf day" had been the day, some seven or eight years earlier, when the judges would not hear the benchers.

There have been changes in the relationship between silks and juniors. In the early part of the nineteenth century, according to Sir John Hollams, it was more common than today for juniors to conduct important jury cases and argue difficult questions of law: "On the argument of special verdicts and demurrers only one counsel was heard, and it was the usage to brief junior counsel to argue, and in cases of importance, leading counsel, from the Attorney-General and Solicitor-General of the day downwards, had briefs to take notes. Their fees were almost nominal, but they attended the argument. The junior counsel who argued had of course a substantial fee. Mr. Crompton and Mr. Willes (both subsequently judges), Mr. Welsby and Mr. Cowling (none of whom were Queen's Counsel), were largely engaged in such cases."[19]

Today, such a procedure seems a strange inversion: the junior conducts a well-paid argument while the silk sits humbly with a noting brief and a nominal fee. Nor does it appear what was the advantage of such arrangements; but doubtless the Victorians had value for their money. In Victorian days, it will be remembered, it was common for a fashionable silk to be engaged in two or more cases at once, dashing from one court to another to cross-examine here and make a speech

---

[18] *Ibid.*, at pp. 211, 212.
[19] Sir John Hollams, *Jottings of an Old Solicitor* (1906), pp. 128–29.

there, with a different junior in each court to provide continuity of endeavour. Today the procedure is reversed: the silk remains faithful to one case at a time, and it is the contented junior, it is said, who from time to time looks in on each of his cases to see that his several leaders and his devils are doing all that they should.

Even today, however, there are occasions when a silk cannot escape simultaneity, and some junior has to go it alone. The reporters' conventional indication that a leader has been absent from a case and has left its conduct to his junior is to use the phrase "with him." Thus "Bower (Moulton Q.C. with him)" means that Mr. Bower alone argued the case, and that Mr. Moulton, Q.C.,[20] though doubtless with him in spirit, was bodily absent. In the case from which this example was taken,[21] Lord Esher M.R., aged 72, spoke with a frankness that some modern law reporters might have eschewed:

> Mr. Moulton, however young he may look, is verging towards middle age[22] as a barrister, and for that reason I should think he must feel extremely happy that other engagements kept him somewhere else, but he certainly did leave the case in the hands of a counsel who has all the refreshing boldness of being a youthful barrister. To us poor faded creatures — no, I will speak for myself[23] — to a faded creature like myself, old and worn out in the law, it is most refreshing to hear bad points, as I said in the course of the argument, put as well as they possibly can be put, and they can only be put well by somebody who has the boldness and freshness of youth. It makes one feel as if one had gone back 40 or 50 years when one used to try to do the same thing oneself in that way, and perhaps sometimes succeed. I mean what I say, I mean that these points were put as well as they could possibly be put; but they consist only in words, they consist in darkening a case which is as clear as any case ever was, in darkening it and confusing it, as some very great people have the gift of doing, darkening and confusing the plainest possible propositions by multitudes of hard words.[24]

---

[20] *Semble*, J.F. Moulton, afterwards Fletcher Moulton L.J. and Lord Moulton.
[21] *City of London Contract Corporation, Ltd.* v. *Styles* (1887) 2 T.C. 239: see at p. 242.
[22] He was then nearly 43 years old.
[23] The other members of the Court were Bowen and Fry L.JJ., aged 52 and 60 respectively.
[24] *City of London Contract Corporation Ltd.* v. *Styles, supra* note 21, at p. 243.

After an examination of the arguments, the judgment ended with: "These revenue cases generally present some difficulty to us. This one has only presented to us the pleasurable excitement of hearing, as I said in the beginning, bad points extremely well put."[25] Over the years the Bar's ability to please has not declined. Nearly a century later, in considering the word "benefit", it was said that "Obviously much is a 'benefit' which is not money or money's worth, ranging from matters such as peace and quiet to the pleasure of listening to the arguments of counsel in this case, and much else besides."[26]

One report of a case in the House of Lords states simply: "Harold Morris (Holman Gregory K.C. with him), for the respondents";[27] but thereby hangs a tale. In another report of the same case it is recorded that when Mr. Morris rose to reply for the respondents, he apologised for the absence of his learned leader, "who was engaged in an important jury case in the High Court." At this, Viscount Haldane L.C. is recorded as having said that "this House had a prior claim to the attendance of counsel, and before absenting himself Mr. Gregory ought to have made application for leave to be absent. The House was very indulgent when cases of absolute necessity were shown, but he wished it to be distinctly understood that the House expected that application for indulgence should be specially and personally made."[28] Later Gregory K.C. attended the House, and his explanation and apology were accepted.[29]

Some ten years later the admonition was repeated. This time the culprit was Sir John Simon K.C.,[30] who was leading C.H. Brown K.C. and A.H.D. Gillies (both of the Scottish bar) in a Scottish appeal. Mr. Brown opened the appeal in the absence of his leader, who, he said, was unable to be present. The next day, the Earl of Birkenhead, who was presiding, addressed Mr. Brown and quoted what Lord Haldane had said. He continued: "Mr. Brown, that was, and still is, the rule of the

---

[25] *Ibid.*, at p. 244.
[26] *Medical Defence Union Ltd.* v. *Department of Trade* [1980] Ch. 82 at 95.
[27] *Vacher & Sons Ltd.* v. *London Society of Compositors* [1913] A.C. 107 at 110.
[28] *Ibid.*, 29 T.L.R. 73.
[29] *Ibid.*
[30] Later Viscount Simon L.C.

House, and it is a rule which their Lordships have no intention of pretermitting. You will be good enough to make this known."[31]

If apprenticeship has retained its essential character over the years, legal education has changed much. Today the Bench rarely exhibits Lord Mansfield's solicitude for legal education in court; there is, indeed, usually little opportunity for it to do so. In one case in which a Mr. Hussey had appeared as counsel, the Court of King's Bench had reserved judgment. Later "Lord Mansfield declared the opinion of the Court; having first desired Mr. Hussey to state the case, for the sake of the students."[32] In another case, Lord Mansfield himself stated the case, saying that he did so "for the sake of the students."[33] But listening was not enough: "Serjeant Maynard, the best old book-lawyer of his time, used to say that the law was *ars bablativa*, which humoursomely enough declares the advantage that discoursing brings to the students of the law."[34] The future Lord Guilford L.K., when a Bar student, "fell into the way of putting cases"; and "he used to say that no man could be a good lawyer that was not a put-case. Reading goes off with some cloud, but discourse makes all notions limpid and just."[35]

Until it was abolished,[36] the customary fee for reading in chambers for a year as a pupil was still the hundred guineas (or the equivalent) that it had been for a very long time. Thus in 1775, when the modern pupillage system was young, a difficulty confronting the future Lord Eldon was that of finding what Lord Campbell described as "the usual fee of a hundred guineas."[37] The style of discussion between bar students, too, seems to have changed. When the future Lord Campbell first dined as a student in Lincoln's Inn hall, a brother student broke a long silence by

---

[31] *Abram Steamship Co., Ltd.* v. *Westville Shipping Co., Ltd.* [1923] *The Times,* May 2. The decision is reported *sub nom. Westville Shipping Co. Ltd.* v. *Abram Steamship Co. Ltd.* 1923 S.C. (H.L.) 68.

[32] *R.* v. *Peters* (1758) 1 Burr. 568 at 571.

[33] *Wilson* v. *Mackreth* (1766) 3 Burr. 1824 at 1826.

[34] North, *supra* note 2, p. 27.

[35] *Ibid.,* at pp. 19, 20.

[36] See *Annual Statement of The Senate of the Inns of Court and the Bar 1977–1978*, p. 52.

[37] 9 Camp. L.CC. 143.

asking him: "Pray, Sir, what is your opinion of the *scintilla juris?*" The questioner was later to become Lord St. Leonards[38] and procure the passage of the Act that abolished the complex and artificial doctrine of *scintilla juris.*[39]

Today, the law student gets most of his law from his law school. "Taught law is tough law",[40] and so "law schools make tough law."[41] The courts have borrowed the thought ("Argued law is tough law"[42]), but the law schools do not retreat. "The business of a law school . . . is to teach law in the grand manner, and to make great lawyers."[43] Yet standards vary. Sir Frederick Pollock's view in 1892 was that if the scheme of lectures then proposed by the Council of Legal Education was worked with zeal and intelligence, "the Inns of Court may possibly, within a few years, be not much inferior as a centre of legal instruction to an average second-rate American law school."[44] To those who complained that the Inns of Court had failed to found a great teaching body such as the Harvard Law School came the answer of Augustine Birrell K.C.: "When I balance a law school against Grand Night at the Inner Temple, my stomach rebels against scholarship."[45] Even in academic circles scholastic enthusiasm varies. One professor's objection to lecturing on Wednesdays was mordantly said to be because it spoiled both weekends for him.

Practitioners, too, tend to be unconvinced. Thus Dicey said, "Jurisprudence is a word which stinks in the nostrils of a practising barrister. A jurist is, they constantly find, a professor whose claim to dogmatise on law in general lies in the fact that he has made himself master of no one legal system in particular, whilst his boasted science consists in the enumeration of platitudes which if they ought, as he

[38] *Ibid.*, at p. 142.

[39] Law of Property Amendment Act 1860, s. 7; and see Megarry & Wade, *Real Property* (5th ed. 1984), p. 1180.

[40] F.W. Maitland, *English Law and the Renaissance* (1901), p. 18.

[41] *Ibid.*, at p. 25.

[42] *Cordell* v. *Second Clanfield Properties Ltd.* [1969] 2 Ch. 9 at 16.

[43] Holmes J., *The Occasional Speeches of Justice Oliver Wendell Holmes* (1962), p. 36; and see p. 46.

[44] (1892) 8 L.Q.R. 19.

[45] 1 *Holmes–Laski Letters* (1953), p. 576.

insists, to be law everywhere, cannot in fact be shown to be law anywhere."[46] So also in America: "Sir James Stephen is not the only writer whose attempts to analyze legal ideas have been confused by striving for a useless quintessence of all systems, instead of an accurate anatomy of one."[47] Bowen's views about jurists were similar but more concise: "A Jurist . . . is a person who knows a little about the laws of every country except his own."[48]

There is no escape from lawbooks. Some, indeed, may be put aside when the last examination has been passed; but all too soon their place will be taken by more books, and bigger. Lawyers, too, have no immunity from the *cacoethes scribendi*[49] of mankind: "Prolificacy has been recognised as an ineradicable characteristic of writers at least since the day of the author of Ecclesiastes and, no doubt, for much longer. The world might not be a worse place if some books went unpublished, but this court is not a censor of literary taste. . . . It is improbable that there are many 'mute inglorious Miltons' about nowadays, but there may be a few, and the likelihood of their muteness would be increased, if publishers were constrained to be less adventurous."[50]

The burdens of authorship seem to be an inadequate deterrent. In the epilogue to his Institutes, Coke reflected on law as compared with labour:

Whilest we were in hand with these foure parts of the Institutes, we often having occasion to go into the city, and from thence into the country, did in some sort envy the state of the honest plowman, and other mechanics; for the one when he was at his work would merrily sing, and the plowman whistle some self-pleasing tune, and yet their work both proceeded and succeeded: but he that takes upon him to write, doth captivate all the faculties and powers both of his minde and body, and must be only intentive

---

[46] A.V. Dicey (1880) 5 Law Mag. & Rev. (4th ser.) p. 382.

[47] O.W. Holmes, *The Path of the Law*, 10 Harv. L. Rev. 457, 475 (1897).

[48] As quoted in Sir Henry Cunningham, *Lord Bowen* (1897), p. 184; and see (1902) 113 L.T.News. 357.

[49] "An itch for writing."

[50] *Re Net Book Agreement, 1957* (1962) L.R. 3 R.P. 246 at 319, 320 (*per* Buckley J.).

to that which he collecteth, without any expression of joy or cheerfulness, whilest he is in his work.[51]

Dr. Johnson's view was that "the greatest part of a writer's time is spent in reading, in order to write: a man will turn over half a library to make one book."[52] For, "Knowledge is of two kinds. We know a subject ourselves, or we know where we can find information upon it."[53] There are, of course, modern aids. But their perilous temptations must be resisted. "Go over the drafts as they come back from the typist and rub and rub and rub again until you have massaged away every muddy word and every waste word."[54]

The profession is not always appreciative: "It is a truth! a lamentable truth! that few books in the law are so precise as to be positively correct."[55] Sometimes the author may be excused. One writer supported the proposition that "estate" was a word derived from "status" by citing Holdsworth's monumental history; and in the proofs the footnote duly read "See 2 H.E.L. 351, 352." To the author's chagrin, however, the footnote as published read "cmfwycmfwy."[56] This provided questionable support for anything, and left the author to reflect on the guidance given by the dictum of Lord Abinger C.B.: "If an author is to go and give a beating to a publisher who has offended him, two or three blows with a horsewhip ought to be quite enough to satisfy his irritated feelings."[57]

Nor are the courts always enthusiastic: "The practice of reading from the law books is an exceedingly dangerous one, and should not be indulged in."[58] There is also authority for saying that "there are callings, even now, in which, to be convicted of literature, is dangerous, though

---

[51] 4 Co.Inst. 365.

[52] Boswell's *Johnson*, vol. 2, p. 8.

[53] *Ibid.*, at p. 22.

[54] E.H. Warren, *Margin Customers* (1941), p. vi.

[55] Preston on *Abstracts*, vol. 1 (2d ed. 1823), p. 218.

[56] Megarry, *A Manual of the Law of Real Property* (2d ed. 1955), p. 9.

[57] *Fraser* v. *Berkeley* (1836) 7 C. & P. 621 at 626.

[58] *Steffenson* v. *Chicago, M. & St. P. Ry. Co.*, 51 N.W. 610, 611 (Minn. 1892) (*per* Collins J.). Yet all that counsel had done was to read to a Minnesota jury a section of the Constitution of Minnesota and part of a judgment of the Minnesota Supreme Court.

the danger is sometimes escaped."[59] For a practitioner, authorship may well be a hostage to fortune: "behold, my desire is . . . that mine adversary had written a book."[60]

There have, however, been triumphs. As is well known, Bentham said that it was Blackstone who, "first of all institutional writers, has taught Jurisprudence to speak the language of the Scholar and the Gentleman."[61] It is less well known that Bentham made Blackstone share this honour with Sir James Burrows, who, said Bentham, compiled "the first book of reports in which the Lawyer has been taught to speak the language of the Scholar and the gentleman."[62] A high place must also be accorded to a publication of 1812 entitled "Hints on the Laws and Customs of Ancient and Modern Times respecting Marriage, Adultery, Polygamy, Seduction, Fornication, Rape, etc., by a Gentleman of the Middle Temple." The other Inns doubtless reflected upon the omni-competence of the Middle Temple in its chosen sphere, turning the pages to find out where the "etc." led; and perhaps bookbinders, seeking brevity for the spine, chose "Hints on Rape, etc., by a Gent."

Lord Eldon recounts that while he was at the Bar, Lord Thurlow L.C. once asked him if he did not think that a wooden machine might be invented to draw bills and answers in chancery; and Eldon welcomed the suggestion. Many years later, when Eldon had become Attorney-General, a bill was filed against a Mr. Macnamara, a friend of Lord Thurlow's; and on Lord Thurlow's advice the answer was sent to Eldon to be perused and settled. Eldon found it "so wretchedly ill composed and drawn" that he told the solicitor "that not a Word of it would do", and that he must get someone who understood pleading to draw the answer from beginning to end. He later went down to the House of Lords to argue a case; and Lord Thurlow came to the bar to him and said: "So I understand you think my friend Mac's answer won't do." "Do!" said Eldon, "my Lord, it won't do at all. It must have been drawn by that

---

[59] *Prince Albert* v. *Strange* (1849) 2 De G. & Sm. 652 at 694 (*per* Knight Bruce V.-C.).
[60] Job 31:35.
[61] Bentham, *Fragment on Government* (1774), p. xli.
[62] Bentham, *A Comment on the Commentaries* (ed. C.W. Everett, 1926), p. 206.

wooden Machine which you formerly told me might be invented to draw Bills and Answers." "That's very unlucky, and very impudent, too," said Thurlow, "if you had known the fact that I drew the answer myself."[63]

Like most things, pleading, however logical, may be carried to excess. In an Australian divorce case in 1970 and 1971,

> pleadings in the cause faltered to a stop only on 1st February, 1971. The document presented on that day was called: "Respondent's Reply to Petitioner's Answer to Amended Cross Petition: Respondent's Rejoinder to Petitioner's Reply to Respondent's Further Supplementary Answer and Supplementary Cross Petition: and Respondent's Rejoinder to Petitioner's Reply to Respondent's Rejoinder to Petitioner's Reply to Respondent's Cross Petition." By this time all parties accepted that it was more convenient just to tell the Court what was in issue rather than put anything in writing. . . . Remembering the story of the man of sudden wealth who bought a library by the ton, I weighed the pleadings in this suit. They weighed just under two pounds.[64]

Advice and argument are skilled far more often than they are foolish. The acumen of Noy[65] has been illustrated by the account of a case in which

> three graziers at a fair left their money with their hostess while they went to the market: one of them returned, received the money, and absconded; the other two sued the woman for delivering what she received from the three, before they all came to demand it together. The cause was clearly against the woman, and judgment was ready to be pronounced, when Mr. Noy, not being employed in the cause, desired the woman to give him a fee,[66] as he could not plead in her behalf unless he was employed; and, having received

---

[63] Lord Eldon's *Anecdote Book* (1960), p. 38, with minor revisions.

[64] *Illich* v. *Illich* [1971] 1 N.S.W.L.R. 272 at 273 (*per* Carmichael J.).

[65] 1577–1634. An amplified version of this story is ascribed to Serjeant Vaughan, afterwards B. (1827) and J. (1834): see *The Bench and the Bar* (1837), vol. 1, pp. 300–08. The story has also been fathered on to Ellesmere, *Law and Lawyers* (1840), vol. 1, pp. 169–71; A. Polson, *Law and Lawyers* (1858), p. 64; J.C. Jeaffreson, *A Book About Lawyers* (2d ed. 1867), p. 138; and see *Watson* v. *Evans* (1863) 32 L.J.Ex. 137 at 138 n.2.

[66] It is not obvious why he should not have appeared gratuitously; but see J.H. Baker (1969) 27 Camb. L.J. 213.

it, he moved in arrest of judgment that he was retained by the defendant, and that the case was this: the defendant had received the money from the three together, and was not to deliver it until the same three demanded it; that the money was ready to be paid whenever the three men should demand it together. This motion altered the whole proceedings.[67]

Such a rule is ancient, and applied alike in Athens, Rome, and Westminster Hall.[68] Perhaps Noy could not have foreseen that one day there would be authority for saying that after a joint deposit, if one is disabled from suing, an action by all will also fail.[69]

This tale may be linked with a story most frequently attributed to Curran (1750–1817). A farmer, visiting a fair, and fearful of thieves, had deposited £100 with the local innkeeper for safe custody, without the precaution of witnesses or a receipt. When the farmer claimed his money, the innkeeper denied having received it; and the disconsolate farmer went to Curran for advice. Curran first told him to make his peace with the innkeeper, and to say that he was sure that he must have left the money with another. He should later go with two reliable witnesses and deposit another £100 with the innkeeper, and then return to Curran for further instructions. The puzzled farmer did as he was bid. He was then told to go by himself and seek the return of the £100, and again come back for further instructions. Still puzzled, the farmer did this, and returned with his money, though still without his initial £100. "Now return to the innkeeper with your two witnesses and demand your £100," said Curran; and acumen defeated dishonesty.[70] Yet the perils are obvious. The fraudulent may all too readily pervert ingenuity in defeating dishonesty into their own engines of fraud.

Difficulties have sometimes arisen about whether counsel has been

---

[67] Noy's *Maxims* (9th ed. 1821), p. viii, by W.M. Bythewood, repeated in *Watson* v. *Evans* (1863) 1 H. & C. 662 at 663–64 (*per* Martin B.).

[68] See Jones on *Bailments* (1st ed. 1781), p. 51.

[69] *Brandon* v. *Scott* (1857) 7 E. & B. 234.

[70] See Leslie Hale, *John Philpot Curran* (1958), p. 91; Croake James, *Curiosities of Law & Lawyers* (1882), p. 151. A similar story is attributed to Thomas Addis Emmet, of the New York Bar, early in the nineteenth century; see C. Edwards, *Pleasantries about Courts and Lawyers of the State of New York* (1867), p. 497.

duly instructed on behalf of a client. The general rule is that the court will not enquire whether counsel who states that he is appearing for one of the parties is in fact properly instructed. Thus Patteson J. once enquired of counsel in a civil trial at Assizes whether he was instructed by any attorney, and on learning that he was not, refused to allow him to address the jury. But the Court of Queen's Bench held that this was wrong, and ordered a new trial.[71] The court approved the general rule of etiquette that prohibits such an appearance, but refused to hold that it bound the court.

In the course of argument, Lord Campbell C.J. observed that the court had recently "heard a motion for a habeas corpus by a woman on behalf of her husband: and I did not hesitate to hear a woman as counsel in such a case."[72] The County Courts Act, 1846, indeed contained a provision in the section dealing with rights of audience in county courts, authorising an appearance by an attorney or by "a Barrister at Law instructed by such Attorney on behalf of the Party,"[73] thus excluding any counsel instructed merely by the client; but the modern version of this section contains no such limitation, for it refers to "a barrister retained by or on behalf of any party."[74]

Per contra, sometimes two or more counsel instructed by different solicitors have each attempted to conduct the case of one of the parties to the litigation. When Knight Bruce V.-C. was confronted by such a situation, he ultimately resolved it by asking the lay client which counsel he wished to have, and then excluding the others.[75] An alternative course of action, once adopted by Plumer M.R., is to adjourn the case with a direction that the solicitors should verify their respective authorities by affidavit.[76]

There have been cases where instead of two counsel seeking to appear

---

[71] *Doe d. Bennett* v. *Hale* (1850) 15 Q.B. 171.

[72] *Ibid.*, at p. 181.

[73] County Courts Act, 1846, s. 91.

[74] County Courts Act, 1934, s. 86 (b) replaced by County Courts Acts 1959, s. 89(b), and 1984, s. 60(1)(b).

[75] *Ex parte Bass* (1849) 18 L.J.Ch. 245 at 247.

[76] *Butterworth* v. *Clapham* (1820) 1 Jac. & W. 673 n.

for the same litigant, two opposing litigants have each had a claim to the same counsel. In a bankruptcy case the question was that of the propriety of counsel appearing on a brief for the bankrupt after he had been retained and had appeared in the case for another person, apparently a creditor; and a petition was presented to the court to restrain counsel from appearing for the bankrupt. Lord Eldon L.C. at first refused to adjudicate the point, and expressed the opinion that, sitting in bankruptcy, he had no jurisdiction to interfere with a barrister in the exercise of his discretion as to the client on whose retainer he might think proper to act. But when counsel concerned solicited the Lord Chancellor to hear the petition, he consented to do so "as 'amicus curiae'"[77] — an engaging transformation. In the event he declared that counsel was bound to appear for the bankrupt. The argument contains much of interest, on both the subject of retainers and the subject of advocacy. The barrister, it was said,

> lends his exertions to all, himself to none. The result of the cause is to him a matter of indifference. It is for the court to decide. It is for him to argue. He is, however he may be represented by those who understand not his true situation, merely an officer assisting in the administration of justice, and acting under the impression, that truth is best discovered by powerful statements on both sides of the question."[78]

Misconduct may be palpable. One book[79] states that "Sir Henry Hawkins relates in his *Reminiscences* how he once found the following in his brief: 'If the case is called on before 3.15, the defence is left to the ingenuity of the counsel; if after that hour, the defence is an alibi, as by then the usual alibi witnesses will have returned from Norwich, where they are at present professionally engaged.'" As told, the story is redolent of impropriety. It also reeks of improbability, and the source cited appears to be innocent of any such tale.[80] But there is no reason to doubt

---

[77] *Ex parte Lloyd* (1822) Mont. 70 n.

[78] *Ibid.*, at p. 72 n.

[79] G.A. Morton & D.A. Malloch, *Law and Laughter* (1913), p. 57.

[80] I have failed to find any trace of it in *The Reminiscences of Sir Henry Hawkins (Baron Brampton)*, ed. Richard Harris K.C. (1904, in two volumes).

that the concluding words of a brief that Lord Coleridge once received were as follows: "It is hoped that an acquittal will be secured as a result of the eloquence of counsel and the Madonna-like appearance of the accused."[81] Such innocent optimism contrasts with the activities of an early-twentieth-century advocate whose style had little appeal to the Bench: without often overstepping the bounds of propriety, his conduct of cases too frequently went to the verge. Once he asked a witness a flagrantly objectionable question, and the judge pounced: "Mr. Blank, you must know that you cannot ask a question like that." But an answer was there: "It had occurred to me that your Lordship might take that view, and so I looked up the authorities. My Lord, it is settled that such a question is not inadmissible; it is merely a gross breach of professional etiquette."[82]

[81] Sir Harold Morris K.C., *The Barrister* (1930), p. 144.
[82] *Ex rel.* Trovato B.

6

~

SHORT OF WATER

MUCH illuminating information about individual styles of advocacy is to be found in a book published in 1819 entitled "Criticisms on the Bar; Including Strictures on the Principal Counsel Practising in the Courts of King's Bench, Common Pleas, Chancery, and Exchequer. By Amicus Curiae."[1] This sets out, in some three hundred pages, a detailed examination of the forensic and legal attainments of 32 leading counsel then in practice, with a prefatory chapter, "On the Decline of Eloquence at the English Bar." It is a book that deserves a modern successor, with its doubtless large royalties going to the Barristers Benevolent Association.

The author is frank, pointed, and constructive in his criticisms, which cannot have gratified all his involuntary subjects. Thus Sir Samuel Shepherd A.-G. had an action that was described as being

> unusually vehement upon all occasions, whether it is or is not required: he resorts to the ordinary expedient of making up for the weakness of his language, by the strength of his corporeal exertions. I do not mean that he throws about his figure in all directions, as Mr. Marryat does, like a porpoise in a storm, for he keeps that uncommonly erect; the motion is confined principally to his arms and feet. His deafness prevents him from properly regulating his voice, and fearing when he is strenuously endeavouring to enforce a particular point, that he shall speak too loud, his words become almost inaudible, while his arms and hands are employed in striking the desk or table with so much violence, that the whole Court resounds. The effect is

---

[1] Cited as *Criticisms.*

rendered still more ludicrous by his rising upon his toes to give his small person importance, and beating time with his heels upon the floor.[2]

This is the Sir Samuel Shepherd who, having refused the offices of C.J.K.B. and C.J.C.P. on account of his deafness, spent eleven happy and popular years as C.B. in Scotland.[3] His translation was no doubt welcome to him, for

of all offices in the gift of the Crown that of Attorney-general is perhaps least to be coveted; for whether the Government be popular or unpopular, the person filling that place can scarcely avoid being the object of general dislike: the rank is only fourth or fifth rate, and the manner in which it has been attained is always suspected, though sometimes unjustly: he is pretty sure to be charged with having ascended by the usual steps of political fawning and judicial servility, and after all he is only to be considered as the servant of servants — the curse of the Israelites.[4]

The office of Solicitor-General, on the other hand,

is perhaps most to be desired. In point of rank the latter is but just inferior to the former, and the Solicitor-General is relieved from a great part of the weight of public odium which his co-adjutor is under the necessity of sustaining. The Attorney-General stands forward, almost alone, as the public spy, informer, and prosecutor: all *ex-officio* informations against the libellers of his patrons, or other supposed delinquents, are filed in his name, and the wrath of the parties, and their supporters, and the dislike of the nation at large are levelled principally against him, while the Solicitor-General fights under his shield and sometimes appears not to enter into the contest at all: if he assist in any public proceeding, by far the larger portion of labour and ostensibility belongs to his leader and superior.[5]

The storm-ridden Mr. Marryat's demerits were not merely physical: "Of wit or humour Mr. Marryat has not a particle: he probably never made nor relished a joke in his life; but he is not deficient in good sense

---

[2] *Criticisms*, p. 74.
[3] See 1 Misc. 15.
[4] *Criticisms*, p. 61.
[5] *Ibid.*, at p. 95.

and its companion — discretion. His greatest excellence is zeal, and his greatest defect ignorance."[6] It is pleasant to record that "the assertion that he once applied for two *mandami* is most likely a libel upon his latinity";[7] but

> he is one of the most clumsy, negligent speakers that ever opened his lips: it has often been remarked of the present Lord Chief Justice [Lord Ellenborough[8]], that he never ends a sentence, and Mr. Marryat, it may be added, never begins one: he involves his speech in innumerable parentheses, and connects the most discordant parts by his favourite words, *and*, *but*, and *so*; running on at a hand-gallop; dashing through thick and thin, floundering here and stumbling there, and bespattering all who come in his way.[9]

Just how sound the author's judgment was may be open to doubt. In discussing Denman (later to become Lord Denman C.J.), he observed that Mr. Peel was "a young man of overrated abilities, and who will never do better than he has done, nor attain a higher rank than that of a debater";[10] yet within fifteen years Peel had become Prime Minister. At least the author's prudent pseudonymity preserved him from the treatment that he once saw Sir Vicary Gibbs administer while at the bar; the author saw him "inflict upon an Attorney a very sound box on the ear in open Court: the man shewed however that it was in some degree merited by his patient submission under it."[11]

The Bar at times suffers from the Bar. Lord Eldon recounted how in about 1782, Boswell, who was on circuit at Lancaster, had been found lying on the pavement one evening, intoxicated. Some of his fellow circuiteers subscribed a guinea, with half a crown for his clerk, and the next morning sent him a brief instructing him to move for a writ *Quare*

---

[6] *Ibid.*, at p. 43.

[7] *Ibid.*, at p. 36, casting doubt upon 2 Misc. 153.

[8] Sir Charles Abbott was C.J.K.B. when the book was published; but it seems reasonably clear that the passage in question was written before November 8, 1818, when Lord Ellenborough resigned: see, e.g., *Criticisms*, p. 16.

[9] *Criticisms*, p. 37.

[10] *Ibid.*, at p. 172.

[11] *Ibid.*, at p. 132.

adhaesit pavimento. The brief contained instructions indicating the need of great learning to explain the writ to the court, but Boswell's strenuous endeavours to find authority in the books were in vain. He nevertheless moved for the writ before an astonished judge and an amazed audience. "The Judge said 'I never heard of such a Writ — what can it be, that adheres *pavimento?* — Are any of you Gentlemen at the Bar able to explain this?' The Bar laughed — At last one of them said, 'My Lord, Mr. Boswell last night *adhaesit pavimento.* There was no moving him for some Time: At last he was carried to bed, and he has been dreaming about himself and the pavement.'"[12]

It is impossible to say how accurate this account is; but certainly Boswell never once mentions Lord Eldon in his *Life of Johnson,*[13] although there are references to many other lawyers of the day. It may be added that it was Boswell who was advised by an airy friend against becoming a lawyer because he would be excelled by plodding block-heads. Dr. Johnson's reply was brief: "Why, Sir, in the formulary and statutory part of law, a plodding blockhead may excel; but in the in-genious and rational part of it a plodding blockhead can never excel."[14]

Good argument has always been highly esteemed by the Bench. In 1409 Hankford J. observed: "Home ne scaveroit de quel metal un campane fuit, si ceo ne fuit bien batu, *quasi diceret,* le ley per bon disputacion serra bien conus."[15] Good argument does not lose its force by being expressed in decorous terms. As Lord O'Brien C.J. once drily said: "In our own courts we constantly hear the phrase 'If your Lordship pleases,' and in the House of Commons members not unfrequently make

[12] Twiss, *Eldon,* vol. 1, p. 93; and see Lord Eldon's *Anecdote Book* (1960), pp. 19, 20. See further Boswell, *The English Experiment, 1785–1789* (I. Lustig & F.A. Pottle eds., 1980), pp. 57–58 (where the same story is recounted but the editors comment that the accuracy of Eldon's anecdote has long been questioned on grounds that it is doubtful whether Boswell could have been tricked by such a writ). Also, *adhaesit pavimento* is in the *Book of Common Prayer* (Psalm 119, vv. 25–32), with which Boswell was familiar.

[13] Sir Arnold McNair, *Dr. Johnson & The Law* (1948), p. 23; and see *Stewart v. Fullarton* (1830) 4 Wils. & Sh. 196 at 210 (Boswell blaming the future Lord Eldon).

[14] Boswell's *Johnson,* vol. 1, p. 314.

[15] Y.B. 11 Hen. 4, Mich., fo. 37 (1409), quoted in *Cordell v. Second Clanfield Properties, Ltd.* [1969] 2 Ch. 9 at 16 (scaveroit: know; campane: bell; batu: beaten). For a variant version, see Co.Litt. 395a.

use of the formula, 'With the permission of the House.' These phrases are accepted as mere expressions of courtesy, and are in no way restrictive of exhaustive argument or elaborate discussion."[16]

In the courts it is in the coherent expression of ideas rather than in vehemence or repetition that persuasion lies, though not always at once. In one case counsel began before Lord Lyndhurst L.C. in a somewhat confused and halting way. " 'What a fool the man is!' muttered the Chancellor. As the speaker advanced, he grew clearer and more to the point. 'Aha!' was the comment, 'not such a fool as I thought!' Warming in his work, counsel proceeded with unmistakable effect. 'Egad!' was the next exclamation. 'It is I that was the fool!'"[17] True, "It is sometimes difficult to get rid of first impressions";[18] but overcoming that difficulty is one of the essentials of judicial office.

Other fields, other ways. Dr. Johnson's advice to Boswell, when he was about to argue before a committee of the House of Commons, was: "You must not argue there, as if you were arguing in the schools; close reasoning will not fix their attention; you must say the same thing over and over again, in different words. If you say it but once, they miss it in a moment of inattention. It is unjust, Sir, to censure lawyers for multiplying words when they argue; it is *necessary* for them to multiply words."[19] Another approach is the devious: "A lawyer should be able to suggest the arguments which will win his case so subtly to the judge that the latter believes he has thought of them himself."[20]

Today simplicity of utterance is venerated more than flowers of speech: "Praised be he who can state a cause in a clear, simple and succinct manner, and then stop."[21] In this respect, if no other, the Bar is the home of scholars; for the object of a true scholar is to make

---

[16] *Ussher* v. *Ussher* [1912] 2 I.R. 445 at 487–88.

[17] Sir Theodore Martin, *Life of Lord Lyndhurst* (1883), p. 286. For a variant version, see *Memoirs of Sir John Rolt 1804–1871* (1939), p. 87.

[18] *Withnell* v. *Gartham* (1795) 6 T.R. 388 at 396 (*per* Lord Kenyon C.J.).

[19] Boswell's *Johnson*, vol. 2, p. 452.

[20] P. Calamandrei, *Eulogy of Judges* (1942), p. 19.

[21] *Jungwirth* v. *Jungwirth*, 115 Or. 668, 240 P. 222, 223 (1925) (*per* Belt J.). There are insignificant variations in font and punctuation between the official and unofficial reports.

profound things clear, whereas the object of a German philosopher (and, indeed, of too many others) is to make clear things profound.[22] Yet simplicity cannot conquer all: "The question in the case is made obscure by an attempt at its simplification."[23] Again, "the facts are less complicated than the proceedings that have grown out of them."[24] The old advice still holds: "First settle what the case is, before you argue it."[25]

The language of argument changes with the years. Today, none would dare to use the words with which Erskine once courted a jury: "Gentlemen of the jury, the reputation of a cheese-monger in the city of London is like the bloom upon a peach. Breathe on it! — and it is gone for ever!"[26] Perhaps it is as well. There were disasters. Defending counsel once reminded a jury that "even the beasts of the field and the birds of the air suckle their young." But Byles J. was vigilant: "If you can establish the truth of that proposition," he said, "you may confidently look for an acquittal."[27] Yet one may shed a tear for the finer flowers. It was the future Platt B. who, while at the Bar, obtained an enhanced award of damages for the young lady for whom he was appearing by reminding the jury: "This serpent in human shape stole the virgin heart of my unfortunate client whilst she was returning from confirmation!"[28] Yet it is comforting to know that the Bench will always be there to shield the jury from excesses at the Bar. "If any whimsical notions are put into you, by some enthusiastic counsel, the court is not to take notice of their crotchets."[29]

Applications for an adjournment on personal grounds do sometimes succeed; but there may be a price. After a bankruptcy appeal had for

---

[22] See Serjeant Robinson, *Bench and Bar* (1889), p. 172.

[23] *U.S. v. New River Co.*, 265 U.S. 533, 545 (1924) (McKenna J., dissenting).

[24] *Kansas City Southern Railway Co. v. Guardian Trust Co.*, 240 U.S. 166, 172–73 (1916) (*per* Holmes J.).

[25] *R. v. Sancroft* (1688) 12 St.Tr. 183 at 342 (*per* Wright C.J.) (Trial of the Seven Bishops).

[26] *Pie-Powder* (1911), p. 79. T.E. Crisp, *Reminiscences of a K.C.* (1909), p. 146, attributes similar words to Serjeant Sleigh.

[27] *Pie-Powder, supra* note 26, p. 136; Montagu Williams Q.C., *Leaves of a Life* (1890), p. 47.

[28] Serjeant Ballantine, *Some Experiences of a Barrister's Life* (8th ed. 1882), p. 10; Crisp, *supra* note 26, p. 146. See also *post* p. 236.

[29] *R. v. Hayes* (1684) 10 St.Tr. 307 at 314 (*per* Jeffreys C.J.).

some while been making its somewhat ponderous progress, a distinguished silk in the case (who may be called Blank Q.C.) asked the judges
whether they would abstain from sitting in the morning of the next day.
He explained that he was a member of an important governmental
committee that was due to meet then, and that the chairman heavily
relied on him for assistance. "Indeed," he said, "if the committee met
without my being there, it would be like playing Hamlet without the
prince." This persuaded the court to grant the application, and the
appeal ground on. Towards the end of the day the judges made little
progress in getting a clear answer from the silk on one point. Finally, as
the court was about to adjourn, Browne-Wilkinson J. said: "Mr. Blank,
perhaps you will have an opportunity of considering the answer to that
question on your return from Elsinore."[30]

Sometimes, however, the last word lies with counsel. In 1834, London
University, then a mere company, petitioned for the grant of a Royal
Charter. Before the Privy Council, the future Lord Langdale M.R. on
behalf of the University of Cambridge, contended that without authority
from the Crown London University could not lawfully confer degrees (this
being an obvious essential of a true university[31]). But Lord Brougham
L.C. questioned this:[32] "Pray, Mr. Bickersteth, what is to prevent the
London University granting degrees *now*?" The reply was crushing: "The
universal scorn and contempt of mankind."[33]

Persuasion comes in many forms. While at the Irish Bar towards the
end of the nineteenth century, Thomas Ebenezer Webb, a brilliant
scholar and afterwards County Court Judge of Donegal, once appeared
on a licensing application, a subject about which he knew little or
nothing. He was assured that the case was a mere formality, but to his
horror he found that the police objected to his client on the score of his
youth. This was too much for Webb. "What!" he cried:

[30] *Re a Debtor, No. 37 of 1976 (Liverpool)* [1979] May 14–22, unrep., *ex rel.* Fox J.

[31] See *St. David's College, Lampeter* v. *Ministry of Education* [1951] 1 All E.R. 559 at 561.

[32] T.D. Hardy, *Memoirs of Lord Langdale* (1852), vol. 1, p. 395. The Royal Charter was
granted on November 28, 1836: see 15 *Halsb. Laws* p. 234.

[33] 1 *Greville Diary* 488. Alternatively, "The utter scorn and contempt of the world": Hardy,
supra note 32, loc. cit.

Alexander the Great at the age of 22 had crossed the Ilyssus, razed the city of Thebes to the ground, and brought the entire Persian Empire under his sway. At 23 Descartes evolved a new system of Philosophy. At 24 Pitt was Prime Minister of Great Britain, over whose realms the sun never sets, and at 25 Napoleon Bonaparte saved the Republic with a whiff of grape shot in the streets of Paris. Is it now to be judicially determined that at 25 my client, Peter Mulligan, is too young to manage a public house in Capel Street?[34]

There are also many ways of inducing receptiveness in the listeners. In one nineteenth-century action for slander, tried at Warwick before Cockburn C.J. and a jury, the plaintiff complained that the defendant had called him "a thief, a damned thief, and a blasted thief." The plaintiff was represented by Macaulay Q.C., Mellor Q.C., and Wills, whose ample junior practice had not interfered with his renown as a mountaineer. Serjeant Hayes, for the defendant, set the tone of his speech in his apposite opening words:

> For a long time I have been utterly unable to understand why, in such a case, there should be such an array of counsel for the plaintiff, but I think that I have, at last, found the key to the mystery. There are three degrees of comparison in the slander, and so it is appropriate that there should be three counsel, each to represent one of the degrees. There is my friend Mr. *Wills*, who has risen to great heights *out* of the profession to which he belongs, and who, we all hope, will rise to a great height *within* it. What more natural than that, young and ingenuous, he should be chosen to represent "*the thief*," pure and simple? But, when it came to "a d—d thief," nothing less than a Queen's Counsel and a Member of Parliament would do; and they have, with equal propriety selected the respectability and gravity of my friend Mr. *Mellor*. Even this is not enough — for "*a blasted thief*," they must obviously have something higher still — and who could possibly answer to such a character but the leader of the circuit — the gifted Mr. *Macaulay*?[35]

A student who turns to crammers or coaches should be aware of a modern version of an ancient puzzle. A Bar student arranged to be

---

[34] *Ex rel.* T.C. Tobias, formerly Under-Treasurer of the King's Inns, Dublin. For a variant but similar version, see James Comyn, *Their Friends at Court* (1973), p. 21.

[35] *Hayesiana* (1892), p. vi.

coached for his examinations on the terms that he would pay half the fee in advance and the rest as soon as he had won a case. The student passed his examinations and was duly called to the Bar, but seemed to be in no hurry to obtain any briefs. At last his tutor sued him for the unpaid moiety of his fee, and each party appeared in person. The tutor contended that whatever the result of the case the money must be payable; for if he won, he would have the judgment of the court in his favour, while if he lost, his former pupil would be liable under the terms of the contract. Not so, said the pupil; for if the claim failed there would have been a finding of the court against the claim, while if it succeeded nothing would be payable according to the terms of the contract. At that, the judge prudently adjourned the case *sine die*.[36] leaving the student to reflect that the price of victory would have been the prospect of certain defeat in further proceedings.

Some plain cases are not. In an action for breach of promise of marriage, the defendant had promised to marry the plaintiff, but then had married someone else. There seemed no doubt. Yet defending counsel had two questions to put to the plaintiff:

Q. The defendant's father is still alive, isn't he?
A. Yes.
Q. And the promise was to marry you when his father was dead, wasn't it?
A. Yes.

At that, counsel said, "That is my case, my Lord." "But," said the judge, "how do you get over the fact that the defendant has already married someone else?" Counsel responded, "That was no breach, my Lord. The defendant's wife may die before his father, or there may be a divorce before then, and the defendant can then carry out his contract; while if either the plaintiff or the defendant predeceases the father, the contract will have been frustrated before the time for performance has arrived." And that was that.[37]

---

[36] Based on *Protagoras* v. *Euathlus*: see Sir William Hamilton, *Lectures on Logic*, vol. 1, p. 467, as cited in David Murray, *Lawyers' Merriments* (1912), p. 2.

[37] Suggested by *Frost* v. *Knight* (1870) L.R. 5 Exch. 322.

Until 1940,[38] Scotland had its own special form of defeat for such actions. If the pursuer established that on the faith of the promise she had allowed herself to be seduced, the very act of seduction might constitute marriage, and so destroy her claim; for an irregular (but valid) form of marriage was by promise *subsequente copula*.[39] More generally, the answer lies in frustration: where one party repudiates a contract before the time for performance, the other party may sue for breach.[40]

In the proceedings in the House of Lords in 1820 in which George IV sought to cast off Queen Caroline for immorality, the defence provided examples of good advocacy and bad. The peroration in Brougham's opening speech is often quoted: "Such, my lords, is the Case now before you! Such is the evidence in support of this measure — evidence inadequate to prove a debt — impotent to deprive of a civil right — ridiculous to convict of the lowest offence — scandalous if brought forward to support a charge of the highest nature which the law knows — monstrous to ruin the honour, to blast the name of an English Queen!"[41] Denman's closing speech is not forgotten either: "With a maladroitness that is almost incredible, he closed his peroration with a reference to the woman in the Gospel of St. Mark[42] — 'Go, and sin no more.'[43] No wonder that the town re-echoed with the over-quoted epigram —

> Gracious lady, we implore,
> Go away, and sin no more,
> And if that effort be too great,
> Go away at any rate."[44]

---

[38] Marriage (Scotland) Act 1939.

[39] See 1 Misc. 126. This is also fully examined in Lord Fraser's *Treatise on Husband and Wife According to the Law of Scotland* (2d ed. 1876), vol. 1, 322–90.

[40] See *Frost* v. *Knight* (1872) L.R. 7 Exch. 111; *Fercometal S.A.R.L.* v. *Mediterranean Shipping Co. S.A.* [1989] A.C. 788 at 798, 799.

[41] Speech on October 3 and 4, 1820, as reproduced in *Speeches of Henry Lord Brougham* (1838), vol. 1, p. 227. A less effective version appears in Nightingale's *Trial of Queen Caroline*, vol. 2 (1821), p. 80; and this, being more nearly contemporary, may more closely represent what was actually said, before being edited. There are other variants: see, e.g., *Hornal* v. *Neuberger Products Ltd.* [1957] 1 Q.B. 247 at 263.

[42] *Sic*: see John 8:11.

[43] See Nightingale, *supra* note 41, vol. 3 (1821), p. 292.

[44] 1 Atlay 256.

At its nadir, advocacy drives out all thought save of escape, even into unconsciousness. In a case before Commissioner Kerr, a verbose member of the Bar observed that one juror that he was addressing had fallen asleep; and he berated the wakeful jurors for displaying so little interest in the case. At this the Commissioner interposed: "Ye just remind me of a meenester in Ayrshire, who was lecturing his congregation for not coming to kirk, and remarked, 'Those of ye who do come are asleep, bar the village idiot,' when a voice said, 'If I'd nae been an ideot I had been asleep too.'"[45]

Times indeed change. Today, most cases are argued but once in each court; but in the sixteenth century it was sometimes otherwise. One case was even said to have been "argued twenty-one times severally."[46] Again, no advocate today expresses his regret to the court that he cannot discuss the case further because he is "short of water"; nor does he have occasion to express his gratitude at being enabled to continue by the generous act of another advocate in the same cause giving him some of his water. Yet in ancient Greece and Rome, such experiences were common; for the length of the speeches in many types of action was regulated by the clepsydra, or water-clock;[47] and one advocate might transfer to another a portion of his water, and so of his allotted time.[48] *Aquam dare* was as generous as *aquam perdere* was foolish. The expression "short of water" does not seem to have survived even in those jurisdictions (such as the Supreme Court of the United States) in which forensic eloquence is curbed by the clock, and not merely by the demeanour of the court. Hughes C.J. was so punctilious a time-keeper that he was said to have stopped a leader of the New York Bar in the middle of the word "if."[49]

Brevity in argument may engender brevity in judgments. The

---

[45] G. Pitt-Lewis, *Commissioner Kerr — An Individuality* (1903), p. 202.

[46] *Butler & Baker's Case* (1591) 3 Co.Rep. 25a at 35b; but there are explanations other than the strictly literal.

[47] The "water stole away" through small holes in the container.

[48] See W. Forsyth Q.C., *Hortensius* (3d ed. 1879), p. 44.

[49] Edwin McElwain, *The Business of the Supreme Court as Conducted by Chief Justice Hughes*, 63 Harv. L. Rev. 5, 17 (1949).

question once arose whether for the purposes of income tax a sewer vested in a local authority was not only "a hereditament capable of actual occupation" but also was capable of "profitable occupation." The House of Lords had no difficulty in affirming the decision that it was. Lord Halsbury, indeed, disposed of the appeal in a little over a page. His concluding words were: "I cannot forbear pointing out that the Attorney-General[50] in the course of exactly seven minutes appeared to me to dispose of the whole day's argument with which we had been entertained. I must say I congratulate him and I am endeavouring to emulate his success by the length of the Judgment which I am now delivering."[51]

There are times when the advocate has much to contend with. His difficulties may lie with the judge, the jury, or his opponent, or, indeed, with all three, quite apart from the intractability of the facts and evidence. The Bench may try to cut short his argument, as Jessel M.R. once did with Herschell. But Herschell would not have it, and retorted that "important as it was that people should get justice, it was even more important that they should be made to feel and see that they were getting it."[52] This pronouncement was, of course, a precursor of Lord Hewart C.J.'s famous statement that it is "of fundamental importance that justice should not only be done, but should manifestly and undoubtedly be seen to be done."[53] It is less well-known that there is judicial authority for saying that in this statement the words "be seen" must be a misprint for the word "seem".[54] However that may be, the statement plainly must not be inverted or perverted: "The continued citation of it in cases to which it is not applicable may lead to the erroneous impression that it is more important that justice should appear to be done than that it should in fact be done."[55] It certainly does

---

[50] Sir J. Lawson Walton.

[51] *Ystradyfodwg and Pontypridd Main Sewerage Board* v. *Bensted* [1907] A.C. 264 at 268.

[52] 2 Atlay 460.

[53] *R.* v. *Sussex Justices, ex parte McCarthy* [1924] 1 K.B. 256 at 259, quoted in 1 Misc. 234.

[54] *R.* v. *Essex Justices, ex parte Perkins* [1927] 2 K.B. 475 at 488 (*per* Avory J.), cited in *R.* v. *Salford Assessment Committee, ex parte Ogden* [1937] 2 K.B. 1 at 26.

[55] *R.* v. *Camborne Justices, ex parte Pearce* [1955] 1 Q.B. 41 at 52 (*per* Slade J., speaking for Lord Goddard C.J., Cassels J., and himself).

not mean that "the appearance of justice is of more importance than the attainment of justice itself,"[56] as Herschell in the course of argument seems to have asserted. What it does mean is that "not only must justice appear to be done, it must be done,"[57] without any comparatives.

Such views are old in the law. Thus they were to be found in the Irish Court of Chancery in 1828:

> It is a great point not only to do justice, but to leave the parties in the certainty that justice has been done. That is the truest justice that the suitor acknowledges, and therefore, the decree which I like best, is that with which both parties are content. Perhaps the next best, is that with which both are dissatisfied. I shall spare no pains to convince parties that their rights have been thoroughly sifted. It is mercy to them to bring them to that state of viewing the case, that no temptation shall induce them to come again into court.[58]

More recent restatements of this approach have appeared. Thus:

> Sometimes I ask students to say whom they consider to be the most important person in a court-room. Many pick the judge; others give a variety of answers. One even opted for the usher, without being able to explain why. My answer, given unhesitatingly, is that it is the litigant who is going to lose. Naturally he will usually not know this until the case is at an end. But when the end comes, will he go away feeling that he has had a fair run and a full hearing? . . . One of the important duties of the courts is to send away defeated litigants who feel no justifiable sense of injustice in the judicial process. . . . Justice in full takes time; but often it is time well spent.[59]

Another aspect of what, after all, is one of the fundamentals of justice sometimes appears when the argument has ended. After reserving judgment, a judge may discover seemingly relevant authorities to which

[56] *R. v. Watson, ex parte Armstrong* (1976) 136 C.L.R. 248 at 262, *per* the majority (Barwick C.J. and Gibbs, Stephen, and Mason JJ.).

[57] *Pentland Park Amusements Pty. Ltd.* v. *Melbourne & Metropolitan Board of Works* [1972] V.R. 540 at 552 (*per* Anderson J.).

[58] *Byrne* v. *Frere* (1828) 2 Molloy 157 at 182 (*per* Sir Anthony Hart L.C.).

[59] R.E. Megarry, *Temptations of the Bench*, 12 Univ. Brit. Colum. L. Rev. 145 at 151, 152 (1978); and see C. Rivers (1979) 123 S.J. 229.

he has not been referred by counsel. The question is then what the judge should do:

> Naturally he wishes to avoid the expense and delay of restoring the case for further argument; yet the paramount consideration is that of avoiding any injustice to litigants or their counsel. It seems to me that a distinction can be made. If the authorities are such as to raise a new point, or to change or modify, even provisionally, the conclusion that the judge has already reached, or to resolve his doubts on a point, I can see no alternative to restoring the case for further argument; and, of course, authorities do not always wear the same aspect after they have been dissected in argument as they appeared to wear before. On the other hand, if the authorities do no more than confirm or support the conclusions that the judge has already reached on a point that has been fairly argued, then in most cases I cannot see that it is wrong for the judgment to refer to them without any further argument. A litigant to whom the authorities are adverse would have been defeated in any event, and a litigant whose cause the authorities support is not likely to object to the advent of reinforcements. Further, if an appeal is contemplated, or if the case is reported, the citation of the additional authorities may be of assistance in showing that they were not overlooked and in preventing them from being overlooked in the future. Similarly, I do not think that objection could fairly be taken to the citation of an authority which could not affect the result but merely, for example, provides an apt phrase or extraneous parallel.[60]

Other views have been expressed. In particular, Lord Denning sometimes did his own researches and then delivered judgment partly based on them without affording counsel any prior opportunity of commenting upon them.[61] In one case he defended his practice, observing that he had "been rebuked before for doing my own researches";[62] but this wholly misses the point. The objection is not to a judge doing his own researches, which is admirable, but to the injustice of using them to the detriment of a litigant who has had no opportunity of meeting them. A judge ought not to do what he would condemn in an inferior court as

---

[60] Canadian Judicial Council's *A Book for Judges* (1980) by Hon. J.O. Wilson at p. 88, quoting *Re Lawrence's Will Trusts* [1972] Ch. 418 at 436.

[61] See, e.g., *Rahimtoola* v. *Nizam of Hyderabad* [1958] A.C. 379; *Goldsmith* v. *Sperrings Ltd.* [1977] 1 W.L.R. 478.

[62] *Goldsmith* v. *Sperrings Ltd.*, *supra* note 61, at p. 486.

being a breach of the rule *audi alteram partem*.[63] The parties must not be deprived of the benefit of "one of the most fundamental rules of natural justice: the right of each to be informed of any point adverse to him that is going to be relied upon by the judge and to be given an opportunity of stating what his answer to it is."[64]

Accidents, however, have happened, even in the most exalted places. In a leading case on the *cy-près* doctrine,[65] counsel for the appellants in the House of Lords appears to have made little progress in his reply before their Lordships (Lord Lyndhurst L.C., Lord Brougham, and Lord Campbell) began to intervene with many comments and questions. Soon counsel seems to have been unable to intervene in the amicable discussion between their lordships; at the top of one page he uttered one sentence, and there then followed four and a half pages of assorted judicial comment, including a page from the Lord Chancellor and a page and a half from Lord Campbell, expressing decided views against the appellant.[66] The Lord Chancellor then addressed a sentence to counsel, who replied: "I feel very awkwardly situated; your Lordships are giving judgment, and I was in the middle of my observations, and had meant to draw your Lordships' attention to one or two matters —", whereat, the report states, "Their Lordships severally expressed their readiness to hear the learned counsel, desiring him to consider what passed only as their impression at the time."[67] Counsel then struggled on for a while, but finally abandoned his efforts with a manifestation of hope that he should not be thought to be obstinately arguing against their Lordships' judgments. He added: "I did not know until Lord Campbell began that you were pronouncing judgment." At this, the Lord Chancellor said: "I am to blame. I am not sure that I did in the outset intend to give judgment. I had no right to pronounce judgment in the course of your argument; however, I have expressed my opinion, and I do not see any

---

63 *Ibid.*, at p. 508 (*per* Bridge L.J.).
64 *Hadmor Productions Ltd.* v. *Hamilton* [1983] A.C. 191 at 232–33 (*per* Lord Diplock).
65 *Ironmongers' Co.* v. *Attorney-General* (1844) 10 Cl. & F. 908.
66 *Ibid.*, at pp. 926–30.
67 *Ibid.*, at p. 930.

reason to depart from it."[68] And with less than half a page more the appeal was dismissed.

At times the Bench is less than satisfied with the Bar. Over six centuries ago, Bereford C.J. said to counsel: "Nous voilloms savoir si vous voillez autre chose dire, qe ceo qe vous dites n'est qe jangle et riot."[69] More recently, Bramwell B., having failed in an attempt to curb the loquacity of counsel, observed: "You never shorten anything by attempting to shorten it: on the contrary, you lengthen it by the length of the attempt."[70] Roxburgh J., who was free from taciturnity, put it as a dilemma: "It seems to me that if a judge interrupts during a case, it drags out interminably. If he keeps quiet, it goes on for ever."[71]

Yet chance may play a hand. The future Hallett J. was one of those whose unquenchable volubility at the Bar even the Court of Appeal found it difficult to stem. In one appeal, while on his second or third cycle, he incautiously said, in injured tones, that on one point the judge had stopped him. In a moment of stunned and incredulous silence the presiding Lord Justice saw his chance: "Tell me, Mr. Hallett, just *how* did the judge do that?" The reply was prompt and indignant: "My Lord, by falsely pretending to be in my favour."[72] The flow was augmented rather than abated by his translation to the Bench in 1939. One harassed junior ultimately turned his back on the judge and declared emphatically to the public benches: "There is too much talking in this court."[73] But temporary relief brought no cure. In 1948, under the caption "The Rule in Hallett's Case",[74] there appeared the quotation "I make it a rule not to

---

[68] See *ibid.*, at p. 933.

[69] S.S. vol. 17 (1903), p. xv ("We wish to know whether you have anything else to say, for as yet you have done nothing but wrangle and chatter."). Bereford was C.J.C.P. from 1309 to 1323.

[70] Earl of Oxford and Asquith, *Memories and Reflections, 1852–1927* (Boston, 1928), vol. 1, p. 79.

[71] [1947] 6 C.L. p. ii.

[72] See Sir Harold Kent, *In on the Act* (1978), p. 16, for a variant.

[73] Lord Elwyn-Jones, *In My Time* (1983), p. 136. The hero was Jenkin Jones, of the Swansea Bar.

[74] A title that none confused with the well-known rule of equity based on *Re Hallett's Estate* (1880) 13 Ch.D. 696.

interrupt counsel in his argument."[75] It is said that when the judge complained bitterly to Lord Goddard C.J. about this, he was met by the bland inquiry: "But tell me, Hallett, *do* you talk too much?" Hallett J. is one of the three[76] who are variously said to have been the judge to whom, when a case was called on, counsel boldly inverted a familiar judicial inquiry by saying: "My Lord, it would be of convenience to counsel if your Lordship would indicate how long this case is likely to last."[77]

Juries are different. In the early 1930s, counsel who was opening a prosecution for housebreaking at Assizes suffered from a fidgety juror. The trouble lay in the juror's mackintosh. He began by keeping it on; then he took it off and sat on it; then, finding this uncomfortable, he put it on the edge of the jury-box; next he put it on the floor under his seat; and finally he picked it up and put it on his lap. This done, he embarked on a discussion with his neighbour in conversational tones, doubtless about the lack of amenities of the jury-box. All this time counsel had been trying to open the case, and he had reached the point when the householder had left his dinner to go into his study, and had there encountered the accused. Yet although counsel had been looking hard and often at the juror, he had continued his performance, undismayed and perhaps oblivious of the unrest that he was creating. His conversation with his neighbour proved to be the last straw. Counsel paused, looked straight at the juror, and said with great emphasis: "Keep still, or I'll knock your fucking[78] block off." For a few seconds there was a deathly hush in court; the judge, perhaps for the first time in his career, was bereft of words. Counsel then continued imperturbably: "Those, members of the jury, were the words which the accused uttered to the householder when he entered his study."[79]

---

[75] [1948] 1 C.L. p. ii.

[76] The others are Wallington and Roxburgh JJ.

[77] [1948] 11 C.L. p. ii.

[78] Contrast 1 Misc. 203.

[79] Counsel concerned, the late W.A. Fearnley-Whittingstall Q.C., kindly but reluctantly confirmed the accuracy of this account from his junior days.

7

~

FIGS AND PIPPINS

THERE have been many eulogies both of the process of trial by jury and of juries themselves. But not all the praise has been undiscriminating: "In this country we consider that a jury is the best possible tribunal yet devised for deciding whether or not a man is guilty, and, subject to the direction in law of the judge, of what offence he is guilty, but no one has ever suggested that a jury is composed of persons who are likely at a moment's notice to be able to give a logical explanation of how and why they arrived at their verdict."[1] This echoes Maule J., who once observed that "trial by jury is not founded upon an absurd supposition that all twelve will reason infallibly from the premises to the conclusion."[2] "Juries are not bound by what seems inescapable logic to judges."[3] Indeed, "the jury has the power to bring in a verdict in the teeth of both law and facts."[4] As Bramwell L.J. once said, "If juries had to give reasons for their verdict, trial by jury would not last five years."[5] The giving of reasons would remove "a serious practical obstacle to an appeal"[6] and open the floodgates.

This approach seems to have been regarded as being at least part of

[1] *R.* v. *Larkin* [1943] K.B. 174 at 176 (*per* Humphreys J.), where the judge had questioned the jury.

[2] *Smith* v. *Dobson* (1841) 3 Man. & G. 59 at 62, where the jury gave a reason.

[3] *Morisette* v. *U.S.*, 342 U.S. 246, 276 (1952) (*per* Jackson J.).

[4] *Horning* v. *District of Columbia*, 254 U.S. 135, 138 (1920) (*per* Holmes, J.).

[5] *Dunkirk Colliery Co.* v. *Lever* (1878) 9 Ch.D. 20 at 28.

[6] *Director of Public Prosecutions* v. *Sabapathee* [1997] 1 W.L.R. 483 at 486 (*per* Lord Hoffmann).

the foundation of the rule that the courts will not receive any evidence from a juror about what occurred in the privacy of the jury box or jury room, as distinct from what occurred in open court,[7] and that it is wrong for jurors to divulge such confidences to the press or the public. As Lord Hewart C.J. put it: "If one juryman might communicate with the public upon the evidence and the verdict, so might his colleagues also, and if they all took this dangerous course, differences of individual opinion might be made manifest which, at the least, could not fail to diminish the confidence that the public rightly has in the general propriety of criminal verdicts."[8] Yet it has been held that it is not necessarily a contempt of court for a periodical to publish a juror's account of the deliberations of the jury in a criminal trial,[9] though statute has now changed the law.[10] This, of course, is entirely different from what is one of a jury's prime duties, namely, to publish its verdict in court both clearly and explicitly. One "extraordinary development" that was "unique in the experience of each member of the court" was that "at the end of a long trial and five hours of deliberation by the jury . . . neither the judge nor counsel had the faintest idea what it was that this man [the appellant] had been convicted of by the verdict returned by the jury."[11] The indictment had contained two similar counts, and the jury had been discharged after convicting on one count and failing to agree on the other, but without revealing which was which.

In charging the jury in a case in which a will was alleged to be a forgery, Grier J. uttered many wise words:

> We easily believe what we wish to be true. We are prone to be satisfied with light proof, or any fallacy in favour of a preconceived opinion, prejudice or feeling. When we suffer ourselves to be thus tempted, we act as tyrants, not as judges. . . . In the midst of our virtuous indignation against fraud, we first

7 *Ellis* v. *Deheer* [1922] 2 K.B. 113; *R.* v. *Thompson* [1962] 1 All E.R. 65.

8 *R.* v. *Armstrong* [1922] 2 K.B. 555 at 568 (*per* Lord Hewart C.J., for himself, Avory, and Shearman JJ.).

9 *Attorney-General* v. *New Statesman & Nation Publishing Co. Ltd.* [1981] Q.B. 1.

10 Contempt of Court Act 1981, s. 8.

11 *R.* v. *Bravery* [1990] *The Times*, May 31 (*per* Russell L.J., for himself, Turner, and Fennell JJ.).

assume it has been committed, and then seek for arguments to confirm, not our judgments, but our prejudice. "Trifles, light as air," then become "strong as proofs of holy writ."[12] Circumstances which to an unprejudiced mind are just as compatible with innocence as guilt; which at best could raise only a suspicion, are set down as conclusive evidence of crime. Those who sit in judgment over men's rights, whether as courts or jurors, should beware of this natural weakness to which we are almost all of us subject. We all fancy ourselves wiser than perhaps others are willing to give us credit for. This feeling is gratified[13] by what we believe to be superior sagacity.[14]

The tale of misconduct by jurors is long. In 1588 the members of a jury retired to consider their verdict, and "remained there a long time without concluding any thing; and the officers of the Court who attended them seeing their delay, searched the jurours if they had any thing about them to eat; upon which search it was found, that some of them had figs, and others pippins." The court examined the jurors upon oath, and two confessed to eating figs before agreeing on the verdict, and three owned up to possessing (but not eating) pippins. The figs cost each juror £5 in fines and the pippins £2; but as none of the fruit had been provided by either of the parties, it was held "upon great advice and deliberation, and conference with the other Judges," that the verdict was "good notwithstanding the misdemeanor aforesaid."[15]

Drink, however, might be cheaper than food. In 1515 a jury that was returning to court to deliver its verdict "saw Rede, Chief Justice,[16] going on the way to see an affray, and they followed him, and in going they saw a cup and drank out of it; and for this, they were fined each forty pence."[17] There were also ways of obtaining free drink. In one case in trespass and ejectment in 1655,

---

[12] *Iago:* Trifles, light as air, / Are to the jealous confirmation strong / As proofs of holy writ. *Othello,* Act 3, sc. 3, ll. 322–24.

[13] *Sic:* perhaps "justified" was meant.

[14] *Turner* v. *Hand,* 3 Wallace Jr. 88 at 107, 112 (1855). See also *post* pp. 235–36.

[15] *Mounson & Wests Case* (1588) 1 Leon. 132; and see *Hall* v. *Vaughan* (1595) Moo. K.B. 599; *Harebottle* v. *Placock* (1604) Cro.Jac. 21.

[16] Robert Rede, C.J.C.P.

[17] *Anon.* (1515) 1 Dy. 37b.

the evidence being long and the weather hot, the jury desired they might have drink, which the Court granted, but said they should have it at the Bar, whereupon drink was sent for for them, and they drunk it there before they went out to consider of the evidence. Roll Chief Justice did then reprove the attorneys and sollicitors for the great charges they used to put their clyents to, in feasting the jury, and ordered that thenceforth no more thon 3s. 4d. should be allowed to any juryman to pay for his dinner. Nota."[18]

Yet in those days, three shillings and four pence would have yielded a truly sumptuous dinner.

The verdict itself could not withstand the clandestine obtaining of food and strong drink. One nineteenth-century jury, after retiring to consider its verdict, let down a string out of a window and pulled up "certain victuals and beer which they had caused to be procured for them." The verdict that the jurors ultimately gave "for a very large sum of money" was later set aside on account of their "gross indecencies in the administration of [justice]."[19]

"Trial by jury is a rough scales at best; the beam ought not to tip for motes and straws."[20] Nor, indeed for the drawing of lots. In one seventeenth-century action for misusing a horse, the jury found itself equally divided, and so "agreed by lot, putting two sixpences into a hat, that which the bailiff took, that way the verdict should go, which was for the plaintiff, and 2d. damages." A new trial was sought, "but the Court denied it, because it appeared only by pumping a juryman, who confessed all; but being against himself, it was not much regarded. Also the Court cannot grant a new trial without punishing the jury, which cannot be by this confession against themselves." Wyndham J. then made the somewhat cryptic observation: "This is as good a way of decision as by the strongest body, which is the usual way, and is suitable in such cases to the law of God"; but Twisden J. "doubted it would be of ill example,

---

[18] *Edwards* v. *Stiff* (1655) Sty. 448.

[19] *Cooksey* v. *Haynes* (1858) 27 L.J.Ex. 371, *per curiam* (Pollock C.B., and Martin, Bramwell, and Channell BB.). And see *R.* v. *Taylor* [1950] N.I. 57 (conviction for murder quashed because the jury exceeded the trial judge's limited permission for an outing); see also *People* v. *Heffernan* [1951] I.R. 206.

[20] *U.S.* v. *Brown*, 79 F.2d 321, 326 (2d Cir. 1935) (*per* Learned Hand J.).

and in *Sir Phillip Acton's Case*, on such verdict, on fillip of counter, a new trial was granted, but here it was denied."[21] Where, however, a Yorkshire jury had found their verdict "by hustling half-pence in a hat,"[22] the court ordered the jurors to be attached. "Per Cur.: Let the jurors all attend to be publickly admonished, that the country may take warning."[23]

Another jury, "having sat up all night, agreed in the morning to put two papers into a hat, marked P. and D. and so draw lots; P. came out, and they found for the plaintiff, which happened to be according to the evidence and the opinion of the Judge." Nevertheless the verdict was set aside.[24] A century later in New York, too, a jury drew lots for a verdict, and the lots favoured the defendants. The constable who was attending the jury then "put before them a paper, intimating that their proceeding was unlawful, and might subject them to punishment; whereupon the jury agreed that the balloting should go for nothing, but determined that the verdict should notwithstanding be for the defendants, and reported accordingly." But the court set aside the verdict.[25] There was the same result when a Glamorgan jury in a trial presided over by the under-sheriff went out and returned smoking cigars. Their sally had not interrupted the proceedings, but some of them had been seen talking to the plaintiff's attorney in a neighbouring public house.[26]

A juror who in 1892 separated from his fellows during an adjournment in a murder trial, and for half an hour was outside the precincts of the court and in communication with other persons, was fined £50 by Kennedy J. for "a gross contempt of Court."[27] Again, in a prosecution at Lewes Assizes in 1894, "while the jury were considering their verdict one of the jurymen was seized with sickness, and rushed out of the Court

---

[21] *Prior* v. *Powers* (1664) 1 Keb. 811.

[22] *Langdell* v. *Sutton* (1737) Barnes 32.

[23] *Ibid.*

[24] *Hale* v. *Cove* (1725) 1 Stra. 642. So also in *R.* v. *Lord Fitz-Water* (1675) 2 Lev. 139, 1 Free.K.B. 414; *Foster* v. *Hawden* (1677) 2 Lev. 205; *Phillips* v. *Fowler* (1736) 2 Com. 525.

[25] *Mitchell* v. *Ehle*, 10 Wend. 595 (1833).

[26] *Hughes* v. *Budd* (1840) 8 Dow.Pr.Cas. 315.

[27] *R.* v. *Macrae* [1892] *The Times*, Nov. 19, p. 10. Oswald, *Contempt of Court* (3d ed. 1910) p. 68, says that the juror's purpose was "to despatch a letter"; but the report is silent as to this. The jury was discharged, and the case was sent to the next Assizes.

before he could be stopped. Mr. Justice Cave said the case must be tried all over again, and he fined the juryman £20 for leaving the jury-box without leave."[28]

On the other hand, it may be claimed that the weather has had a preservative effect on verdicts. When in a case in 1499 it appeared that some of the jurors had left the court without leave, the reason for their departure was said to have been on account of "tiel tempest de thunder et de pluye." One of them even had a drink with friends of the defendant, who told him that the defendant had a better case than the plaintiff. After the storm, the jurors returned and no challenge was made by either party. In the Exchequer Chamber there was much argument, but in the end it was held that the verdict was good, though the offending jurors were duly fined.[29]

Business is another matter; the upshot of a case recounted by Lord Eldon does not appear, though it is not difficult to guess. The case was before Gould J. at York, and after it had been proceeding for some two hours the judge noticed that there were only eleven jurors in the box. When he asked where the twelfth was, one of the jurors replied: "Please you, my Lord, . . . he has gone away about some business, but he has left his Verdict with me."[30]

In cases of alleged misconduct the court has long been tender of the confidences of the jury room. It was not always so. In 1602 a jury acquitted one Wharton and three others of murder, contrary to the evidence, and found it to be manslaughter. "Wherefore Popham, Gaudy, and Fenner *fuerunt valde irati*,"[31] and the jurors were punished. There seems to have been some investigation of the secrets of the jury room, for three of the principal jurors, suspected of corruption, were

> to pay 20 marks apiece to the King for a fine, and to be bound to their good behaviour, and for the good behaviour of the prisoners acquitted by them: and to remain in prison for a year. . . . Six other less suspitious were fined

[28] *R. v. Rhoder* [1894] *The Times*, Feb. 12, p. 6.

[29] (1499) Y.B. 14 Hen. 7, Trin., pl. 4; (1500) 15 Hen. 7, Hil., pl. 2.

[30] Lord Eldon's *Anecdote Book* (1960), pp. 70, 71.

[31] *Wharton's Case* (1602) Yelv. 24 ("were exceedingly angry").

£10 a piece, and to be bound in a recognizance for the good behaviour of the prisoners, and of the other 3 jurors before. And the last three because they much disagreed, and did not consent, until by long time and perswasion they were mislead by the others, contrary to their evidence, and because they had not so declared themselves, and pray'd advice of the Court before verdict given; they were committed to prison, and to pay £5 a piece.[32]

Times, however, were changing. The entire report of a case before Foster J. in 1640 is as follows:

The Judge would not suffer a grand-Jury man to be produced as a witness to swear what was given in evidence to them, because he is sworn not to reveal the secrets of his companions. See if a witness is questioned for a false oath to the grand Jury, how it shall be proved if some of the Jury be not sworn in such case, and in a case before between *Hitch* and *Mallet* such a case was about an oath made before a grand Jury, *Quaere* what became of it.[33]

Two centuries later a mere affidavit by an attorney that a juror had told him that the jury had reached its verdict by tossing up was held insufficient to disturb the verdict.[34] The result was the same even where two jurors themselves swore an affidavit recounting the tossing up.[35]

It is otherwise if there is the direct evidence of some other person who had "seen the jurymen toss up, or put dice into a box."[36] Thus in one case the bailiff in charge of the jury swore in an affidavit that "the jury being a long time in debate on their verdict, it was at length agreed amongst them, that they would try the matter by the event of the falling of a sixpence, if pile for the plaintiff, if cross for the defendant; and the chance being for the plaintiff they unanimously gave their verdict for him." On this evidence, the verdict was quashed "for the ill behaviour of the jury, who put their consciences in the power of chance . . . and the

[32] *Ibid.*; Noy, at pp. 48, 49.

[33] *Anon.* (1640) Clayton 84. What indeed ? I have found no trace of it.

[34] *Straker* v. *Graham* (1839) 7 Dow.Pr. 223.

[35] *Vaise* v. *Delaval* (1785) 1 T.R. 11; and see *Stewart* v. *Fraser* (1838) 5 Murray's Jury Cas. 166.

[36] *Straker* v. *Graham, supra* note 34, at 224 (*per* Lord Abinger C.B.); and see *Vaise* v. *Delaval, supra* note 35 (*per* Lord Mansfield C.J.)

jurors being of the County of Northumberland should attend the Court the next term, unless cause this term shewn."[37]

The Court of Criminal Appeal once refused to look at affidavits made by two Welsh jurors, stating that their knowledge of the English language had been insufficient to enable them to follow the proceedings.[38] But the Judicial Committee later dissented from the reasoning of this decision in an Indian case in which a juror did not understand English, the language in which some of the evidence as well as the addresses of counsel and the judge's charge had been given: "The question whether a juror is competent for physical or other reasons to understand the proceedings is not a question which invades the privacy of the discussions in the jury box or in the retiring room. It does not seek to inquire into the reasons for a verdict."[39] As for the argument that although such matters might be put right during the course of the trial, in the interests of finality the court would not later interfere: "Finality is a good thing, but justice is a better."[40]

This decision was reached without reference to a case in 1835, where the plaintiff had sued in trespass. The burden of proof, however, lay on the defendant, and so he opened the case. The jury found in his favour, but then the plaintiff produced affidavits from two of the jurors swearing that they had been misled by the defendant's making the first argument, and that they had thought that they were finding a verdict for the plaintiff. The plaintiff's attorney also stated in a further affidavit that one of the jurors had spoken to him of the verdict as being for the "defendant Bridgewood," whereas in fact Bridgewood was the plaintiff. The plaintiff accordingly moved for a new trial, but the Court of King's Bench refused to grant it, holding that "though this verdict might probably have been given under a mistake, the jury as such being now separated, the affidavits of any individuals composing the jury cannot be

---

[37] *Fry* v. *Hordy* (1677) T.Jo. 83.

[38] *R.* v. *Thomas* [1933] 2 K.B. 489.

[39] *Ras Behari Lal* v. *King-Emperor* (1933) 102 L.J.P.C. 144.

[40] *Ibid.*, at p. 147 (*per* Lord Atkin); cp. *Nanan* v. *The State* [1986] 3 All E.R. 248. Contra *Gilman* v. *City of Philadelphia*, 70 U.S. 713, 724 (1865) (stating, *per* Swayne J., that it is sometimes more important that the law be settled than that it be settled correctly).

received."[41] Again, where the clerk of assize visited the jury room twice, and on each occasion discussed the case with the jury, the court refused to hear evidence by three of the jurors about the circumstances of the visits, though on a report by the clerk of assize the conviction was quashed.[42]

The right to challenge jurors is sometimes used by the accused on general rather than individual grounds. In a discussion in the House of Lords on an alleged practice of challenging all women jurors in prosecutions for driving while under the influence of drink, Lord Stoneham once said: "Frankly, the only such case I know of was one where the defendant, a married man, said he was not drunk but had visited his mistress and was very tired, and his legal adviser felt that defence was unlikely to appeal to a female jury."[43]

The prime objective, of course, is to secure an impartial jury. In a federal prosecution in the District of Columbia, the accused had been convicted by a jury composed entirely of employees of the Federal Government, and this attracted comment: "On one proposition I should expect trial lawyers to be nearly unanimous: that a jury, every member of which is in the hire of one of the litigants, lacks something of being an impartial jury. A system which has produced such an objectionable result and always tends to repeat it, should, in my opinion, be disapproved by this Court in exercise of its supervisory power over federal courts."[44] Still, "the defendant's right is a neutral jury. He has no constitutional right to friends on the jury."[45] With a prejudiced juror on the jury, "the doom of mere sterility was on the trial from the beginning."[46] Even if there is initial impartiality, it "cannot survive in the shadow of threats to a juror's reputation and livelihood."[47]

---

[41] *Bridgewood* v. *Wynn* (1835) 1 H. & W. 574; and see *Boston* v. *W.S. Bagshaw & Sons* [1966] 1 W.L.R. 1135; *R.* v. *Roads* [1967] 2 Q.B. 108.

[42] *R.* v. *Willmont* (1914) 30 T.L.R. 499.

[43] (1966) 275 Hansard H.L. (5th ser.) 780.

[44] *Frazier* v. *U.S.*, 335 U.S. 497, 514 (1948) (Jackson J., dissenting).

[45] *Fay* v. *N.Y.*, 332 U.S. 261, 288–89 (1947) (*per* Jackson J.).

[46] *Clark* v. *U.S.*, 289 U.S. 1, 11 (1933) (*per* Cardozo J.).

[47] *Dennis* v. *U.S.*, 339 U.S. 162, 181 (1950) (Black J., dissenting).

Impartiality may be sapped by what occurs at the trial; and not even the most zealous of judicial attempts can wholly undo what has been done. Indeed, "The naive assumption that prejudicial effects can be overcome by instructions to the jury all practicing lawyers know to be unmitigated fiction."[48] The remedy is otherwise: "If counsel knew that an unfair presentation to the jury would prevent the jury being allowed to pass upon his case, he would be careful not to transgress — unless he were a fool: there is no known cure for that."[49]

Sometimes the Bench is not wholly without fault. In one case,[50] a woman had obtained judgment for £300 for breach of promise of marriage. The defendant obtained an order for a new trial on the ground of surprise and fresh evidence. Pollock C.B. was due to preside at the new trial, and when the case came on he enquired of Cockburn, for the defendant, whether the case was to be tried again, as the new trial had been granted in the expectation of a compromise. After some discussion, Pollock C.B. said to Cockburn: "I know your case for the defence from the affidavits which were made on the application for the new trial — in my opinion it would be insanity in the defendant to call witnesses for the defence."[51] Cockburn at once vigorously protested at such language in the hearing of the jury who were to try the case, and the next day when the case was called on, he applied to postpone the trial. Pollock C.B. asserted that his expressions "were not and could not be understood by anyone except a gentleman of the bar,"[52] and he refused to hear Cockburn in argument. Cockburn said: "Your Lordship stated in open court that having looked through the affidavits it would be insanity in the defendant to call witnesses," and Pollock replied: "I say so now."[53] In the end Cockburn withdrew from the case.

This time the jury awarded £400 damages, and again the defendant applied for a new trial. Six of the jurors swore affidavits denying that the

[48] *Krulewitch* v. *U.S.*, 336 U.S. 440, 453 (1949) (*per* Jackson J.).

[49] *Dale* v. *Toronto R.W. Co.* (1915) 34 Ont.L.R. 104 at 109 (*per* Riddell J.).

[50] *Goldicut* v. *Beagin* (1848) 11 Jur. 544.

[51] *Ibid.*, at p. 544.

[52] *Ibid.*

[53] *Ibid.*, at p. 545.

remarks of Pollock C.B. had influenced them, and Pollock C.B. in his notes on the case said that his remarks were made with reference to the plaintiff being given a right of reply if the defendant called evidence. Parke B. (with whom Alderson, Rolfe, and Platt BB. concurred) said that the observations by Pollock C.B. "would have been better spared," but said that Cockburn "might have interposed and made such observations as would have induced the Lord Chief Baron to withdraw the expressions he had used, and explain that he had only intended to observe generally on the dangerous conduct of calling witnesses for the defence in cases of this nature."[54] But on the professed ground that although the jury had not been misled, Cockburn had, a new trial was ordered on certain terms. Nearly twenty years later, when Cockburn was Chief Justice and was giving judgment refusing a new trial, he referred to the observations made by Pollock C.B. and said that the Chief Baron had "added others which do not appear in the report."[55] But a defendant can always hope that the judge will tell the jury to remember that "generosity is not a virtue when dealing with the property of others."[56]

Although jurors are entitled and expected to use their general knowledge, any specialised knowledge that they have must be excluded from their deliberations unless, indeed, the jurors in question give evidence. Thus in one case in 1836 a witness for the prosecution valued a watch at £7, and Vaughan J. said to the jury: "If you see any reason to doubt the evidence on the subject, you are at liberty to do so. Any knowledge you may have on the subject you may use. Some of you may perhaps be in the trade." But Parke B. promptly replied, "If a gentleman is in the trade, he must be sworn as a witness. That general knowledge which any man can bring to the subject may be used without; but if it depends on any knowledge of the trade, the gentleman must be sworn." There was no response to this invitation, and the verdict found the watch to be of a value under £5.[57]

[54] *Ibid.*, at p. 546.
[55] *Lloyd* v. *Jones* (1866) 7 B. & S. 475 at 476.
[56] *Cashion* v. *Western Union Tel. Co.*, 31 S.E. 493, 494 (N.C. 1898) (*per* Douglas J.).
[57] *R.* v. *Rosser* (1836) 7 C. & P. 648 at 649.

A few years later, in the course of an undefended action on a bill of exchange, a juror asserted that the stamp on the bill was a forgery. Tindal C.J. said: "The gentleman of the jury who says that the stamp is a forgery, should be sworn as a witness to give evidence to his brother jurors, before they can act on his opinion." But the juror declined to be examined as a witness, and on the directions of the judge a verdict was found for the plaintiff.[58] These statements follow earlier authority:[59] "If a jury give a verdict upon their own knowledge, they ought to tell the Court so; but the fair way had been, for such of the jury as had knowledge of the matter, before they are sworn, to tell the thing to the Court, and be sworn as a witness."[60]

If a juror does testify, it is not clear whether he can thereafter return to the jury-box. Holmes J., indeed, once said: "It is well settled that a juror can join in the verdict after he has given evidence on oath in open Court";[61] but he gave no authority for this statement, and merely made some general reference to peers giving evidence in trials in the House of Lords and afterwards taking part in the decision of the case. In 1663, however, one juror in a civil case "done evidence publiquement a ces companions & uncore continue del jury."[62] Yet it ill-accords with modern ideas that one person should occupy the dual position of juror and witness, duly assessing what weight to give to his or her own evidence.

There is also old authority for the view that such a juror ought not to be sworn as a witness but should give evidence upon his oath as a juror. A case of 1650 is ambiguous upon this point, for it was said: "If either of the parties to a tryall desire that a juror may give evidence of something of his own knowledge, to the rest of the jurors, . . . the Court will examine him openly in Court upon his oath, and he ought not to be

---

[58] *Manley* v. *Shaw* (1840) Car. & M. 361.

[59] See, e.g., *Smith* v. *Hollings* (1791) 6 St.Tr. 1012.

[60] *Wright* v. *Crump* (1702) 7 Mod. 1 at 2 (*per* Holt C.J.); and see S.C. *sub nom. Anon.* (1702) 1 Salk. 405.

[61] *R. (Giant's Causeway &c. Tramway Co.)* v. *Justices of Co. Antrim* [1895] 2 I.R. 603 at 657.

[62] *Fitz-James* v. *Moys* (1663) 1 Sid. 133.

examined in private by his companions."[63] But six years later in the King's Bench, there is an explicit statement: "One Mr. *Beverly* of Suff. a Barrister was returned of the Jury, who (having been at a Tryal of the same Cause above 20 years before in the Cheq. [Exchequer] and heard there great Evidence to make a Deed fraudulent, which was now the Contest) demanded of the Court, whether he ought to inform the rest of the Jury privately of this, or conceal it, or declare it in open court? The Court ordered him to come into Court, and deliver all his knowledge which he heard then proved (which Evidence was not now given, because the parties were dead) and so he did, being not sworn again, but only upon the Oath taken as a Juryman."[64]

Although Beverly was a barrister, it was as a juror and not as counsel that he appeared in the case. It is clear that no barrister ought to take part in a case both as counsel and as witness; if he is one, he should not be the other,[65] except, no doubt, as to evidence given by counsel about a compromise or other occurrence in the course of a case.[66] The position of justices of the peace is similar to that of jurors, not judges. A magistrate who is a medical practitioner may thus express to his fellow justices his appreciation, based on his specialised knowledge, of the evidence that they have heard on medical matters, though he must not attempt to overbear his fellows, or give them what is in effect evidence contradictory of the evidence that they have heard.[67] Nor may magistrates rely on their recollections of previous proceedings between the parties that have come before them, without giving the parties an opportunity of dealing with those recollections.[68] Arbitrators, like jurors, may use their general knowledge of the locality in question, but must

---

[63] *Bennet* v. *Hundred of Hartford* (1650) Sty. 233.

[64] *Duke* v. *Ventres* (1656) G. Duncombe, *Tryals per Pais* (2d ed. 1682), p. 427.

[65] *R. v. Secretary of State for India, ex parte Ezekial* [1941] 2 K.B. 169 at 175. In *Re Vandervell's Trusts (No. 2)* [1947] Ch. 269 at 283, a silk elected to continue as counsel in the case rather than give evidence and then retire from it.

[66] See 2 Misc. 91–93.

[67] *Wetherall* v. *Harrison* [1976] Q.B. 773.

[68] *Thomas* v. *Thomas* [1961] 1 W.L.R. 1.

not rely on their detailed knowledge of particular facts that have not been put in evidence.[69]

Judges are in much the same position as jurors concerning evidence of particular facts. Thus there seems to be little doubt about the proper course to be adopted if it emerges that a judge has personal knowledge of some fact that is relevant to a trial before him. This appears as settled law as early as 1406. In a case in that year Tirwhit (of counsel) asserted in argument that if a judge saw one man kill another, and afterwards a third man was indicted before the judge for the murder, and convicted, the judge should no doubt respite judgment, and make representations to the King for a pardon; but he should not acquit him, and so give judgment of his own private knowledge. At this, Gascoigne C.J. observed that the King had once put that very case to him, and he had replied that the law was as counsel had just stated it; and the King "fuit bien please que la ley fuit tiel."[70]

Again, at the trial of the regicides "Secretary Morris and Mr. Annesly, President of the Council, were both in commission for the tryal of the prisoners, and sate upon the Bench, but there being occasion to make use of their testimony against Hacker, one of the prisoners, they both came off from the Bench, and were sworn, and gave evidence, and did not go up to the Bench again during that man's tryal; and agreed by the Court they were good witnesses, tho' in commission, and might be made use of."[71] The practice, however, was not uniform. Thus at the trial of the Earl of Essex, Popham C.J. was one of the nine judges summoned to advise the House of Lords. Nevertheless, he not only testified against the accused at the trial, but also consulted with the peers in private at the conclusion of the hearing.[72]

The results of disagreement in the jury are various. At the turn of the

---

[69] *Reynolds* v. *Llanelly Associated Tinplate Co. Ltd.* [1948] 1 All E.R. 140.

[70] Y.B. 7 Hen. 4, Pasch., fo. 41a, pl. 5 (1406); cited e.g. in *Partridge* v. *Strange* (1553) 1 Plowd. 77 at 83; *Marriot* v. *Pascall* (1558) 1 Leon. 159 at 161; *R. (Giant's Causeway &c. Tramway Co.)* v. *Justices of Co. Antrim, supra* note 61, at 650. Today the judge would refuse to try the case, and would leave it to be heard by another judge.

[71] *Trial of the Regicides* (1660) Kel. 7 at 12.

[72] See *R.* v. *Earl of Essex* (1600) 1 St.Tr. 1333 at 1340, 1342, 1355.

century, the decision in *Bright* v. *Walker*[73] gave rise to high controversy in Ireland. Holmes L.J. observed that it was a case on which counsel had often asked the court to give a direction, but he could not remember this having been done:

> *Love* v. *Taylor* [unreported] was in its time a well-known case, famous for the sturdy spirit of both plaintiff and defendant. I held a brief in it at six Assizes, at three of which it was tried out; but the jury always disagreed. It was tried again on either one or two occasions after I had left the circuit, with the same result. It was known to counsel on both sides that unless the passages I have quoted from *Bright* v. *Walker*[74] were disregarded, there must be judgment for the plaintiff; but successive Judges, although strongly pressed for a direction at the plaintiff's risk, declined to give it. At length the late Lord Justice Barry announced his intention to direct, whereupon the parties, finding that the battle would be transferred to another field, agreed to refer the whole subject in dispute to arbitration, which resulted, I believe, in a bad award."[75]

In days gone by, thirst and hunger often induced agreement. The entire report of a case in 1310 is as follows:

> In a writ of entry *sur* disseisin an inquest was joined. And after the inquest was sworn, they could not agree.
>
> STANTON J. Good people, you cannot agree?
>
> STANTON J., to John Allen [apparently the marshal]: Go and put them in a house until Monday, and let them not eat or drink.
>
> On that commandment John put them in a house without [food or drink]. At length on the same day about vesper-time they agreed. And John went to Sir Hervey and told him that they agreed. Then STANTON J., gave them leave to eat. Then on the Monday the inquest came and wanted to give a verdict in gross [i.e., a general verdict]. And STANTON J., said that he wanted the story told. So the inquest told the story etc.[76]

---

[73] (1834) 1 Cr. M. & R. 211.
[74] *Ibid.*
[75] *Hanna* v. *Pollock* [1900] 2 I.R. 664 at 708, 709.
[76] Y.B. 4 Edw. 2, Mich. (22 S.S.) 188.

Again, in 1346 there were a number of challenges to jurors, and the triers of these challenges failed to agree. When the point was reached of there being five triers who were divided three to two, "the five were commanded to abide in one chamber, without eating or drinking, until they agreed. And on the morrow they had agreed."[77]

In another fourteenth-century case the jury could not agree, and the court, tired of waiting, went home to dinner.[78] When it was reported that the jury had at last agreed, Thorpe J. after dinner took the verdict at St. Clement's Church, which presumably was near his home. Afterwards, Serjeant Pole challenged the verdict, as having been taken out of court and not at a proper time. But Scot C.J. would have none of it: "We can take a verdict by candle-light if the jury will not agree," he said; "and if the Court were to move, we could take the jurors about in carts with us, and so Justices of Assize have to do."[79]

The ancient practice of carting a jury was controversial;[80] but whatever uncertainty there may be about the practice in England,[81] there seems to be little doubt that at one time it flourished in Ireland. There is, for example, a contemporary account of the course of justice in a case at Roscommon Assizes in 1793, *R. v. McDiarmid*:

> McDiarmid was indicted for having, on 21st of May, feloniously, with several persons unknown, broken open the house of Thomas Tennison, Esq., and thereout stolen several articles of plate, wine &c., &c. To this he pleaded not guilty. Be it remembered that if the value of the property then stolen exceeded a certain small sum, the penalty was death. The following gentlemen were professionally engaged: Serjeant Stanley, the Solicitor-General, Mr. Tiller, John Blosset, and James Whitestone, for the prosecution; while the counsel for the prisoner were John Geoghegan and Owen McDermott, Esqrs.
> The indictment was opened by junior counsel for the prosecution, and the

---

[77] Y.B. 20 Edw. 3, Trin. (R.S.) 488.

[78] See W.C. Bolland, *The Year Books* (1921), p. 66; *A Manual of Year Book Studies* (1925), pp. 97, 98.

[79] (1345) Y.B. 19 Edw. 3 (R.S.) 178 at 184.

[80] See 1 Misc. 185, and add to the authorities cited G. Duncombe, *Tryals per Pais* (2d ed. 1682), p. 422.

[81] See generally 1 Misc. 185–87.

Serjeant stated the case, we are told, with great ability and ingenuity. Several witnesses were examined on both sides, and a very able and discriminating charge was delivered by the Chief Baron.[82] The jury retired about 10 p.m., but as it was not probable that they would agree, the Court was adjourned until the following morning, when they reassembled; and as an agreement was still unlikely, they were informed by the Court that carts would be ready at three o'clock to cart them to the bounds of the county, fifteen miles off, there to be discharged. Such was the punishment usually inflicted in those days upon disagreeing juries. Now, the weather was cold and cheerless, and the majority were determined to enforce their arguments upon the minority in some way likely to ensure their coming to an unanimous decision. The foreman, accordingly, insisted that those differing from him, four in number, should give way, and find the prisoner guilty. They, with equal determination, resisted all persuasion. A hand-to-hand fight ensued. Fortunately, the only fire-arms in the room were the fire-irons, but even those were too freely used. The uproar reached the ears of the judge; the halberdmen rushed upstairs, broke open the door, and, with the aid of the military, succeeded in dragging the jurors, all battered and bleeding, into Court. Each party swore that "they'd have the other's lives." His lordship then administered a severe lecture to them, and they were led down to the carts, three in number, which were ready to receive them. On they moved, attended by the sub-sheriff, on horseback, and by a troop of the 14th Light Dragoons. As the jury were leaving the town, those that had been for acquitting the prisoner consented to find him guilty of stealing property to the value of 4s. 9d., to which the others assented. The compromise, however, came too late, as the judge had left town, and so they must travel on for hours before those awkward vehicles could reach him; for the rugged roads, up hill and down dale, were almost impassable to wheel carriages — and such carriages! The wheels, revolving on wooden axles, which were never oiled, made a detestable half-screaming and half-whistling sound, as they rolled along into ruts and out of them as best they could! We cannot say that either in their jury-room or in their equipage we envy these twelve men![83]

In England, the days of special juries[84] and grand juries are no more.

[82] Then Yelverton.

[83] I am indebted to the late Professor V.T.H. Delany for this passage. He cites Oliver J. Burke, *Anecdotes of the Connaught Circuit* (Dublin, 1885), p. 163, quoting from *Walker's Hibernian Magazine*, Oct. 1793, pp. 96–380. It is not clear how far the book directly quotes from the magazine; the passage seems mainly a paraphrase, though circumstantial enough.

[84] The survival of the City of London special jury for cases in the Commercial List ended with the Courts Act 1971, s. 4, and the repeal of R.S.C., Ord. 72, r. 9, by S.I. 1971, No. 1955.

Oddly enough, the earliest case to establish the practice of summoning special juries seems to have been an action for slander brought in 1623 in the Court of Chancery; and this case reveals that the practice had been in existence since 1584.[85] Not long afterwards there was a jury that at least sounded very grand. When on circuit at Huntingdon Assizes, Dodderidge J. "found fault with the Sheriff for impanneling men not qualified for the grand-jury; he, being a merry man, resolved to fit the Judge (with sound at least)." Accordingly, at the next Assize in 1619, the "true List of the Jury impanneled" was as follows: the sheriff, by "calling over the . . . names emphatically," made the judge "believe he had indeed a jury of gentility" (no doubt the misplaced commas and the capitals represent the emphasis):

Mamilian, KING of Tozland.	George, GENTLEMAN of Spaldock
Henry, PRINCE of Godmanchester	Robert, YEOMAN of Barham.
George, DUKE of Somersham.	Stephen, POPE of Weston.
William, DUKE of Weston.	Humphrey, CARDINAL of Kimbolton.
William, MARQUIS of Stukeley.	William, BISHOP of Bugden.
Edward, EARL of Hartford.	John, ARCHDEACON of Paxton.
Robert, LORD of Warsley.	John, ABBOT of Stukeley.
Richard, BARON of Bythorpe.	Richard, FRIAR of Ellington.
Robert, BARON of Winwich.	Henry, MONK of Stukeley.
Edmund, KNIGHT of St. Neots.	Edward, PRIEST of Graffham.
Peter, ESQUIRE of Euston.	Richard, DEACON of Catworth.[86]

Centuries later, a similar cull among practising solicitors produced Popes, Priors, Priests, Kings, Princes, and Dukes aplenty, as well as Birds, Herons, and much else besides.[87]

America has produced instances of both coincidental juries and imaginary juries. The coincidental juries were to be found in New York

[85] *Philpot* v. *Feeler* (1623) Cro.Jac. 672; and see *Vickery* v. *London, Brighton and South Coast Railway Co.* (1870) L.R. 5 C.P. 165 at 169.

[86] *Harleian Miscellany*, vol. 3 (1809), p. 499. Euston apart, all the places are still to be found in Huntingdonshire, though there are variant spellings. There is a Euston in neighbouring Suffolk, but I have found none in Huntingdonshire; possibly "Easton" has been misspelled.

[87] (1893) 5 *Green Bag* 484.

in February 1958, before Birdie Amsterdam J., the first woman to become a justice of the New York Supreme Court. Although jurors were selected by lot from large panels, the same twelve jurors were empanelled in two successive cases[88] that were entirely unconnected with each other.[89]

The imaginary jury was Californian. In 1862 the State Supreme Court said:

> This action was tried by the Court without the intervention of a jury. Of course, in such cases the Court not only performs its peculiar and appropriate duty of deciding the law, but also discharges the functions of a jury, and passes upon the facts. The counsel of the appellants impressed, as it would seem, with this dual character, requested the Court to charge itself as a jury, and handed in certain instructions for that purpose. The Court thereupon formally charged that part of itself which was thus supposed to be separated and converted into a jury, commencing the charge with the usual address, "Gentlemen of the jury," and instructing that imaginary body, that if they found certain facts they should find for the plaintiff, and otherwise for the defendants, and that they were not concluded by the statements of the Court, but were at liberty to judge of the facts for themselves. The record does not inform us whether the jury thus addressed differed in their conclusions from those of the Court. These proceedings have about them so ludicrous an air that we could not believe they were seriously taken, but for the gravity with which counsel on the argument referred to them. . . . The mode [of presentation] adopted in the present case, though highly original, is not of sufficient merit to be exalted into a precedent to be followed.[90]

---

[88] *Lebell* v. *N.Y. City Transit Auth.*; and *Santiago* v. *Coczzino*. Neither case was published.

[89] *N.Y.L.J.*, March 25, 1958; letter by Mr. Julius Chaiet.

[90] *Touchard* v. *Crow*, 20 Cal. 150, 163 (1862) (*per* Field C.J.).

8

~

LIVING IN OUR ANCESTORS

BOTH AT home and abroad, the common law once attracted many panegyrics, of varying degrees of cogency. For example:

The common law is truly entitled to our highest veneration; and, although it has been said by some to have been instituted by Brutus, the grandson of Aeneas, and the first king of England, who died when Samuel was judge of Israel, and who wrote a book in the Greek tongue, which he called the Laws of the Britons, and which he had collected from the laws of the Trojans, it is nevertheless not entitled to our veneration on account of its antiquity; for nearly all that is valuable in it is comparatively of modern date. (See Preface to Third Reports.) Neither is it entitled to our respect on account of the ancient, absurd, and superstitious modes of trial; none of which have the slightest resemblance to our present trial by jury. Still less is it entitled to our admiration on account of the feudal system, which imposed a restraint upon every effort to improve the jurisprudence of the country, and which prevented the adoption of those maxims of justice and equity, which now render it the admiration of the enlightened jurist, and the favourite of the people.

It is, however, entitled to our veneration, because it has, within the last two centuries, been moulded by the wisdom of the ablest statesmen, and a succession of learned and liberal minded judges, into a flexible system, expanding and contracting its provisions, so as to correspond to the changes that are continually taking place in society, by the progress of luxury and refinement. As the youthful skin of a vigorous child expands with its growth, and accommodates itself to every developement, which the body, in its progress to maturity, makes of its powers, capacities and energies, so does

137

the common law, in order to suit the exigencies of society, possess the power of altering, amending, and regenerating itself.[1]

It has been truly and eloquently said that "it is the law of a free people, and has freedom for its end; and under it we live both free and happy. When we go forth it walks silently and unobtrusively by our side, covering us with its invisible shield from violence and wrong. Beneath our own roof, or by our own fireside, it makes our home our castle. All ages, sexes and conditions, share in its protecting influence. It shadows with its wings the infant's cradle, and with its arm upholds the tottering steps of age. It is the duty of the judiciary not only to guard it with vigilance against incongruous innovations, but also to extend the operation of its principles, so as to embrace all the new and various interests, which arise among an active and enterprising people. Thus much for the common law."[2]

At that, the court (no doubt reluctantly) came down from the heights and considered the issue before it, relating to the admissibility of certain evidence. Today, such extravagances find little favour.[3]

The reference above to "Preface to Third Reports" is, of course, to the Preface to volume 3 of Coke's Reports. This today is somewhat less highly regarded than most of the writings of that pre-eminent judge. It refers to things published in the ancient books of the law —

concerning the antiquity and honour of the common laws: first, they say that Brutus the first King of this land, as soon as he had settled himself in his kingdom, for the safe and peaceable government of his people, wrote a book in the Greek tongue, calling it the Laws of the Britons, and he collected the same out of the Laws of the Trojans: this King, say they, died after the creation of the World 2860 years, and before the Incarnation of Christ 1103 years, Samuel then being Judge of Israel. I will not examine these things in a quo warranto; the ground thereof I think was best known to the authors and writers of them: but that the laws of the ancient Britons, their contracts and other instruments, and the records and judicial proceedings of their Judges, were wrote and sentenced in the Greek tongue, it is plain and evident by proofs luculent and uncontrollable . . . .[4]

[1] See also 2 Misc. 112.
[2] *Snowden* v. *Warder*, 3 Rawle 101, 103 (Pa. 1831) (*per* Ross J.). I have subdivided the text.
[3] See, e.g., C.P. Harvey, Q.C., *The Advocate's Devil* (1958), c. 5.
[4] 3 Co.Rep., Pref., xiv; and see the faint Hellenic echo in 3 Mod. (5th ed. 1793), Pref., ix.

Today, the views of a later Chief Justice seem preferable. The common law is "coeval with civilised society itself, and was formed from time to time by the wisdom of man. Good sense did not come in with the Conquest, or at any other one time, but grew and increased from time to time with the wisdom of mankind."[5] It has even been put as a matter of choice: "We ourselves of the present age, chose our common law, and consented to the most ancient acts of parliament, for we lived in our ancestors 1,000 years ago, and those ancestors are still living in us."[6]

Whatever their source, laws ought at least to be readily discoverable. It is Caligula who is said to have made one of his horses a consul, and to have placed his laws high on a pillar so that they could not be read. But Suetonius is less sweeping about each of these legends. Caligula indeed provided a splendid stable and household for one of his chariot-steeds named Incitatus; but the consulship seems to have been at most *in fieri*: "It is reported, moreover, that he meant to prefer him unto a consulship."[7] As for the laws on a pillar, complaints had been made that Caligula had imposed many new and unfamiliar taxes, including a tax on the "takings of common strumpets, as much as they earned by once lying with a man," and also "that wedded persons should pay for their use of marriage." Yet "after these and such-like taxes were denounced by proclamation, but not yet published abroad in writing, whenas through ignorance of the written law many trespasses and transgressions were committed, at length, upon instant demand of the people, he [published] indeed the act, but written in very small letter and within as narrow a place so that no man might exemplify the same or copy it out."[8] The real complaint, it seems, was not height but legibility.

For the law to be discoverable does not necessarily mean that it will be intelligible, especially to the layman. Many have been suspicious and resentful of the "innumerable wyles, craftys, sotyltes and delayes that be

---

[5] *R.* v. *Rusby* (1800) Peake Add.Cas. 189 at 192 (*per* Lord Kenyon C.J.).

[6] *Godden* v. *Hales* (1686) 11 St.Tr. 1165 at 1204 (*per* Sir Robert Atkyns, previously J., and later C.B.) in a tract published later but appended to the report.

[7] Suetonius, *History of Twelve Caesars* (tr. P. Holland, 1606, ed. J.H. Freese (n.d.)), p. 219.

[8] *Ibid.*, at pp. 209, 210.

in the lawe."[9] Modern courts are far less enamoured of technicality than courts once were. Thus Story J.: "In new cases, not governed by antecedent authorities, I should not incline to support mere technical niceties, or to give them a wider range. The days for such subtleties are, as I trust, in a great measure passed away."[10] Cardozo J. concurred: "The law has outgrown its primitive stage of formalism when the precise word was the sovereign talisman, and every slip was fatal."[11]

Yet technicality is not to be condemned *per se*. Frankfurter J. observed that there are some matters that to laymen "may seem technicalities in a derogatory sense of the term. But this is only one phase of an attitude of mind that thinks ill of law which does not accord with private wishes. When informed by a legal adviser that to carry out his desires would encounter 'technical legal difficulties,' a strenuous President of the United States impatiently observed that 'all law is technicality.'"[12] Yet "legal refinements are not always the worse for eluding the quick understanding of a layman."[13] A contemporary American judge, Wiley J., essentially agreed that "lawyers know, if others do not, that what may seem technical may embody a great tradition of justice — or a necessity for drawing lines somewhere between great areas of law; that, in other words, one cannot always segregate the technique from the substance or the form from the reality."[14]

Today little is heard of information of intrusion or the privilege of palace; but they were matters of controversy in 1865. In that year the sheriffs of Middlesex executed a writ of fieri facias in the suite of apartments in Hampton Court Palace occupied by Lady Henry Gordon, whose husband was the debtor. Thereupon the Attorney-General laid an information of intrusion against the sheriffs, claiming that the palace

[9] Sir Charles Ogilvie, *The King's Government and the Common Law* (1958), p. 21, citing H. Brinklow, *Complaint of Roderick Mors* (J.M. Cooper ed.), Early English Text Society (1874), p. 20.

[10] *Bottomley* v. *U.S.*, 1 Story 135, 152 (1840) (*per* Story J.).

[11] *Wood* v. *Duff-Gordon*, 222 N.Y. 88, 91 (1917) (*per* Cardozo J.).

[12] *U.S.* v. *Storer Broad. Co.*, 351 U.S. 192, 214 (1956) (Frankfurter J., dissenting).

[13] *Pacific Coast Dairy, Inc.* v. *Dept. of Agriculture of Cal.*, 318 U.S. 285, 298 (1943) (Frankfurter J., dissenting).

[14] *Kotteakos* v. *U.S.*, 328 U.S. 750, 761 (1946) (*per* Rutledge J.).

was a royal residence and so had the privilege of palace against execution by a sheriff. The Court of Exchequer agreed that the privilege of palace attached to any place that was a residence of the Sovereign and that the Sovereign's mere intention to resume residence at one of the palaces sufficed without actual personal residence at the time; but the court was divided on the status of Hampton Court Palace. The view of Kelly C.B. was that the use to which the palace was then being put was not inconsistent with an intention by the Sovereign to resume residence there, so that the information should succeed. But Martin and Bramwell BB. held that the palace was occupied in such a way that the Sovereign could not immediately resume occupation, and so the information should fail.[15] Hampton Court was contrasted with the state of Kensington Palace in 1809, when part of the palace was kept in a constant state of preparedness for the King if at any time he wished to reside there; and it had been held that apartments there occupied by the Duke of Sussex were covered by the privilege.[16]

No doubt an appeal was encouraged by the division in the Court of Exchequer; but the Exchequer Chamber was also divided, though equally, and so the appeal failed. Willes, Keating, and Montague Smith JJ. would have allowed the appeal, but Blackburn, Mellor, and Lush JJ. were in favour of dismissing it.[17] Blackburn J.[18] cited with approval the statement of Lord Gifford M.R. in relation to the Palace of Holyrood that the privilege was given "not merely because otherwise the King might be deprived of the services of his domestics, but that it is not seemly that the royal palace, or the royal presence, should be exposed to be made a scene of disturbance or confusion."[19] "The foundation of the whole", said Blackburn J., "depends on the reverence due to the person of the sovereign."[20] An information of intrusion, it may be added, was in the nature of an action for trespass *quare clausum fregit*.[21]

---

[15] *Attorney-General* v. *Dakin* (1867) L.R. 2 Exch. 290.

[16] *Winter* v. *Miles* (1809) 10 East 578.

[17] *Attorney-General* v. *Dakin* (1868) L.R. 3 Exch. 288.

[18] *Ibid.*, at p. 293.

[19] *Earl of Strathmore* v. *Laing* (1826) 2 Wils. & Sh. 1 at 6.

[20] *Attorney-General* v. *Dakin, supra* note 17, at 293.

[21] The information of intrusion was a form of Latin information, and so was replaced by

The equal division of judicial opinion presaged an appeal to the House of Lords; and in due course five judges (three of whom had already delivered judgments in the case) were summoned to advise the House.[22] The four who spoke were equally divided: Cleasby B. (a newcomer) and Keating J. were for allowing the appeal, whereas Mellor and Blackburn JJ. remained steadfast for dismissing it. But Keating J. was able to announce that Brett J. agreed with him,[23] and so the majority advice was that the appeal should be allowed. With this, Lord Hatherley L.C. agreed; but Lord Chelmsford and Lord Colonsay thought otherwise, so that in the end the appeal was dismissed and the action of the sheriffs was held to be lawful.

The furthest point to which the privilege of palace seems to have been pressed was a contention that the privilege rendered null and void a sentence of deprivation against a clerk in holy orders pronounced by Lord Penzance, Dean of Arches; for the sentence was pronounced in Committee Room E in the House of Lords, and this, it was said, was subject to the privilege of palace as being part of the Palace of West-minster.[24] The contention was that such a place was exempt from the jurisdiction of any of the civil or ecclesiastical courts, and was subject only to the jurisdiction of officers specially appointed by the Crown.[25] Without deciding whether the committee room was within the precincts of the old Palace of Westminster, which had been used as a royal residence, both Chitty J. and the Court of Appeal held that the sentence was valid; for the new Palace of Westminster, though used by the Queen for certain purposes, was no royal residence.

The territorial ambit of law has many facets. Apart from the ancient three-mile limit, there is the doctrine of *inter fauces terrae*, namely, that "within limits inlets of the sea into the land are part of the territory of

---

an ordinary action by the Crown Proceedings Act 1947: see s. 13, 1st Sched. Yet the Intrusion Act 1623, which allowed the subject to plead the general issue in certain informations of intrusion, remained on the statute book until removed by the Statute Law Revision Act 1958.

[22] *Attorney-General* v. *Dakin* (1870) L.R. 4 H.L. 338.

[23] *Ibid.*, at p. 359.

[24] *Combe* v. *De la Bere* (1882) 22 Ch.D. 316.

[25] *Ibid.*, at p. 337.

the State which owns the land on both sides."[26] But what limits? What of a point in the Bristol Channel some ten miles from the nearest land on either side? As Hill J. put it, "What are the inland waters contained within the land? What are bays, gulfs, or estuaries *inter fauces terrae?* What is the metaphor, the open mouth of a man or of a crocodile?"[27] Before him, the crocodile succeeded, but on appeal the man prevailed.

The common law has attracted many metaphors. For Diplock L.J. its beauty was that it was "a maze and not a motorway."[28] Others have turned from land to the water, though with biological frailty. On some subjects, it is said, the stream of the law can be followed, turbid though it is. But then "the common law itself is not a clear stream. Its waters are muddy, but the mud is rich and fertilizing. If the waters of the stream of the common law were clear they would be sterile and lifeless."[29] The essence is not clarity but motion: "Moving waters are full of life and health; only in the still waters is stagnation and death."[30]

Problems of jurisdiction are not, indeed, confined to this world. In *United States ex rel. Mayo* v. *Satan and His Staff,*[31] the relator sought leave to file *in forma pauperis* a complaint against the defendants for violation of his civil rights. He alleged that Satan had on numerous occasions caused him misery and placed obstacles in his path, and by causing his downfall had deprived him of his constitutional rights. In the United States District Court in Pennsylvania, Weber J. found a variety of insuperable difficulties in the application. He seriously doubted whether there was a cause of action upon which the court could grant relief. He also questioned whether the court had any jurisdiction. The complaint made no allegation that the defendant resided within the district of the court, and it had also failed to include "the required form of instructions

[26] *The Fagernes* [1927] P. 311 at 320 (*per* Bankes L.J.).

[27] *The Fagernes* [1926] P. 185 at 189.

[28] See 2 Misc. 113.

[29] *Wong* v. *Benning* (1968) 70 S.R. (N.S.W.) 290 at 315 (*per* Jacobs J.A.); reversed *sub nom. Benning* v. *Wong* (1969) 122 C.L.R. 249.

[30] See (1898) 15 Nat'l Corp. Rep. 848 at 849; *per* Brewer J. Though uttered in another context, the words are apt here.

[31] 54 F.R.D. 282 (W.D. Pa. 1971).

for the United States Marshal for directions as to service of process."[32] Further, even if the action was maintainable as a class action, it could not be determined whether "the representative party will fairly protect the interests of the class."[33] A more fundamental difficulty in the action was not even mentioned: and so the case may be claimed to be an authority *sub silentio* that the principal defendant does in fact exist, at least in America. In Canada, on the other hand, the question whether God was a person was fully argued.[34]

The priority between England and Scotland in the judicial condemnation of slavery has been the subject of serious question. A Scottish view is that

> There is a popular superstition that in *Sommersett's Case*[35] the English courts vindicated personal liberty and condemned slavery generally. This was not the case. Lord Mansfield held that contracts for slaves were quite valid in England, but that a slave who was actually in England could not be sent back to a colony for punishment. In Scotland, however, as early as 1757 the Court of Session had ordered full argument on the question whether the law would countenance the institution of absolute slavery of negroes, but, unfortunately, the slave died during the hearing by the Whole Court.[36] Thus it was not until *Knight* v. *Wedderburn*[37] in 1778 that a judicial pronouncement was made on this matter. The Scottish courts went much further than Lord Mansfield. They held "that the dominion assumed over this Negro, under the law of Jamaica, being unjust, could not be supported in this country to any extent." Further, they expressly approved the Sheriff's interlocutor "that the state of slavery is not recognised by the laws of this kingdom, and is inconsistent with the principles thereof."[38]

This, no doubt, strikes a shrewd blow for Scotland, and shows how backward and half-hearted England was: but is it right? *Somersett's Case*

---

[32] *Ibid.*, at p. 283 (*per* Weber J.).

[33] *Ibid.*

[34] *R.* v. *Davie* (1980) 17 C.R. (3d) 72.

[35] "(1772) 20 St.Tr. 1."

[36] "*Sheddon* v. *Negro* (1757) Mor. 14545." The pursuer's name in fact appears as "*Sheddan*."

[37] "(1778) 33 Mor. 14545." See at p. 14549.

[38] T.B. Smith, Q.C., *British Justice: The Scottish Contribution* (1961), p. 196.

was argued in 1772 on a return to a writ of habeas corpus. The owner, a Mr. Stewart, had purchased the slave in Jamaica and had brought the slave to England to attend him. Stewart intended to take him back to Jamaica to be sold; and while he was in the custody of the captain of the *Ann and Mary* awaiting departure from the Thames, the writ of habeas corpus was issued. In giving judgment, Lord Mansfield said:

> The state of slavery is of such a nature, that it is incapable of being introduced on any reasons, moral or political, but only by positive law, which preserves its force long after the reasons, occasion, and time itself from whence it was created, is erased from memory. It is so odious, that nothing can be suffered to support it, but positive law. Whatever inconveniences, therefore, may follow from the decision, I cannot say this case is allowed or approved by the law of England; and therefore the black must be discharged.[39]

That, it seems, is the case of which it is wrong to say that it "vindicated personal liberty and condemned slavery generally." In holding six years later that "the dominion assumed over this Negro, under the law of Jamaica, being unjust, could not be supported to any extent," the Scottish court, it is said, went "much further than Lord Mansfield." Perhaps in Scotland "unjust" is a much stronger word than "odious." Lord Mansfield's judgment says nothing to the effect that "a slave who was actually in England could not be sent back to a colony for punishment"; the slave was to be sent back for sale, not punishment.

As for the hint of Scottish priority, achieved in 1778, let Holt C.J. speak in 1696 and 1706 and Lord Henley L.C. in 1762. Holt C.J. held that neither trespass[40] nor trover would lie for a slave, saying that "there is no such thing as a slave by the law of England."[41] Lord Henley said: "As soon as a man sets foot on English ground he is free: a negro may maintain an action against his master for ill usage, and may have a

---

[39] *Sommersett's Case* (1772) 20 St.Tr. 1 at 82; *sub nom. Somerset* v. *Stewart* (1772) Lofft 1 at 19.

[40] *Chamberlain* v. *Harvey* (1696) Carth. 396; 1 Ld.Raym. 146.

[41] *Smith* v. *Gould* (1706) 2 Ld.Raym. 1274 at 1275.

Habeas Corpus if restrained of his liberty."[42] He held that the administrator of a deceased woman who had been given a slave had no claim to
property given by the deceased to the slave as a *donatio mortis causa.*
These cases, as well as *Somersett's Case,* were all cited in the Scottish case
of *Knight* v. *Wedderburn,*[43] so that it may at least be doubted whether the
Court of Session regarded itself as blazing a new trail.

One purpose of a constitution is to provide protection against the
misuse of power, as judges have long recognised:

- "History shows that all officers tend to be officious."[44]

- "Evil men are rarely given power; they take it over from better men to
  whom it had been entrusted."[45]

- "It is from petty tyrannies that large ones take root and grow. . . .
  Seedlings planted in that soil grow great and, growing, break down the
  foundations of liberty."[46]

Nor should it be forgotten that "there are village tyrants as well as village
Hampdens."[47] Yet there are limits to what can be achieved by any
constitution: "This is a power which may be abused; but that is no
argument against its existence. For protection against abuses by
legislatures the people must resort to the polls, not to the courts."[48]

The precious right of privacy has a special need for constitutional
protection: "The right to be let alone is indeed the beginning of all
freedom,"[49] and "once privacy is invaded, privacy is gone."[50] Invasion by
loud speakers in the open is an obvious menace: "The unwilling listener

---

[42] *Shanley* v. *Harvey* (1762) 2 Eden 126 at 127. See generally 1 Misc. 128; but cp. *The Slave
Grace* (1827) 2 Hagg.Adm. 94.

[43] See *supra* note 37 at p. 14549.

[44] *Frank* v. *Maryland,* 359 U.S. 360, 382 (1959) (Douglas J., dissenting).

[45] *Screws* v. *U.S.,* 325 U.S. 91, 160 (1945) (Roberts, Frankfurter, and Jackson JJ., dissenting).

[46] *Thomas* v. *Collins,* 323 U.S. 516, 543 (1944) (*per* Rutledge J.).

[47] *West Virginia St. Bd. of Educ.* v. *Barnette,* 319 U.S. 624, 638 (1943) (*per* Jackson J.).

[48] *Munn* v. *Illinois,* 94 U.S. 113, 134 (1876) (*per* Waite C.J.).

[49] *Public Util. Commn. of D.C.* v. *Pollak,* 343 U.S. 451, 467 (1952) (Douglas J., dissenting);
and see 2 Misc. 207 (quoting *Olmstead* v. *U.S.,* 277 U.S. 438, 478 (1928)).

[50] *Pollak,* 343 U.S. at 469 (Douglas J., dissenting).

is not like the passer-by who may be offered a pamphlet in the street but cannot be made to take it. In his home or on the street he is practically helpless to escape this interference with his privacy by loud speakers except through the protection of the municipality."[51] True, "Free speech carries with it some freedom to listen";[52] but "surely there is not a constitutional right to force unwilling people to listen."[53] Today other intrusions are less obvious and more sinister: "Science has perfected amplifying and recording devices to become frightening instruments of surveillance and invasion of privacy, whether by the policemen, the blackmailer, or the busybody."[54]

Freedom of speech has always demanded a special position:

- "Free speech is not to be regulated like diseased cattle and impure butter. The audience (in this case the judge or the jury) that hissed yesterday may applaud today, even for the same performance."[55]

- "Freedom to differ is not limited to things that do not matter much. That would be a mere shadow of freedom. The test of its substance is the right to differ as to things that touch the heart of the existing order."[56]

- "History teaches us that there have been but few infringements of personal liberty by the state which have not been justified, as they are here, in the name of righteousness and the public good, and few which have not been directed, as they are now, at politically helpless minorities."[57]

- "Even when the use of its public streets and sidewalks is involved, . . . a municipality may not empower its licensing officials to roam essentially at will, dispensing or withholding permission to speak,

---

[51] *Kovacs* v. *Cooper*, 336 U.S. 77, 86 (1949) (*per* Reed J.).
[52] *Richmond Newspapers, Inc.* v. *Virginia*, 448 U.S. 555, 576 (1980) (*per* Burger C.J.).
[53] *Saia* v. *N.Y.*, 334 U.S. 558, 563 (1948) (Frankfurter J., dissenting).
[54] *Irvine* v. *California*, 347 U.S. 128, 132 (1954) (*per* Jackson J.).
[55] *Kingsley Books Inc.* v. *Brown*, 354 U.S. 436, 447 (1957) (Douglas J., dissenting).
[56] *West Virginia St. Bd. of Educ.* v. *Barnette*, 319 U.S. 624, 642 (1943) (*per* Jackson J.).
[57] *Minersville Sch. Dist.* v. *Gobitis*, 310 U.S. 586, 604 (1940) (Stone J., dissenting).

assemble, picket, or parade, according to their own opinions regarding the potential effect of the activity in question on the 'welfare,' 'decency,' or 'morals' of the community";[58] "and experience tells us that sometimes, when minorities insist on their rights, they ultimately prevail."[59]

Today, universal acceptance can hardly be claimed for the proposition that "Where vituperation begins, the liberty of the press ends."[60]

The courts have interpreted the United States Constitution on broad lines: "The Constitution does not make it a condition of preventive legislation that it should work a perfect cure. It is enough if the questioned act has a manifest tendency to cure or at least to make the evil less."[61] The courts will not be deterred by "the phantoms of attenuated and unfounded doubts concerning the meaning of the Constitution."[62] Indeed, in some respects the courts will be bold: "Constitutional law like other mortal contrivances has to take some chances."[63] Yet chances do not include contradictions: "A provision of the Constitution . . . does not admit of two distinctly opposite interpretations. It does not mean one thing at one time and an entirely different thing at another time. . . . If the provisions of the Constitution be not upheld when they pinch as well as when they comfort, they may as well be abandoned."[64] Even so, "The interpretation of constitutional principles must not be too literal. We must remember that the machinery of government would not work if it were not allowed a little play in its joints."[65]

---

[58] *Shuttlesworth* v. *City of Birmingham*, 394 U.S. 147, 153 (1969) (*per* Stewart J.).

[59] *Young* v. *South African & Australian Exploration & Development Syndicate* [1896] 2 Ch. 268 at 278 (*per* Kekewich J.).

[60] *R.* v. *Burdett* (1820) 1 St.Tr. (N.S.) 1 at 120 (*per* Best J.).

[61] *Louis K. Liggett Co.* v. *Baldridge*, 278 U.S. 105, 115 (1928) (Holmes J., dissenting).

[62] *Newberry* v. *U.S.*, 256 U.S. 232, 268 (1921) (*per* White C.J.).

[63] *Blinn* v. *Nelson*, 222 U.S. 1, 7 (1911) (*per* Holmes J.).

[64] *Home Bldg. & Loan Assn.* v. *Blaisdell*, 290 U.S. 398, 448, 483 (1934) (Sutherland J., dissenting).

[65] *Bain Peanut Co. of Texas* v. *Pinson*, 282 U.S. 499, 501 (1931) (*per* Holmes J.); and see *Missouri, Kansas & Texas Ry. Co.* v. *May*, 194 U.S. 267, 270 (1904); *Tyson* v. *Banton*, 273 U.S. 418, 446 (1927).

A basic principle was laid down early in the nineteenth century: "It is but a decent respect due to the wisdom, the integrity, and the patriotism of the legislative body, by which any law is passed, to presume in favour of its validity, until its violation of the constitution is proved beyond all reasonable doubt."[66] State action ought not to be held unconstitutional "by interpreting the law of the state as though, to use a phrase of Mr. Justice Holmes, one were fired with a zeal to pervert."[67] The process of the Supreme Court itself contributes to this approach. "It is asking more than rightfully may be asked of ordinary men to take an oath that a method is not 'unconstitutional' or 'illegal' when constitutionality or legality is frequently determined by this Court by the chance of a single vote."[68]

The powers of the Supreme Court sometimes, indeed, provide an incentive to excesses in the language of attack. Thus in speaking of an argument assailing the United States Securities and Exchange Commission,[69] Cardozo J. once said: "A Commission which is without coercive powers, which cannot arrest or amerce or imprison though a crime has been uncovered, or even punish for contempt, but can only inquire and report, the propriety of every question in the course of the inquiry being subject to the supervision of the ordinary courts of justice, is likened with denunciatory fervor to the Star Chamber of the Stuarts. Historians may find hyperbole in the sanguinary simile."[70] Yet a contravention is a contravention, however small: "If it is interstate commerce that feels the pinch, it does not matter how local the operation which applies the squeeze."[71]

Explicit statements, implications, and omissions all contribute to interpretation. The separation of powers is, of course, written into the

---

66 *Ogden* v. *Saunders*, 25 U.S. 213, 270 (1827) (*per* Washington J.).

67 *Milk Wagon Drivers Union of Chicago, Local 753* v. *Meadowmoor Dairies, Inc.*, 312 U.S. 287, 298 (1941) (*per* Frankfurter J.). The actual words of Holmes J. were: "fired with a desire to pervert": *Paraiso* v. *U.S.*, 207 U.S. 368, 372 (1907).

68 *Am. Commun. Assn., C.I.O.* v. *Douds*, 339 U.S. 382, 420 (1950) (*per* Frankfurter J.).

69 For which Alger Hiss was one of the counsel on the brief.

70 *Jones* v. *SEC*, 298 U.S. 1, 33 (1936) (Cardozo J., dissenting).

71 *U.S.* v. *Women's Sportswear Mfrs. Assn.*, 336 U.S. 460, 464 (1949) (*per* Jackson J.).

constitution, with all that flows from it: "The sound application of a principle that makes one master in his own house precludes him from imposing his control in the house of another who is master there."[72] Yet "a great principle of constitutional law is not susceptible of comprehensive statement in an adjective."[73] Familiar expressions must be scrutinised with care. The phrase "the preferred position of freedom of speech" is "mischievous because it radiates a constitutional doctrine without avowing it."[74] Yet the language of the constitution itself carries with it all proper implications: "The power to regulate implies the existence and not the destruction of the thing to be controlled."[75]

Some reasoning is more dubious. Without the nation's consent, it has been said, a nation cannot be sued in the courts that it has set up, for "the creature cannot rule the creator."[76] One view attaches less weight to what is said than to what is not: "Perhaps even more than by interpretation of its written word, this Court has advanced the solidarity and prosperity of this Nation by the meaning it has given to these great silences of the Constitution."[77] Yet there is a danger in over-zealous building: "This Court is forever adding new stories to the temples of constitutional law, and the temples have a way of collapsing when one story too many is added."[78] The existing storeys, too, must be appraised truly. The quest is for equal justice for all, but it should not be forgotten that "it was a wise man who said that there is no greater inequality than the equal treatment of unequals."[79]

---

[72] *Rathbun* v. *U.S.*, 295 U.S. 602, 630 (1935) (*per* Sutherland J.).

[73] *Carter* v. *Carter Coal Co.*, 298 U.S. 238, 327 (1936) (Cardozo J., dissenting). The adjective was "direct," in "direct relation."

[74] *Kovacs* v. *Cooper*, 336 U.S. 77, 90 (1949) (*per* Frankfurter J.).

[75] *Grand Trunk Western Ry.* v. *City of South Bend*, 227 U.S. 544, 555 (1913) (*per* Lamar J.).

[76] *Kansas* v. *Colorado*, 206 U.S. 46, 83 (1907) (*per* Brewer J.).

[77] *H.P. Hood & Sons, Inc.* v. *Du Mond*, 336 U.S. 525, 535 (1949) (*per* Jackson J.).

[78] *Douglas* v. *City of Jeannette*, 319 U.S. 157, 181 (1943) (*per* Jackson J.).

[79] *Dennis* v. *U.S.*, 339 U.S. 162, 184 (1950) (Frankfurter J., dissenting).

9

~

All Deliberate Speed

In England, a remedy in civil matters can usually be obtained only by applying to the court by writ, summons, or motion. In other jurisdictions this is not always an essential. The ancient institution of the Clameur de Haro[1] lives on in the Channel Islands, a concept as unfamiliar in England as the rule in *Foss* v. *Harbottle*[2] doubtless is over there.[3] The clameur has much the effect of an instant injunction, obtained without reference to the court. It is a purely civil remedy that restrains the commission of some alleged wrong to property or rights of property until the courts have adjudicated upon it. It may be used to resist the invasion of property, or dispossession, but not to recover possession once lost.[4]

A person seeking to raise the clameur must do so at the place where the act is being committed, or as near as possible to it. On bended knees, bareheaded and with his hands together, he must cry aloud, in the presence of two bareheaded witnesses, "Haro! Haro! Haro! à l'aide mon Prince: on me fait tort." If he does this in Guernsey or Alderney, he must then recite the Lord's Prayer in French; in Sark the formula is somewhat

---

[1] This account is mainly based on C.S. Le Gros, *Traité du Droit Coutumier dé l'Ile de Jersey* (1943), pp. 28–35, and R. Lemprière, *Customs, Ceremonies and Traditions of the Channel Islands* (1976), pp. 22, 51–53. See also 4 Bl.Comm. 293.

[2] (1843) 2 Hare 461.

[3] See *Heyting* v. *Dupont* [1964] 1 W.L.R. 843 at 848 (*per* Russell L.J.).

[4] *Re Kirk* [1985] Apr. 16, Guernsey C.A., unrep., *affirmed* [1986] Jan. 26, P.C. Appeal No. 49 of 1985, unrep.

different. Thereupon the alleged wrongdoer must desist from what he is doing.

Steps then have to be taken to bring the matter before the court. In Jersey, the raiser of the clameur must forthwith report it to the Attorney-General, who will then see that the matter comes to court. In Guernsey and Alderney, on the other hand, the raiser must within 24 hours make a written declaration and duly register it. Either the raiser or the person enjoined may then commence proceedings within twelve months, to support or oppose the complaint. If the clameur has been improperly raised, the raiser is liable to be fined; but if it was rightly raised, it is the defendant who is liable to a fine. In Guernsey there was formerly a liability to imprisonment for 24 hours; and in Sark the raiser has to make a deposit of cash which is liable to forfeiture if the raiser's claim is not upheld.

The word "Haro" is said to be a corruption of "O Rollo" or "Ha Rollo." Rollo was a Norseman who in 911 was recognised as the first Duke of Normandy. He is said to have introduced the clameur, though more probably the cry is simply a call for attention, like "Here!" or "Hear!" The clameur has also been said to be related to the old English hue and cry. Despite its age, the clameur is far from obsolete. In Guernsey, it was raised 7 times between 1900 and 1947, 12 times between 1968 and 1982, and 19 times by a Mr. and Mrs. Kirk.[5] A modern example is the clameur raised by Mrs. A.J. Le Touzel on 4 May 1974 in the parish of St. Ouen, Jersey, in a land dispute. Twenty days later the Royal Court held that she had properly raised the clameur, fined the defendant £1, with £5 costs, and ordered him to restore the disputed land, together with the potatoes grown on it.[6] Given adequate safeguards against abuse, a process of self-help in the law has much to commend it, not least in speed and economy. One day the Law Commission might do worse than consider whether, instead of framing new concepts, reform in England in this field might not be better promoted by borrowing

[5] See *Re Kirk*, C.A., *supra* note 4, at pp. 5, 12.

[6] See Lemprière, *supra* note 1, p. 51. Between pp. 32 and 33 there is a photograph of the raising of this clameur.

from Norman antiquity: "If kept under proper supervision by the courts, is there not some place for instant 'Do-it-yourself' remedies in the law?"[7]

From speedy relief to delay, and judicial delay at that. Some jurisdictions have legislated against delay in decision. For over a century California has provided that no judge of a court of record may receive any judicial salary while any cause before the judge "remains pending and undetermined for 90 days after it has been submitted for decision."[8] It does not appear that any allowance is made for unusually massive and complex cases that require very lengthy judgments.[9] For the Courts of Appeal in California, a case is treated as being "submitted" when the court has heard oral argument (or has approved a waiver of oral argument), and the time for submission of all papers has expired.[10]

This rule, however, does not apply to the Supreme Court of California itself, which for many years now has been neatly sidestepping this part of the Constitution. This has been done by the simple means of ruling that a case is not "submitted" until an order of submittal is signed, and then by not signing any such order until the judgments are ready to be delivered. This allows great latitude. Thus in one case[11] argued on August 31, 1977, judgment was not delivered until November 9, 1978, 435 days later.[12] It is thus that the guardians of the Constitution of California have been guarding it.

There are, of course, degrees of speed. It was the great racial desegregation case in the United States in 1954[13] that gave prominence to a

---

[7] See *Cost of Justice* (The Canadian Institute for the Administration of Justice: Toronto, 1980), p. 151.

[8] Constitution of California, Art. 6, s. 19 (replacing similar provisions dating from 1879; the process is one of suspension, not forfeiture).

[9] See, e.g., *Tito v. Waddell (No. 2)* [1977] Ch. 106.

[10] Rule 22.5(a) of the Judicial Council, 1978, as cited in P. Stolz, *Judging Judges* (1981), p. 264.

[11] *People v. Levins*, 586 P.2d 939 (Cal. 1978).

[12] P. Stolz, *supra* note 10, at pp. 264, 265. The Chief Justice had (apparently in error) signed a submittal order on August 15, 1978, 87 days before judgment was given, just in time.

[13] *Brown v. Bd. of Educ. of Topeka*, 347 U.S. 483 (1954).

phrase which in England had fallen into desuetude. The order of the
Supreme Court was for such orders and decrees as were necessary and
proper to admit pupils to public schools on a racially non-discriminatory
basis "with all deliberate speed."[14] It has been suggested that this phrase
was drawn from Francis Thompson's *The Hound of Heaven*:

> But with unhurrying chase,
> And unperturb'd pace,
> Deliberate speed, majestic instancy,
> They beat — and a Voice beat
> More instant that the Feet —
> "All things betray thee, who betrayest Me."

But it seems more probable that the phrase harks back to an old Chancery
term that had found lodgment in the Supreme Court practice.[15] Thus
Holmes J. once said that "a State cannot be expected to move with
the celerity of a private business man; it is enough if it proceeds, in the
language of the English Chancery, with all deliberate speed."[16] In 1954
the phrase, which had dropped out of the Chancery vocabulary in
England,[17] may well have come from Frankfurter J., who had often used
it before.[18] In one case he said that "mere speed is not a test of justice.
Deliberate speed is. Deliberate speed takes time. But it is time well
spent."[19] A cousin to the phrase is "with all convenient speed," which is

---

[14] *Brown* v. *Bd. of Educ. of Topeka*, 349 U.S. 294, 301 (1955) (*per* Warren C.J.).

[15] See Charles P. Curtis, *Commonplace Book* (1957), p. 111; Paul A. Freund, *Storm over the American Supreme Court*, 21 Mod. L.R. 345, 351 (1958).

[16] *Virginia* v. *West Virginia*, 222 U.S. 17, 19–20 (1911). Holmes once described it as "chancery's delightful phrase": *Holmes–Pollock Letters*, vol. 1, p. 152.

[17] In 1960 it was unknown in the Chancery Registrar's Department: *ex rel.* Mr. Registrar C.M. Kidd.

[18] See, e.g., *Chrysler Corp.* v. *U.S.*, 316 U.S. 556, 568 (1942) (Frankfurter J., dissenting); *Addison* v. *Holly Hill Fruit Prods. Inc.*, 322 U.S. 607, 619 (1944); *Radio Station WOW Inc.* v. *Johnson*, 326 U.S. 120, 132 (1945); *Sutton* v. *Leib*, 342 U.S. 402, 414 (1952) (Frankfurter J., concurring).

[19] *First Hydro-Electric Corp.* v. *Federal Power Commn.*, 328 U.S. 152, 188 (1946) (Frankfurter J., dissenting).

to be found in Shakespeare,[20] in Isaac Walton's "Life of John Donne",[21] and in nineteenth-century rules of court.[22]

Long trials are a burden to all, and nobody thinks that litigation is getting more concise. In the nineteenth century, perhaps the best-known test of endurance was the *Tichborne* case, where the civil hearing lasted 103 days and the criminal 188 days.[23] But in the twentieth century India did much better, in its own version of the *Tichborne* case.[24] It began on July 24, 1930; and the facts were striking. The Rajah of Bhowal died in 1901, leaving his vast estates in East Bengal in equal shares among his three sons. In April 1909, his second son, Mejo Kumar, fell ill in Darjeeling, and on May 8, 1909, he was taken for dead. His body was forthwith prepared for cremation, and on May 9, after a funeral procession, a body was cremated. His widow thereupon proceeded to recover on a life policy taken out by her husband, and to enjoy her widow's interest in one third of the Bhowal raj.

Twelve years later, in December 1920 or January 1921, a sanyasi (an itinerant ash-smeared naked ascetic, with long matted hair and a beard) appeared in Dacca and took up a position at which he remained seated day and night, with an ascetic's fire burning before him. On May 4, 1921, the sanyasi publicly declared that he was Mejo Kumar. His story was that although he had been taken for dead, he was in fact still living. His unconscious body had been placed in position for cremation, but almost at once there was a violent storm of rain, and the mourners fled for shelter. The rain had partly revived him, and hearing certain sounds from his body on the abandoned pyre, four passing sanyasis had released him and taken him with them. When he fully recovered consciousness, he found that he had lost all memory of himself or his antecedents. The body that had been cremated was, he said, another body, procured by his

---

[20] *Merchant of Venice*, Act III, sc. 4, l. 56.

[21] Isaac Walton, *Lives* (3d ed. 1817), vol. 1, p. 90. Originally this was prefixed to the first volume of Donne's *Sermons*, printed in 1640: see *ibid.*, at 37.

[22] Regulae Generales, Hil., 2 Will. 4, 1832, r. 87: see 2 Tyr. 341 at 349.

[23] *R.* v. *Castro* (1873–1874) L.R. 9 Q.B. 219.

[24] See (1939) 55 L.Q.R. 181; (1946) 62 L.Q.R. 310; *Srimati Bibhabati Devi* v. *Kumar Ramendra Narayan Roy* [1946] A.C. 508.

relations when they found that his body had disappeared. Eventually he remembered that he had come from Dacca, and so he had returned there. People had then begun to recognise him as the second Kumar, and this recognition was greatly increased after removal of the ashes. The issue, of course, was whether or not he was truly the second Kumar.

The trial lasted 608 days, spread over some two and a half years; and some 1,500 witnesses were called. Finally, in 1936, judgment was given for the claimant. In 1940 the High Court in Calcutta, by a majority, dismissed an appeal. The war delayed the inevitable appeal to the Judicial Committee of the Privy Council, but in 1946 there was a hearing which lasted 28 days; and on July 30, 1946, the appeal was dismissed. Four days later the newspapers reported the death of the claimant in India; and this time there was no mistake.

In one respect the judicial function is plain: "It is the business of judges to send into the world, not doubts but decisions."[25] Yet doubts may later crystallise; and judicial second thoughts have many ways of emerging. It was Lord King L.C. who said: "I always thought it a much greater reproach to a judge to continue in his error than to retract it."[26] Lord Mansfield C.J. was forthright when a direction that he had given to a jury was attacked in the King's Bench: "This case has been remarkably well argued; so well, indeed, that whilst the learned counsel [Erskine] was supporting my direction, I began to think I had been in the right, whereas I never was more mistaken in my life; I totally misunderstood the case and misdirected the jury — So there must be a new trial and without costs."[27]

Chancery was equally unvarnished. Lord Hardwicke L.C. once refused to grant relief in equity,[28] but on a rehearing nearly two years later[29] he reversed his decision and said: "I am thoroughly convinced that my

---

[25] *Lindo* v. *Belisario* (1795) 1 Hag.Con. 216 at 220 (*per* Sir William Scott); and see *Re Flynn* [1968] 1 W.L.R. 103 at 108.

[26] *Galton* v. *Hancock* (1743) 2 Atk. 427 at 439.

[27] (1818) 38 Hansard (1st ser.) 1082 (*per* Lord Erskine).

[28] *Walmesley* v. *Booth* (1739) 2 Atk. 25.

[29] *Walmesley* v. *Booth* (1741) 2 Atk. 27.

former decree was wrong."[30] Lord Eldon, too, was uncharacteristically laconic when concurring with Lord Redesdale in reversing a decision of his own reached nearly ten years earlier, saying: "The Court below did not rightly apprehend the case, as it now appears."[31] Later he became his true periphrastic self again:

> I feel bound to add, with respect to the case of *ex parte Wylie*,[32] which has been so repeatedly appealed to during the argument, that as the first duty of a judge is to endeavour, in the case before him, to decide rightly, — and that his next is, if in any future case of the like kind he has reason to apprehend that his judgment was not upon such sound principles as it appeared to be when he pronounced it, he should not hesitate to rectify his error, — looking at both these obligations, I feel myself bound to state that I must, when I decided the case, have seen it in a point of view, in which, after most laborious consideration, I cannot see it now.[33]

Sometimes a lower appellate decision has provided a spur to self-reversal at last instance. In one case, Lord Tenterden C.J. delivered an unhesitating judgment of the Court of King's Bench in favour of the plaintiffs.[34] But the Court of Exchequer Chamber reversed this decision,[35] and the plaintiffs carried the matter to the House of Lords. There, Lord Tenterden presided as Deputy Speaker, and delivered the only reported speech. His advice to their lordships, which was accepted, was that he was "inclined to think that the judgment of the Court of Exchequer Chamber is right; and I shall have no hesitation on this occasion, and I hope I never shall have any hesitation, in acknowledging any error which I may have committed in the seat of justice, and in endeavouring, as far as I can, to correct that error."[36]

---

[30] *Ibid.*, at p. 27.

[31] *Jackson* v. *Innes* (1819) 1 Bli. 104 at 135, reversing *Innes* v. *Jackson* (1809) 16 Ves. Jun. 356.

[32] (1816) 2 Rose 393.

[33] *Ex parte Nolte* (1826) 2 Gl. & J. 295 at 307. Contrast the pithy dictum of Bramwell B. in *Andrews* v. *Styrap*, cited *post* pp. 158, 159; 1 Misc. 316.

[34] *Colvin* v. *Newberry* (1828) 8 B. & C. 166.

[35] *Newberry* v. *Colvin* (1830) 7 Bing. 190.

[36] *Colvin* v. *Newberry* (1832) 1 Cl. & F. 283 at 301.

In Nova Scotia, Johnstone J. did his best. He gave judgment for the plaintiff at first instance, but then, sitting on appeal in a court that otherwise was equally divided, joined with the two judges who were in favour of reversing his decision. Yet he was to be reversed once more, for the Judicial Committee of the Privy Council held that his first judgment had been "right in its reasoning and sound in its conclusion."[37]

In this field, the palm should perhaps be accorded to Maule J. for determination and to Jackson J. for thoroughness. Maule J. once gave a certain ruling at a trial in favour of the plaintiff, and the defendant afterwards applied to the Court of Common Pleas to reverse the ruling. Tindal C.J., Cresswell J., and Erle J. all held the ruling to be correct, but despite this support Maule J., in a lonely minority of one, not only dissented but also delivered a judgment longer than the other three judgments put together, demonstrating the error of his earlier ruling.[38]

As for Jackson J., in a case in 1950 on the deportation of an alien it fell to him to consider the soundness of an opinion that he, as Attorney General, had given in 1940: "I am entitled to say of that opinion what any discriminating reader must think of it — that it was as foggy as the statute the Attorney General was asked to interpret. It left the difficult borderline questions posed by the Secretary of War unanswered, covering its lack of precision with generalities which, however, gave off overtones of assurance that the Act applied to nearly every alien from a neutral country caught in the United States under almost any circumstances which required him to stay overnight."[39] After considering a number of relevant matters, the judgment continued by saying that precedent was —

> not lacking for ways by which a judge may recede from a prior opinion that has proven untenable and perhaps misled others. See Chief Justice Taney, *License Cases*, 5 How. 504, recanting views he had pressed upon the Court as Attorney General of Maryland in *Brown* v. *Maryland*, 12 Wheat. 419. Baron Bramwell extricated himself from a somewhat similar embarrassment by

---

[37] *McLean* v. *McKay* (1873) L.R. 5 P. C. 327 at 330 (*per* Sir Montague Smith).

[38] *Martindale* v. *Falkner* (1846) 2 C.B. 706.

[39] *McGrath* v. *Kristensen*, 340 U.S. 162, 176 (1950) (Jackson J., concurring).

saying, "The matter does not appear to me now as it appears to have appeared to me then." *Andrews* v. *Styrap*, 26 L.T.R. (N.S.) 704, 706.[40] And Mr. Justice Story, accounting for his contradiction of his own former opinion, quite properly put the matter: "My own error, however, can furnish no ground for its being adopted by this Court . . . ." *United States* v. *Gooding*, 12 Wheat. 460, 478. Perhaps Dr. Johnson really went to the heart of the matter when he explained a blunder in his dictionary — "Ignorance, sir, ignorance."[41] But an escape less self-deprecating was taken by Lord Westbury, who, it is said, rebuffed a barrister's reliance upon an earlier opinion of his Lordship: "I can only say that I am amazed, that a man of my intelligence should have been guilty of giving such an opinion."[42] If there are other ways of gracefully and good-naturedly surrendering former views to a better considered position, I invoke them all.[43]

In brief, "I see no reason why I should be consciously wrong today because I was unconsciously wrong yesterday."[44]

Judges who have remained unconvinced of error in their decisions have been known to seize an opportunity of leaping to their own rescue. Thus in 1864 Sir John Romilly M.R. held that a particular shareholder in a company should not be placed on the list of contributories in the winding up of the company.[45] On appeal, Lord Westbury L.C. reversed this decision,[46] and there was a further appeal to the House of Lords. By the time this came to be heard, a timely ennoblement[47] had enabled the Master of the Rolls to sit in the appeal; and sit he did. As Lord Romilly, he spoke and voted in favour of reversing the Lord Chancellor, and he recruited Lord St. Leonards to his cause; but the voices of Lord Cranworth, Lord Chelmsford, and Lord Colonsay combined to prevent the reversed from reversing the reverser.[48] A reverser has even accom-

[40] See 1 Misc. 316. Contrast Lord Eldon's comma-bestrewn ramble, *ante* p. 157.

[41] In fact, "Ignorance, madam, pure ignorance": Boswell's *Johnson*, vol. 1, p. 181.

[42] For another version, see 2 Atlay 260.

[43] *McGrath*, 340 U.S. at 177–78. For a brief-writer's use of this passage in a motion, see Garner, *The Winning Brief* (2d ed. 2004), pp. 419–20.

[44] *Massachusetts* v. *U.S.*, 333 U.S. 611, 639 (1948) (Jackson J., dissenting); cited 2 Misc. 136.

[45] *Re Agriculturist Cattle Ins. Co., Spackman's Case* (1864) 12 W.R. 1133.

[46] *Re Agriculturist Cattle Ins. Co., Spackman's Case* (1865) 34 L.J.Ch. 321.

[47] He became Lord Romilly on January 3, 1866.

[48] *Spackman* v. *Evans* (1868) L.R. 3 H.L. 171.

panied the reversed upstairs in self-defence. Thus in one case where Page
Wood V.-C. had been reversed by Lord Chelmsford L.C., each of them
sat in the final appeal, Page Wood presiding as Lord Hatherley L.C.
Neither changed his mind, and the upshot was that after reserving
judgment for nearly a year, Lord Westbury and Lord Colonsay joined in
leaving Lord Hatherley in isolation.[49]

Today, all is changed. A judge can no longer sit in an appeal from one
of his own decisions. This became law for civil appeals in the late
nineteenth century.[50] Crime was different. When the Criminal Appeal
Act 1907 established the Court of Criminal Appeal, the Act contained
nothing to prevent the trial judge from sitting in an appeal; and in days
when criminal law and criminal procedure were much simpler than
today, and most criminal appeals much shorter, many a trial judge sat
in the appeal.[51] But when in 1966 the jurisdiction of that court was
transferred to the Criminal Division of the Court of Appeal, the Act
precluded the trial judge from sitting in an appeal.[52] Even so, there still
seems to be nothing in law to prevent a judge who is a peer from sitting
in the House of Lords in an appeal against a decision of his, as the Earl
of Reading C.J. once did (reversing himself).[53] Yet procedural changes
now preclude this; for since 1948 appeals to the House have normally
been heard by an appellate committee of the House, and a latter-day
Lord Romilly would not find himself a member of the committee.

In the Court of Session, it was formerly the practice for the judge who
had presided at a jury trial to sit with the Division of the Inner House
hearing a motion for a new trial. Sometimes that judge would concur in
holding that a direction to the jury was incorrect.[54] This practice was
later discontinued.

Prompt self-reversal is another matter; for a judge may still alter his

---

[49] *Knox* v. *Gye* (1872) L.R. 5 H.L. 656, cited 2 Misc. 65.

[50] See Judicature Acts 1873, s. 54; 1875, s. 54; 1925, s. 68(4); Supreme Court Act 1981,
s. 56.

[51] See, e.g., *R.* v. *Lovegrove* (1951) 35 Cr. App. R. 30 (*per* Lynskey J.).

[52] Criminal Appeal Act 1966, s. 2(3).

[53] *Director of Public Prosecutions* v. *Beard* [1920] A.C. 479.

[54] E.g., *Hendry* v. *Clan Line Steamers*, 1949 S.C. 320.

decision at any time before the formal order of the court has been perfected. Changes may even be made while the judgment is in course of delivery, as where the judge suddenly realises that the Court has no jurisdiction. The pure theory of jurisdiction may demand an instant halt to the proceedings, and oblivion for all that has been said; but at least when the judgment is in progress towards dismissing an appeal, pragmatism may encourage the judge to complete his unjurisdictional judgment, professedly *de bene esse*, and even make an order for costs.[55]

The time that a case takes naturally depends on the time spent in talking; and occasionally the Bench will exonerate counsel. Starke J. once began a judgment by saying: "This is an appeal from the Chief Justice, which was argued by this Court over nine days, with some occasional assistance from the learned and experienced counsel who appeared for the parties. The evidence was taken and the matter argued before the Chief Justice in two days. The case involves two questions, of no transcendent importance, which are capable of brief statement, and could have been exhaustively argued by the learned counsel in a few hours."[56] A year earlier, Scrutton L.J. had observed of a court consisting of Lord Hanworth M.R., himself, and Romer J. that "the Court, with occasional assistance from counsel, took more than a day in discussing this case."[57]

In the nature of things it is unlikely that the law reports will set out such arguments *in extenso*; yet the quest is not hopeless. Thus in 1926 a Chancery Divisional Court held that two infants had wrongly been adjudicated bankrupt, and then had to consider whether the Official Receiver might retain the assets against his costs. Astbury J. thought he could, but P.O. Lawrence J. thought not; and most of the three pages of the report is occupied by their argument on this point, with minor contributions by counsel. In the end, as the court was equally divided no

---

[55] *Aire Property Trust* v. *Treeweek* [1989] 7 E.G. 74 (*per* Kerr L.J.).

[56] *Federal Commissioner of Taxation* v. *S. Hoffnung & Co. Ltd* (1928) 42 C.L.R. 39 at p. 62.

[57] *Elliott* v. *Duchess Mill Ltd.* [1927] 1 K.B. 182 at 201. See also (1927) 3 Camb. L.J. 1 at pp. 8, 9 (*per* Atkin L.J.); *R.* v. *Young* (1925) 43 S.A.L.J. 48.

order could be made on the point, and so Lawrence J., who had spoken less than Astbury J., in effect prevailed.[58]

In the 1880s, *Ex parte Stanford, Re Barber*,[59] ran no ordinary course in the Court of Appeal. The question was whether a mortgage bill of sale was void as not being in the statutory form; and a Queen's Bench Divisional Court had held that it was valid. On appeal, the appellant raised a point not taken below, to the effect that the grantor had assigned the chattels "as beneficial owner," and that these words, by importing the complex covenants for title of the Conveyancing Act 1881, section 7, provided an additional ground of invalidity.[60] But this was of no avail: without even calling on counsel for the respondent, the court dismissed the appeal. Lord Esher M.R. began his judgment with the words: "In my opinion there is no blemish to be found in this bill of sale";[61] and Lindley and Lopes L.JJ. joined him in rejecting the point on the phrase "as beneficial owner," though Lopes L.J. observed that he had some doubt on the matter.[62]

That ended Round 1; more was to follow. Perhaps the doubts of Lopes L.J. took root. At all events, the court soon expressed a desire to hear further argument on the point, and a week after the appeal had been dismissed, there was Round 2. After full argument on both sides, the court, constituted as before, unanimously reversed itself and allowed the appeal; but tribute was paid to the earlier decision by giving leave to appeal to the House of Lords.[63] A month passed, and then counsel returned to the court to point out that by statute the decision of the Court of Appeal was final,[64] and so there was no power to allow an appeal to the House of Lords. All that the court could then do it did: the case was directed to be argued yet again, but this time before the full court. Six days later the court sat again, with Cotton, Bowen, and Fry

---

[58] *Re A & M* [1926] Ch. 274.
[59] (1885) 17 Q.B.D. 259; 34 W.R. 168.
[60] (1886) 17 Q.B.D. 259 at 263.
[61] *Ibid.*
[62] *Ibid.*, at p. 265.
[63] (1886) 34 W.R. 287.
[64] Bankruptcy Appeals (County Courts) Act 1884, s. 2.

L.JJ. added to the strength.[65] The result of Round 3 was that the court unanimously adhered to its second decision allowing the appeal, and held the bill void.[66] And that was really that.

The running of time is ever a fertile subject for dispute. A statutory provision[67] that prohibited any appeal unless a notice of appeal was given "within three weeks" of the decision was clear enough: but the following words were "unless such time is extended by the Court of Appeal." On this, the contention was that once the three weeks had run, no extension could be made; for how could something non-existent be "extended"? But the House of Lords would have none of it; and Lord Hatherley L.C. uttered words pregnant with possibilities. "Time is not a material with respect to which it may be said that the matter itself having ceased, there is no farther subject to operate upon."[68]

Few would think of enquiring how the House of Lords came to be the highest court in the land in England; but Scotland is another matter. The first Earl of Rosebery has received scant credit outside Scotland — and sometimes within it — for establishing that in civil cases[69] the House of Lords is the final court of appeal from Scotland, Europe apart. This occurred in a curiously muffled way. On May 1, 1707, the United Kingdom of Great Britain came into existence in accordance with the Articles of Union 1706 and the Union with Scotland Act 1706. Article XIX dealt at length with the Court of Session and other Scottish courts, but said not a word about appeals from the Court of Session. For very different reasons, all concerned wished such appeals to lie to the House of Lords; yet the potential of the respective sleeping dogs that would have been aroused by explicitness was decisive.[70] Statute said nothing,

---

[65] (1886) 17 Q.B.D. 259 at 268.

[66] (1886) 17 Q.B.D. 259; 34 W.R. 507. Fry L.J. dissented on another point. Lord Esher seems to have abandoned his dissent in Round 2 on another point: compare 34 W.R. 287 at 288 with the judgment in Round 3.

[67] Companies Act 1862, s. 124.

[68] *Banner* v. *Johnston* (1871) L.R. 5 H.L. 157 at 170–71.

[69] In criminal cases there is no such appeal. For the curious history of this, see A.J. MacLean, *The House of Lords and Appeals from the High Court of Justiciary, 1707–1887*, 1985 Jurid. Rev. 192.

[70] See A.J. MacLean (1983) 4 Jnl.Leg.Hist. (No. 3) 50; *The Laws of Scotland*, vol. 6 (1988), pp. 337–41.

and the point was not resolved by judicial decision; instead, there was a somewhat singular process of assumption *sub silentio.*

Within a year of the Union, Lord Rosebery had taken what proved to be the decisive step. On February 1, 1695, he had been defeated in proceedings in the Court of Session relating to "a Fishing in Common . . . in the Water of Cramond."[71] Undeterred by the elapse of some 13 years, he presented a petition and appeal to the House of Lords; and on February 16, 1708, the House ordered the respondent to put in his answer on March 15, 1708.[72] This was not done, and on March 24, 1708, 49 Lords Committees were appointed to consider a motion by the petitioner for the House to fix a peremptory day for the answer to be put in.[73] Three days later, the committees reported that in their opinion "the Respondents, in this and all other Cases of Appeals from Scotland," should put in their answers, as respondents did in cases of appeals from the courts in England, within the time appointed by the House.[74] The House forthwith agreed with this report, and ordered accordingly.[75] That proved to be that: no more was needed. An order cast in a form like this was a plain assertion of a general jurisdiction in civil appeals from Scotland; and that assertion seems never to have been questioned. That was the end of Lord Rosebery's contribution; for some 12 years later his appeal, in company with 34 other aging appeals, was dismissed for want of prosecution.[76] Long before then, on March 10, 1709, the first reported case of such an appeal[77] had been decided, reversing the Court of Session; and that made assurance double sure.

Safebreaking at the behest of the court is rare but not unknown. In

---

[71] *Archibald, Earl of Roseberie* v. *Sir John Inglis*: see (1708) 18 Lds. Jnl. 464.

[72] (1708) 18 Lds. Jnl. 464.

[73] *Ibid.,* at p. 550.

[74] *Ibid.,* at p. 555.

[75] *Ibid.,* at p. 556. It was also ordered that Sir John Inglis should have until April 20, 1708, to answer the appeal.

[76] (1720) 21 Lds. Jnl. 283, 284.

[77] *Gray* v. *Duke of Hamilton* (1709) Robert.App. 1; 18 Lds. Jnl. 660. On December 14, 1708, an order had been made for an answer on or before January 25, 1709: see 18 Lds. Jnl. 591; and see 18 Lds. Jnl. 614, 641, 656. Ireland was different: see 6 Geo. 1, c. 5, 1719; 23 Geo. 3, c. 28, 1783.

one case in 1955 two sisters who were trustees refused to take any part in a proper sale of the trust property, or to comply with an order of the court directing them to deliver the title deeds of the property to their co-trustee, who was their brother. They even barricaded themselves in their house and fixed barbed wire round the ground-floor windows; and in due course they were committed for contempt and lodged in Holloway Prison. This, however, did little to facilitate the sale, for the sisters remained recalcitrant: the deeds were in a safe in their house, and it was not known where the keys were. Their brother accordingly applied to the court for a writ of assistance, a remedy that had become rare. After some discussion, Upjohn J. ordered the writ to issue, directing the sheriff to enter the house and if necessary break open the safe, though the brother's solicitor was first to go to the prison and explain to the sisters what would happen if they did not indicate where the deeds were and deliver up the keys.[78] The rest is silence.

---

[78] *Re Klingelhoefer's Will Trusts* [1955] *The Times*, Mar. 19.

10

~

LE NEEDFULNESS DE EUX

FOR OVER seven centuries law reporters of one kind or another have been recording words uttered by judges and counsel in cases in the English courts. These have ranged from solemn pronouncements of law to the cut and thrust of argument, casual comments, and much else besides. It is indeed remarkable that in one branch of learning there should have been the systematic, contemporaneous, and verbatim reporting of so much of what was said in daily life so long ago. Thus when in 1286 Brompton J. said during argument: "Won mon avez mon yenne avez loverd to,"[1] he was only stating a feudal adage; yet there it stands, for all to read today, even without comprehending that it merely states that for every man there is a feudal lord.

Through the centuries much has changed in the type and style of law reports; but the essential of satisfying the need for accurate and discriminating contemporaneity has always been at the core. One of the many changes was the introduction of the side-note, and later the head-note. The side-notes in Sir Gregory Lewin's two volumes of criminal law reports have a reputation all their own; indeed, posterity has failed to resist the temptation to gild some of his lilies, and to father upon the reports much that is not truly theirs. Of the true-born, pride of place must go to the celebrated side-note to *Clement's Case*:[2] "Possession in Scotland evidence of stealing in England." This tendency to the

---

[1] *Oger of Kernick* v. *D'Aumale* (1286) 112 S.S. (1996) 256.
[2] (1830) 1 Lewin C.C. 113, cited 1 Misc. 289.

sweeping assertion was manifest in other side-notes, such as "A party is bound to retreat by a back door to avoid a conflict":[3] *secus*, no doubt, a front door, a side door, or even French windows. Again:

- "Encouragers are guilty."[4]

- "Omitting the word 'unlawfully' is fatal."[5]

- "A loft under the same roof may be described as a dwelling-house."[6]

- "An acquittal of murder includes an acquittal of concealment."[7]

Brute creation added its quota: "Hens must be described as tame, or they will be taken to be *ferae naturae*."[8] Further, "The word sheep is *nomen generalissimum* and includes all ages and sexes. R. v. Puddefoot overruled,"[9] so that it is not surprising to find "a dead sheep held to be a sheep."[10]

Some of the side-notes do not attempt to state propositions, but merely indicate what was in issue. Even so, brevity can be carried too far. The side-note to *Thorpe's Case*[11] is in four cryptic words: "Fighting up and down." And *Knight's Case*[12] is not much better: "Sitting inside a cart instead of attending at the horse's head." There are glimpses of the obvious, too: "The handwriting of prisoner not in itself *prima facie* evidence of forgery,"[13] and "compulsory performance of statutory duty not evidence of the adoption of a way."[14] Sometimes matters are left in

---

[3] *Dakin's Case* (1828) 1 Lewin C.C. 166.

[4] *Nelson's and Others' Case* (1828) 1 Lewin C.C. 249.

[5] *Turner and Reader's Case* (1830) 1 Lewin C.C. 226.

[6] *Thompson's Case* (1824) 1 Lewin C.C. 212.

[7] *Calverley's Case* (1830) 1 Lewin C.C. 44.

[8] *Tate and Another's Case* (1833) 1 Lewin C.C. 234.

[9] *M'Cully's Case* (1828) 2 Lewin C.C. 272.

[10] *Boaz Puckering's Case* (1830) 1 Lewin C.C. 225.

[11] (1829) 1 Lewin C.C. 171.

[12] (1828) 1 Lewin C.C. 168.

[13] *Musgrave's Case* (1829) 1 Lewin C.C. 112.

[14] *R. v. Mellor* (1828) 1 Lewin C.C. 158.

the air, as in "Drunkenness is no excuse for crime, unless, &c."[15] But it is *Sarah Hobson's Case*[16] that takes pride of place. While the side-note impeccably[17] asserts, "Better that ten guilty escape than that one innocent should suffer," the index proclaims "INNOCENT, better that ten guilty should suffer than one innocent."[18] Why only ten?

In the United States, law reporters have at times exercised a sturdy independence in their head-notes. Thus to one proposition in a head-note is appended a footnote that reads: "The reporter does not believe that the opinion in this case was intended to change the settled rule of law, as laid down in the several cases cited, and he has therefore made the head-note conform to those cases, and not to the language of the opinion."[19] Nor can reporters be expected to achieve the impossible. One head-note of a case in the United States Supreme Court reads:

> This case involves deciding whether the defendants in error are liable for the damage occasioned to certain property, resulting from a fire which occurred on October 28, 1894, in a railroad yard at East St. Louis, Illinois. . . . At the time of the fire [Bosworth] was operating the railway as receiver. The decision depends largely, if not entirely, on facts, which are stated at great length by the court, both in the statement of the case, and in its opinion. These papers are most carefully prepared. While both deal with facts, those facts are stated with clearness, with fullness, with completeness, and with unusual care. They leave nothing untouched. Without treating them with the same fullness, the reporter feels himself unable to prepare a headnote which could convey an adequate and just account of the opinion and decision of the court. Under these circumstances he deems it best not to attempt an impossibility, but to respectfully ask the readers of this headnote to regard the opinion of the court in this case as incorporated into it.[20]

The head-note thus became, by incorporation, some twenty pages long.

---

[15] *John Burrow's Case* (1828) 1 Lewin C.C. 75; *William Rennie's Case* (1825) 1 Lewin C.C. 76.

[16] (1831) 1 Lewin C.C. 261.

[17] See 4 Bl.Comm. (15th ed. 1809), p. 358.

[18] 1 Lewin C.C. 353.

[19] *Drake* v. *State*, 51 Ala. 30 (1874) (*per* J.W. Shepherd, Reporter).

[20] *Huntting Elevator Co.* v. *Bosworth*, 179 U.S. 415 (1900) (*per* J.C. Bancroft Davis, Reporter).

In 1870 the House of Lords was emphatic in its disapproval of a number of Scottish appeals. In one case, the head-note ended with the words "Censure of a seven years' litigation, and disallowance of costs on both sides."[21] Lord Westbury regretted very much that the taxpayers should "have to pay the expenses of a most improper and unpardonable litigation."[22] In another case (under the catchwords "*The Litigation — Regret expressed*") the head-note ends with the words: "*Per* The Lord Chancellor: — Mrs. Reid is to be pitied for the course into which she has been dragged, — evidently without any consciousness on her part of the extreme folly of these proceedings."[23]

Again Lord Westbury made his contribution: "It may be instructive to the people of Scotland to examine this case a little further in order that they may see the lamentable consequences which arise from the state of the procedure in their Law Courts, and the abuses of that procedure which take place."[24] A week later, he began a speech by saying: "It is to me a constant subject of grief that there should be in Scotland the power to litigants of coming on the most trifling matters to your Lordships' House. The result is, that the time of the greatest tribunal in the land is occupied with the most insignificant matters; and further, the expense and misery occasioned are augmented indefinitely by this power of prolonged litigation."[25] But perhaps the most striking case at this time was one in which the whole of the catchwords and head-note were as follows:

Costly Litigation — Expressions of Regret.
Per Lord Chelmsford: — It is really lamentable to think of the enormous expense incurred in this case.
Per Lord Westbury: — Such things occur in the appeals from Scotland day by day.[26]

---

[21] *Campbell's Trustees & Executors* v. *Police Commissioners of Leith* (1870) L.R. 2 Sc. & D. 1.
[22] *Ibid.*, at p. 4.
[23] *Keith* v. *Reid* (1870) L.R. 2 Sc. & D. 39; see at p. 40 (*per* Lord Hatherley L.C.).
[24] *Ibid.*, at p. 41.
[25] *Gray* v. *Turnbull* (1870) L.R. 2 Sc. & D. 53 at 54.
[26] *Fraser* v. *Crawford* (1870) L.R. 2 Sc. & D. 42.

Law French added its peculiar riches to the reports.[27] There were striking contributions in nuisance and murder. Lord Denning once referred to a case in the year books about a tannery in which it was said that "L'utilite de la chose excuse le noisomeness de la stink."[28] Unfortunately it has not proved possible to trace this imperishable phrase; but perhaps it was derived from *Rankett's Case* in the King's Bench in 1605. The note of this in Rolle's *Abridgement* reads as follows: "Si home fait Candells deins un vill, per que il cause un noysom sent al Inhabitants, uncore ceo nest ascun Nusans, car le needfulness de eux dispensera ove le noisomness del smell."[29] This suggests a process of striking a balance between good and evil, with the court examining an ethical and utilitarian balance sheet, and determining whether the defendant was in credit or faced a deficit. Tanners were in like case with candle makers, for as Hyde C.J. once said, "Un tan-house est necessary, car touts wear shoes":[30] even they must walk.

Yet any such incipient doctrine was short-lived; for in *Morley* v. *Pragnel*,[31] decided less than 35 years later, it was held that an action for nuisance lay for the erection and operation of a tallow furnace. Despite the argument "that an action lies not, for he, being a tallow-chandler, ought to use his trade, which cannot be said to be a nusance," the court held that the claim succeeded, "for every one ought sic uti suo, quod alienum non laedat."[32] This decision reduced the books to making unhappy distinctions: the action lay for a "Tallow-Furnace" (citing *Morley* v. *Pragnel*[33]), "But, if he be a Chandler, *Quaere*" (citing *Rankett's Case*).[34]

In one action for nuisance the plaintiff, who was registrar of an ecclesiastical court, complained that his neighbour, whose house was a mere 16 feet away, had erected "un brewhouse, & quandum latrinam, &

---

[27] See also 1 Misc. and 2 Misc., *passim*.
[28] [1955] *Year Book of the Canadian Bar Association* 154.
[29] 2 Roll.Abr. 139, Common Nusans, pl. 2.
[30] *Jones & Powell* (1628) Palm. 536 at 539.
[31] (1638) Cro.Car. 510.
[32] *Ibid*. For the value of the maxim, see *post* p. 211.
[33] (1638) Cro.Car. 510.
[34] 1 Comyns' *Digest* (1762) 232.

en le dit mease use l'art & mystery d'un brewer: et en le use de ceo arde seacole en grand quantity; & que horribiles vapores & insalubres surge del brewhouse, & privy avantdit, que ratione inde le plaintiff ne poit user son mease ne office, & que per ceo ses biens & utensils fueront spoil per le smoke."[35] It was held to be no nuisance merely to erect a privy or brewhouse, or to burn sea coal in it, "car est natural fuel, coment n'est cy sweet come wood."[36] But it was different when the privy and brewhouse were erected so close to the plaintiff's house that "ses biens sont spoiled, & il ne poet inhabiter son mese."[37] In other cases there were other steps that the complainant could take: "Si home est cy tender nosed, que ne poit indurer sea-cole, il doit lesser son mease."[38] Further, "In cesty matters le ley est come apparel, que alter ove le temps."[39]

As for murder:

> Holloway fuit indict pur le Murther d'un Paine, pur tyer luy al un horse tayle ex Malitia, &c. ove un rope, & faire le horse a dragger luy sur le terre per three furlongs, issint que le Shoulder de Paine fuit infreint, & il morust de ceo instanter; Et sur non culp': le Jury trove special verdict.
>
> Le Seignior Denby fuit seisie de Osterley Parke in Middlesex in fee, & fait le dit Holloway son Woodward del dit Parke, & que Paine un puer vient in le Parke pur prender Wood la, & veyent Holloway, climbe en un arbre de occulter luy mesme; Et Holloway veyant luy, command luy de descender, sur le quel le Garson descend, Et donque Holloway struck le boy bis, & donque espyant le fine del un rope, que fuit tyde circa le wast del Garson dependant, tye ceo al tayl de son Chival, sur que il viegne adonque en le Parke, & percute le Garson arere, sur que le Chival ranne away, & drag le dit Garson, tanque le shoulder del Garson fuit infreint per ceo, & le Garson de ceo instanter morust; Et Holloway prist Payne, & eject luy en un bush arere le pale del Parke. Et si super totam materiam, &c.[40]

---

[35] *Jones & Powell* (1628) Palm. 536: mese, mease (house); arde (burn).

[36] *Ibid.*, at p. 537 (*per* Whitlocke J.): coment (although).

[37] *Ibid.*, at p. 539 (*per* Hyde C.J.). See also S.C., Hut. 135 at 136 (finding by jury).

[38] *Ibid.*, at p. 538 (*per* Dodderidge J.).

[39] *Ibid.*

[40] *Hollowaye's Case* (1628) Palm. 545. There is little need for a translation, for there is little to translate; but the following indications may be useful: ove (with); issint que (so that); infreint (broken); puer vient (boy comes); veyent (seeing); occulter (hide); viegne adonque (had then come).

After much argument, the case was adjourned; but in the next term, "fuit adjudge per le Court, que ceo fuit murder, & Holloway fuit pendus pur ceo; mes le Court ne declara les reasons overtment."[41]

Law reporters today have little opportunity of displaying their command of law French; but there have been achievements in modern French. When in 1971 Casey J. in the Quebec Court of Appeal mentioned that at one point the respondent had had "a change of heart," he can hardly have foreseen a report that would refer to the respondent's "transplantation de coeur,"[42] least of all when the respondent was a club that had been incorporated as a limited company.

Sometimes a judge is confronted with a report of an argument that he put forward when at the Bar. The argument of Twisden, of counsel, in one case[43] was cited nearly twenty years later, when he was Twisden J. Counsel said: "We beg leave to mention especially what you Mr. Justice Twisden said there; though indeed we do not know, nor can be very confident that it is reported right." At this, Twisden J. said: "I do protest not one word of it is true they went about."[44] In the end, Twisden J. dissented from his brethren, Morton and Rainsford JJ. In his words: "I cannot so easily as my brothers slubber over all the authorities cited."[45]

Even when a report is accurate, posterity sometimes plays the editor, as it has done to the famous words uttered by Maule J. over 160 years ago on bigamy and the problems of divorce. A contemporary report of these words deserves reproduction in full:

MIDLAND CIRCUIT

Warwick, Tuesday, April 1
Thomas Hall, *alias* Thomas Rollins,[46] a poor man not possessed of a farthing, or a farthing's worth, in the world, aged 35, was indicted for having,

---

[41] *Hollowaye's Case, supra* note 40, at 548.

[42] *Tamarack Construction Inc.* v. *The United Services Club Ltd.* [1971] C.A. 334 (see the catchwords). The Corrigenda substitute "changement d'idée."

[43] *Weld* v. *Rumney* (1651) Sty. 318.

[44] *Foxwith* v. *Tremain* (1670) 1 Mod. 296.

[45] *Ibid.*, at p. 297.

[46] Not "Pallins," as stated in 2 Atlay 71, nor "Pollins," as stated in R. Walton, *Random Recollections of the Midland Circuit* (1869), p. 154.

on the 18th of April, 1830, at the parish of Northleach, in the county of Gloucester, taken for his wife Mary Ann Nicholls, and afterwards, on the 15th of February, 1840, at the parish of Hampden-in-Arden, in this county, married and taken to wife Maria Hadley, his former wife being then alive, *contra forman.*

The offence was clearly proved, but he stated that within a year or two of his marriage with Mary Ann, she robbed him, and sallied forth with the child, and he had never since seen either, though he had at the time obtained a special warrant for her apprehension, armed with which he proceeded to the region of her seclusion or retirement, where he got sadly handled by ruffians, and was made heartily glad to make the best of his way home to save his life, leaving his baggage in his precipitate departure from that profligate retreat. The substance of this, or at least much of it, he elicited from the witnesses for the prosecution. He had, however, represented to Maria that he had never entered into the holy state, and she had given birth to two children by him.

He was, of course, under these circumstances, convicted, and Mr. Justice Maule, in passing sentence, said, that it did appear that he had been hardly used. It was hard for him to be so used, and not be able to have another wife to live with him, when the former had gone off to live in an improper state with another man. But the law was the same for him as it was for a rich man, and was equally open for him, through its aid, to afford relief; but, as the rich man would have done, he also should have pursued the proper means pointed out by law whereby to obtain redress of his grievances. He should have brought an action against the man who was living in the way stated with his wife, and he should have obtained damages, and then should have gone to the Ecclesiastical Court and obtained a divorce, which would have done what seemed to have been done already, and then he should have gone to the House of Lords, and, proving all his case and the preliminary proceedings, have obtained a full and complete divorce, after which he might, if he liked it, have married again. The prisoner might perhaps object to this that he had not the money to pay the expenses, which would amount to about £500 or £600 — perhaps he had not so many pence — but this did not exempt him from paying the penalty for committing a felony, of which he had been convicted. His Lordship might, perhaps, have visited the crime more lightly if the prisoner had not misrepresented himself as a bachelor to Maria Hadley, and so deceived her. If he had told her the circumstances, and said, "Now I'll marry you if you like to take the chance," &c.; but this he had not done, and thus he had induced her to live with him upon terms which she perhaps else would not have done. It was a serious injury to her, which he had no right to inflict because his wife and others had injured him. For this offence he must receive some punishment, and the sentence was, that he be imprisoned and kept to hard labour for four months, which he hoped would operate as a warning how people trifled with matrimony.[47]

If this report is compared with the versions usually current today,[48] it will be seen that, even after allowing for the damping effect of *oratio obliqua*, the original language has been amplified and polished, and that the sentence was not the derisory "one day"[49] that is so often stated.

For another pronouncement by Maule J., there is no authority save tradition. When sentencing a deaf old man for an offence of indecency he ended by saying: "Though you are aged, for such prurience as yours you must go to prison for eight months. Gaoler, repeat my words to the prisoner." The gaoler, who had been inattentive, shouted in the prisoner's ear: "The judge says you are a prudent old man and must go to quod for eighteen months." At this, the judge said: "Gaoler, I can tolerate the liberty that you have taken with my words, but I cannot allow you to alter my sentences."

Possibly there are some law reporters who still do not realise that they stand in a functional line of descent from Moses; for he "was the first reporter or writer of law in the world."[50] Like Moses, some reports achieve the impossible. Thus there is one case[51] that, as reported in The Reports,[52] carries the footnote: "A typical instance of an unreportable case." It is strange that a word indicating impossibility should have come to be treated as being apt for what is perfectly possible but not worth the doing.

Watkins, the conveyancer, had no affection for unreported cases:

---

[47] *R. v. Hall* [1845] *The Times*, April 3, p. 7; and see *Report of the Royal Commission on Divorce and Matrimonial Causes*, 1912 (Cd. 6478), p. 12.

[48] See, e.g., 1 Misc. 116, 117.

[49] Nor three months, as stated in 2 Atlay 72.

[50] *Calvin's Case* (1608) 7 Co.Rep. la at 12b.

[51] *In b. Crawshay* [1893] P. 108.

[52] 1 R. 477.

Is the law of England to depend upon the private note of an individual, and to which an individual can only have access? Is a Judge to say — "Lo! I have the law of England, on this point, in my pocket. Here is a note of the case, which contains an exact statement of the whole facts, and the decision of my Lord A. or my Lord B. upon them. He was a great, a very great, man. I am bound by his decision. All you have been reading was erroneous. The printed books are inaccurate. I cannot go into principle. The point is settled by this case." Under such circumstances, who is to know when he is right or when he is wrong? If conclusions from unquestionable principles are to be overthrown in the last stage of a suit by private *memoranda*, who can hope to become acquainted with the laws of England? And who, that retains any portion of rationality, would waste his time and his talents in so fruitless an attempt? Is a paper evidencing the law of England to be buttoned up in the side-pocket of a Judge, or to serve for a mouse to sit upon in the dusty corner of a private library? If the law of England is to be deduced from adjudged cases, let the reports of those adjudged cases, be certain, known, and authenticated.[53]

Yet the remedy of leaving nothing unreported seems worse than the ill. In the United States, the number of judgments sent for publication by federal and State courts rose from 27,336 in 1964 to 66,500 in 1992.[54]

The reasons for a judgment remaining unreported are various. In Pennsylvania, Musmanno J. once not only took proceedings for mandamus against the official reporter to require him to publish a dissenting judgment of his in the official reports, but also appears to have argued his case in person, at any rate on the appeal to his brethren in the State Supreme Court.[55] That court would have contented itself with affirming the dismissal of the claim —

---

[53] C. Watkins, *Principles of Conveyancing* (2d ed. 1804), Introduction, p. xiv.

[54] See Robert J. Martineau, *Restrictions on Publication and Citation of Judicial Opinions: A Reassessment*, 28 Univ. Mich. J.L. Reform 119, 143–44 (1994). Some 35,000 additional opinions were added to Westlaw's electronic database, for a total of about 100,000 research-able opinions. For 2003, West estimates that it received 52,000 opinions for publication and 80,000 to 90,000 other opinions to add to its database.

[55] "Michael A. Musmanno, in pro. per., and . . . for appellant": *Musmanno v. Eldredge* 114 A.2d 511, 511 (Pa. 1955) (*per curiam*); and see the first sentence of the judgment quoted above.

had not the appellant, during the course of his oral argument, publicly voiced a grave charge against the other members of this court which cannot be permitted to go unanswered. The appellant asserted that we discriminated against him in the matter of the filing and publication of dissenting opinions, — that there is one rule for him and a different rule for the other members of the court. Never once have we withheld, nor have we any intention of ever withholding, from publication in the official State Reports a dissenting opinion of any member of the court if in accord with established rules and practices. In the little more than three years that the appellant has been a member of this court he has filed and has had published in the official State Reports, with this court's full approval, more dissenting opinions than all the other members of the court combined.

The appellant's opinion in the *Tribune Review Publishing Company* case,[56] the non-publication whereof in the official State Reports constitutes the gravamen of his present complaint, was never circulated among the members of the court nor even shown to any one of them prior to it being lodged by appellant with the Prothonotary for the Western District after this court had entered an order dismissing the Tribune's petition for a writ of prohibition on the ground that the petition did not present a justiciable question. . . . The order of this court . . . did not discuss, much less decide, the merits of the very important legal question involved. It merely held that there was nothing justiciable before us for decision, dismissed the petition without prejudice, and suggested that a proper test case might be presented. The appellant's opinion, instead of confining itself to the subject matter of the order, went on to discuss and decide the merits of the controversy which the petitioner had endeavored to litigate prematurely and as to which this court had expressed no views whatever. It is, to say the least, unfortunate that appellant saw fit to write and hand out for publication an opinion pre-judging a question which has yet to come before the court.

Not only, as already stated, did appellant file his opinion in the Tribune case without circulating it among the other members of the court, but he filed it after the court had adjourned its sessions for the summer and its members were scattered. Thus we were effectually denied the opportunity, indeed the fundamental right, of seeing, reading, or considering the dissent before the appellant made it public.[57]

[56] *In re Tribune Review Publg. Co.*, 113 A.2d 861 (Pa. 1954).

[57] *Musmanno* v. *Eldredge*, 114 A.2d 511, 512 (1955) (*per curiam*) (Stern C.J. and Stearne, Jones, Bell, Chidsey, and Arnold JJ.).

Bell J. observed: "Dissenting opinions sometimes become, after circulation and consultation, the majority opinion of the Court, and at other times have caused the majority opinion to be modified or rewritten."[58] He added that Musmanno J. had "agreed in this case to the Opinion of the Court and thereby, in my judgment, waived his right to have any dissenting opinion of his published in the official Reports."[59] Certainly the report of the case in question shows Musmanno J. as one of six judges concurring in an opinion *per curiam*.[60] Yet the dissent was not long to be denied the light of day; for two years later, in company with many others,[61] it appeared in a book entitled *Justice Musmanno Dissents*.[62]

Sometimes a judgment that has had no difficulty in getting reported provides intrinsic grounds for regret that it ever emerged from obscurity. This view may well be taken of a report of an American case that appeared almost entirely in rhyme.[63] Head-note, annotations, the judgment itself, footnotes, and the order, all save the list of counsel appearing in the case and the quotation of part of a statute are in verse, of a sort. Verse even seems to have invaded the briefs, if not the pleadings. In one respect the report is welcome; for the precedent that it sets is overwhelming. So lame is most of the verse, so forced is much of the rhyming, and so contorted is some of the language, that the case is strongly persuasive against any attempt at repetition. When to that is added the impropriety of allowing the choice of the appropriate language even to be suspected of having been affected by the demands of rhyming or scansion, it was hoped that the case would be left to enjoy an inglorious solitude. Sometimes what has been done at least has the value

---

[58] *Ibid.*, at pp. 511–12.

[59] *Ibid.*, at p. 513.

[60] *In re Tribune Review Publg. Co.*, 113 A.2d at 861.

[61] One other opinion in the book that did not appear in the state reports is Justice Musmanno's dissent in *Haefele* v. *Davis*, 110 A.2d 233 (Pa. 1955). Michael Angelo Musmanno, *Justice Musmanno Dissents* (Bobbs-Merrill 1956), pp. 537–39. The book does not indicate who compiled or edited it. For some Musmannodicts, see *post* pp. 205–09.

[62] Musmanno, at pp. 15–29.

[63] *Mackensworth* v. *Am. Trading Transp. Co.*, 367 F. Supp. 373 (E.D. Pa. 1973). An unhappy precursor has since been found: *Wheat* v. *Fraker*, 130 S.E.2d 251 (Ga. App. 1963).

of demonstrating what ought never to be done again. But all too often hopes are dashed; emulations of this sorry example have since appeared, both whole[64] and partial.[65] One imitator, indeed, seems to have jettisoned two centuries of Independence when he obtained a rhyme for "A prosecutor named Brown" by continuing "Representing the Crown."[66] Later he was removed from office, though not for this reason.[67] An alternative to verse is pastiche. Some judges have descended to mimicry of Mark Twain[68] or even the Old Testament.[69]

An award for Garrulous Irrelevance might well be claimed by the judgment in an unsuccessful action for damages for diverting and destroying fish in a navigable river.[70] After the initial two sentences, the first six columns of the report contain what the judge called his "prologue."[71] It ranged wide. *Inter alia*, there were the fifth day of the Creation, the Devil,[72] Nimrod, Isaac Walton, the twelve Apostles, the

---

[64] See *In re Rome*, 542 P.2d 676, 680, 681 (Kan. 1975); *Fisher* v. *Lowe*, 333 N.W.2d 67 (Mich. App. 1983), a rare example of regular scansion, apart from one lame line. See also *Brown* v. *State*, 216 S.E.2d 356, 357 n.3 (Ga. 1975), written in verse to meet a convivial challenge by a fellow judge; *Nelson* v. *State*, 465 N.E.2d 1391 (Ind. 1984), where one may hope that it was the verse that induced the lone dissent; *Devine* v. *Byrd*, 667 F. Supp. 414 (N.D. Tex. 1982), written in brief free verse.

[65] *U.S.* v. *Ven-Fuel Inc.*, 602 F.2d 747, 749, 750, 751, 753 (5th Cir. 1979) (14 lines at beginning of judgment; also cross-headings); *U.S.* v. *Batson*, 782 F.2d 1307, 1309, 1316 (5th Cir. 1986) (10 lines at beginning and 5 at end, all in limerick metre); and see *Anderson, Greenwood & Co.* v. *NLRB*, 604 F.2d 322, 323 (5th Cir. 1979).

[66] See *In re Rome*, 542 P.2d at 680.

[67] *State ex rel. Commn. on Judicial Qualifications* v. *Rome*, 623 P.2d 1307 (Kan. 1981).

[68] *State* v. *Knowles*, 739 S.W.2d 753, 754 (Mo. App. 1987) (*per* Nugent P.J.).

[69] *Zim* v. *Western Publg. Co.*, 573 F.2d 1318, 1320 (5th Cir. 1978) (*per* Goldberg J.). For other judgments by this judge, see A. Jordan, *Imagery, Humor, and the Judicial Opinion*, 41 Univ. Miami L. Rev. 693, 709–14 (1987). On judicial humor generally, see *The Judicial Humorist: A Collection of Judicial Opinions and Other Frivolities* (William L. Prosser ed., 1952). On American judicial humor, see George Rose Smith J., *A Critique of Judicial Humor*, 43 Ark. L. Rev. 1 (1990). See also *Amicus Humoriae: An Anthology of Legal Humor* (Robert M. Jarvis et al. eds., 2003).

[70] *Hampton* v. *North Carolina Pulp Co.*, 49 F. Supp. 625 (E.D.N.C. 1943) (*per* Meekins J.), *rev'd*, 139 F.2d 840 (4th Cir. 1944) (*per curiam*).

[71] *Hampton*, 49 F. Supp. at 628.

[72] The Devil, as a business man, "is a working success. He sat in the original game, not with one fruit tree, but with the cash capital of one snake, and now he has half the world grabbed and a diamond hitch on the other half": *ibid.*, at pp. 625–26.

miracle of the loaves and fishes, a "joke" about fish as a brain-food, Noah, Jonah, Capt. John Smith, and Herbert Hoover. There were then some statistics about the Great Flood and Mount Everest, a fable about Manu, more about Jonah and "a muzzle-loading leviathan,"[73] and John Smith again. Next there were General Lee, Shylock, the price of fish, the Woolsack, the introduction of wigs in England (and how they are made), Shadrach, Meshach and Abednego, the frequency of the judge being reversed by the Circuit Court,[74] Lord Thurlow, Charles Lamb, a "good story going around" about a man who sued his city in tort (and won, but suffered the reversal of the judgment in "precisely one sentence"[75]), and Selden and the Chancellor's foot.[76] Only then did the judgment turn to what the case was about; and in another seven columns, with some backward glances at the "prologue," the claim was dismissed. A mild comment was that by this judgment the judge had "proved himself to be unfit to be a judge."[77]

---

[73] *Ibid.*, at 626.

[74] "Oh, well, now, yes, of course, the Circuit Court gives me a lot of trouble. But 'hit ain't as bad as it mought be.' If I am not reversed in more than nine cases out of ten, I feel from fair to middling." *Hampton*, 49 F. Supp. at 628. The opinion has its own style of sleazy jocularity.

[75] *Ibid.* The case is plainly *Robinson* v. *Pioche, Bayerque & Co.*, 5 Cal. 460 (1855), where the judgment was four sentences long.

[76] *Hampton*, 49 F. Supp. at 628.

[77] George Rose Smith J., *A Primer of Opinion Writing, for Four New Judges*, 21 Ark. L. Rev. 197, 211 (1968).

11

~

STATUTES AT LARGER

THE BOUNDS of statute law seem limitless. The days are long past when it could be said: "The common law is nothing else but statutes worn out by time."[1] Nor are claims of primacy unquestioned: "All occasions do not arise at once. . . . A statute very seldom can take in all cases, therefore the common law, *that works itself pure* by rules drawn from the fountain of justice, is for this reason superior to an act of parliament."[2] Today, many a statute has been worked pure in the hands of the courts; and what cannot be worked pure but does too much or too little can readily be amended or repealed.

One instance of a well-meaning tropical reform appeared in Hong Kong. The Judicial Proceedings (Adjournment During Gale Warnings) Ordinance 1969[3] was enacted "to provide for the adjournment of judicial proceedings during a gale warning and for matters incidental thereto or connected therewith"; and "gale warning" was appropriately defined.[4] As would be expected, the main provisions of the Ordinance dealt with the adjournment and resumption of judicial proceedings. But then there was section 10: "In computing time for the purposes of any Ordinance, any day on which — (a) a gale warning is in force . . . shall not be reckoned in the computation of that time."

---

[1] *Collins* v. *Blantern* (1765) 2 Wils. K.B. 341 at 348 (*per* Wilmot C.J.), cited by Willes J. in *Pickering* v. *Ilfracombe Railway Co.* (1868) L.R. 3 C.P. 235 at 250.

[2] *Omychund* v. *Barker* (1744) 1 Atk. 21 at 33, *per* the future Lord Mansfield, when arguing as S.-G.

[3] No. 37 of 1969.

[4] By ss. 2, 5.

This had a wide-ranging effect.[5] There was not only the extension of many statutory periods, including periods of limitation and the perpetuity period, but also, perhaps, the postponement of the date on which a person attained full age. With a well-timed gale, many an act that would otherwise have been a day late might emerge as being a day early. Yet sometimes the section destroyed rather than saved. Thus if the minimum period of 21 clear days' notice had been given for a company meeting at which a special resolution was to be proposed, the advent of a gale warning while the notice was running would invalidate the meeting. After some 14 years of uneasy life, with many possibilities still unresolved, in 1983 the section was retrospectively repealed.[6]

There are, of course, many differences in style in legislative drafting, as in so many other things. The military style is simplicity itself. A mere parliamentary draftsman, for instance, must wrestle with the question of the person to make liable for any fault in a chattel: is it to be the manufacturer, the vendor, the possessor, the custodian, or who? Such problems have little appeal to the military mind. Thus during the U.S. Army administration of Hawaii in 1942, a legislative order was made to control dogs. With martial simplicity all problems of responsibility were avoided by enacting that —

1.   All dogs will be confined during the hours of blackout.

2.   All dogs will wear at all times except when actually confined, license tags issued by the proper authorities.[7]

Command, and it will be done: only a lawyer would quibble.

Australia did it differently. Army regulations provided for members of the forces to forfeit one-third of their pay while absent from duty suffering from acquired venereal disease.[8] But then there was what

---

[5] As pointed out by P.G. Willoughby (1981) 11 H.K.L.J. 60–62.

[6] By the Interpretation and General Clauses (Amendment) (No. 2) Ordinance 1983, No. 43 of 1983. This Ordinance took effect 60 days after publication, thereby allowing for the tally of some 55 gale days since the enactment of the Ordinance of 1969.

[7] General Order No. 54 (dated January 20, 1942), s. IV, reproduced in J. Garner Anthony, *Hawaii Under Army Rule* (1955), p. 147.

[8] War Financial (Military Forces) Regulations and Instructions, 1944, reg. 25(1).

became known as the Mata Hari proviso. This excluded forfeiture by any member of the forces "who acquired the disease while acting in the course of his duty."[9]

At the other extreme there is pomp and circumstance. Most lawyers who wished to make it plain in a statute that references to a "Schedule" were to a "Schedule to this Act" would simply say so in the definition section. But this was too unimpressive a course for the draftsman of the Brighton Corporation Act 1931. He provided that in the Act: "'The First Schedule' 'the Second Schedule' 'the Third Schedule' 'the Fourth Schedule' 'the Fifth Schedule' 'the Sixth Schedule' 'the Seventh Schedule' 'the Eighth Schedule' 'the Ninth Schedule' 'the Tenth Schedule' 'the Eleventh Schedule' 'the Twelfth Schedule' and 'the Thirteenth Schedule' mean respectively[10] the First Second Third Fourth Fifth Sixth Seventh Eighth Ninth Tenth Eleventh Twelfth and Thirteenth Schedules to this Act."[11] At least this brings more speedy comprehension than a definition set out in some Regulations in 1983.[12] It runs: "In these Regulations a reference to a Regulation is a reference to a Regulation contained therein, a reference in a Regulation or the Schedule to a paragraph is a reference to a paragraph of that Regulation or the Schedule and a reference in a paragraph to a sub-paragraph is a reference to a sub-paragraph of that paragraph."[13]

The draftsman of the Brighton Corporation Act 1931 plainly did not stand alone. His family name must have been Thorough; and the best-known family product may be set out in all its ponderous inglory, omitting only the formal and referential details. It is the Control of Tins Cans Kegs Drums and Packaging Pails (No. 10) Order, 1943:[14]

---

[9] *Ibid.*, reg. 25(2)(c). The object was to protect medical orderlies in treating infected patients.

[10] The touch of a master hand.

[11] 21 & 22 Geo. 5, c. cix, 1931, s. 6(54).

[12] The Teachers (Compensation) (Advanced Further Education) Regulations 1983, S.I. 1983 No. 856.

[13] Reg. 2(2). *Quaere* how this was intended to operate for references to paragraphs or sub-paragraphs in a specified Act (the Employment Protection (Consolidation) Act 1978): see, e.g., reg. 5(2).

[14] S.R. & O. 1943 No. 1216.

Whereas it appears to the Minister of Supply to be necessary for maintaining supplies and services essential to the life of the community and expedient that this Order should be made:

Now therefore the Minister of Supply in exercise of the powers conferred on him by Regulations 55 and 98 of the Defence (General) Regulations, 1939, hereby orders as follows: —

1.   The Control of Tins Cans Kegs Drums and Packaging Pails (No. 5) Order, 1942, as varied by the Control of Tins Cans Kegs Drums and Packaging Pails (No. 6) Order, 1942, the Control of Tins Cans Kegs Drums and Packaging Pails (No. 7) Order, 1942, the Control of Tins Cans Kegs Drums and Packaging Pails (No. 8) Order, 1942, and the Control of Tins Cans Kegs Drums and Packaging Pails (No. 9) Order, 1942, is hereby further varied in the Third Schedule thereto (which is printed at p. 2 of the printed (No. 6) Order), in "Part II, Commodities other than Food," by substituting for the reference "2A" therein, the reference "2A(1)"; and by deleting therefrom the reference "2B."
2.   This Order shall come into force on the 25th day of August, 1943; and may be cited as the Control of Tins Cans Kegs Drums and Packaging Pails (No. 10) Order, 1943, and this Order and the Control of Tins Cans Kegs Drums and Packaging Pails (Nos. 5–9) Orders, 1942, may be cited together as the Control of Tins Cans Kegs Drums and Packaging Pails (Nos. 5–10) Orders, 1942-3.

Dated this 19th day of August, 1943

That was all, save for a merciful explanatory note printed at the end of the Order: "The above Order enables tinplate to be used for tobacco and snuff tins other than cutter-lid tobacco tins."

The renown of this Order[15] encouraged imitators. One Order, dating from the days when the ill-fated post-war Government ground-nuts venture was slowly being forgotten, was said to provide: "In the Nuts (Unground) Other than Groundnuts Order, the expressions 'nuts' shall have reference to such nuts other than groundnuts as would, apart from this Amending Order, fail to qualify as nuts (unground) (other than

---

[15] I had the honour of knowing its draftsman.

groundnuts) by reason of their not being nuts (unground)."[16] The Order
has its appeal, but, alas, it is plain that it is an Order That Never Was,[17]
despite an assertion[18] that a judge of the Court of Session had put it
forward for recognition as the most inexplicable statute. But one
undoubted Order of 1944, with the accustomed majestic opening, brings
forth its *ridiculus mus*:

> In exercise of the powers conferred upon him by Regulation 55 of the
> Defence (General) Regulations, 1939, and of all other powers him enabling,
> the Minister of Food hereby makes the following Order:—

> The Food (Section Scheme) Order, 1943, as amended, shall be further
> amended by inserting in the Second Schedule thereto (which sets out the
> articles of food and drink to which the provisions of the said Order do not
> apply) the entry "Nuts."[19]

And that, apart, from the date of commencement, was all. Yet later that
year, at Bastogne, that *mus* was to become *gloriosus* in the mouth of
Brigadier General Anthony C. McAuliffe in his celebrated monosyllabic
reply on December 22 to the German invitation in the Ardennes to
surrender honorably.

It is not surprising that judges sometimes look wistfully at possibilities of escape. Certain provisions of the Finance Act 1940[20] related to

> the charging of estate duty in respect of certain benefits received by a
> deceased person from certain companies. It was these provisions that in *St
> Aubyn (LM) v Attorney-General (No. 2)*[21] Lord Simonds described as being
> "of unrivalled complexity and difficulty and couched in language so

---

[16] This is a conflation of the versions appearing at (1951) 95 S.J. 87, (1951) 157 E.G. 97,
and Ivor Brown, *I Break My Word* (1951), p. 84. The first of these versions substitutes
"underground" for "unground"; but this blunts the point (or a point). It has been asserted
that the "Order" was made in April 1956 (K. Hudson, *The Jargon of the Professions* (1978),
p. 40); if so, it was enacted five years after it had been ridiculed.

[17] Information from high drafting circles.

[18] *The Guinness Book of Records*, 22d ed. 1975, p. 191; 32d ed. 1985, p. 201.

[19] S.R. & O. 1944 No. 1198.

[20] Sects. 46–51, 58, 7th Sched.

[21] [1952] A.C. 15 at 30, cited 1 Misc. 351.

tortuous and obscure that I am tempted to reject them as meaningless." It is my misfortune that it has fallen to me to be required to attempt to call these provisions out of obscurity. The passage of a quarter of a century has not brought enlightenment, and counsel for the Crown and counsel for the company were at one in accepting and asserting that these provisions set exceptional problems. I am indeed grateful to them for their assistance, and in particular for suffering the multiplicity of questions that I put to them in my attempts to understand what Parliament has said. During the argument I think that all concerned must at times have regretted that Lord Simonds had not yielded to temptation; and I certainly regretted the failure of the expedient resorted to by Kay J in *Brown* v. *Collins*.[22] Confronted by difficulty, he expressed the desire that the case be taken direct to the Court of Appeal; but when the parties got there, the court not surprisingly held that it lacked jurisdiction, and so the case was returned to the judge for decision.[23]

On its return, a day's argument duly produced some four pages of extempore judgment that, not surprisingly, seems to have escaped appeal; for both counsel advanced the same contentions. The former Court of Appeal in Chancery was more yielding; for some ten years earlier, when Wickens V.-C. had felt "pressed by the conflicting decisions on the point," his request for the case to be taken for decision by the Court of Appeal had been granted.[24]

A statute may command simplicity of utterance without itself achieving it. One Minnesota statute governing certain insurance policies requires all insurers "to use policy and contract forms which are written in simple and commonly used language, which are logically and clearly arranged, which are printed in a legible format, and which are generally understandable."[25] This is reinforced by provisions that require such policies to be filed with a commissioner and to be "written in language easily readable and understandable by a person of average intelligence and education."[26] In determining whether for this purpose any such

---

[22] [1883] W.N. 155; 25 Ch.D. 56 at 57.

[23] *Inland Revenue Commissioners* v. *Standard Industrial Trust Ltd.* [1977] S.T.C. 330 at 332 (*per* Megarry V.-C.); *affirmed* [1979] S.T.C. 372.

[24] *Re Bignold's Settlement Trusts* (1872) 41 L.J.Ch. 235 at 236; 7 Ch.App. 223; 20 W.R. 345.

[25] Readability of Insurance Policies Act, Minn. Stat. s. 72C.02 (1984).

[26] *Ibid.*, ss. 72C.06(1), 10(1).

policy is "readable," the commissioner is directed to consider a variety of factors, including the simplicity of the sentence structure, the shortness of the sentences used, the extent to which commonly used and understood words are employed, and the extent to which legal terms are avoided.[27]

These precepts, though admirable, plainly leave considerable scope for argument; and so the statute sought to clothe "readability" with a form of mathematical certainty. The Act provides that the commissioner "shall disapprove" any policy if it is not "accompanied by a certified Flesch scale analysis readability score of more than 40";[28] and "'Flesch scale analysis readability score' means a measurement of the ease of readability of a policy or contract made pursuant to the procedures prescribed in section 72C.09."[29] By that section, the entire contract must be analysed if it contains not more than 10,000 words of text, though a sampling process is permitted if the contract is longer than that.[30] The section then lays down[31] a threefold process of analysis: "(i) The number of words and sentences in the text shall be counted and the total number of words divided by the total number of sentences. The figure obtained shall be multiplied by a factor of 1.015. (ii) The total number of syllables shall be counted and divided by the total number of words. The figure obtained shall be multiplied by a factor of 84.6. (iii) The sum of the figures computed under (i) and (ii) subtracted from 206.835 equals the Flesch scale analysis readability score for the policy or contract."[32]

Without resorting to the fine degree of precision given by three places of decimals, it can readily be seen that a contract that averages ten words to a sentence and two syllables to a word would easily fail the test.[33] Yet

[27] *Ibid.*, s. 72C.06(2).

[28] *Ibid.*, s. 72C.10(2)(a).

[29] *Ibid.*, s. 72C.04(3). For the Flesch test, see Rudolf Flesch, *The Art of Readable Writing* (25th ed. 1974), pp. 247 *et seq.*

[30] Readability of Insurance Policies Act, Minn. Stat. s. 72C.09(1).

[31] *Ibid.*, s. 72C.09(2)(a).

[32] Section 72C.09(2)(b) defines such matters as what counts as one word (e.g., "Vice-President" but not "Vice President"), and what counts as a sentence (a new sentence begins after every period, colon, or semicolon).

[33] The score would be 10.15 under (i) and 169.2 under (ii), making 179.35. Subtracted from 206.835, this gives 27.485, far less than the requisite 40.

one beneficial side-effect of the statute may be the restoration to favour of the definite article, so long abandoned in much American legal drafting. "The insured" averages 1.5 syllables a word, instead of the 2.0 of "Insured."

Sad to relate, the Flesch Scale Analysis Readability Score of the statute itself is nowhere revealed: yet plainly there must be grave suspicions. To take one of the shortest subsections, section 72C.04(7) runs: "'Person' means any individual, corporation, partnership, association, business trust or voluntary organization." This fails the test miserably, falling short of the requisite 40 points by nearly 100.[34] Perhaps insurance corporations have built up a collection of monosyllabic clauses with little or no significance that can be inserted in policies to preserve them from the perils of a high polysyllabic count. Even so desperate a failure as the subsection quoted above could be made to sail triumphantly through the test by abjuring attempts at brevity and simply adding suitable syllabic diluents such as "If you do not know what this means, do not give up. Look up the words that are not clear to you. Then read it once more." The score for the four sentences would be 9.896 under (i) and 134.492 under (ii). Subtracted from 206.835, this gives 62.447, which is well over the requisite 40. Diluents can achieve much. Over two-thirds of the massive 1,269 that "antidisestablishmentarianism" scores under (ii) (or the clown's "honorificabilitudinitatibus" in *Love's Labours Lost*[35]) could be removed by simply adding "Rah! Rah! Rah!"

Some formulae emerge from the Bench rather than the Legislature. Thus in the United States it has been said that in deciding the often difficult question whether an interlocutory (or preliminary) injunction should be granted, the court should use the help of "a simple formula: grant the preliminary injunction if but only if $P \times H_p > (1 - P) \times H_d$, or, in words, only if the harm to the plaintiff if the injunction is denied, multiplied by the probability that the denial would be an error (that the plaintiff, in other words, will win at the trial), exceeds the harm to the

---

[34] The score would be 12.18 under (i) and 246.75 under (ii), making 258.93. Subtracted from 206.835, this gives minus 52.095.

[35] Act 5, sc. 1; or words more than half as long again: see 2 Misc. 160.

defendant if the injunction is granted, multiplied by the probability that granting the injunction would be an error."[36] But this stroke of invention attracted dissent; the necessity and the wisdom of adopting a formula were both questioned, especially as the variables remained unquantified and there was no provision for measuring P or H_p or H_d. Thus, "Like a Homeric Siren the majority's formula offers a seductive but deceptive security."[37]

Some statutory provisions are indeed far-reaching. England once provided embanked continuity by enacting that where one of its many Rent Acts had "become applicable to any dwelling-house, . . . it shall continue to apply thereto whether or not the dwelling-house continues to be one to which this Act applies."[38] Judicial comment was mild: the only practical effect of this "still-unsolved conundrum" in its half-century life appeared "to be to waste time in its abortive discussion."[39] In Western Australia, internal paramountcy was established by enacting that "the provisions of this section have effect in respect of shops to which these provisions apply, notwithstanding any of the other provisions of this Act."[40] Florida went further, producing a summit of universal applicability worthy of insertion in almost any Act almost anywhere: "Whenever applicable, the provisions of this Act shall apply notwithstanding any provision of this Act to the contrary."[41] Brevity could scarcely balance tautology with contrariety more neatly: the Act applies if it is applicable even if it provides that it is not to apply. Wartime Britain evolved a provision to which King Canute would no doubt have been pleased to give the Royal Assent. The Minister of Agriculture, Fisheries and Food was given wide powers to prevent the spread of pests or diseases among bees, including power to make an

[36] *Am. Hosp. Supply Corp.* v. *Hospital Prods. Ltd.*, 780 F.2d 589, 593 (7th Cir. 1986) (*per* Posner J., speaking for himself and Pell J.).

[37] *Ibid.*, at pp. 609, 610 (*per* Swygert J.).

[38] Increase of Rent and Mortgage Interest (Restrictions) Act 1920, s. 12(6), not repealed until Rent Act 1968, Sched. 17.

[39] Coghlan, *Law of Rent Restriction in Eire* (2d ed. 1950), p. viii (*per* Black J.).

[40] Factories and Shops Act, 1963, s. 92(2) (Western Australia).

[41] 1963 Fla. Laws, ch. 63-379, s. l(3).

order (which every law-abiding bee would no doubt have respected) "for prohibiting or restricting the movement of bees."[42]

One drafting triumph is to give a statutory instrument a title that contains an unusual word and then to mention the word nowhere else in the instrument. An example is The Zoonoses Order 1975.[43] What are zoonoses? The *Oxford English Dictionary*[44] knows them not, and although the Order includes a number of definitions (including "animal" as meaning "any kind of mammal, except man, and any kind of four-footed beast which is not a mammal"[45]), neither in the definitions nor elsewhere does it mention zoonoses or say what they are, though "designated organisms" abound. Then, with his creation complete and unexplained, the draftsman makes an exultant gesture of omniscience by appending an explanatory note that forms no part of the Order. There at last zoonoses stand revealed as "diseases which man can contract from animals or birds." The Zoonoses Order 1988[46] omits even this; and nowhere is there the diaeresis that would aid pronunciation. America is richer, with the term itself defined, and over a dozen related words, including zoonosis, zoonoses, zoonotic, zoopaleontology, and zoopery.[47]

The draftsman, however, can do better than that. It is, of course, hardly fair to present a referential enactment without setting out the provisions to which it refers. Yet few would expect even the most ample quotations of every subsection mentioned to bring clarity to a subsection such as this: "Subject to subsection (4) of this section, subsections (3) and (4) of section twenty-five of this Act shall apply where the provisions of section twenty-three of this Act have effect as applied by subsection (1) of this section as they apply where those provisions have effect as applied by subsection (1) or subsection (2) of the said section twenty-five."[48] It is better, of course, if referentialism can

---

[42] Agriculture (Miscellaneous Provisions) Act, 1941, s. 11(1)(c).

[43] S.I. 1975 No. 1030.

[44] (2d ed. 1989), vol. 20, p. 824.

[45] Art. 2(1).

[46] S.I. 1988 No. 2264.

[47] See Funk & Wagnall's *New Standard Dictionary* (1927) and Webster's *Third New International Dictionary* (1971).

[48] Land Compensation Act 1961, s. 26(3).

be combined with some esoteric concept such as a doctrine of continuous revival: and this Ontario achieved with section 450 of its Municipal Act:[49]

> In all cases where land is sold for arrears of taxes whether such sale is or is not valid, then so far as regards rights of entry adverse to a bona fide claim or right, whether valid or invalid, derived mediately or immediately under such sale, section 10 of The Conveyancing and Law of Property Act[50] does not apply, to the end and intent that in such cases the right or title of a person claiming adversely to any such sale shall not be conveyed where any person is in occupation adversely to such right or title, and that in such cases the Common Law and sections 2, 4 and 6 of the statute passed in the 32nd year of the reign of King Henry VIII, and chapter 9,[51] be revived, and the same are and shall continue to be revived.

On inquiry as to the prospects for this survival, a distinguished Ontario judge sagely said that it was very dangerous to repeal what you do not understand; but in 1984[52] Ontario took the risk, and the revival is no more.

There is great scope in "deeming"[53] and its associated operations. Thus the Leasehold Reform Bill 1967, as passed by the House of Commons, contained important amendments to the Places of Worship (Enfranchisement) Act, 1920, s. 2. One of these provided that "for purposes of sections 77 to 85 of the Railways Clauses Consolidation Act 1845 the use of the premises as a place of worship or minister's house, whether in conjunction with other purposes or not, shall be deemed to be the railway and the trustees shall be deemed to be the railway company."[54] But this imperishable concept did not, alas, survive the Committee stage in the House of Lords.[55] On the other hand, there

---

[49] Revised Statutes of Ontario, 1980, c. 302.

[50] The section enables contingent, executory, and future interests in land, and possibilities coupled with an interest, to be disposed of by deed.

[51] 32 Hen. 8, c. 9, 1540 (Maintenance, Champerty, and Embracery).

[52] C. 48; and R.S.O. 1990 accordingly omits it.

[53] Lord Radcliffe once spoke kindly of it: *St. Aubyn* v. *Attorney-General* [1952] A.C. 15 at 53.

[54] See the Bill as introduced into the House of Lords (June 21, 1967) cl. 41(3).

[55] See the clause as revised and renumbered, cl. 40(4), in the draft dated July 12, 1967.

is one sublime sentence that so held Parliament in thrall that it managed to appear, almost unchanged,[56] in at least sixteen National Insurance Acts[57] in little more than twenty-five years. It runs: "For the purpose of this Part of this Schedule a person over pensionable age, not being an insured person, shall be treated as an employed person if he would be an insured person were he under pensionable age and would be an employed person were he an insured person."

In Ireland, deeming has been carried into the family. For certain death duty purposes, "relative" has been defined as meaning "a husband or wife, ancestor, lineal descendant, or brother or sister or descendant of a brother or sister."[58] But to this comprehensible concept has been added a provision that, for these purposes, "a company which is controlled by any one or more of the deceased and relatives of the deceased shall be regarded as being itself a relative of the deceased."[59] This gives rise to many speculations. Is my aunt's company my aunt or my uncle? Is one to say "My sister was wound up yesterday"? And what of the prohibited degrees of relationship? If your sister's company merges with your brother's company, what is the status of all their little subsidiaries? The possibilities seem boundless. Indeed, these examples of the boundless variety of drafting fully justify one of the provisions of the California Civil Code, with its charming side-note: "*§1597. Impossibility, what.* Everything is deemed possible except that which is impossible in the nature of things."[60]

Outside California, however, there is decency to be considered. As

---

[56] In the first five Acts, "purpose" is in the singular, whereas in the other ten it is in the plural. The contrast doubtless carries one deep into the arcana of legal drafting.

[57] Acts of 1946, 1952, 1953, 1954, 1957, 1959, 1960, 1963, 1964, 1965, 1967, 1969, 1971, 1972, 1973, and 1974. Each is entitled "National Insurance Act," save that the Act of 1952 has the prefatory words "Family Allowances and"; the Act of 1954 has "(No. 2)" after "Insurance"; the Act of 1964 achieves an "&c." after "Insurance"; and the Act of 1973 has "and Supplementary Benefits" after "Insurance." The provision knows its place: it is always in Part II of a Schedule. This is usually the First Schedule, but in the Acts of 1960, 1973, and 1974 it is the Second Schedule, and in the Acts of 1952, 1954, and 1957 it is the Third Schedule. The Acts thus leaven constancy with variety.

[58] Finance Act, 1965, s. 20(1) (Ireland).

[59] *Ibid.*, s. 20(2)(b).

[60] Enacted 1872: see Deering's *California Code* (1960).

Lord Macnaghten once pointed out: "Everything is possible. Even a Lord Chancellor may possibly make a mistake. But one must use one's common sense, and there are some mistakes which it is hardly decent to attribute to the Court."[61] So too in relying upon definition clauses (such as the general provision[62] that the singular includes the plural and that words importing one gender include the other[63]), technical accuracy should be tempered by a reasonable discretion, a precept forgotten in the draft of a police regulation that began: "When a policeman is pregnant . . . ."[64]

---

[61] *Hatton* v. *Harris* [1892] A.C. 547 at 564.

[62] See Interpretation Act 1978, s. 6.

[63] In Canada, "all other genders," postulating at least four: see 2 Misc. 184.

[64] The source is unimpeachable.

12

~

A PLAIN AND SIMPLE QUESTION

THOUGH justly esteemed, simplicity of utterance is not a universal judicial achievement.[1] Kelly C.B. was not noted for it. To one witness he was reported to have said:

My good woman . . . you must give me an answer, in the fewest possible words of which you are capable, to the plain and simple question, whether, when you were crossing the street with the baby on your arm, and the omnibus was coming down on the right side, and the cab on the left side, and the brougham was trying to pass the omnibus, you saw the plaintiff between the brougham and the omnibus, or between the brougham and the cab, or between the omnibus and the cab, or whether and when you saw him at all, and whether or not near the brougham, cab, and omnibus, or either or any two, and which, of them respectively — or how was it?[2]

A century later Kelly C.B. found a spiritual descendant in Frankfurter J., in the United States Supreme Court during the argument in a racial desegregation case concerning the Little Rock School Board.[3] The subject was the implications of previous decisions of the Supreme Court, and the Board's desire to postpone integration. The judge was reported as saying to counsel for the Board:

Mr. Butler, why aren't the two decisions of this court, the first one, which laid down as a Constitutional requirement that this court unanimously felt

[1] See also 2 Misc. 161.
[2] *A Generation of Judges* (1886), pp. 51–52.
[3] *Cooper* v. *Aaron*, 358 U.S. 1 (1958).

compelled to agree upon, and the second opinion recognizing that this was a change of what had been supposed to be the provisions of the Constitution, and recognizing that and the kind of life that has been built under the contrary conception said, as equity also has said, you must make appropriate accommodation to the specific circumstances of the situation instead of having a procrustean bed where everybody's legs are cut off or stretched to fit the length of the bed, and who is better to decide that than the local United States Judges, why isn't that a National policy?[4]

The transition from a multitude of words to the singular brings no assurance of lucidity; for so many words have multiple meanings that shatter the clarity. Partnerships vary greatly, from long-standing partnerships to partnerships in a single venture;[5] and today more "partners" are linked by sex than by business. Again:

> "Home" is a somewhat nebulous concept, incapable of precise definition. Nor would it be possible to obtain any measure of agreement between reasonable men as to the essential constituents of a real home. For example, uxorious persons might consider that a real home cannot exist without a wife and children; hardened bachelors might take an entirely opposite view. Some people might hold that there can be no real home without television; others that there can be none with it.[6]

Under the poor law, the maxim was that "a man's home is where his wife lives,"[7] or "ubi uxor ibi domus."[8]

Lord Blackburn had "no doubt that in common talk, the language of men not speaking technically, a 'person' does not include an artificial person, that is to say, a corporation. Nobody in common talk if he were asked, Who is the richest person in London, would answer, The London and North-Western Railway Company. The thing is absurd."[9] Again, an

---

[4] H.S. Thomas, *Felix Frankfurter, Scholar on the Bench* (1960), p. 356, citing a press report of the stenographic record.

[5] *Mann* v. *D'Arcy* [1968] 1 W.L.R. 893 at 899.

[6] *Herbert* v. *Byrne* [1964] 1 W.L.R. 519 at 528 (*per* Salmon L.J.).

[7] *Wellington* v. *Whitchurch* (1863) 32 L.J.M.C. 189 at 192 (*per* Cockburn C.J.).

[8] See the argument in *R.* v. *Norwood* (1867) L.R. 2 Q.B. 457 at 459.

[9] *Pharmaceutical Society* v. *London & Provincial Supply Association Ltd.* (1880) 5 App.Cas. 857 at 869. For the Old Bailey meaning of "person," see 2 Misc. 166.

agent is, strictly speaking, a person who has authority to act on behalf of another, particularly in making contracts. Yet in daily life the term is used to embrace many others: "No word is more commonly and constantly abused than the word 'agent.'"[10] Bowen characteristically resorted to Latin. When making a claim to land on the basis that his client's donkey had been habitually pastured on it, he was asked by the judge whether the plaintiff was claiming through his accredited agent. The reply was prompt: "Yes, my Lord. My contention is Qui facit per asinum facit per se."[11] But some words are immune. When a judge refers to "murder" as "a term of art,"[12] the lawyer knows what he means, though the layman may at first be a little puzzled. A modern phrase that is well set in its progress towards becoming a term of art is "work to rule." This "has a perfectly well known meaning, namely 'Give the rules a meaning which no reasonable man could give them and work to that.'"[13]

The term "bum-bailiff" is not lacking in etymological interest. The word is usually said to have been derived from "bum," a vulgarism for buttocks or bottom. A bailiff employed to make arrests or distraints, it is said, is "so called because he attacks from the rear," or "comes behind to make arrests," and is in "close pursuit of debtors"; he is the bailiff "that is close at the debtor's back, or that catches him in the rear," and he is "a bailiff of the meanest kind."[14]

This chorus is impressive but unconvincing. Many a bailiff is fully frontal in his approach, and a directional derivation ignores the usage of more than two centuries:

Bailiffs, or sheriff's officers, are either bailiffs of hundreds, or special bailiffs. Bailiffs of hundreds are officers appointed over those respective districts by

[10] *Kennedy* v. *De Trafford* [1897] A.C. 180 at 188 (*per* Lord Herschell).

[11] (1902) 113 L.T.News. 357.

[12] *Holford* v. *Bailey* (1850) 13 Q.B. 426 at 446 (*per* Parke B.): "terms of art, such as the words 'felony,' 'murder,' 'burglary.'"

[13] *Secretary of State for Employment* v. *Associated Society of Locomotive Engineers and Firemen (No. 2)* [1972] 2 Q.B. 455 at 466 (*per* Sir John Donaldson P.).

[14] *Oxford Dictionary of English Etymology* (1966), s.v.; Chambers' *Twentieth Century Dictionary* (1972), s.v.; Webster's *Third New International Dictionary* (1961), s.v.; *O.E.D.* (2d ed. 1989), s.v. Funk & Wagnall's *New Standard Dictionary* (1927) eschews any derivation.

the sheriffs, to collect fines therein, to summon juries, to attend the judges and justices at the assises and quarter sessions, and also to execute writs and process in the several hundreds. But, as these are generally plain men, and not thoroughly skilful in this latter part of their office, that of serving writs, and making arrests and executions, it is now usual to join special bailiffs with them; who are generally mean persons, employed by the sheriffs on account only of their adroitness and dexterity in hunting and seising their prey. The sheriff being answerable for the misdemeanors of these bailiffs, they are therefore usually bound in an obligation with sureties for the due execution of their office, and thence are called bound-bailiffs; which the common people have corrupted into a much more homely appellation.[15]

Other words are far more indefinite and laden with overtones. In 1668 there arose the question whether a man might lawfully marry his great-uncle's widow; and it was held that he could. In the course of the case there appears to have been some argument as to what intercourse was "unnatural"; and Vaughan C.J. had something to say on this:

> To speak strictly what is unnatural, it is evident that nothing which actually is, can be said to be unnatural; for Nature is but the production of effects from causes sufficient to produce them; and whatever is, had a sufficient cause to make it be, else it had never been; and whatsoever is effected by a cause sufficient to effect it, is as natural as any other thing effected by its sufficient cause. And in this sense nothing is unnatural but that which cannot be, and consequently nothing that is, is unnatural; and so no Copulation of any Man with any Woman, nor an effect of that Copulation by Generation, can be said unnatural; for if it were, it could not be; and if it be, it had sufficient cause.[16]

Two centuries later Tweedledee was to be recorded as saying: "Contrariwise, if it was so, it might be; and if it were so, it would be: but as it isn't, it ain't. That's logic."[17]

Then there is the supernatural. Those who regard Westminster Hall as doing little more than providing a housing for the courts of law before

---

[15] 1 Bl.Comm. 345.

[16] *Harrison* v. *Burwell* (1668) Vaugh. 206 at 221.

[17] Lewis Carroll, *Through the Looking-Glass* (1871), c. 4.

the Royal Courts of Justice were erected in the nineteenth century should consider an annuity granted by Edward VI on May 16, 1547, to Sir Anthony Denny. The motive for giving the annuity appears from the grant, which records that Henry VIII had granted Sir Anthony certain premises for life, including "the houses and mansions called Paradise and Hell within Westminster Hall," and also "the house or mansion called Purgatorie within the said hall," but that the King had later taken into his own hands, as storage for the records and rolls of the Exchequer, "the said houses called Paradise, Hell and Purgatorie."[18]

Hell, of course, was properly staffed. It was officially recorded that on November 28, 1626, Charles I informed Sir Thomas Richardson (who had that day become C.J.C.P.) that "the Lord Chief Justice of the Common Pleas has been used to appoint a clerk of the Treasury, anciently called the Clerk of Hell, for keeping the records of that Court. It is the King's pleasure that as soon as Sir Thos. had the Chief Justiceship he would admit Edward Nicholas to the said clerkship."[19] Nor was Hell an English monopoly: the old Four Courts in Dublin were formerly approached from a lane bearing the name "Hell," and in that lane many lawyers had their chambers. This led to advertisements of the type: "To be let, furnished apartments in Hell. They are well suited for a lawyer."[20] The contrast with ordinary people who on earth do dwell is striking; for there is high authority for the view that the Almighty has appointed the earth "as the suburbs of heaven to be the habitation of man."[21]

Commercial medicine has long been a rich source of inventive titles. An example is provided by a style of parliamentary drafting that is with us no more. The Schedule to an Excise Act of 1812[22] sets out a long list of medicines that were subject to duty. Examples show how dull are the names of today: Addison's Re-animating European Balsam; Aetherial

---

[18] *Calendar of Patent Rolls, 1547–1548* (1924), p. 248.

[19] *Calendar of State Papers (Domestic) 1625–1626* (1858), p. 482.

[20] J.R. O'Flanagan, *The Munster Circuit* (1880), pp. 70, 71.

[21] Co.Litt. 4a.

[22] 52 Geo. 3, c. 150, 1812.

Anodyne Spirit; American Alterative Pills; Antapoplectic Pills; Arquebusade Water; Asiatic Bilious Pills; Bateman's Golden Spirit of Scurvy
Grass; Boldersome's Worm Cakes; Brodum's Nervous Cordial; Cornwell's
Opodeldoc; Dalmhoy's Sal Poignant; Essence Kayou Pouti; Felton's
Mucilage of Marsh Mallows; Grand Specific or Infallible Antidote to
Consumptions; Guest's Welcome Guest; Hewitt's Analambanic Pills;
Imperial Anodyne Opodeldoc; James's Analeptic Pills; James's Tin
Powder for the Worms; Jesuits' Drops; Lucas's Pure Drops of Life;
Ormskirk Medicine for the Bite of a Mad Dog; Robert's Worm Sugar
Plums; Roe's English Coffee for Nervous Disorders; Senate's Aromatic
Steel Lozenges, or Lozenges of Steel; Shaw's Sovereign Itch Ointment;
Simson's Infallible Aethereal Tincture; Smellome's Eye Salve; Smith's
Cooling Opening Pills; Spinliff's Aromatic Bilious Cordial; Sterne's
Tincture of Gout Drops; Swinfen's Electuary; Ward's Liquid Sweat; and
Zimmerman's Stimulating Fluid.

Then there are little-known pockets of law, living but obscure. An
examination candidate might well feel aggrieved if he were required to
discuss and explain *jus liquidissimum* and *rusticum judicium*; for he
could with justice point to the absence of these terms even from books
such as *Jowitt, Stroud, Words and Phrases*, and the index to *Halsbury's
Laws of England*.[23] Yet the terms are to be found in the law reports. It is
the right of salvage that is "what the law calls *jus liquidissimum*, the
clearest general right that they who have saved lives and property at sea
should be rewarded for such salutary exertions; and those who say that
they are not bound to reward, ought to prove their exemption in very
definite terms, and by arguments of irresistible cogency."[24]

Rusticum judicium, on the other hand, is to be found not only at sea,
but also embedded in copyright; and its potential for extension is great.[25]

[23] *Jowitt's Dictionary of English Law* (2d ed. 1977; Supp. 1985); *Stroud's Judicial Dictionary*
(5th ed. 1986); *Words and Phrases Judicially Defined* (3d ed. 1990); *Halsbury's Laws of
England, Consolidated Index* (1996). Across the Atlantic, there is partial redemption in
Black's Law Dictionary (8th ed. 2004), p. 1361.

[24] *The Waterloo* (1820) 2 Dods. 433 at 435 (*per* Sir William Scott); and see *France Fenwick
Tyne and Wear Co. Ltd.* v. *H.M. Procurator General* [1942] A.C. 667 at 690.

[25] E.g., to the determination of the capital value of an annuity *dum casta et sola*: see 2 *Misc.*
232. For the broad axe, see *post* p. 367. For an export to the Pacific, see *Tito* v. *Waddell
(No. 2)* [1977] Ch. 106 at 338, 341.

If without A's permission B publishes a book or a periodical that includes A's copyright material, the damages for conversion that A can claim must to some extent depend upon how much of the book or periodical consists of what is A's. His involuntary contribution may be long but of little importance, or it may be short though of great value. The appropriate fraction of the total selling price of the book or periodical thus cannot "be arrived at by any exact method of calculation. I think," said Lord Wright M.R., that "it must be a matter of what has been called rusticum judicium."[26] Soon afterwards Crossman J. proceeded to assess damages on this basis,[27] only to be told that his use of the term was "an excess of modesty, considering the industry he has expended";[28] but in the end his assessment prevailed.[29]

Misplaced words are another matter; and "only" is often in peril. Long years ago, a notice exhibited in the gardens of Lincoln's Inn moved a very learned Chancery junior, Arthur Cole, to address some verses to his former pupil-master and one of the benchers, Sir Arthur Underhill. It ran as follows:[30]

From a tree in our gardens our Benchers have hung
A new notice "DOGS only admitted if led":
May an equity draftsman respectfully ask
Whether what they intended is what they have said?

"Dogs only"? Not men, women, children or cats?
And "only admitted"? Not fondled or fed?
These are doubts which should be expected to be
Overcome by a junior only if led.

English claims less precision than Latin or Greek,
In the classics our Benchers have nothing to learn:

---

26 *Ash* v. *Dickie* [1936] Ch. 655 at 664.

27 *Sutherland Publishing Co. Ltd.* v. *Caxton Publishing Co. Ltd.* [1937] Ch. 294 at 304.

28 S.C., [1938] Ch. 174 at 195 (*per* MacKinnon L.J., dissenting).

29 S.C., [1939] A.C. 178, reversing the majority in the Court of Appeal; and see at p. 194 (*per* Lord Roche).

30 This has been slightly revised from a copy found in circulation many years later. It has less trouble with its feet than the version in *Verses from Lincoln's Inn* (n.d.: pub. 1975), p. 4.

> But why have they placed this poor "only" between
> The only two words that it does not concern?

Sir Arthur replied, invoking the then Under-Treasurer of the Inn, Rowe:

> A fallacy lurks in your excellent rhyme,
> And I'll have you and others to know
> Your Benchers, to save themselves trouble and time,
> Left the words of that notice to Rowe.

> But if for the future your accurate mind
> Would prefer *Key & Elphinstone's* aid,
> Your name I will mention, if it's not unkind,
> To their Worships as draftsman — unpaid.

> So, finding this rhyming has made a large hole
> In the time which to clients is due,
> Believe me sincerely, my dear Arthur Cole,
> I'm your quondam instructor A.U.

Time has not brought impeccability. In 1965 a Practice Direction[31] gravely informed the world: "The Lord Chancellor and the Lords of Appeal in Ordinary have agreed that from the beginning of next term Queen's Counsel appearing before the Appellate Committee of the House of Lords will only wear full-bottomed wigs when their Lordships are sitting in the Chamber either for the hearing of appeals or for delivering judgments." Punctuation may also be potent in making a document intelligible or the reverse. Thus if a home-made will gives a number of legacies ranging from £25 to £250, and then leaves a residue of over £14,000 to be "divided between those beneficiaries who have only received small amounts," the presence or absence after "beneficiaries" of a comma or its equivalent may be of much significance.[32] A jingle that was current over two centuries ago illustrates the power of punctuation:

---

[31] Practice Direction of April 13, 1965 [1965] 1 W.L.R. 727.
[32] See *Re Steel* [1979] Ch. 218.

> Every Lady in this Land
> Hath *twenty* Nails upon *each* Hand;
> *Five and twenty* on Hands *and Feet*:
> And this is *true*, without Deceit.[33]

The question, of course, is what changes in the punctuation have to be made in order to bring sense to the rhyme.[34] Other examples abound. Consider "X said Y is a thief" and the inversion produced by a pair of commas: "X, said Y, is a thief." Consider also the ten-fold "had": the question is how to punctuate into intelligibility the words, "where X had had had Y had had had had had had had my approval."[35]

Mixed metaphors and euphuism are another matter; and the reaper may gather from the law a rich harvest of excesses.[36] Some are ancient. It was Coke who observed of certain expired statutes that "they were so like labyrinthes, with such intricate windings and turnings, as little or no fruit proceeded of them."[37] But that is as nothing when compared with the preface or foreword to a seventeenth-century volume of law reports, here deservedly reproduced in its entirety. It is probably unrivalled as an exhibitionist exercise in tortuosity, emphasising that the office of language is to conceal thought.[38] Some may take pleasure in teasing some meaning from its multilingual thickets, and perhaps essay a précis more ample than "Man, being vile, needs law: here is some of it." Others may prefer to do no more than glance through the next two pages, and reflect on the prudence of the second edition[39] of the reports ("carefully Corrected and Amended") in wholly omitting the preface. But on any footing, it deserves rescue from its centuries of oblivion, to serve as an

---

[33] J. Burrow, *An Essay on Punctuation* (1772), p. 11. The rhyme was quoted in *Marshall* v. *Cottingham* [1982] Ch. 82 at 88.

[34] The semicolon in line 2 should be moved three words back, and a semicolon should be inserted after the first word in line 3.

[35] "Where X had had 'had' Y had had 'had had'; 'had had' had my approval."

[36] See also *ante*, pp. 8–9.

[37] 3 Co.Inst. 204.

[38] See *post* p. 306.

[39] 1675.

outstanding demonstration of the perils of excess. Some may even find that familiarity breeds a strange affection:

> Upon the strict survey of natures products, there is nothing to be found, whether in the bosome of its causes, or in its singularities, within the convexity of the universe, which being contemplated at an intellectuall distance, beyond the magnetick effluvium of our senses, doth not felicitate with more certainty, nedum, probability, as more obsequious to the prototype of its projection, then Man: the very cronologie of whose errors doth compute his existency, an ingratefull returne for the dignity of his essence, which unmolested and freed from the procacity of his junior and inferior faculties, would have fixt him in the harmonious orbe of his motion, and have secured him, as well against the scandal of a planetique, as the ecclipse of his native glory: But alas! the doome is past, ex Athaeniis in barathrum, hee's now benighted with ignorance, Phainomena's, and verities; an ignis fatuus, and a linck-boy, are eodem calculo; which condition imposes upon him something more then metaphorically, the semblance of a moth-flye, which is in nothing so solicitous, as in its owne ruine: neverthelesse had privation in his judgement been the onely losse, hee could then have undergone; but his poco di matto, but his will, and too too cereous potestatives, have stigmatiz'd him in all his habitudes, undiqueversum, with a more reproachfull sobriquet of vellacazo teso, in which shamefull state, forgetting his constitutive nature, and rudely breaking through his divisive difference, he seems now to be lost, if perchance he is not found in the confused thickets and forests of his genus; where measuring his actions (rather ausa furosa) by the cubit of his strength, he giddyes himselfe into a maze of inquietudes, shuffling the malefactor and judge into one chaire, to make up the riddle of all injustice, because all things are just; hence was the no lesse opportune, then needfull venu of Cicero's Vir magnus quidem & sapiens, &c. Hence the blissefull emergency of all laws, the limitting repagula's of his insolency, and the just monuments of his depravity: but hinc polydacrya, he is yet so unwilling to forgoe his bainefull appetite (reasons too potent competitor) that he is still perswaded he may safely act without controlment; though like a partridge in a net, he finds no other guerdon for his bussle, then a more hopelesse irretition: and as if he were damned to be a fury to himselfe, he will not admit that wholesome and thriving councell, That obedience to laws is a much more thriving peice of prudence then sacrifice; and as much differenced as innocency, and guilt ignorant of its expiation. Whence I conceive by a just title, to keep the world

from combats, and the reward of vertue from violation, the wisest in all ages have had the priviledge, not onely of prescribing, but of coacting the orders of regiment amongst others, who by necessary complot have engaged for observance; which somthing seems to repaire the loss; yet so, as by our dianoeticks, we have opportunity enough to see, and like the satyre in the fable, to feare, our idaeated humanity, although in a more sublime contemplation, it may fall out otherwise, in respect that the law of essences are more certaine, and of a far more facile direction, then those of existency; which is so necessarily entituled to infinite incertainty, from approximation of accidents, that it would now be an equall madnesse for the governour to think he can, or the governed to fancie hee should, constitute laws, adaequate to humane velleity, since the wills of no two sons of Adam did ever mathematically concenter, nor were ever two humane actions shaped with parallel circumstances; which, as it seems necessarily to import the deficiency of the rule, so also to imply the evident reason of debating and reporting of cases in our law: and the denoting of limitations in that of the empire; which first, properly are, or (a notatione) at least should be, no other then exceptions to the rules generall, from a due consideration of individuating circumstances. For the expediment of which knowledge, this gentleman, the painfull collector of these ensuing relations, for his owne benefit, whilst yet living, and for the good of others, who by natures decree should see his pyre, did think it tanti to make his observations legible: there now remaines nothing, but thy boni consule, in which thou wilt oblige the publisher to continue thy freind in all like opportunities."[40]

This was over 350 years ago; but the fount, though varied and less ample, has not run dry. In Pennsylvania the middle of the twentieth century brought Musmanno J. His style was indeed diverse: Musmanno-dicts have a quality that is all their own.[41] Many take to the water:

---

[40] Brownlow's *Reports, Part II* (1652), p. iii. I have eliminated variations of type and many capital letters, but otherwise the text is as it appears in the original. For those who are not classical scholars, a brief glossary follows. Nedum — still more; ex Athaeniis in barathrum — from the [civilized] Athenian into the abyss; Phainomena — extraordinary appearance; ignis fatuus — will o' the wisp; eodem calculo — reckoned the same; poco di matto — little foolishness; cereous potestatatives — waxen powers; undiqueversum — from every angle; vellacuzo teso — overstrung titillation; ausa furosa — mad attempts; Vir magnus quidem & sapiens — great and wise man; repagula — barrier in circus or racecourse to prevent horses from straying; hinc polydacrya — hence many tears; irretition — lack of power of retention; a notatione — by choice; tanti — worth-while; boni consule — good consideration.

[41] See 2 Misc. 154–57. For proceedings brought by Musmanno J. seeking to have a judgment of his reported, see *ante* pp. 176–78.

"Having these well-considered and wise precedents to guide us, standing out as they do like bell buoys, excellently marking the course of sound judgment, why must we drift out into the confusing and churning sea of doubt, uncertainty and decision-by-chance?"[42] Or this: "A gift given by a man to a woman on condition that she embark on the sea of matrimony with him is no different from a gift based on the condition that the donee sail on any other sea. If, after receiving the provisional gift, the donee refuses to leave the harbor, — if the anchor of contractual performance sticks in the sands of irresolution and procrastination — the gift must be restored to the donor."[43] Again, "Why did [the court] subject the plaintiff to the expenditure of time and expense and the ordeal of a second trial when it could have told him the first time that his aspirations were but fragile bubbles on the sea of a meaningless hope, that his anticipations were but sterile buds on the bleak tree of unrealizable yearning, and that, no matter what his efforts, he was in the end to wind up in the inextricable swamp of a judgment n.o.v.?"[44]

Indeed, Pennsylvania's case-law is awash with sea-going Musmanno-dicts:

- "The expression *common sense* is one much abused in everyday parlance, but it is still the mountain peak of reason which projects above the ever-rising flood of legal formulae, complicated termin-ology, dicta, syllabi, clauses and phrases pouring from the reservoirs of formal law."[45]

- "A man's good name is as much his possession as his physical prop-erty. It is more than property, it is his guardian angel of safety and security; it is his lifesaver in the sea of adversity, it is his parachute

---

[42] *Costack* v. *Pennsylvania R.R. Co.*, 102 A.2d 127, 136 (Pa. 1954) (Musmanno J., dissenting).

[43] *Pavlicic* v. *Vogtsberger*, 136 A.2d 127, 130 (Pa. 1957) (*per* Musmanno J.).

[44] *Hartigan* v. *Clark*, 165 A.2d 647, 654 (Pa. 1960) (Musmanno J., dissenting). A judgment "n.o.v." is a decision against a litigant despite a verdict of the jury (*non obstante veredicto*) in his favour.

[45] *Jeanette Glass Co.* v. *Indemnity Ins. Co. of North Am.*, 88 A.2d 407, 412 (Pa. 1952) (Musmanno J., dissenting).

when he falls out of the sky of good fortune, it is his plank of rescue in the quicksands of personal disaster."[46]

- "It is supposed that the Judge presiding over a trial will tranquilize with deliberative manner and speech the turbulent waves of thought and feeling aroused and agitated by the battling attorneys. Here, however, the Judge did not pour the oil of serenity on the billows of debate."[47]

- One contention assumed that "a stream of fault loses its identity once it enters into a gulf of subsequent circumstance."[48]

Other Musmannodicts turn to transport by land or air:

- "The Majority Opinion sweeps over the evidence in this case like an express train shooting across a trestle, ignoring signals, semaphores and swinging lanterns. It says that the plaintiffs proved no negligence on the part of the railroad. Like a wreck train blowing alarm warnings as it pushes its way through an enveloping fog, the record shouts negligence throughout the entire length of its 200 pages."[49]

- "The attainment of true justice is over the highway of realities and not through the alley of technicalities."[50]

- "It was this Court which took the subject into the sylvan labyrinths of illogicality, complexity, and injustice; it is, therefore, up to this Court to bring it back to the highway of logic, order, and justice."[51]

[46] *Purcell* v. *Westinghouse Broad. Co.,* 191 A.2d 662, 665 (Pa. 1963) (*per* Musmanno J.).

[47] *Commonwealth* v. *Cisneros,* 113 A.2d 293, 298 (Pa. 1955) (Musmanno J., dissenting).

[48] *Thornton* v. *Weaber,* 112 A.2d 344, 346 (Pa. 1955) (*per* Musmanno J.).

[49] *Grotefend* v. *Pennsylvania R.R. Co.,* 110 A.2d 362, 363 (Pa. 1958) (Musmanno J., dissenting).

[50] *Potter Title & Trust Co.* v. *Lattavo Bros. Inc.,* 88 A.2d 91, 93 (Pa. 1952) (Musmanno J., dissenting).

[51] *Commonwealth ex rel. Norman* v. *Banmiller,* 149 A.2d 881, 887 (Pa. 1959) (Musmanno J., dissenting).

- "No amount of bodily disablement or annoyance will invalidate a testator's resolution, if his mind, like a high-flying plane, clears the mountain peaks of pain, cuts with a clear keel through the storm of importunity and insistence, and lands successfully at the destination of an accomplished desire."[52]

Then there are the powers of darkness:

- "It is because there are persons who defy goodness and honor and who accept the cut rates of Mr. Satan at his sulphuric supermarket rather than pay the just price which decency and justice demand, that evil still walks the earth."[53]

- "Does not the simplest reflection dictate that the time to attack juvenile delinquency is when it is forming in the bud of adolescent irresponsibility, and not when it has developed into the deadly nightshade of consummate criminality?"[54]

- "A judicial decision should be a searchlight before it becomes a guillotine."[55]

- "The law should represent the truth at all times. Fiction should be for the novelists and fantasy for the clairvoyants. Labyrinthian and sophistical explanations should be for superannuated philosophers resting in the shade of melancholy maples as the sun of reality disappears into the mystic darkness of conjecture and supposition."[56]

- One proposal to pay was said to represent "the very essence of indefiniteness, wrapped in vaporous obscurity and hidden in the vague, amorphous shell of enigmatic conjecture."[57]

---

[52] *In re Erdeljac's Estate*, 131 A.2d 97, 100 (Pa. 1957) (*per* Musmanno J.).

[53] *Commonwealth* v. *Brown*, 131 A.2d 367, 373 (Pa. 1957) (Musmanno J., dissenting).

[54] *Barth* v. *Sch. Dist. of Philadelphia*, 143 A.2d 909, 923 (Pa. 1958) (Musmanno J., dissenting).

[55] *In re Trombetta*, 156 A.2d 107, 111 (Pa. 1959) (Musmanno J., dissenting).

[56] *Meisel* v. *Little*, 180 A.2d 772, 781 (Pa. 1962) (Musmanno J., dissenting).

[57] *Klingensmith* v. *Klingensmith*, 100 A.2d 76, 79 (Pa. 1953) (*per* Musmanno J.).

Finally, there are the joys of the ear: "A juke box confined to 'jazz' records may be a nuisance. It robs the air of sweet silence, it substitutes for the gentle concord of stillness the wailings of the so-called 'blues singer,' the whining of foggy saxophones, the screeching of untuned fiddles, the blasts of head-splitting horns, and the battering of ear-shattering drums. It makes a mockery of music, it replaces harmony with cacophony, tonality with discord, and peace with annoyance."[58] Again, "Throughout the entire length of the Judge's charge, which ran 20 printed pages, the defendant's case travelled on a big wheel while the plaintiffs rode a small wheel. The defendant's case strode on long legs, the plaintiffs' case stumbled on short legs. The defendant's case was trumpeted with a bass horn, the plaintiffs' case squeaked through a piccolo. The Trial Judge's charge was unilateral, partisan, partial, warped, unequal, inequitable, and unjust."[59]

Musmanno J. is not alone, either in authorship or in style. In America, a conviction may be sustained on appeal despite error at the trial if the error is harmless. Yet this doctrine, it has been said, "must be sparingly employed. A miniscule error must coalesce with gargantuan guilt, even where the accused displays an imagination of Pantagruelian dimensions."[60] The opening sentence of another judgment promised equally well: "This appeal confronts us with a paragon of unclarity, a paradigm of mutuality, and a plethora of pittances."[61] In due course, the promise was fulfilled: "On the one hand, the contract between the two is a bipartite umbilical cord fed by Medicare and Medicaid funds . . . . On the other hand, the parameters limned by the Supreme Court . . . constrain us to hold that . . . ."[62] But enough, and more than enough.

---

[58] *Fierro* v. *City of Williamsport*, 120 A.2d 889, 891 (Pa. 1956) (Musmanno J., dissenting).

[59] *Bizich* v. *Sears, Roebuck & Co.*, 139 A.2d 663, 668 (Pa. 1958) (Musmanno J., dissenting).

[60] *Chapman* v. *U.S.*, 547 F.2d 1240, 1250 (5th Cir. 1977) (*per* Goldberg J.). *Quaere* if the error is minuscule.

[61] *Frazier* v. *Bd. of Trustees of North-West Mississippi Regl. Med. Ctr.*, 765 F.2d 1278, 1280 (5th Cir. 1985) (*per* Goldberg J.).

[62] *Ibid.*, at p. 1295.

13

~

MAXIMA

MAXIMS have had a chequered career in the law. Once lauded and often quoted, today's shrinking Latinity has encouraged their move into the shadows, both in Academe and in the courts. Over the last two centuries judicial comment has greatly varied, with a tendency towards the discouragement of those who place reliance on maxims, or, indeed, on Latin phrases of any kind.[1] The view of Erle J. was that "The maxim, Sic utere tuo ut alienum non laedas,[2] is mere verbiage. A party may damage the property of another where the law permits; and he may not when the law prohibits: so that the maxim can never be applied till the law is ascertained; and, where it is, the maxim is superfluous."[3] Holmes J. concurred: a general proposition such as that maxim "teaches nothing but a benevolent yearning."[4] Again, "General maxims are oftener an excuse for the want of accurate analysis than a help in determining the extent of a duty or the construction of a statute."[5] And nearly a century later: "Legal maxims, said Salmond, are the proverbs of the law, with the same merits and defects of other proverbs, being brief and pithy statements of partial truths."[6]

---

[1] See, e.g., 1 Misc. 25; 2 Misc. 158, 159.

[2] "Use your own property in such a way that it will not injure the property of another." See *Black's Law Dictionary* (8th ed. 2004), p. 1757.

[3] *Bonomi* v. *Backhouse* (1858) E.B. & E. 622 at 643; *reversed*, E.B. & E. 646; reversal *affirmed*, 9 H.L.C. 503. For an example, see *ante* p. 171.

[4] Oliver Wendell Holmes Jr., *Privilege, Malice, and Intent*, 8 Harv. L. Rev. 1, 3 (1894).

[5] *Ryalls* v. *Mechanic's Mills*, 22 N.E. 766, 767 (Mass. 1899) (*per* Holmes J.).

[6] *Government Insurance Office (N.S.W.)* v. *K.A. Reed Services Pty. Ltd* [1988] V.R. 829 at

Others differed. Parke B. once austerely[7] observed: "It is of much more importance that we should adhere strictly to legal maxims, than attempt to evade them in order to meet the supposed intention of the parties."[8] Sir John Neligan, the Recorder of Cork, was also often technical and learned; but the Bar was vigilant. "Mr. Barry," Neligan once said to counsel, "has your client never heard *Sic utere tuo ut alienum non laedas?*" The reply was prompt: "Not a day passes, your Honour, on which he does not hear it. It is the sole topic of conversation where he lives at the top of Mushera mountain."[9] The Englishman's attachment to the law is less passionate: "There are topics of conversation more popular in public houses than the finer points of the equitable doctrine of the constructive trust."[10]

Lord Reid showed scant enthusiasm: "It is a rule of law that an employer, though guilty of no fault himself, is liable for damage done by the fault or negligence of his servant acting in the course of his employment. The maxims respondeat superior and qui facit per alium facit per se[11] are often used, but I do not think that they add anything or that they lead to any different results. The former merely states the rule baldly in two words, and the latter merely gives a fictional explanation of it."[12] Moody J. had been milder: "The reason for the rule is not clarified much by the Latin phrases in which it is sometimes clothed."[13]

The number of legal maxims in common use today is indeed small; and it is sometimes not realised what a tiny part of the whole they are. In England, *Broom's Legal Maxims*[14] lists 625, all in Latin but considerately translated for increasingly unlatinized times. Yet that is as nothing:

---

834 (*per* Brooking J., citing *Salmond on Jurisprudence* (Glanville Williams ed., 10th ed. 1947), in an appendix jettisoned from the 12th edition (1966) as being "no longer worthy of inclusion": p. viii).

7 The adverb is Lord Sumner's: *Eastwood* v. *Ashton* [1915] A.C. 900 at 914.

8 *Llewellyn* v. *Earl of Jersey* (1843) 11 M. & W. 183 at 190.

9 A.M. Sullivan, *The Last Serjeant* (1952), p. 48.

10 *Attorney-General's Reference (No. 1 of 1985)* [1986] Q.B. 491 at 506 (*per* Lord Lane C.J.).

11 "Let the principal be answerable," and "He who acts through another acts himself."

12 *Staveley Iron & Chem. Co. Ltd.* v. *Jones* [1956] A.C. 627 at 643.

13 *Standard Oil Co.* v. *Anderson*, 212 U.S. 215, 220 (1909).

14 10th ed. 1939, pp. xiii–xxvi.

Scotland achieved much more. In 1823 *A Collection of Latin Maxims &
Rules, in Law and Equity* by Peter Halkerston[15] was published in
Edinburgh. It contains some 1,400 Latin maxims, each translated into
English. In the preface the author, who attained a place in the *Dictionary
of National Biography*,[16] spoke of his translations with a modesty
befitting his "L.L.D." on the title page. They had cost him "some labour,"
but while not supposing them to be "in every respect perfect," he trusts
that on the whole they will be found to be "pretty correct." Sometimes
his labours were unwittingly increased by errors in transcribing the Latin
from the sources that he cites, as where "Ignorantia juris non excusat"[17]
appears also as "Ignorantia non excusat legem" ("Ignorance does not
excuse the law").[18] And consistency is avoided when a maxim is set out
twice on the same page with different translations.[19]

The shape of things to come appears on the first page: "From the
impossibility of a thing to its nonentity, the argument or proof follows
of necessity, negatively, though not affirmatively." An alternative
translation of *A non posse ad non esse sequitur argumentum necessarie
negative, licet non affirmative*[20] is "From the impossibility of doing a
thing necessarily follows the conclusion that it has not in fact been done;
but the converse does not hold."

To some extent the book has become legendary. Other authors have
not hesitated to ascribe to it (though without mentioning its name)
maxims and mistranslations that it does not contain. Thus it has been
said that *Actor sequitur forum rei* means "The agent must be in court

---

[15] Cited as "Halk."

[16] Vol. 24, p. 47. He was a solicitor in the Supreme Court of Scotland. The entry is silent
about the source of his honorary LL.D.

[17] Halk. 56.

[18] Halk. 56.

[19] See Halk. 120 (*Paribus sententiis reus absolvitur*). The first translation, at the top of the
page, is "A guilty person is absolved by an equal number of votes for or against him." The
second, at the bottom, is "The accused is acquitted by an equal number of votes for or
against him."

[20] "From impossibility to nonexistence the inference follows necessarily in the negative,
though not in the affirmative." *Black's Law Dictionary* (8th ed. 2004), p. 1706. See *Lord
Sheffield* v. *Ratcliffe* (1621) Hob. 334 at 336.

when the case is going on."[21] And there is said to be a maxim *Catella realis non potest legari*, translated as "A genuine little whelp cannot be left in legacy."[22] In fact, the first maxim is translated, "The agent attends the court where the business is carried on"[23] (instead of "A plaintiff must sue in the jurisdiction to which the defendant is subject"). And the second maxim is *Catella juste possessa amitti non possunt*, translated as "A little whelp, (perhaps cattle), lawfully possessed, cannot be lost"[24] ("The ownership of lawfully owned chattels is not destroyed merely because they are lost").

The book is rich in variant curiosities, and it has been said to be "exceedingly rare, some malicious person having put the author up to their absurdity."[25] Many law libraries lack the book. Sometimes it seems impossible to get both the Latin and the English right at the same time. Thus one page proclaims *Urbi concurrent commune jus et jus scriptum communi juri standum*, translated as: "When common law and written law disagree, we must stand by the common law." Yet five pages earlier *Urbi* and *juri* had instead been *Ubi* and *jure*, and *disagree* had been *agree*.[26] There are also exercises in double negatives, as in *Lex Angliae nunquam sine Parliamento mutare non potest*, where either the *non* or the *nunquam* must be expelled in order to justify the translation: "The law of England cannot undergo a change, without the interference of Parliament."[27]

Perhaps it is by way of compensation that sometimes there is a deficiency of negatives: "In those things which are conceded to all by common right, the custom of any country or place is to be alleged"[28] does not sound very cogent. The true maxim is *In hiis quae de jure*

---

[21] J. Larwood, *Humour of the Law* (1903), p. 131; F.F. Heard, *Oddities of the Law* (1921), p. 153; A.H. Engelbach, *Anecdotes of Bench and Bar* (1913), p. 245.

[22] Larwood, *supra* note 21, p. 131; Heard, *supra* note 21, p. 152; Engelbach, *supra* note 21, p. 245.

[23] Halk. 4.

[24] Halk. 18; see Jenk.Cent. 28 ("catalla").

[25] Heard, *supra* note 21, at 153.

[26] Halk. 177, 182; see Lofft's *Maxims* (1776) (cited as "Lofft") No. 602 ("ubi" and "juri").

[27] Halk. 78; see 2 Co.Inst. 618, dispensing with "nunquam".

[28] Halk. 62.

communi omnibus conceduntur, consuetudo alicujus patriae vel loci non est alleganda[29] ("In those things that by common right are conceded to all, the custom of a particular country or place is not to be adduced");[30] but as well as producing *consedentur*, Halkerston omits the *non*.

Errors apart, Halkerston's strongest suit was one of gentle incoherence. To say, "It is the property of a judge to administer justice, not to give it"[31] (*Judicis est jus dicere, non dare*) is an oblique way of asserting that a judge should declare the existing law, and not make new law. Again, "Such an interpretation ought to be made, as that a thing may either rather prosper than perish"[32] (*Interpretatio fienda est ut res magis valeat quam pereat*) does not plainly reveal that a document ought to be construed so that the transaction will be effective rather than ineffectual.

Res ipsa loquitur: this handful of examples is striking enough. But what is truly remarkable is the sheer bulk of obscure English. Some readers may be content with speculating on what rational meaning can be given to each example; the learned may exercise their skills in deducing the Latin from the crabbed English that it is said to have spawned, with resort in case of doubt to the more orthodox versions set out in the Codicil.[33] Others may prefer merely to glance through the collection before turning to other things. A substantial selection of what was put forward as being the concise embodiment of distilled legal wisdom deserves its place here.

At times Halkerson is contra-suggestible. Thus "A common error makes law necessary" (1), and "Ignorance does not excuse the law" (2), though "Inability excuses law" (3). Then "One day is a complete term, in law" (4), and "To whom more is allowed, that which is less ought not to be allowed" (5). Yet "Spoliation of all things ought to be restored" (6). Great liberty is given by the precept, "We must not dispute against a person denying first principles" (7). And does human (or political)

---

[29] *The Case of Monopolies* (1602) 11 Co.Rep. 84b at 85b.

[30] *Black's Law Dictionary* (8th ed. 2004), p. 1724.

[31] Halk. 73; see Lofft No. 42.

[32] Halk. 70; see Jenk.Cent. 198.

[33] See *post* pp. 217–21. The numerals in brackets refer to this. Because Halkerston arranged the maxims alphabetically according to the Latin, page references are omitted here.

experience confirm that "What hath once been approved of, in elections, cannot any longer displease" (8)?

At times, there are glimpses of the obvious: "A case omitted is to be considered as omitted" (9), and "The right of accrescing is preferable to burdens" (10). Then "The law is safest for the poor" (11), yet "The oaths of the poor are to be kept" (12). Further "No one seems to obtain that which it is necessary for him to restore unto another" (13), and "The estimation of a past transgression never increases from an after-deed" (14). Yet "No one can derive advantage from his own proper injury" (15).

Sometimes there is a Shakespearean echo: "The appointment of an action for a certain day, is said to take place, when any thing in an uncertain case happens, which may have a tendency to be or not to be" (16). There is a Draconian flavour, too, about "All things are presumed in hatred of a defrauder" (17), especially as "Denial cannot be proved" (18). At times the maxims even verge on the treasonable. Thus it is said: "The king is a mixed character" (19) with the barest hint of a "crazy mixed-up king"; and so "No time occurs to the king" (20), although he must remember that "Application is the life of rule" (21), comforted by the thought that "Derivative power cannot be greater than primitive" (22). There is an equivocal flavour, too, about "Nothing is so peculiar to empire, as to live by the laws" (23), especially as "Every one is the ruler and empire of his own affairs" (24). There may even be a trace of sedition in the latter part of "It is a part of established law, that bargains have no force which are made against laws, and constituted authorities are against good manners" (25).

Perhaps Halkerston gives the greatest pleasure when he makes obscurity more obscure: "It a blessed exposure when the thing is redeemed from destruction" (26), just as "Dominion cannot be over a thing depending" (27). So also "Craft is inconsistent in general" (28), perhaps because "The crafty man is employed in universals" (29). And "The craft of an author does not hurt his successor" (30), although "An assignee enjoys the privilege of his author" (31). Yet "Nobody is a pirate, who hath told down the price" (32), for "Injury is not anticipated" (33).

It should also be remembered that "The law is the army, trial is the safest leader" (34), while "Nobody can certify against a record through the country" (35). Yet "What labours under no internal fault, but yields to an opposing obstacle, the obstacle being removed, it emerges of it self" (36). Similarly, "What is destitute of remedy, in fact, is valid, if it be not faulty" (37), unless, perhaps, "The substance is prior, and more worthy than what is eventual" (38). Even so, "Superfluous things oppose, defective things destroy" (39), and "The union of three witnesses always ought to happen, when the jurors can have better information" (40). Again, "The appointment of an action preceding, ought to take place before any effect can follow" (41), whereas "The first act of a trial, is the approbatory act of the judge" (42), who must remember that "One eye witness is more valid, than ten ear witnesses" (43). Further, "The disposal of the law is stronger and later than that of a man" (44), and "An excess of cautionary does no harm" (45). After all, "As often as there is no ambiguity in words, no explanation ought to be made against words" (46). Perhaps that is Halkerston's real defence: no explanation ought to be made against words.

CODICIL

Halkerstoniana

1. *Communis error facit jus:*[34] common error ripens into law.
2. *Ignorantia non excusat legem* [*legum*]:[35] ignorance of the law is no excuse.
3. *Impotentia excusat legem:*[36] impossibility of performance is a dispensation from compliance with the law.
4. *Universus terminus in lege dies unus:*[37] a whole term is in law but a single day.

---

[34] 4 Co.Inst. 240; Lofft No. 509. The numbers in this Codicil refer to those on pp. 215–17, *ante.*

[35] *Mildmay's Case* (1584) 1 Co.Rep. 175a at 177b; *Manser's Case* (1584) 2 Co.Rep. la at 3b ("ignorantia juris non excusat" in each place).

[36] Co.Litt. 29a.

[37] Lofft No. 486: and see 4 Bl.Comm. 363.

5. *Non debet, cui plus licet, quod minus est non licere:*[38] a man may lawfully do a lesser thing if he is entitled to do a greater.
6. *Spoliatus debet ante omnia restitui:*[39] restitution to the despoiled ought to be made before anything else.
7. *Non est disputandum contra principia negantem:*[40] one cannot argue with a man who disputes first principles.
8. *Quod semel placuit in electionibus amplius displicere non potest:*[41] where an election has once been made it cannot be altered.
9. *Casus omissus pro omisso habendus est:*[42] an omitted case is to be treated as having been purposely omitted.
10. *Jus accrescendi prefertur oneribus:*[43] the right of survivorship takes precedence over incumbrances.
11. *Lex est tutissima casis [cassis]:*[44] the law is the safest helmet.
12. *Sacramenta pauperum sunt servanda:*[45] the law-suits of poor persons are to be protected.
13. *Non videtur quisquam id capere, quod ei necesse est alii [alio] restituere:*[46] nobody is to be taken as taking something that others are bound to restore to him.
14. *Nunquam crescit ex post facto praeteriti delicti aestimatio:*[47] the gravity of an offence is not increased by any subsequent event.
15. *Nullus commodum capere potest de injuria sua propria:*[48] nobody can gain an advantage by his own wrong.
16. *Condictio [Conditio] dicitur, cum quid in casum incertum, qui potest tendere ad esse aut non esse, confertur:*[49] it is called a condition when

---

[38] Corpus Juris Civilis, Digest, Bk. 50, tit. 17, para. 21; and see *Gravenor* v. *Todd* (1593) 4 Co.Rep. 23a.

[39] 2 Co.Inst. 714; Lofft No. 449.

[40] Co.Litt. 343a.

[41] Lofft No. 284; Co.Litt. 146a. See *Scarf* v. *Jardine* (1882) 7 App.Cas 345 at 360.

[42] Erskine, *An Institute of the Law of Scotland* (ed. 1828: cited as "Ersk.Inst."), p. 24.

[43] Co.Litt. 185a

[44] 2 Co.Inst. 56, 526; Lofft No. 65.

[45] Ersk.Inst. 193 has "puberum" for "pauperum."

[46] Corpus Juris Civilis, Digest, Bk. 50, tit. 17, para. 51.

[47] *Ibid.*, para. 1381; and see Bacon's *Maxims* (1630), p. 38.

[48] Co.Litt. 148b.

[49] *Ibid.*, at p. 201a.

something is given on an uncertain event that may or may not occur.

17. *In odium spoliatoris omnia praesumuntur:*[50] all possible presumptions should be made against him who destroys or suppresses evidence.

18. *Negatio non potest probari:*[51] a negative cannot be proved.

19. *Rex est mista persona:*[52] the King combines several legal personalities.

20. *Nullum tempus occurrit regi:*[53] time never runs against the Crown.

21. *Applicatio est vita regulae:*[54] the application is the soul of a rule.

22. *Derivativa potestas non potest esse major primitiva:*[55] derived power cannot be greater than the power whence it springs.

23. *Nihil tam proprium est imperii quam legibus vivere:*[56] nothing is more characteristic of supreme power than to abide by the laws.

24. *Rerum suorum [suarum] quilibet est moderator et arbiter:*[57] everyone is the manager and judge of his own affairs.

25. *Pacta quae contra leges constitutionesque vel contra bono[s] mores fiunt, nullam vim habere indubitati juris est:*[58] it is undoubted law that agreements contrary to the laws and constitutions, or contrary to good morals, have no force.

26. *Benedicta est expositio quando res redimitur a destructione:*[59] blessed is the exposition by which anything is saved from destruction.

[50] See *Dalston* v. *Coatsworth* (1721) 1 P.Wms. 731 at 732; *Williamson* v. *Rover Cycle Co.* [1901] 2 I.R. 189, 615.

[51] Lofft No. 581.

[52] Lofft No. 567; *Bishop of Winchester's Case* (1596) 2 Co.Rep. 43b at 44a; *Case of Modus Decimandi* (1608) 13 Co.Rep. 12 at 17; *The Case of the Master and Fellows of Magdalene College in Cambridge* (1615) 11 Co.Rep. 66b at 70a; *Sydowne* v. *Holme* (1635) Cro.Car. 422 at 423; and see *Tito* v. *Waddell (No. 2)* [1977] Ch. 106 at 320.

[53] Jenk.Cent. 83; Lofft No. 13; 2 Co.Inst. 273.

[54] *Craske* v. *Johnson* (1613) 2 Bulstr. 74 at 79.

[55] Noy's *Maxims* (9th ed. 1821), p. 15; Wingate's *Maximes of Reason* (1658) (cited as "Wing."), p. 66 ("derivata").

[56] 2 Co.Inst. 63.

[57] Lofft No. 167; Co.Litt. 223a.

[58] Corpus Juris Civilis, Codex, 2, 3, 6.

[59] *Melwich* v. *Luter* (1588) 4 Co.Rep. 26a at 26b; Lofft No. 488.

27. *Dominium non potest esse in pendenti:*[60] the ownership of property cannot be in suspense.

28. *Dolus versatur in generalibus:*[61] fraud lurks in generalities.

29. *Dolosus versatur in universalibus:*[62] a deceiver deals in generalities.

30. *Dolus auctoris non nocet successori:*[63] a man's fraud does not harm his successors in title.

31. *Assignatus utitur jure auctoris:* an agent may enjoy the rights of his principal.[64]

32. *Nemo praedo est, qui pretium numeravit:*[65] nobody who has paid the price is a robber.

33. *Injuria non praesumitur:*[66] a wrong is not to be presumed.

34. *Lex est exercitus, judicium [judicum] tutissimus ductor:*[67] the law is the safest guide for the army of judges.

35. *Nemo potest contra recordum verificare per patriam:*[68] no man can take the verdict of a jury as to the correctness of a decision.

36. *Quod nullo interno vitio laborat at objecto impedimento cessat, remoto impedimento per se emergit:*[69] that which is halted not by any inherent defect but by an obstacle in its path proceeds under its own power when the obstacle is removed.

37. *Quod remedio destituitur ipsa re valet si culpa absit:*[70] that which

---

[60] Ersk.Inst. 220.

[61] *Doddington's Case* (1594) 2 Co.Rep. 32b at 34a; *Twyne's Case* (1601) 3 Co.Rep. 80b at 81a; Jenk. 48; Wing. 636; and see the next maxim.

[62] *Stone* v. *Grubham* (1614) 2 Bulstr. 225 at 226; Lofft No. 532; and see the last preceding maxim.

[63] Stair's *Institutions,* Bk. I, tit. 9, para. 10 (ed. J.S. More, 1832, vol. 1, p. 80), adding "*nisi in causa lucrativa.*"

[64] Or "An assignee may enjoy the rights of his principal." Broom, *supra* note 14, cited Halk. p. 14 as the only source of this maxim: Halk. cites none.

[65] Corpus Juris Civilis, Digest, Bk. 50, tit. 17, para. 126 pr.

[66] Co.Litt. 232b.

[67] 2 Co.Inst. 526. Halk. has a comma after "exercitus."

[68] 2 Co.Inst. 380; Lofft No. 29.

[69] Lofft No. 647.

[70] Lofft No. 270; Bacon's *Maxims* (1630), p. 40.

lacks a remedy suffices of itself if there is no fault in the party seeking to enforce it.[71]

38. *Substantia prior et dignior est accidente:*[72] the substance [of a judgment] will prevail over any formal defects in it.

39. *Superflua obstant; defectiva perimunt:*[73] [in the presentation of a case] too much hinders, but too little destroys; or irrelevancies hinder the conduct of a case, whereas lacunae lose it.

40. *Triatio ibi semper debet fieri, ubi juratores meliorem possunt habere notitiam:*[74] a jury trial always ought to be in the place where the jurors will be better informed.

41. *Condictio [Conditio] praecedens adimpleri debet priusquam sequatur effectus:*[75] a condition precedent must be fulfilled before the effect can follow.

42. *Primus actus judicii est judicis approbatorius:*[76] the first step in a trial is the acceptance of the jurisdiction of the court.

43. *Plus valet oculatus testis unus, quam auriti decem:*[77] one eye-witness is worth more than ten witnesses who speak only from hearsay.

44. *Fortior et posterior [potentior] est dispositio legis quam hominis:*[78] the will of the law is of greater force and potency than that of man.

45. *Abundans cautela non nocet:*[79] excessive precautions can do no harm.

46. *Quoties in verbis nulla est ambiguitas, ibi nulla expositio contra verba fienda est:*[80] where there is no ambiguity in the words, no interpretation contrary to them may be adopted.

---

[71] E.g., the former preferential right of an executor to retain money in satisfaction of a debt due to himself.

[72] Macdonnel's *Manual of Quotations* (ed. E.H. Michelsen, 1856), p. 274. At p. 179 "non est factum" is translated as "it is untrue."

[73] Lofft No. 412.

[74] See *Bulwer's Case* (1587) 7 Co.Rep. la at 1b.

[75] Co.Litt. 201a (omitting "praecedens").

[76] Ersk.Inst. 46.

[77] 4 Co.Inst. 279; Lofft No. 111; and see Halk. 175.

[78] Co.Litt. 234a.

[79] *Heydon's Case* (1612) 11 Co.Rep. 5a at 6b.

[80] Co.Litt. 147a (verba expressa fienda est); Wing. 24.

14

~

ANDORANDORORAND

WORDS can be both a delight and a torment. The law is rich, and judges, despite any initial lack of enthusiasm, perforce become "philologists of the highest order."[1] Sometimes there are questions of sound; and there may be much ado about a single letter. In 1304 Hengham C.J. held that "h" was not a letter, so that there was no variance between Hersam and Ersam.[2] Equally, "abilem" was as good as "habilem," as Babington J. held in 1430.[3] A year later the question whether W was interchangeable with V seems to have been the subject of judicial difference. Paston J. (of whom Sam Weller would have approved) took the view that there was no significant difference between Willelmus and Villelmus, for W was no more than two V's. Cottesmore, J., on the other hand, would not have it that J. Wise and J. Vise were the same person; and he pointed out that words with an initial W were pronounced differently from words with an initial V. Babington C.J. seems to have expressed no views on the point.[4] He might perhaps have observed that Paston's doctrine — that two things were substantially the same if one were merely double the other — would carry him into strange waters; if the proverbial last straw would break the camel's back,[5] would the same be done by halving the straw, and then halving it again, and so on, *ad infinitum*?

---

[1] *Ex parte Davis* (1857) 5 W.R. 522 at 523 (*per* Pollock C.B.); and see 1 Misc. pp. 25 *et seq.*
[2] (1304) Y.B. 32 Edw. 1 (R.S.) 128, 129.
[3] (1430) Y.B. 9 Hen. 6, Mich., pl. 37, fo. 53.
[4] (1431) Y.B. 9 Hen. 6, Pasch., pl. 15, fo. 7.
[5] See *post* p. 359.

Some four centuries later it was established that "Shakespeare" was not *idem sonans* with "Shakepear."[6] In a later case an indictment for larceny and for receiving stated that the chattels in question were the property of "Darius Christopher"; but at the trial, at Dorset Quarter Sessions, it emerged that his name was "Trius Christopher," and although for this reason the defence objected to the indictment, the objection was overruled. The chairman first laid down "the rule as to names being *idem sonantia*," and then, "the Court being of opinion that the names Darius (pronounced in the Dorset dialect D'rius) and Trius sounded alike," the trial proceeded to conviction. On appeal, the Court for Crown Cases Reserved quashed the conviction, for it had not been left to the jury to say whether in fact the two names were *idem sonans*; and no court could say as a matter of law that they were.[7] Latterly, an application of the concept of names being *idem sonans* has made its way into company law, benevolently.[8]

More often the problem is one of meaning rather than sound; and many words that seem simple are not. Some are insidious: "Such words as 'right' are a constant solicitation to fallacy."[9] Others have concealed opulence. Consider the riches of "but." Counsel once argued in the House of Lords that "The word 'But' is not necessarily in opposition to what precedes it. It is a conjunction, as well as a preposition. In one case it is derived from *be out*, and is equivalent to *except* or *without*." At this, Lord Brougham interjected: "As in the motto of the Macphersons, 'Touch not a cat but [without] a glove!'"[10] Again, in a case in 1744 the two chief justices disagreed over the construction of the word "or" in a phrase referring to death under 21 "or without issue"; but Lord Hardwicke

[6] *R.* v. *Shakespeare* (1808) 10 East 83.

[7] *R.* v. *Davis* (1851) 20 L.J.M.C. 207; see also 1 Misc. 43, 44, 264.

[8] See *Re Vidiofusion* [1974] 1 W.L.R. 1548 at 1549.

[9] *Jackman* v. *Rosenbaum Co.*, 260 U.S. 22, 31 (1922) (*per* Holmes J.).

[10] *Abbott* v. *Middleton* (1858) 7 H.L.C. 68 at 76; and see *Duke of Devonshire* v. *Smith* (1833) Alc. & N. 442 at 471. Consider also "baht" (e.g., "On Ilkla' Moor baht hat."). Dictionaries say that "baht" means "both", or is "the basic monetary unit of Thailand" (see J.O. Halliwell, *Dictionary of Archaic and Provincial Words* (1847); O.E.D. (2d ed. 1989) s.v.), but for Yorkshire it plainly means "without."

L.C. considered it a "very plain case" of "or" in effect meaning "and."[11] In the twentieth century this view was roundly condemned as being "a cowardly evasion. In truth one word is substituted for another. For 'or' can never mean 'and.'"[12] Equally, "the proposition that 'and' can sometimes mean 'or' is true neither in law or in English usage."[13] Doubtless similar comments would today be applied to the word "hereinafter" in a will being treated as being "hereinbefore."[14] The explanation of cases to the contrary is that the context has shown that one word was being used by mistake for the other. After all, a will giving "the black cow on which I ride to hounds" will carry the black horse on which the testator rode to hounds without establishing that "cow" means "horse."[15]

Problems of meaning may be intensified when invention takes a hand. The nineteenth century was not content to allow "and" and "or" to continue their discrete lives, but fashioned the conjoint "and/or": *hinc illae lacrimae*. The judicial welcome, though certainly not warm, might indifferently be described as being either hot or cold.[16] There is admirable authority for the proposition that the expression forms no part of the English language. The Constitution of the State of Illinois provides[17] that judicial proceedings are to be conducted and preserved in the English language. Counsel once submitted to a trial judge in that State certain findings of fact and conclusions of law that used the term "and/or"; and a splendid appellate court roundly condemned this. After discussing some instances of judicial and other castigations of the

[11] *Walsh* v. *Peterson* (1744) 3 Atk. 193 at 194, applying *Soulle* v. *Gerrard* (1596) Cro.Eliz. 525, *sub nom. Sowell* v. *Garret* (1596) Moo.K.B. 422.

[12] *Sutherland Publishing Co., Ltd.* v. *Caxton Publishing Co., Ltd.* [1938] Ch. 174 at 201 (*per* MacKinnon L.J., dissenting).

[13] *Re The Licensing Ordinance* (1968) 13 F.L.R. 143 at 147 (*per* Blackburn J.).

[14] *Bengough* v. *Edridge* (1827) 1 Sim. 173 at 270; *affirmed sub nom. Cadell* v. *Palmer* (1833) 1 Cl. & F. 372 (there being no appeal on this point: see at p. 373 n.).

[15] See *Morgan* v. *Thomas* (1882) 9 Q.B.D. 643 at 645 (*per* Jessel M.R.); 1 Misc. 29. Lord Hoffmann pointed out that "no one . . . has any difficulty in understanding Mrs. Malaprop when she says, 'She is as obstinate as an allegory on the banks of the Nile' ": *Mannai Investment Co. Ltd.* v. *Eagle Star Life Assurance Co. Ltd.* [1997] A.C. 749 at 774.

[16] See 1 Misc. 28.

[17] See Schedule, s. 18.

term,[18] the court referred to many vituperations, including "freakish fad," "accuracy-destroying symbol," "pollution of the English language," "unsightly hieroglyphic," "device for the encouragement of mental laziness," "a bastard sired by Indolence (he by Ignorance) out of Dubiety," and "barbarism."[19] The conclusion was emphatic: the findings and conclusions, it was held, "cannot be said to be in the English language."[20] Over thirty years later there was an Anglo-Scottish echo of this view, though less trenchant: "The symbol 'and/or' is not yet part of the English language."[21] Perhaps a more tolerant view is to call it "an abuse of the English language."[22] The title of *Words and Phrases Legally Defined*[23] enabled it to include the "abuse" without indicating whether it is word or phrase and/or both.[24]

The destructive hand of the term has reached far. Thus the generous use of this "unwarranted combination"[25] in pleadings may produce a "mass of vagueness"[26] that would invalidate them: "It is doubtful whether the interloper 'and/or' has any appropriate place in the English language, but it is certain that it has no place in pleading, where the law requires that the pleader must state his cause of action or ground of defense with certainty to a common intent."[27] The "dubious term" is one that "imports uncertainty where clarity and definiteness are required."[28] Other victims of the expression have been indictments,[29] complaints,[30]

---

[18] See, e.g., *Preble* v. *Architectural Iron Workers' Union of Chicago, Local No. 63*, 260 Ill. App. 435, 442 (1931).

[19] *Tarjan* v. *National Surety Co.*, 268 Ill. App. 232, 240–42 (1932).

[20] *Ibid.*, at p. 242 (*per* O'Connor J.); and see *Gully* v. *Jackson Intl. Co.*, 145 So. 905, 906 (Miss. 1933).

[21] *John G. Stein & Co. Ltd.* v. *O'Hanlon* [1965] A.C. 890 at 904 (*per* Lord Reid, Lord Hodson and Lord Wilberforce concurring).

[22] *Thibodeaux* v. *Upton Mtrs. Corp.*, 270 Ill. App. 191, 193 (1933) (*per* Matchett J.).

[23] 3d ed. 1988.

[24] But *Employers' Mut. Liab. Ins. Co.* v. *Tollefsen*, 263 N.W. 376, 377 (Wis. 1935), denies it either title. The *O.E.D.* defines *and/or* as a "formula." (vol. 1, p. 449, 2d ed. 1989).

[25] *Kornbrodt* v. *Equitable Trust Co.*, 2 P.2d 236, 237 (Or. 1931) (*per* Rand J.).

[26] *Grandchamp* v. *Costello*, 194 N.E. 837, 838 (Mass. 1935) (*per* Rugg C.J.).

[27] *Clay County Abstract Co.* v. *McKay*, 147 So. 407, 408 (Ala. 1933) (*per* Brown J.).

[28] *Irving Trust Co.* v. *Rose*, 67 F.2d 89, 90 (4th Cir. 1933) (*per* Soper J.).

[29] *Compton* v. *State*, 91 S.W.2d 732 (Tex. Crim. App. 1936).

[30] *State* v. *Jefferson*, 23 A.2d 406 (N.J. 1941).

petitions in equity,[31] affidavits,[32] a decision by a commission based on findings that used the term,[33] the result of a ballot in which the expression had appeared in the question,[34] a writ of fieri facias,[35] and a city ordinance.[36] A state statute,[37] on the other hand, survived, despite using the term 32 times, since this had failed to make the Act vague and uncertain enough to obscure the legislative intent.[38] Verdicts, however, are different. A verdict of Guilty fixing the punishment at a fine of $250 "and/or" confinement in the county jail was reversed for uncertainty;[39] and a verdict fixing the punishment "at a fine of $0.00 and/or confinement in the County Jail of 30 days" fared no better.[40]

The language of condemnation has not been limited to the comments quoted above. The "senseless and/or"[41] is a "meaningless symbol,"[42] "a kind of verbal teratism"[43] that is a "linguistic abomination."[44] It is "as devoid of meaning as it is incapable of classification by the rules of grammar and syntax,"[45] and it "has no place in pleadings, findings of

[31] *Shadden* v. *Cowan*, 96 S.E.2d 608 (Ga. 1957). Cp. *State ex rel. Adler* v. *Douglas*, 95 S.W.2d 1179 (Mo. 1936), where the decision was reached by "wholly ignoring the use of this meaningless symbol."

[32] *Ralls* v. *E.R. Taylor Auto Co.*, 42 S.E.2d 446 (Ga. 1947); and see *Shadden*, 96 S.E.2d at 609 ("or and"). See also *Rosenberg* v. *Bullard*, 15 P.2d 870 (Cal. App. 1932).

[33] *Putnam* v. *Indus. Commn.*, 14 P.2d 973 (Utah 1932).

[34] *Drummond* v. *City of Columbus*, 285 N.W. 109 (Neb. 1939).

[35] *Saylor* v. *Williams*, 92 S.E.2d 565 (Ga. App. 1956).

[36] *City of Washington* v. *Washington Oil Co.*, 145 S.W.2d 366 (Mo. 1940), where the use of the term contributed to invalidating the ordinance.

[37] 1933 Nev. Stat. c.165.

[38] *Ex parte Iratacable*, 30 P.2d 284 (Nev. 1934).

[39] *James* v. *State*, 139 S.W.2d 587 (Tex. Crim. App. 1940).

[40] *Cobb* v. *State*, 139 S.W.2d 272, 273 (Tex. Crim. App. 1940). The obscurity of a footnote must be sought for the reluctant admission that the term has been found in the Law Reports in judgments in the House of Lords: see *D.* v. *National Society for the Prevention of Cruelty to Children* [1978] A.C. 171 at 241; *United Scientific Holdings Ltd.* v. *Burnley Borough Council* [1978] A.C. 904 at 923; *Sovmots Investments Ltd.* v. *Secretary of State for the Environment* [1979] A.C. 144 at 179. See also *Federal Steam Navigation Co. Ltd.* v. *Department of Trade & Industry* [1974] 1 W.L.R. 505 at 522, 523.

[41] *Gallopin* v. *Continental Cas. Co.*, 7 N.E.2d 771, 772 (Ill. App. 1937) (*per* McSurely J.).

[42] *State ex rel. Adler* v. *Douglas*, 95 S.W.2d 1179, 1180 (Mo. 1936) (*per* Frank J.).

[43] *Gallopin*, 7 N.E.2d at 771 (*per* McSurely J.).

[44] *State* v. *Smith*, 184 P.2d 301, 303 (N.M. 1947) (*per* McGhee J.).

[45] *Am. Gen. Ins. Co.* v. *Webster*, 118 S.W.2d 1082, 1084 (Tex. App. 1938) (*per* Combs J.).

fact, conclusions of law, judgments or decrees, and least of all instructions to a jury."[46] It is even criminal: "The presiding judge murdered the King's, the Queen's, and everybody's English by using the monstrous linguistic abomination 'and/or' in this portion of the order."[47] The "literary fraction 'and/or'" is one of "the ingenious inventions of scriveners to confuse and befuddle," and it is the "latest and lustiest of these pests."[48] It is "a fractional form of expression"[49] that, as ordinarily used, is "a deliberate amphibology; it is purposely ambiguous. Its sole usefulness lies in its self-evident equivocality."[50] The "baffling symbol" is "a disingenuous modernistic hybrid, inept and irritating,"[51] for which draftsmen have a "common and deplorable affection."[52]

Perhaps the most thorough condemnation of the expression is to be found in a Wisconsin judgment:

> We are confronted with the task of first construing "and/or," that befuddling, nameless thing, that Janus-faced verbal monstrosity, neither word nor phrase, the child of a brain of some one too lazy or too dull to express his precise meaning, or too dull to know what he did mean, now commonly used by lawyers in drafting legal documents, through carelessness or ignorance or as a cunning device to conceal rather than express meaning with view to furthering the interest of their clients. We have even observed the "thing" in statutes, in the opinion of courts, and in statements in briefs of counsel, some learned and some not.[53]

Australia was less forthright but more succinct: "and/or" was said to be "an elliptical and embarrassing expression which endangers accuracy

---

[46] *State* v. *Smith*, 184 P.2d at 303.

[47] *Brown* v. *Guaranty Estates Corp.*, 80 S.E.2d 645, 653 (N.C. 1954) (*per* Ervin J.).

[48] *Equitable Life Assur. Socy.* v. *Hemenover*, 67 P.2d 80, 82 (Colo. 1937) (*per* Burke C.J.).

[49] *Fisher* v. *Healy's Special Tours Inc.*, 1 A.2d 848, 849 (N.J. 1938) (*per* Parker J.); *State* v. *Jefferson*, 23 A.2d 406, 407 (N.J. 1941) (*per* Flannagan J.).

[50] *Bank Bldg. & Equip. Corp.* v. *Georgia St. Bank*, 209 S.E.2d 82, 84 (Ga. App. 1974) (*per* Webb J.), quoting from 17 Am.Jur. 2d 698, Contracts, § 283. See also *Ex parte Bell*, 122 P.2d 22, 29 (Cal. 1942) (*per* Traynor J.).

[51] *Bell* v. *Wayne United Gas Co.*, 181 S.E. 609, 618 (W. Va. 1935) (Maxwell J., dissenting).

[52] *Millen* v. *Grove* [1945] V.L.R. 259 at 260 (*per* Gavan Duffy J.).

[53] *Employers Mut. Liab. Ins. Co.* v. *Tollefsen*, 263 N.W. 376, 377 (Wis. 1935) (*per* Fowler J.).

for the sake of brevity."[54] On this issue, Alberta stands between Australia and the United States. Thus in 1929 Harvey C.J.A. said that "no sensible meaning can be attached to this hybrid method of trying to express two alternatives by a short cut and there is no reason why the Courts should encourage it by permitting its use in pleadings which by our rules of practice are required to state plainly and definitely what is intended."[55] More recently, Johnson J.A. adhered to this view, saying that "one can hardly be termed a purist" for calling attention to "the impropriety in the use of such an abbreviation in pleadings and affidavits."[56]

In South Africa, it was said of one indictment that it "bristles" with the expression "and/or." The defence not surprisingly "complained about the extravagant use of the conjunction 'and/or.' It was suggested that if all the 'and/or's' are added together, the number of combinations possible under paras. 1, 2 and 4 of part B of the main charge is 498,015. While not wishing to condone this type of conjunction, we think it necessary to state that the total number of combinations looks more menacing that it really is."[57] This relaxed approach contrasts with the United States, where a criminal charge was held void for uncertainty because it used the "abominable combination of a conjunctive and a disjunctive" in averring the theft of "money and/or property" to a stated value.[58]

The courts have struggled against their distaste. Two main strands run through the cases: one may be called "selection" and the other "identification." Selection may be taken first. If under a charterparty a shipper is to ship a full and complete cargo of "X, Y and/or Z," what is his range of choice? One view was that the cargo could consist of X, Y, and Z; or of X and Y; or of Z.[59] Another view was that it could consist of

---

[54] *Fadden* v. *Deputy Federal Commissioner of Taxation* (1943) 68 C.L.R. 76 at 82 (*per* Williams J.).

[55] *Mason* v. *Livingston* [1929] 1 W.W.R. 295 at 300.

[56] *Bell Bros. Transport Ltd.* v. *Cummins Diesel Power Ltd.* (1962) 40 W.W.R. 169 at 172.

[57] *R.* v. *Adams* 1959(1) S.A. 646 at 650, 657 (*per* Rumpff, Kennedy, and Bekker JJ., cited by Megarry J. in *May* v. *Tower Construction Co. Ltd.* [1967] Nov. 17, unrep., where the complaint was merely of some 700 possible combinations).

[58] *U.S.* v. *Autrey*, 12 U.S.C.M.A. 252, 254 (1961) (*per* Homer Ferguson J.).

[59] *Cuthbert* v. *Cumming* (1855) 10 Exch. 809 at 814 (*per* Alderson, B., speaking for himself, Platt, and Martin BB.: see 3 C.L.R. 401).

X, Y, and Z; or of X and Y.[60] Later other views emerged. One was that the cargo could at least consist of X or Y or Z.[61] Another was that it could be X; or X and Y; or X and Z; or X, Y, and Z.[62] Yet another view was that the cargo could consist of X or Y or Z, or any combination of them;[63] and this, the most wide and comprehensive view, is surely the most persuasive. When instead of three categories there are only two, such as a charterparty under which the ship is to proceed to X and/or Y at the charterer's option, it is plain that the charterer may send her to X alone, to Y alone, or to both X and Y.[64] The "or" and the stroke may even be expelled, so that "and/or" will mean "nothing more than 'and'."[65]

Identification is a different matter. What is the effect if a will gives the residue of the estate "to W and/or H," a married couple? Farwell J. managed to avoid holding the gift void for uncertainty, and construed it as a gift to the two in joint tenancy, but as a gift to H alone if W failed to survive the testator.[66] Again, bank accounts have stood in the name of "A and/or B"; but in one case the difficulties created by the bank's choice of such a nomenclature were overcome by referring to the instructions given by the depositor.[67] Yet some cases are beyond salvation: a judgment entered in favour of A "and/or" B has been held void for uncertainty.[68] Yet the entire blame cannot be laid on the expression as a whole; a simple "and" may leave doubts. If a testator makes a bequest of "all my black and white horses," and he dies leaving six black, five white, and four piebald horses (coloured only black and white), does the

---

[60] *Cuthbert* v. *Cumming* (1855) 11 Exch. 405 at 408 (*per* Coleridge J.); but this mainly relied on custom: cp. *per* Cresswell J., at 409.

[61] *Stanton* v. *Richardson* (1875) 45 L.J.Q.B. 78 at 85 (*per* Lord O'Hagan).

[62] *Ibid.*, at p. 85 (*per* Lord Hatherley): this seems to be the meaning of what was said.

[63] *Ibid.*, at p. 83 (*per* Lord Cairns L.C.).

[64] *Gurney* v. *Grimmer* (1932) 38 Com.Cas. 7 at 13 (*per* Scrutton L.J.); and see *Furness* v. *Charles Tennant, Sons & Co.* (1892) 66 L.T. 635, which was not cited.

[65] *Neame* v. *Neame's Trs.* 1956 S.L.T. 57 at 62 (*per* Lord President Clyde).

[66] *Re Lewis* [1942] Ch. 424.

[67] *Fadden* v. *Deputy Federal Commissioner of Taxation* (1943) 68 C.L.R. 76; and see at pp. 80, 82 (in effect, joint tenancy).

[68] *Sproule* v. *Taffe*, 13 N.E.2d 827 (Ill. App. Ct. 1938).

bequest pass the six and the five but not the four, or the four but not the five and the six, or all of them?[69]

The expression is protean: neither stroke nor sequence seems to be essential. An early version preferred a pair of brackets or a horizontal line to a stroke: "$\{ \frac{and}{or} \}$"[70] or "$\frac{and}{or}$"[71] and a little later there were neither brackets nor a line but merely location: "$\frac{and}{or}$".[72] The choice of one statute was a comma in place of the stroke: "and, or";[73] and the Supreme Court of Louisiana repelled an attack on this for being uncertain and ambiguous by the simple means of deleting the "or" as being mere surplusage.[74] As for sequence, surely "or/and"[75] must be just as good — or bad. And both punctuation and the usual sequence may be discarded so as to produce "or and."[76] This approach has even invaded Magna Carta, 1215, where "vel" in the famous chapter 39 has been translated as "or/and";[77] others have preferred "or[and]"[78] or "and (or)."[79] The ultimate simplicity surely lies in a union that rejects all punctuation and produces the single word "andor," or "orand." It seems that Georgia can take the credit (if that is the word) for a stroke of pioneering zeal that produced the first of these words.

---

[69] Consider 1 Misc. 298–301 (piebalds said to be mares).

[70] *Cuthbert* v. *Cumming* (1855) 3 C.L.R. 401, 1301; 3 W.R. 244 (cp. *Cuthbert* v. *Cumming*, 3 W.R. at 553).

[71] *Cuthbert* v. *Cumming*, as reported at 10 Exch. 809; 11 Exch. 405; 24 L.J.Ex. 198, 310; 1 Jur. N.S. 686; 25 L.T. (O.S.) 235 (cp. *Cuthbert* v. *Cumming*, 25 L.T. (O.S.) 23, which omits the "and" and the line).

[72] *Bowes* v. *Shand* (1877) 46 L.J.Q.B. 561; 25 W.R. 730: cp. the reports at 2 App.Cas. 455 and 3 Asp.M.L.C. 461, which insert a horizontal line. The parties disappointingly agreed the meaning of the term: see 2 App.Cas. 462.

[73] Louisiana, Act 78 of 1924, s. 2.

[74] *State* v. *Dudley*, 106 So. 364 (La. 1925).

[75] See, e.g., *Olsen Water & Towing Co.* v. *U.S.*, 21 F.2d 304, 305 (2d Cir. 1927).

[76] *Ralls* v. *E.R. Taylor Auto Co.*, 42 S.E.2d 446 (Ga. 1947) (affidavit condemned on this account); and see *Ralls* v. *E.R. Taylor Auto Co.*, 42 S.E.2d 656 (Ga. App. 1947).

[77] 1 Holdsworth H.E.L. 59 (no freeman shall be taken "vel" imprisoned, etc., save by the lawful judgment of his peers "vel" the law of the land).

[78] W.S. McKechnie, *Magna Carta* (2d ed. 1914), p. 375.

[79] Pollock & Maitland, *History of English Law* (2d ed. 1898), vol. 1, p. 173. 1 Holdsworth H.E.L., *supra* at 61, expresses this as "$\frac{and}{or}$".

In 1953 the Georgia House of Representatives passed a Bill[80] "to create a new word to be known as 'andor,' to define its use and meaning, and for other purposes." The four short sections of the Bill may be quoted in full:

Section 1. That there is hereby created a new word to be known and spelled "andor."

Section 2. That the word "andor" shall mean "either," "or," "both"; "and," "and or or"; and "and and or."

Section 3. That the said word "andor" may be used whenever the conjunctive and disjunctive is[81] desired or when the conjunctive or disjunctive is desired to be used in writing or speaking.

Section 4. That all laws or parts of laws in conflict herewith are hereby repealed.

An unsympathetic Senate left the Bill as a mere Bill. Section 2 promised well. To say "A and/or B" at present offers two possibilities, namely, "A and B," and "A or B." But "A andor B" would have been far richer. "A and B" and "A or B" would still have been there: but what splendid arguments there might have been about "A either B," "A both B," "A and or or B," and "A and and or B." For section 2 was not qualified by any cowardly reference to "unless the context otherwise requires or admits," or, as a semantic enthusiast might have put it, "unless the context otherwise requires andor admits." Lovers of brevity, too, might well point out that law reform begins at home, and that section 3 is hardly a model of drafting. The substitution of "andor" for the first "and" would at least have made redundant the words "or when the conjunctive or disjunctive is desired."

---

[80] H.B. No. 526. First reading, Feb. 11; passed by the Committee on Education, Feb. 17; second reading, Feb. 18; third reading, Feb. 19; passed by 111 votes to 15.

[81] Some would say "are."

15

~

Dark with Excessive Brightness

THE PRELUDE to evidence is the oath; and usually this is uneventful. But there have been exceptions. In a county court case on the Munster Circuit between Gaelic-speaking litigants, one Michael MacNamara was the court interpreter. He was also counsel for the plaintiff, and he feared that the defendant would swear himself out of the debt by barefaced perjury. When the defendant came to the witness box to be sworn, there was a colloquy in Gaelic:

Interpreter:	Take the Book in your right hand and listen to your oath — repeat after me: If I do not tell the truth in this case —
Defendant:	If I do not tell the truth in this case —
Interpreter:	May all my sheep be clifted.
Defendant:	My God, Counsellor, I never heard an oath like that.
Interpreter:	I shall tell His Honour that you refuse to be sworn if you do not repeat —
Defendant:	May all my sheep — but Counsellor, I have three hundred sheep.
Interpreter:	Are you going to repeat the oath?
Defendant:	May all my sheep — may all — may all — may all my sheep be clifted — God help the poor sheep.
Interpreter:	(sternly:) May all my cattle die of the murrain.
Defendant:	Oh Counsellor, I have only three little beasts.
Interpreter:	Very well, you will be decreed.
Defendant:	But this is dreadful altogether — May all — may all — may all my cattle die of the murrain — I'm a ruined man.
Interpreter:	And may all my potatoes be blighted, and rot in the ground.
Defendant:	What?!!

Interpreter: Go on, Sir, and repeat your oath.
Defendant: (laying down the Bible:) Oh Counsellor, I'll admit the debt,
             I'm only asking for time.

When afterwards taxed with this, MacNamara "not merely admitted its truth, but took great pride in it. 'Wasn't I right?' he asked. 'What is an oath? Isn't it a calling on God to punish you if you don't say what is true? And what was I doing but bringing home to him the perils he was running?'"[1]

The logic of the rules of evidence is noteworthy neither for cogency nor for coherence: "It illustrates Judge Hand's suggestion that the system may work best when explained least."[2] True, "in the classic phrase of Lord Chancellor Hardwicke,[3] 'the public has a right to every man's evidence.'"[4] Yet —

> How frail and fallible is memory! History records a few examples, of men of whom it may be said, that whatever knowledge they acquired, either sensible or intellectual, remained as indelibly fixed upon their mind, as if it was engraved on a rock. Seneca reports of Hortensius, that he could repeat at night, the prices and purchasers of every article sold at auction throughout the day; and of himself, that he repeated two thousand names in the same order in which they were spoken to him; and it is told of Cyrus, that he could salute all the soldiers in his vast army by their names, respectively; and of an Englishman, that he recited *verbatim*, one of *Voltaire's* great poems, from having heard it read once by its author to Frederick of Prussia. But these are rare instances. Usually, the impressions made on the memory resemble much more the traceless track of the arrow through the air, than the enduring hieroglyphics upon the pyramids and obelisks of ancient Egypt. Many memories are mere seives. And I would sooner trust the smallest slip of paper for truth, than the strongest and most retentive memory ever bestowed on mortal man.[5]

---

[1] This account combines oral tradition, A.M. Sullivan, *Old Ireland* (1927), pp. 125, 126, and M. Healy, *The Old Munster Circuit* (1939), pp. 160–62.

[2] *Michelson* v. *U.S.*, 335 U.S. 469, 481 (1948) (*per* Jackson J.).

[3] Lord Hardwicke was in fact merely repeating a phrase used by the Duke of Argyll, substituting "right" for "claim": see (1742) 12 Parl.Hist. (1812), cols. 675, 693.

[4] *U.S.* v. *Monia*, 317 U.S. 424, 432 (1943) (Frankfurter J., dissenting).

[5] *Miller* v. *Cotten*, 5 Ga. 341, 348 (1848) (*per* Lumpkin J.).

Indeed, "some instances of strength of memory are very surprising."[6] As Popham C.J. once said, it would be inconvenient if "matters in writing made by advice and upon consideration, and which finally import the certain truth of the agreement of the parties should be controlled by averment of the parties to be provided by the uncertain testimony of slippery memory."[7] A belief that destroying a document puts an end to any liability under it can still persist. A Canadian guarantor, when called upon to pay, tore his signature from the guarantee and swallowed it. When told that his signature could still be proved by the witness to the guarantee, he tore off and swallowed the witness's signature as well; but then the police arrived.[8]

Sometimes interest is at fault: "How easily and insensibly words of hope or expectation are converted by an interested memory into statements of quality and value when the expectation has been disappointed."[9] Further:

> Witnesses not unfrequently turn inference into recollection, and a person by long dwelling on a subject thinks a thing may have happened, and at last comes to a belief that it actually did happen. This arises more particularly on questions of pedigree; but in these cases it is material to consider whether the witness is indifferent to the result. Slight and casual circumstances, however, awaken the recollection. A witness may be asked if he can recollect a particular transaction: it may be forgotten. In one instance, however, a diary was produced in the handwriting of the witness, who had made an entry of what he had done on a particular day; he had forgotten the transaction: but seeing the diary he remembered not only the transaction, but all the surrounding circumstances, which were proved to be true by the evidence of other witnesses.[10]

The frailty of human recollection is proverbial. Sometimes the

---

6 *Coleman* v. *Wathen* (1793) 5 T.R. 245 (*per* Buller J.).

7 *Countess of Rutland's Case* (1604) 5 Co.Rep. 25b at 26a.

8 *Royal Bank of Canada* v. *Kiska* [1967] 2 O.R. 379; see at p. 381. Contrast wills: see, e.g., *Hobbs* v. *Knight* (1838) 1 Curt. 768, where the signature was excised but not eaten.

9 *Deming* v. *Darling*, 20 N.E. 107, 109 (Mass. 1889) (*per* Holmes J.); and see *ante* p. 119.

10 *Peirce* v. *Brady* (1856) 26 L.J.Ch. 257 at 260 (*per* Romilly M.R.). Cp. S.C. *sub nom. Pierce* v. *Brady* (1856) 23 Beav. 64 at 70.

evidence is merely incredible: "I did not believe the evidence of either the defendant or his wife, and it would not have required very much equally to disregard that of the plaintiff."[11] Sometimes the evidence is credible but contradictory. Where the plaintiff's horse-carriage and a tram-car had collided, the judge said:

> The evidence is extremely conflicting as to the manner in which this accident occurred. There is evidence that the carriage was going eastwardly, and also that it was going westwardly; that the car was an open car; also that it was a closed car; that the left hind wheel of the carriage was struck by the car; also, that the fore-wheel, and not either of the hind wheels was struck; that there was only one vehicle in the vicinity on the occasion, and that there were two. Probably I have not exhausted the list of contradictions, but the statement of one of the witnesses, that the horse was heading east and west, seems to cap the climax, and, possibly, resolves some of the other contradictions in the case by the hypothesis of a two-headed horse.[12]

The lapse of time between the accident and the hearing of the case is responsible for much: "The courts . . . are full of honest witnesses, whose memories as the years go by become more and more certain and less and less accurate."[13]

Counsel may be forceful in smiting falsity. Serjeant Vaughan once caught sight of one of his adversary's witnesses, Brown, standing with his hands in his pockets: "And then we come to Brown. Ah, there the impudent and deceitful fellow stands just like a crocodile, with tears in his eyes and his hands in his breeches pockets."[14] Montagu Williams assailed two of the opposing witnesses as being "excellent in vice and exquisite in fraud — the cunning of a cat teeming from the eyes of one; the oily serpent-like treachery of deceit trickling from the mouth of the other."[15] All this is explicable: "The arsenal of every advocate holds two bundles of adjectives for witnesses — such ones as 'reluctant,' 'unbiased,'

---

[11] *Albert* v. *Marshall* (1915) 49 N.S.R. 417 at 418 (*per* Meagher J.).

[12] *Lancaster* v. *The Halifax Electric Tram Co.* (1917) 50 N.S.R. 386 at 387 (*per* Russell J.).

[13] *Per* Macnaghten J.: Henry Cecil, *Just Within the Law* (1975), p. 8.

[14] R. Walton, *Random Recollections of the Midland Circuit* (1869), p. 13.

[15] *Pie-Powder* (1911), p. 176; and see *ante* p. 104.

'disinterested,' and 'honest' are reserved for his own; others, such as 'partisan,' 'eager,' 'interested,' 'hostile,' and even 'perjured,' for those of his adversary."[16] Yet peril lies in pitching a claim too high. In a medical negligence case, counsel characterised the status of one of his witnesses, Professor T, as being "Olympian." Perhaps he repented of this when the judge said: "My recollection of classical mythology is that the gods on Olympus were no strangers to error."[17]

The Bench is given to greater moderation: "It is true the court does not find that the witnesses have sworn falsely, but that is not essential even when that is its belief. To say that the testimony is not satisfactory is more polite and less offensive, and at the same time equally sufficient."[18] As Hilbery J. once observed, "I have often reflected that we lawyers would be out of work if everyone told the truth. I sometimes think, after sitting on the bench for 23 years, that nothing is improbable with human beings."[19] There may also be extenuating circumstances. As Dr. Johnson said, "The writer of an epitaph should not be considered as saying nothing but what is strictly true. Allowance must be made for some degree of exaggerated praise. In lapidary inscriptions a man is not upon oath."[20] The same principle may apply to autobiographies,[21] and explain why librarians have been known to classify them firmly under "Fiction." There are even witnesses of whom it may be said that "he would not stoop to a lie when a half-truth would do."[22]

Yet there are many distinctions to be made: "Honesty and sincerity are not the same as prudence and reasonableness. Some of the most sincere people are the most unreasonable; and Mr. Scargill told me that he had met quite a few of them."[23] Sincerity coupled with dogmatic impetuosity

---

16 *Kingsland* v. *Dorsey*, 338 U.S. 318, 324 (1949) (Jackson J., dissenting).

17 *Clark* v. *MacLennan* [1983] 1 All E.R. 416 at 422 (*per* Peter Pain J.).

18 *Stone* v. *U.S.*, 164 U.S. 380, 382 (1896) (*per* Brewer J.).

19 *Gray* v. *Ralli* [1958] *The Times*, Feb. 13.

20 Boswell's *Johnson*, vol. 2, p. 53.

21 A list of examples would be long and invidious.

22 An interlocutory comment by Powell J. [1986] *The Times*, Dec. 20, in *Attorney-General for the United Kingdom* v. *Heinemann Publishers Australia Pty. Ltd.* (1987) 8 N.S.W.L.R. 341 (the *Spycatcher* case).

23 *Cowan* v. *Scargill* [1985] Ch. 270 at 289.

breeds fanatics, and all that goes with them: "It is a matter of human experience that political zealots, as some of the appellants seem to have been, can so delude themselves about reality that lying is unnecessary for them."[24] Indeed, politics tend to make answering superfluous. In politics, "there is an increasing and regrettable tendency for questions not to be answered, but rather for the so-called reply to consist of a blistering attack on the interrogator himself."[25]

Expert evidence has attracted much comment. In the latter half of the nineteenth century, Sir Frederick Bramwell was one of the best-known engineering witnesses of the day.[26] He was a brother of Bramwell B., whose classification of witnesses beyond belief was into "liars, damned liars, and expert witnesses, . . . [and] my brother Frederick."[27] Lord Campbell left no doubt about his views. Of one expert witness he said: "I dare say he is a very respectable gentleman, and did not mean to give any evidence that was untrue; but really this confirms the opinion I have entertained, that hardly any weight is to be given to the evidence of what are called scientific witnesses; they come with a bias on their minds to support the cause in which they are embarked."[28]

The passage of a century brought no change: "The testimony relating to this footing of the case has been profuse and illuminating. As too often happens, the experts disagree, leaving the problem, as Tennyson[29] might say, dark with excessive brightness."[30] Indeed, expert opinion has been described as "only an ordinary guess in evening clothes."[31] Luck should surely have no part to play. Yet in one case a Canadian judge was accused of a grossly indecent assault on a woman by making a

[24] *Lloyd* v. *McMahon* [1987] A.C. 625 at 644 (*per* Lawton L.J.).

[25] *Re Australian Postal & Telecommunications Union, ex parte Wilson* (1979) 28 A.L.R. 330 at 335 (*per* Sheppard J.).

[26] And an arbitrator: see e.g., *East & West India Dock Co.* v. *Kirk & Randall* (1887) 12 App.Cas. 788 at 789; *London Street Tramways Co.* v. *London County Council* [1894] A.C. 489 at 490.

[27] See *Pie-Powder* (1911), p. 180.

[28] *The Tracy Peerage* (1843) 10 Cl. & F. 154 at 191.

[29] See Milton, *Paradise Lost*, Bk. 3, l. 380 ("dark with excessive bright").

[30] *Intl. Pulverizing Corp.* v. *Kidwell*, 71 A.2d 151, 156 (N.J. 1950) (*per* Jayne J.).

[31] *Earl M. Kerstetter, Inc.* v. *State*, 171 A.2d 163, 165 (Pa. 1961) (*per* Bok J.).

remarkable use of his hands. A retired professor of anatomy who was called as an expert witness asserted that the alleged process was an anatomical impossibility. His own hand, he said, was fairly big, and "I can tell you from practical experience that I've had no luck in doing it."[32]

Curt and sweeping condemnations, however, resolve little. It was Bowen L.J. who put in telling words the strength and the weakness of expert evidence in the law courts:

> If we are to act in the present instance, we must fall back upon the opinions of experts, and I wish emphatically to state my view, that in a matter like the present, so far from thinking the opinions of experts unsatisfactory, it is to the opinion of experts that I myself should turn with the utmost confidence and faith. Courts of Law and Courts of Justice are not fit places for the exercise of the inductive logic of science. Life is short; it is impossible to place endless time at the disposal of litigants; and the laws of evidence are based upon this very impossibility of prolonging enquiries to endless length. There is hardly a scientific theory in the world which, if we were to examine into it in Law Courts, might not take year after year of the whole time of a tribunal.
>
> Supposing, for a moment, one had brought in question the circular theory of storms, and were to propose before a tribunal like this to examine it, not by reference to the opinions of the most experienced persons who have made it a subject of study and investigation, but to enquire ourselves into all the special circumstances of storms, with which witnesses could favour us, who had crossed the Atlantic or the Eastern Seas in order to form our opinion, assisted, no doubt, by scientific men, as to the circular theory of storms, with all the qualifications which might be adopted, and with all the definitions in which it might be embodied. Take another instance of a law which is very far from likely to be accepted by science, but most probably would be rejected as pure theory, and as utterly beyond reason. I believe there are many persons in India who endeavour to connect the existence of famine raging over tracts of country with spots on the sun. Supposing that theory were brought up in an English Court of Law, we should be bound to embark on an endless enquiry into all the instances in which spots on the sun had been found to be coincident with famine in India.
>
> The truth is, when you are dealing with scientific theories, it is hopeless for Courts of Law to do more than to take the evidence of the scientific men,

---

[32] *The Globe and Mail* (Canada), Oct. 8, 1993.

subject, no doubt to cross-examination, which may or may not condescend to particular instances, which may be brought home to them to show, if it exists, the uncertainty of the grounds upon which their opinions are founded. The result of the admission of this evidence, assuming it, as I do, to be admissible, has been, in my judgment, to show that the endeavour to utilise such evidence launches us upon an inquiry fit only for the leisure of learned and scientific men, but for which the jury system and the judicial system are probably inadequate.[33]

And, Bowen added, "it would be most dangerous to form an independent opinion on a scientific question from the smatterings of science that might be picked up during the hearing of a case."[34]

It was also Bowen L.J. who famously asserted that "the state of a man's mind is as much a fact as the state of his digestion";[35] but it was Harman J. who added the pendant that "the doctors know precious little about the one; and the judges know nothing about the other."[36] The courts rarely investigate the supernatural, though in a dispute on the sale of a house in New York an appellate court once held that "as a matter of law, the house is haunted."[37] This conclusion, however, was based not on spectral or expert evidence but on the vendor being estopped from denying the local reputation that she had fostered.

One frailty of expert evidence lies in its provenance. Expert-shopping is no novelty, as Sir George Jessel M.R. once made plain on a motion for an interlocutory injunction:

In the present instance I have, as usual, the evidence of experts on the one side and on the other, and, as usual, the experts do not agree in their opinion. There is no reason why they should. As I have often explained since I have had the honour of a seat on this Bench, the opinion of an expert may be honestly obtained, and it may be quite different from the opinion of another expert also honestly obtained. But the mode in which expert

---

[33] *Fleet* v. *Metropolitan Asylums Board* (1886) 2 T.L.R. 361, as cited in Cunningham, *Lord Bowen* (1897), p. 162.

[34] *Ibid.*, 2 T.L.R. at p. 363.

[35] *Edgington* v. *Fitzmaurice* (1885) 29 Ch.D. 459 at 483; 1 Misc. 243.

[36] 1955 S.L.T.News. 206 *Semble*, the case was *Re Cutts* [1955] Dec. 12, unrep.: in C.A., [1956] 1 W.L.R. 728. See Williams & Muir Hunter, *Bankruptcy* (19th ed. 1979), p. 348.

[37] *Stambovsky* v. *Ackley*, 572 N.Y.S.2d 672 (1991) (*per* Rubin J.).

evidence is obtained is such as not to give the fair result of scientific opinion to the Court. A man may go, and does sometimes, to half-a-dozen experts. I have known it in cases of valuation within my own experience at the Bar. He takes their honest opinions, he finds three in his favour and three against him; he says to the three in his favour, Will you be kind enough to give evidence? and he pays the three against him their fees and leaves them alone; the other side does the same. It may not be three out of six, it may be three out of fifty. I was told in one case, where a person wanted a certain thing done, that they went to sixty-eight people before they found one. I was told that by the solicitor in the cause. That is an extreme case no doubt, but it may be done, and therefore I have always the greatest possible distrust of scientific evidence of this kind, not only because it is universally contra-dictory, and the mode of its selection makes it necessarily contradictory, but because I know of the way in which it is obtained. I am sorry to say the result is that the Court does not get that assistance from the experts which, if they were unbiassed and fairly chosen, it would have a right to expect.[38]

Only after emerging from cross-examination at the trial could any expert hope for his credibility to be established.

Like judgments, expert evidence may be right for the wrong reasons. Thus Lord Blackburn once said:

I am not inclined to reject the evidence of practical men as to a fact, merely because they give a bad theoretical reason for it, and I am not able myself to furnish the right one. I have been told that some years ago the pilots in the English channel uniformly asserted that there was a current setting towards the French shore, and to allow for that supposed current they always steered to the north of the course which by the chart and compass they should have held. It was ascertained that there was no such current, and some ships were lost because their commanders disregarded the rule of the pilots, because their reason for it was wrong. On further investigation it was found that the deflexion of an unadjusted compass from the action of the iron in most ships was such as to make it right, when the ship's head lay either east or west, to steer to the north of the course by chart as indicated by that compass. The pilots were quite right in the fact which they had observed, though quite wrong in their reason. Whether what I have been told is accurate or not, it is a good illustration of what I mean.[39]

---

[38] *Thorn* v. *Worthing Skating Rink Co.* (1876) 6 Ch.D. 415 at 416.
[39] *Orr Ewing* v. *Colquhoun* (1877) 2 App.Cas. 839 at 863.

Not surprisingly, affidavits remain targets for the Bench: "It is true that the affidavits contain many other statements which are not evidence and are not trustworthy. They revel in rumours, they abound in hearsay, they contain many exaggerations and some extravagancies, and after all they are affidavits."[40] Yet little today is heard of what Lord Hardwicke L.C. once laid down: "Vying and revying in affidavits is intirely discountenanced in the Court of King's Bench, *a fortiori* in a court of equity."[41] The territory of expert witnesses, too, is not quite what it once was; for Parliament has taken a hand. Where it is contended that a three-dimensional object infringes the copyright in a two-dimensional artistic work, statute[42] provided that there was no infringement if the object would not appear "to persons who are not experts in relation to objects of that description" to be a reproduction of the artistic work. In one case a company made spare parts for looms, and the manufacturer of the looms contended that these spare parts infringed the copyright in his drawings for the looms. The judge's comment was that although he felt very well qualified as one of the persons mentioned in the subsection, he could not say whether it contemplated evidence being given by expert non-experts.[43]

Much has been spoken and written about the weight to be given to circumstantial evidence. Pollock C.B. once gave an estimate: "It has been said that circumstantial evidence is to be considered as a chain, and each piece of evidence as a link in the chain, but that is not so, for then, if any one link broke, the chain would fall. It is more like the case of a rope composed of several cords. One strand of the cord might be insufficient to sustain the weight, but three stranded together may be quite of sufficient strength."[44] Indeed, "in law, unlike plane geometry, the whole may be greater than the mere sum of the parts."[45]

---

[40] *The Proton* [1918] A.C. 578 at 583 (*per* Lord Sumner).

[41] *Mellish* v. *De Costa* (1737) 2 Atk. 14.

[42] Copyright Act 1956, s. 9(8).

[43] *British Northrop Ltd.* v. *Texteam Blackburn Ltd.* [1974] R.P.C. 57 at 72.

[44] *R.* v. *Exall* (1866) 4 F. & F. 922 at 929.

[45] *U.S.* v. *DeLeon*, 641 F.2d 330, 336 (5th Cir. 1981) (*per* Rubin J.).

Perhaps the best appraisal was once given by Lord Coleridge J.:

Circumstantial evidence varies infinitely in its strength in proportion to the character and variety, the cogency, the independence, one of another, of the circumstances; I think one might describe it as a network of facts cast around the accused man. That network may be a mere gossamer thread, as light and unsubstantial as the very air itself. It may vanish at a touch. It may be that, strong as it is in part, it leaves great gaps and rents, through which the accused is entitled to pass in safety. It may be so close, so stringent, so coherent in its texture that no efforts on the part of the accused can break through. It may come to nothing. On the other hand, it may be absolutely convincing. If we find a variety of circumstances all pointing in the same direction, convincing in proportion to the number and variety of those circumstances and their independence one of another, although each separate piece of evidence, standing by itself, may admit of an innocent interpretation, yet the cumulative effect of such evidence may be, I do not say that it is, overwhelming proof of guilt. The law does not demand that you should act upon certainties and certainties alone. In the passage of our lives, in our acts, in our thoughts, we do not deal with certainties. We ought to act — we do, in fact act — on just and reasonable convictions founded upon just and reasonable grounds. Juries ought to act upon the evidence. The law asks for no more, and the law demands no less.[46]

To this must be added Lord Normand's caveat:

Circumstantial evidence may sometimes be conclusive, but it must always be narrowly examined, if only because evidence of this kind may be fabricated to cast suspicion on another. Joseph commanded the steward of his house, "put my cup, the silver cup, in the sack's mouth of the youngest,"[47] and when the cup was found there Benjamin's brethren too hastily assumed that he must have stolen it. It is also necessary before drawing the inference of the accused's guilt from circumstantial evidence to be sure that there are no other co-existing circumstances which would weaken or destroy the inference.[48]

[46] *Per* Lord Coleridge J., summing up in *R.* v. *Dickman* (1910), as reported in *The Trial of J.A. Dickman* (Notable British Trials Series) (2d ed. 1926) p. 186–87.

[47] *Genesis* 44:2.

[48] *Teper* v. *The Queen* [1952] A.C. 480 at 489.

The weight of evidence plainly varies with the circumstances: "It is a rule of evidence . . . that positive testimony is entitled to more weight than negative testimony, but by the latter term is meant negative testimony in its true sense and not positive evidence of a negative, because testimony in support of a negative may be as positive as that in support of an affirmative."[49] Again, "the production of weak evidence when strong is available can lead only to the conclusion that the strong would have been adverse. . . . Silence then becomes evidence of the most convincing character."[50] "It is certainly a maxim that all evidence is to be weighed according to the proof which it was in the power of one side to have produced, and in the power of the other to have contradicted."[51] Yet silence, though sometimes eloquent, must be weighed most cautiously: "In my opinion nothing is more dangerous than to say that a thing does not exist because it is not mentioned, except in cases when the thing would inevitably be mentioned if it existed. Long ago it was said that that argument would lead to the conclusion that Tobit's dog had no tail because the tail is not mentioned in the story of *Tobit*.[52] That is precisely the line of argument which has been addressed to us in this case."[53]

However numerous the witnesses and however forthright their evidence, it is for the trial judge to decide whether to believe it:

> When you come to consider the evidence, you, being the person to decide on the effect of it, must not only look at what people say, but you must exercise your own opinion as to whether what they are saying is sensible or can be accepted. If a man was to come and tell me that a horse was like a cat, he might swear to it, and you might get fifty persons to swear to it, but I should not act on such evidence, because it is pure nonsense; and if people come and tell me that all the natives of India are of the same class of intelligence, and some people think they are all exceedingly sharp, and some think that they are all exceedingly stupid, I have a right to bring my own knowledge of

[49] *Blackburn* v. *State*, 254 P. 467, 472 (Ariz. 1927) (*per* McAlister J.).

[50] *Interstate Circuit, Inc.* v. *U.S.*, 306 U.S. 208, 226 (1939) (*per* Stone J.).

[51] *Blatch* v. *Archer* (1774) 1 Cowp. 63 at 65 (*per* Lord Mansfield C.J.).

[52] See *Tobit*, v:16 ("So they went forth both, and the young man's dog with them"); xi:4 ("So they went on their way, and the dog went after them").

[53] *Re Taurine Co.* (1883) 25 Ch.D. 118 at 141 (*per* Fry L.J.).

the world into play; I have a right to bring to bear that knowledge which all educated people have who have read about India or who have known the history of India, and to say that such evidence is simply absurd. . . . There are some of them as clever as any Europeans, and some of them more clever, and some of them as stupid as any Europeans, and I suppose it is difficult to be more stupid.[54]

There are many grounds on which the credibility of a witness may be supported. When he was nearly 82, Lord Esher M.R. had to consider the evidence of one Ritchie, who "had been at some other mill where there was an old man — they called him an old man — of 65, and some people seem to think that 65 is an end of you, and that you are worth nothing afterwards; we shall find that out by and by . . . ." Ritchie —

came before the court, it is said, with all the appearance of an honest old man, and, amongst other things, to show he appeared as an honest old man, it was said that he wore a white beard. I do not myself quite agree that that is a great sign of honesty, but it is certainly not a sign of dishonesty. He gave his account of his life and mode of living, which seems to me, so far as it goes, to be very good evidence of his being a respectable and God-fearing man. He had a bible. It is something in these days to have a bible. He kept a bible, and it was his family bible. He did not say he was in the habit of reading it to his wife or children, but I am perfectly certain he did; and he did that which very respectable people have been in the habit of doing for hundreds of years in this country — he put down in this bible the date of his marriage, and the name of his wife, and the names of his children as they were born, and the dates of their births. I have seen such family bibles, and I have seen them when that thing was done by people whom I revere, and who are as respectable people as any in this kingdom; and I do think it is a very good specimen of what sort of a man Ritchie was. It is not at all conclusive, and he may be a horrible rogue notwithstanding; but still it is something. Nobody ever said he had been a rogue before. When he came as a witness he had not the slightest reason why he should favour one side more than the other. The people in whose favour he gave evidence were not his masters, and never had been; and they were not his relations, and never had been. Well, he says this, and is supported by the other two men I have mentioned, who had no interest to say what was not true. "Then," says Mr. Moulton, "what does that

[54] *Re Christiansen's Trade Mark* (1886) 3 R.P.C. 54 at 60 (*per* Lord Esher M.R.).

signify; they were conspiring to tell lies; they were liars all of them, and they were conspiring to do it." He has not any evidence such as the most virulent judge in the country ever left to a jury of a conspiracy. There is no evidence that it was a conspiracy. What happened? The judge was not bound to believe them, although they were not conspiring; but he saw them, and he gives an account of what he did see, and he says, "I confess I see no reason to doubt the correctness of their evidence in any respect." That is upon the view of them, and of what they said . . . .[55]

And that carried the day.

Success in cross-examination may topple into disaster. In a case before Upjohn J.,[56] a mother had settled some investments on her daughter, but had omitted to transfer them to the trustees, who were her two sons. After a while the mother, who had retained a life interest in the investments, forgot about the settlement and began to deal with some of the investments as if they were still her own. Some 14 years later she died, and, not surprisingly, problems then emerged. One of the sons was cross-examined about his own degree of forgetfulness.

Q.C.:   You executed the settlement, did you not?
Son: Yes.
Q.C.:   Surely you knew then that your mother had only a life interest?
Son: Yes, I did.
Q.C.:   A year after the settlement was made, you hadn't forgotten it, had you?
Son: No.
Q.C.:   Nor two years later?
Son: No.
Q.C.:   And you hadn't forgotten it four years later, had you?
Son: No, I don't think so.
Q.C.:   And five years later you still knew it?
Son: (hesitantly:) I *think* I did.
Q.C.:   (clinching it:) And when did you first remember that you had forgotten it?

---

[55] *Haggenmacher* v. *Watson, Todd & Co.* (1897) 14 R.P.C. 631 at 634 (*per* Lord Esher M.R.).

[56] *Re Wale* [1956] 1 W.L.R. 1346.

To this there was no reply save laughter, not least from the Bench. (An alternative version of the last question is "Then tell my Lord, when did you first forget it?" followed, after a long pause, by "I can't remember."[57])

Finally, there is the doctrine of judicial notice, which can make the adduction of evidence unnecessary: "There comes a point where this court should not be ignorant as judges of what we know as men."[58] But the extent to which the doctrine may be carried has often troubled the court. In a case arising out of the operations in the Dardanelles during the First World War, Lord Dunedin once observed that he would not feel that he was justified —

> in resting any conclusion which I formed on such things as the particular dates when certain operations of war were begun or were in progress, when those dates had not been proved but had to be supplied from my own private knowledge. On the other hand, it is settled by authority that a judge may be aware that there is a state of war; and by that I do not understand a vague consciousness such as may have been felt by an ancient Roman when he noticed that the Temple of Janus was open, but an intelligent apprehension of the war as it is and the theatre of the operations thereof.[59]

Lord Sumner's view was similar:

> To require that a judge should affect a cloistered aloofness from facts that every other man in Court is fully aware of, and should insist on having proof on oath of what, as a man of the world, he knows already better than any witness can tell him, is a rule that may easily become pedantic and futile. Least of all would it be possible to require this detached and blindfold attitude towards events which the course of the late war has burnt into the memories of us all. It does not, however, seem to me, as at present advised, that the month and day at or about which a particular military movement was carried out, or that the existence between the Gallipoli Peninsula and Mudros Bay of the relation of active front to supply base, are matters as to

---

[57] This account combines the recollections of counsel for the trustees, (Sir) Raymond Jennings Q.C. and Raymond Walton (Walton J.).

[58] *Watts* v. *Indiana*, 338 U.S. 49, 52 (1949) (*per* Frankfurter J.).

[59] *Commonwealth Shipping Representative* v. *Peninsular & Oriental Branch Service* [1923] A.C. 191 at 205.

which everybody can be deemed to be fully and accurately informed or of which judges can be required, in the legal sense of the words, to take judicial notice.[60]

A more recent view is succinct: "Judicial knowledge is the knowledge of the ordinary wide-awake man, used by one who is trained to express it in terms of precision."[61]

In 1661, Twisden J. illustrated the ambit of judicial notice by citing an unreported case in the time of James I where the action was "pur ceux parolls, As sure as God governs the world, and King James this kingdom, so sure hath J.S. committed treason, &c. in cest case fuit adjudge que J.S. poit bien maintainer son action sans averring that God governs the world, ou King James this kingdom, car sont choses apparent."[62] Some years earlier the defence to an action for assault was that the plaintiff had been trespassing and that the defendant had only thrown stones at him "gently." But this failed: "les Judges disont que home ne poet jecter pierres molliter."[63]

---

[60] *Ibid.*, at p. 211.

[61] *Brisbane City Council* v. *Attorney-General for Queensland* [1979] A.C. 411 at 423 (*per* Lord Wilberforce).

[62] *Dacy* v. *Clinch* (1661) 1 Sid. 52 at 53.

[63] *Cole* v. *Maunder* (1635) 2 Rolle Abr. 548 ("the judges said that man is unable to throw stones gently").

16

~

AN UNCHARTED SEA OF
DOUBT AND DIFFICULTY

TO THE doctrine of *stare decisis* all common-law jurisdictions subscribe. Obedience is the rule, though at times unwelcome decisions are met by "distinguishing" them on grounds that are wafer-thin. Cases of outright rebellion are rare, but there was a little-known outbreak among the nineteenth-century Vice-Chancellors. They were a sturdy race, not unduly impressed by appellate decisions of the Lord Chancellor or the Court of Appeal in Chancery, and scorning fine distinctions. An example is the treatment accorded to *Hensman* v. *Fryer*,[1] in which Lord Chelmsford L.C. had reversed an order of Kindersley V.-C. Two years later a similar point came before Stuart V.-C.; and he disposed of it in four sentences. One of these was "The decision in the case of *Hensman* v. *Fryer* is clearly a mistaken decision; I must therefore decline to follow it."[2] Three years later Malins V.-C. took the same view, saying: "The Court is not bound to follow a decision even of the Court of Appeal if clearly erroneous. There were in my recollection no less than three decisions of Lord Westbury which Vice-Chancellor Stuart declined to follow. One of the cases in which he did so was *Drummond* v. *Drummond*,[3] which afterwards went to the Court of Appeal,[4] and the decision was affirmed."[5]

---

[1] (1867) 3 Ch.App. 420.

[2] *Collins* v. *Lewis* (1869) L.R. 8 Eq. 708 at 709.

[3] (1866) L.R. 2 Eq. 335.

[4] (1866) 2 Ch.App. 32 (Lord Chelmsford L.C. and Turner L.J., Knight Bruce L.J. concurring): see at p. 47.

[5] *Dugdale* v. *Dugdale* (1872) L.R. 14 Eq. 234 at 235.

Two years later the Court of Appeal tried again, in *Lancefield* v. *Iggulden*.[6] Lord Cairns L.C. and James L.J. reversed the decision of Bacon V.-C. and held that *Hensman* v. *Fryer* was both right and a binding authority. But even that did not suffice. The next year Malins V.-C. once more refused to apply *Hensman* v. *Fryer*, and treated *Lancefield* v. *Iggulden* as being confined to another point.[7] A year later Hall V.-C., in a mere three sentences, preferred the views of his brother Vice-Chancellors to those of the Court of Appeal, and decided the case accordingly.[8] Vice-Cancellarian persistence seems to have prevailed over dutiful obedience.

Some points are free from the constraints and assistance of authority: "The clearer a thing is, the more difficult it is to find any express authority or any *dictum* exactly to the point."[9] And "as Lord Macnaghten said, the plainer a proposition is the harder it often is to find judicial authority for it."[10] Lord Dunedin expressed the view in abecedarian form: "To hold that one of the fundamental doctrines of real property can be called in question because it has not been in terms laid down by a judgment of the House of Lords is, in my opinion, to invest the judicial proceedings of this House with an authority to which they are not entitled. The A B C of the law is generally not questioned before your Lordships, just because it is the A B C."[11] Lord Mansfield phrased the idea magisterially: "Precedent, though it be evidence of law, is not law in itself; much less the whole of the law."[12]

James L.J. once illustrated this view in an Italian excursion:

> If a man hired a *vetturino* to take him from one place to another, and found that the *vetturino*, after he had accepted the hiring, had conspired with his

6 (1874) 10 Ch.App. 136.

7 *Tomkins* v. *Colthurst* (1875) 1 Ch.D. 626.

8 *Farquharson* v. *Floyer* (1876) 3 Ch.D. 109.

9 *Panama & South Pacific Telegraph Co.* v. *India Rubber, Gutta Percha & Telegraph Works Co.* (1875) 10 Ch.App. 515 at 526 (*per* James L.J.).

10 *Kimber* v. *Gas Light & Coke Co.* [1918] 1 K.B. 439 at 447 (*per* Scrutton L.J.); and see 1 Misc. 304.

11 *Johnston* v. *O'Neill* [1911] A.C. 552 at 592–93 (*per* Lord Dunedin).

12 *Jones* v. *Randall* (1774) Lofft 383 at 385 (*per* Lord Mansfield C.J.).

servant to rob him on the way, he would be entitled to get rid both of the *vetturino* and the servant. So, if a man sits down in a tavern or *osteria* to play at cards or dice with another man for a stake, and finds that his opponent has provided himself with cogged dice or marked cards, the man would be immediately entitled to leave the table, and would not be obliged to procure proper cards or honest dice. I am not aware, however, of any express decision on either of the cases I have suggested.[13]

When the court does make new law, however, it can "only be done on principles of private justice, moral fitness, and public convenience; which, when applied to a new subject, make common law without a precedent."[14]

The success of hymn books as sources of law has been limited. When it was attempted to obtain an injunction to restrain foreign shipowners from removing from the jurisdiction the insurance money to which they were entitled after their ship had been lost at sea, questions were raised as to the jurisdiction to make such an order. To Lord Denning M.R. there was no difficulty, and no need to wait for the Rule Committee to change the law:

> I ask, why should the judges wait for the Rule Committee? The judges have an inherent jurisdiction to lay down the practice and procedure of the courts: and we can invoke it now to restrain the removal of these insurance moneys. To the timorous souls I would say in the words of William Cowper:
>
> > "Ye fearful saints, fresh courage take,
> > The clouds ye so much dread
> > Are big with mercy, and shall break
> > In blessings on your head."
>
> Instead of "saints," read "judges." Instead of "mercy," read "justice." And you will find a good way to law reform.[15]

---

13 *Panama & South Pacific Telegraph Co.* v. *India Rubber, Gutta Percha & Telegraph Works Co.*, (1875) 10 Ch.App. 515 at 526.
14 *Millar* v. *Taylor* (1769) 4 Burr. 2303 at 2312 (*per* Willes J.).
15 *Siskina* v. *Distos Compania Naviera S.A.* [1979] A.C. 210 at 236.

But Bridge L.J. dissented: "The clouds in Lord Denning M.R.'s adaptation of William Cowper may be big with justice but we are neither midwives nor rainmakers";[16] and it was this that proved to be the accurate forecast of the climate in the House of Lords,[17] though this did not discourage Lord Denning for long,[18] or at all.

Legal authors, however venerable, have their critics:

One may, perhaps, wonder how far either the practicality or the attractiveness of the Roman Dutch Common Law is demonstrated to modern eyes, and whether the law is made more comprehensible to present day practitioners, by learned, but seemingly rather agonizing, searches for, and consideration of, statements made — quite often without the support of reasoned argument so far as appears — by commentators and legal pundits of the 17th and 18th centuries, who cite, as authority for the statements they make, statements similarly made by other writers, of some of whom many lawyers now in practice have not ever heard before, and to whose works the large majority of them have no access. It is, at times, difficult not to link with some of these commentators the words of Berowne[19] in "Love's Labour's Lost":

> "Small have continual plodders ever won,
> Save base authority from others' books.
> These earthly godfathers of heaven's lights,
> That gave a name to every fixed star,
> Have no more profit of their shining nights
> Than those that walk, and wot not what they are."

I, certainly, find it difficult to suppose that a present-day man of affairs is likely to acquiesce more readily in some legal rule which, in his view, frustrates, or unduly restricts, him in the advantageous employment or management of property left by will, for the reason that it represents the opinion of, say, Guido Papa, or Peregrinus or Michael Graffus, or all of them. Indeed I rather think this information might dispose him to align himself with Mr. Bumble in his opinion of the law.[20]

---

[16] *Ibid.*, at p. 243.

[17] *Siskina* v. *Distos Compania Naviera S.A.* [1979] A.C. 210.

[18] See, e.g., *Croke* v. *Wiseman* [1982] 1 W.L.R. 71 at 76, dissenting.

[19] (Or Biron), in Act 1, sc.1, ll. 86–91.

[20] *Ex parte Administrator Estate Dickins*, 1953(1) P. H., G. 39 at 42 (*per* Selke J.).

Judgments that have never been delivered are an improbable source of law, but not impossible. In 1864, in the Court of Queen's Bench, a yearly tenant and his wife successfully sued the reversioner on the defective condition of part of the premises demised.[21] The reversioner then appealed to the Court of Exchequer Chamber, and judgment was reserved.[22] The next day, the court recommended the tenant and his wife to accept a stay of the proceedings, saying that if they did not, judgment would be delivered some three weeks later. "The parties having, after some delay, acceded to this, Erle C.J. now said, as the plaintiff had consented to a stet processus it will not be necessary to deliver the judgment we have prepared."[23] The plain inference was that the appeal would have succeeded; indeed, another report stated that there was an intimation to that effect.[24] But judgment was there none; and for some five years the Queen's Bench judges were left in the unhappy state of knowing that they had been wrong but not knowing why. Then in a volume of reports published in 1870 the undelivered judgment appeared, under the heading "Trin. Vac.1865" but without explanation.[25] All seven judges of the Exchequer Chamber had concurred in reversing the decision below, and it is this undelivered "judgment" that has been treated as establishing the law.

The proper use of authority is one of the great crafts of the law: "It is always a most dangerous thing to take a somewhat wide expression of a learned judge and separate it altogether from its context and the facts of the case and say: 'Now that is something which has to be followed in every other case.' The learned judge, in ninety-nine cases out of a hundred, never meant anything of the kind."[26] Interlocutory observations are in a special category. Lord Simon L.C. once pointed out that such observations "were not judicial pronouncements. They did not decide anything, even provisionally. They were made to elucidate the

---

[21] *Gandy* v. *Jubber* (1864) 5 B. & S. 78.

[22] *Ibid.*, (1865) 5 B. & S. 485.

[23] *Ibid.*, at p. 494.

[24] 13 W.R. 1022.

[25] *Gandy* v. *Jubber* (1865) 9 B. & S. 15.

[26] *Scranton's Trustee* v. *Pearse* [1922] 2 Ch. 87 at 124 (*per* Lord Sterndale M.R.).

argument, to point the question, or to indicate what were the matters which the judicial spokesman thought needed to be investigated, and that was all."[27] So too Jessel M.R.: "I distrust *dicta* in all cases, and especially *dicta* during argument."[28]

Willes C.J. introduced another category of unreliability, referring to "the *obiter dicta*, which in many cases were *nunquam dicta*; but barely the words of the reporters; for upon examination I have found many of the sayings ascribed to that great man, Lord Chief Justice Holt, were never said by him."[29] And it was Baron Bramwell (not "Lord Bramble," as *The Times* once made Lord Goddard C.J. allege[30]) who bewailed the absence of any "Statute of Limitations to protect judges against their old *obiter dicta*."[31] Eyre J. would have agreed; for nearly a century and a half was to pass before a *dictum* of his[32] was to receive a cruel cut at the hands of Lord Abinger C.B. The Chief Baron said of it: "It was not only an obiter dictum, but a very wide divaricating dictum."[33]

In an article in *Punch* (which was alleged, unsuccessfully, to be a contempt of court), the author, who within three years was to be seated on the Woolsack, enunciated the "golden rule for judges in the matter of obiter dicta. Silence is always an option."[34] Yet even if the option is rejected, obiter dicta are not simply to be thrust aside. They may carry great weight, especially if many distinguished judges have concurred in them: "A battery of howitzers off the target is more impressive than a pop-gun on it,"[35] not least when there are seven in the battery with the calibre of Viscount Simon L.C., Lord Thankerton, Lord Russell of Killowen, Lord Macmillan, Lord Wright, Lord Porter, and Lord Clauson.[36]

---

[27] Practice Note [1942] W.N. 89, J.C.

[28] *Wallis* v. *Smith* (1882) 21 Ch.D. 243 at 265.

[29] *Ellis* v. *Smith* (1754) 1 Ves.Jun. 11 at 13.

[30] *R.* v. *Cheltenham Justices, ex parte Martin* [1955] *The Times*, Dec. 21.

[31] *Pie-Powder* (1911), p. 180; and see 1 Misc. 306.

[32] In *Newton* v. *Trigg* (1691) 1 Show. K.B. 268 at 269.

[33] *Sunbolf* v. *Alford* (1838) 3 M. & W. 248 at 252 ("spreading out").

[34] *R.* v. *Commissioner of Police of the Metropolis, ex parte Blackburn (No. 2)* [1968] 2 Q.B. 150 at 154. The author, Quintin Hogg Q.C., had vehemently and inaccurately attacked the Court of Appeal for decisions that had in fact been made by other courts.

[35] *Re Grosvenor Hotel, London (No. 2)* [1965] Ch. 1210 at 1223 (*per* Ungoed-Thomas J.).

[36] In *Duncan* v. *Cammell, Laird & Co. Ltd.* [1942] A.C. 624.

Salmon L.J. mused: "This is undoubtedly true, but a battery of howitzers off target sometimes does great damage to what is intended to be preserved."[37]

Obiter dicta do not stand alone. There are dicta and dicta and dicta:

> Some authorities distinguish between obiter dicta and judicial dicta. The former are mere passing remarks[38] of the judge, whereas the latter consist of considered enunciations of the judge's opinion of the law upon some point which does not arise for decision on the facts of the case before him, and so is not part of the ratio decidendi. But there is, I think, a third type of dictum, so far innominate. If instead of merely stating his own view of the point in question the judge supports it by stating what has been done in other cases, not reported, then his statement is one which rests not only on his own unsupported view of the law but also on the decisions of those other judges whose authority he has invoked. He is, as it were, a reporter pro tanto. Such a statement of the settled law of accustomed practice carries with it the authority not merely of the judge who makes it but also of an unseen cloud of his judicial brethren. A dictum of this type offers, as it seems to me, the highest authority that any dictum can bear; and I think that a judge would have to be very sure of himself before he refused to follow it.[39]

As for judicial dicta, "a mere passing remark, or a statement or assumption on some matter that has not been argued, is one thing; a considered judgment on a point fully argued is another, especially where, had the facts been otherwise, it would have formed part of the ratio. Such judicial dicta, standing in authority somewhere between a ratio decidendi and an obiter dictum, seem to me to have a weight nearer to the former than the latter."[40]

Even if a statement is no mere dictum and plainly contains the ratio decidendi, many warnings must be heeded. For example: "It by no means follows that the rule is co-extensive with the reasons given in support of it."[41] The courts must not "confound the reasons for the rule with the

---

[37] *Re Grosvenor Hotel, London (No. 2)*, *supra* note 35, at p. 1257.

[38] And see *Flower* v. *Ebbw Vale Steel, Iron & Coal Co. Ltd.* [1934] 2 K.B. 132 at 154 (*per* Talbot J.: "statements by the way").

[39] *Richard West & Partners (Inverness) Ltd.* v. *Dick* [1969] 2 Ch. 424 at 431–32.

[40] *Brunner* v. *Greenslade* [1971] Ch. 993 at 1002–03.

[41] *O'Connor* v. *Marjoribanks* (1842) 4 Man. & G. 435 at 445 (*per* Maule J.); 1 Misc. 249–50.

rule itself."[42] Again, "It may be well to bear in mind that not every passing expression of a judge, however eminent, can be treated as an ex cathedra statement. It must be read in its context, and the most that can be expected is that it should be accurate enough for the matter in hand."[43] Principles outweigh the words in which they are expressed: "The expressions of every judge must be taken with reference to the case on which he decides, otherwise the law will get into extreme confusion. That is what we are to look at in all cases. The manner in which he is arguing it is not the thing; it is the principle he is deciding."[44] Furthermore, "We should not indulge in the fiction that the law now announced has always been the law. . . . It is much more conducive to law's self-respect to recognize candidly the considerations that give prospective content to a new pronouncement of law."[45] Again, "A court by announcing that its decision is confined to the facts before it does not decide in advance that logic will not drive it further when new facts arise."[46] At the same time, "A proposition may be generally applicable and yet involve embarrassment when pushed to a logical extreme."[47]

Distinctions are important:

- "The more we read, unless we are very careful to distinguish, the more we shall be confounded."[48]

- "Upon questions of construction when no arbitrary rule is involved, it is always more important to consider the words and the circumstances than even strong analogies in earlier decisions. The successive neglect of a series of small distinctions, in the effort to follow precedent, is very liable to end in perverting instruments from their plain meaning.[49]

---

[42] *Re Wingham* [1949] P. 187 at 196 (*per* Denning L.J.); and see (1941) 57 L.Q.R. 481 at 482, 483.

[43] *London Graving Dock Co. Ltd.* v. *Horton* [1951] A.C. 737 at 748 (*per* Lord Porter).

[44] *Richardson* v. *Mellish* (1824) 2 Bing. 229 at 248 (*per* Best C.J.).

[45] *Griffin* v. *Illinois*, 351 U.S. 12, 26 (1956) (*per* Frankfurter J.).

[46] *Haddock* v. *Haddock*, 201 U.S. 562, 631 (1906) (Holmes J., dissenting).

[47] *Davis* v. *Cleveland, Cincinnati, Chicago & St. Louis Ry. Co.*, 217 U.S. 157, 177 (1910) (*per* McKenna J.).

[48] *Taylor d. Atkyns* v. *Horde* (1757) 1 Burr. 60 at 110 (*per* Lord Mansfield C.J.).

[49] And see 1 Misc. 160.

In no other branch of the law is so much discretion required in dealing with authority."[50]

- "If once we go upon niceties of construction, we shall not know where to stop: for one nicety is made a foundation for another; and that other for a third; and so on, without end."[51]

Yet distinctions may be carried too far: "It is desirable that the law should be uniform, and that people should not be tempted to bring experimental new suits on minute differences of fact."[52] Distinctions may also be obscure. Roxburgh J., in a case[53] in which he confessed to "considerable bewilderment,"[54] was forthright: "I am convinced — though I do not know what the distinction is — that there must be a very great distinction between *James* v. *Vane*[55] and the present case."

Instead of relying on an undiscoverable distinction, a judge may base a decision on an undisclosed principle. When Swinfen Eady Q.C. cited *Conway* v. *Fenton*[56] to North J., the judge's comment was pointed: "I am tired of hearing that case quoted, Mr. Eady. It does not establish any rule."[57] In his judgment the judge discussed the case, and said that in it Kekewich J. had cited *Re Household*,[58] "in which he seems to have found a principle, on which he was able to make the order, but unfortunately he does not state what the principle was."[59] Jessel M.R. was emphatic. At first instance, when confronted by two decisions of the Court of Appeal, he said: "It is very dangerous for a Judge who does not agree with particular decisions, to deal in distinctions from those decisions."[60]

---

50 *Merrill* v. *Preston*, 135 Mass. 451, 455 (1883) (*per* Holmes J.).

51 *R.* v. *Inhabitants of Caverswell* (1758) Burr. Sett.Cas. 461 at 465 (*per* Wilmot J.).

52 *Johns* v. *James* (1878) 8 Ch.D. 744 at 752 (*per* James L.J.).

53 *Read's Trustee in Bankruptcy* v. *Smith* [1951] 1 All E.R. 406 at 410.

54 S.C. [1951] Ch. 439 at 445: see (1951) 67 L.Q.R. 443.

55 (1860) 29 L.J.Q.B. 169.

56 (1888) 40 Ch.D. 512.

57 *Re Lord de Tabley* (1896) 75 L.T. 328 at 328.

58 (1884) 27 Ch.D. 553.

59 *Re Lord de Tabley*, *supra* note 57, at p. 329.

60 *Re International Pulp & Paper Co., Knowles' Mortgage* (1877) 6 Ch.D. 556 at 559.

Instead, he said that he did not consider the decisions as being absolutely binding upon him, because "as I do not know the principle on which the Court of Appeal founded their decisions, I cannot tell whether I ought to follow them or not. If those decisions do lay down any principle I am bound by it, but I have not the remotest notion what that principle is."[61] In due time the House of Lords laid the two cases to rest, still unexplained.[62]

A major divergence is between those who would follow precedent closely and those who feel less constrained by its shackles. The passage of years is often used as a foundation for the latter view: "Precedents drawn from the days of travel by stage coach do not fit the conditions of travel to-day."[63] The Middle Ages are *a fortiori*: "It is revolting to have no better reason for a rule of law than that so it was laid down in the time of Henry IV. It is still more revolting if the grounds upon which it was laid down have vanished long since, and the rule simply persists from blind imitation of the past."[64] Indeed, "No one really doubts that the common law is a body of law which develops in process of time in response to the developments of the society in which it rules. Its movement may not be perceptible at any distinct point of time, nor can we always say how it gets from one point to another; but I do not think that, for all that, we need abandon the conviction of Galileo that somehow, by some means, there is a movement that takes place."[65] Both abuse and ambiguity have made their contributions: "The life of the law has been in the unceasing abuse of its elementary ideas."[66] More charitably, "The common law has often (if sometimes unconsciously) thrived on ambiguity and it would

---

[61] *Ibid.*

[62] *Wright* v. *Horton* (1887) 12 App.Cas. 371.

[63] *MacPherson* v. *Buick Motor Co.*, 111 N.E. 1050, 1053 (N.Y. 1916) (*per* Cardozo J.).

[64] O.W. Holmes J., *The Path of the Law*, 10 Harv. L. Rev. 457, 469 (1897).

[65] *Lister* v. *Romford Ice & Cold Storage Co. Ltd.* [1957] A.C. 555 at 591–92 (*per* Lord Radcliffe, dissenting).

[66] S.F.C. Milsom, *Historical Foundations of the Common Law* (1969), p. xi (cp. 2d ed. 1981, p. 6).

be mistaken, even it if were possible, to try to crystallize the rules of this, or any, aspect of public policy into neat propositions."[67]

In support of a less flexible approach much has been said. Emphasis has been on matters of width: "It is better to submit to a particular inconvenience than to introduce a general mischief."[68] Again, "The hardship of the particular case is no reason for melting down the law. For the sake of fixedness and uniformity, law must be treated as a solid, not as a fluid. It must have, and always retain, a certain degree of hardness, to keep its outlines firm and constant. Water changes shape with every vessel into which it is poured; and a liquid law would vary with the mental conformation of judges, and become a synonym for vagueness and instability."[69]

The ancient proposition that hard cases make bad law[70] is to be found in this camp. Lord Denning M.R. put forward an equivalent only to anathematize it: "It comes to this: 'Unjust decisions make good law': whereas they do nothing of the kind."[71] Without pausing to examine the logic of this exegesis, one may turn to Lord Blackburn's inversion of the proposition: "There is a legal proverb that hard cases make bad law; but I think there is truth in the retort that it is a bad law which makes hard cases."[72] Lord du Parcq turned to the past: "Historically one may say, perhaps, that hard cases made Equity, but the most prejudiced common lawyer would not say to-day that Equity was bad law."[73]

For that peer of equity lawyers, Jessel M.R., the temptation to make bad law was one to be resisted most resolutely. The House of Lords agreed: "Hard cases offer a strong temptation to let them have their proverbial consequences. It is a temptation that the judicial mind must

---

[67] *Esso Petroleum Co. Ltd.* v. *Harper's Garage (Stourport) Ltd.* [1968] A.C. 269 at 331 (*per* Lord Wilberforce).

[68] *Dent* v. *Basham* (1854) 9 Exch. 469 at 471 (*per* Alderson B., applying *Emerson* v. *Lashley* (1793) 2 Hy.Bl. 248 at 252, *per* Gould J.).

[69] *Southern Star Lightning Rod Co.* v. *Duvall*, 64 Ga. 262, 268 (1879) (*per* Bleckley J.).

[70] See, e.g., *Ex parte Long* (1854) 3 W.R. 18 at 19 (*per* Lord Campbell C.J.); and see *Winterbottom* v. *Wright* (1842) 10 M. & W. 109 at 116 (*per* Rolfe B.); 1 Misc. 305.

[71] *Re Vandervell's Trusts (No. 2)* [1974] Ch. 269 at 322.

[72] *River Wear Commissioners* v. *Adamson* (1877) 2 App.Cas. 743 at 770.

[73] *Aspects of the Law* (Presidential Address to the Holdsworth Club, 1948), p. 9.

be vigilant to resist."[74] Again, "My Lords, this is a hard case — and we all know where hard cases can take a judge."[75] There is a kinship with great cases: "Great cases like hard cases make bad law. For great cases are called great, not by reason of their real importance in shaping the law of the future, but because of some accident of immediate overwhelming interest which appeals to the feelings and distorts the judgment. These immediate interests exercise a kind of hydraulic pressure which makes what previously was clear seem doubtful, and before which even well settled principles of law will bend."[76]

Ultimately, the question is one of discrimination: "There is an old and somewhat foolish saying that 'Hard cases make bad law,' and therefore the law must be left as it is. It would be equally true to say, 'Bad law makes hard cases,' and therefore the law must be amended. The real truth lies somewhere between. Mere freaks of fortune should not be made an excuse for weakening a law which is sound. But a law which is seen to multiply hard cases, not through any accident but by its necessary elements, is not worth preserving, for the law was made for man, not man for the law."[77]

The fault in the less flexible approach, if it be a fault, is a fault on the right side: "If I must either attribute to some Judges a reverence more for the letter than the spirit, caution carried too far, and over-anxiousness to keep themselves within the most clearly defined limits of their authority, or ascribe to others an arbitrary and unwarrantable assumption of legislative power, I elect the former."[78] In constitutional law this attitude is of special weight: "We should not be so unmindful, even when constitutional questions are involved, of the principle of *stare decisis*, by whose circumspect observance the wisdom of this Court as an institution transcending the moment can alone be brought to bear on the difficult problems that confront us."[79] On this, there have been some forceful

---

[74] *Gibson* v. *Manchester City Council* [1979] 1 W.L.R. 294 at 299 (*per* Lord Diplock).

[75] *Ibid.* (*per* Lord Edmund-Davies).

[76] *Northern Secs. Co.* v. *U.S.*, 193 U.S. 197, 400–01 (1904) (Holmes J., dissenting).

[77] *Pale* v. *Pale*, A.P. Herbert, *Uncommon Law* (1935) 425 at 455 (*per* Wool J.).

[78] *Boyse* v. *Rossborough* (1854) 3 De G.M. & G. 817 at 845 (*per* Knight Bruce L.J.).

[79] *Green* v. *U.S.*, 355 U.S. 184, 215 (1957) (Frankfurter J., dissenting).

protests in the United States Supreme Court: "The tendency to disregard precedents in the decision of cases like the present has become so strong in this court of late as, in my view, to shake confidence in the consistency of decision and leave the courts below on an uncharted sea of doubt and difficulty without any confidence that what was said yesterday will hold good tomorrow . . . ."[80]

The formidable team of Boswell and Dr. Johnson once stood on this side. In a case in the Court of Session Boswell attempted to persuade the court to return to the strictness of a rule that had come to be relaxed. He failed, but then applied to the court for a revision and alteration of the judgment; and Dr. Johnson composed an argument. In this, he said:

> Concerning the power of the Court to make or to suspend a law, we have no intention to inquire. It is sufficient for our purpose that every just law is dictated by reason; and that the practice of every legal Court is regulated by equity. It is the quality of reason to be invariable and constant; and of equity, to give to one man what, in the same case, is given to another. The advantage which humanity derives from law is this: that the law gives every man a rule of action, and prescribes a mode of conduct which shall entitle him to the support and protection of society. That the law may be a rule of action, it is necessary that it be known; — it is necessary that it be permanent and stable. The law is the measure of civil right; but if the measure be changeable, the extent of the thing measured never can be settled.
>
> To permit a law to be modified at discretion, is to leave the community without law.[81] It is to withdraw the direction of that publick wisdom, by which the deficiencies of private understanding are to be supplied. It is to suffer the rash and ignorant to act at discretion, and then to depend for the legality of that action on the sentence of the Judge. He that is thus governed, lives not by law, but by opinion: not by a certain rule to which he can apply his intention before he acts, but by an uncertain and variable opinion, which he can never know but after he has committed the act on which that opinion shall be passed. He lives by a law (if a law it be,) which he can never know before he has offended it. To this case may be justly applied that important principle, *misera est servitus ubi jus est aut incognitum aut vagum.*[82]

[80] *Mahnich v. Southern Steamship Co.*, 321 U.S. 96, 113 (1944) (Roberts J., dissenting).

[81] See also 1 Misc. 219; 2 Misc. 194.

[82] 1 Boswell's *Johnson* 441 ("Obedience is wretched where the law is either unknown or unsettled").

But the application failed,[83] though one of the judges recognised the hand of Johnson.[84]

In the nineteenth century Bentham was to generalise Dr. Johnson's last point: "It is judges . . . that make the common law. Do you know how they make it? Just as a man makes laws for his dog. When your dog does anything you want to break him of, you wait till he does it, and then beat him for it. This is the way you make laws for your dog; and this is the way the judges make law for you and me. They won't tell a man beforehand what it is he *should not do* — they won't so much as allow of his being told:[85] they lie by till he has done something which they say he should not *have done*, and then they hang him for it."[86] Some have even seen this type of peril in so well-tried a concept as what is "reasonable." Thus it has been described as being "that irrepressible, vague and delusive standard which at times threatens to engulf the entire law, including the Constitution itself, in a sea of judicial discretion."[87]

The control of discretion, of course, does not cure all: "However much men may honestly endeavour to limit the exercise of their discretion by definite rule, there must always be room for idiosyncrasy; and idiosyncrasy, as the word expresses, varies with the man. But there is, besides this, that of which every student of legal history must be aware, the leaning of the courts for a certain time in a particular direction, balanced at least, if not reversed, by the leaning of the courts for a certain time in a direction opposite. The current of legal decision runs often to a point which is felt to be beyond the bounds of sound and sane control, and there is a danger sometimes that the retrocession of the current should become itself extreme."[88]

---

[83] *Wilson v. Armour and Smith* (1772) 1 Hailes' Dec. 482; *sub nom. Wilson v. Smith and Armour* (1772) Mor. 9833; 6 Fac.Col. 41.

[84] *Wilson v. Armour and Smith, supra* note 83, at p. 483 (*per* Lord Hailes).

[85] This seems to refer to the former rule that it was a contempt of court to publish a report of a judgment; yet this did not apply to reports by authorised reporters: see 1 Burr. v.

[86] Bentham, *Works*, vol. 5 (1843), p. 235.

[87] *Green v. U.S.*, 356 U.S. 165, 197 (1958) (Black J., dissenting and disagreeing on a "reasonable" punishment for contempt).

[88] *R. v. Labouchere* (1884) 15 Cox C.C. 415 at 425 (*per* Lord Coleridge C.J.).

The use of precedents requires full understanding, accurate expression, and sound reasoning. As was said by one Lord-Justice Clerk of Scotland: "The more I am able to collect of English law, I am only the more confident that we do not understand nine out of ten of the cases which are quoted to us, and that, in attempts to apply that law, we run the greatest risk of spoiling our own by mistaking theirs."[89] In the words of Holmes J., a case may involve "one of those general truths which become untrue by being inaccurately expressed."[90] It was he who used to say of Horace Gray J. that "the premise of his opinion and the conclusion stood forth like precipices, with a roaring torrent of precedents between, but he never quite understood how Gray got across."[91] In this, there may have been some echo of the comment of Lord Eldon L.C. on Sir Richard Arden M.R.:[92] "He was seldom wrong in saying what was the law, though he sometimes had a difficulty in explaining why it was law."[93]

Although exceptions sometimes aid reasoning, they can sometimes imperil it: "It is not a case where an exception can prove the rule; it is one where the exception destroys the rule."[94] Again, some would-be exceptions are merely imposters: "The exception which exhausts the principal rule must be incorrect, if the rule itself be admitted as a correct one."[95]

"Strong decisions" are in a special category. They were once delineated by Erle C.J.: "I have known judges, bred in the world of legal studies, who delighted in nothing so much as a strong decision. Now a strong decision is a decision opposed to common sense and to common convenience. . . . A great part of the law made by judges consists of strong decisions, and as one strong decision is a precedent for another a little stronger, the law at least on some matters becomes such a nuisance, that equity intervenes, or an Act of Parliament must be passed to sweep

---

[89] *M'Cowan* v. *Wright* (1852) 15 D. 229 at 232 (*per* Lord Justice-Clerk Hope).

[90] *Damon* v. *Hawaii*, 194 U.S. 154, 160 (1904) (*per* Holmes J.).

[91] Francis Biddle, *Mr. Justice Holmes* (1942), p. 103.

[92] Later Lord Alvanley C.J.

[93] *Cockerell* v. *Barber* (1826) 2 Russ. 585 at 598.

[94] *De Lima* v. *Bidwell*, 182 U.S. 1, 211 (1901) (McKenna J., dissenting).

[95] *The Atalanta*, 16 U.S. 409, 426 (1818) (*per* Johnson J.).

the whole away."[96] As Lord Blackburn pointed out: "Certainly Chief Justice Erle when he saw justice and convenience on the other side of the hedge was not a man whom it was easy to keep on the technical side of it."[97] It was also Erle C.J. who said: "It is easy for a judge to be impartial between plaintiff and defendant, indeed, he is almost always so; it is difficult to be impartial between counsel and counsel."[98] Judicial suspicion may be easily aroused: "Lord Denman said, that he suspected a case very much when he found it continually quoted immediately after its decision."[99] Lindley L.J. explained where he directed his suspicion: "When I am sought to be driven to a conclusion which appears to me unreasonable and unjust, I at once suspect the validity of the premises, even if I can detect no flaw in the reasoning from them."[100]

Much difficulty may be avoided by restraint or abstention. In one case the Court of Appeal was confronted with an earlier decision of the same court, named *Re National Funds Assurance Co.*,[101] in which the judgments were far from consistent with each other. The two senior members of the court each delivered a judgment discussing and explaining the earlier case, but the junior member of the court, Scrutton L.J., contented himself with a single sentence: "In view of the warning given by the report of *In re National Funds Assurance Co.* against three members of the Court of Appeal stating a rule in three different sets of words, I propose to add nothing except that I agree."[102] Twenty years later MacKinnon L.J. followed suit: "I have had the advantage of reading the judgment which has just been read by the Master of the Rolls, and that which is about to be read by Clauson L.J. It will be apparent that in the process of reasoning by which each arrives at the same conclusion as

---

[96] N.W. Senior, *Conversations with Distinguished Persons During the Second Empire* (1880), vol. 1, p. 321.

[97] *Metropolitan District Railway Co. v. Sharpe* (1880) 5 App.Cas. 425 at 445.

[98] N.W. Senior, *supra* note 96, p. 316.

[99] *Bamford v. Turnley* (1862) 3 B. & S. 66 at 87 (*per* Bramwell B.).

[100] *Re Holford* [1894] 3 Ch. 30 at 45.

[101] (1876) 4 Ch.D. 305.

[102] *Lawson v. Financial News Ltd.* [1918] 1 Ch. 1 at 8; and see *Selvage v. Charles Burrell & Sons Ltd.* [1921] 1 K.B. 355 at 368.

I do, they differ upon one point, which is among the nicest and sharpest quillets of the law as administered in Courts of equity. Since we all reach the same result, I can pretend to no regret that it is unnecessary for me to indicate my opinion upon this point of difference between them. But let no one suppose that, if it had been necessary, I should have completed the quotation from Shakespeare."[103]

Where the court is a court not of three but of five, as in the House of Lords, or nine, as in the Supreme Court of the United States, the possibilities of diverse reasoning are, of course, greatly enhanced:[104] nine judges could in theory deliver nine different judgments reaching nine different results for nine different reasons, or, indeed, sets of reasons. But theory is not practice, and some unison is usually to be found even in profound discord. In a mathematical rarity among Supreme Court opinions the Supreme Court of the United States set aside a conviction of a white man for burglary on the ground that blacks had been excluded from the jury, even though no objection had been made at the trial and the accused did not suggest that race was relevant to the proceedings. In reaching this result the court divided itself into thirds. Three justices based their decisions on broad constitutional grounds, three more relied on a statute making it criminal to exclude any person on account of "race, color or previous condition of servitude,"[105] and the other three would have upheld the conviction, and so dissented.[106]

Where a point is merely hypothetical, the judge's course is usually clear: to abstain from deciding it. In one case the judge said that he would do this. But then he incautiously added: "Sufficient unto the day, I think, is the judgment which I have given."[107] Yet few would put the judgment into the category that the quotation[108] suggests. Of American

---

[103] *Re Warwick's Settlement Trusts* [1938] Ch. 530 at 541–42. The quotation is: "But in these nice sharp quillets of the law,/ Good faith, I am no wiser than a daw": *Henry VI, Part I*, Act II, sc. iv, ll. 17–18.

[104] For the House of Lords, see 2 Misc. 144.

[105] 18 U.S.C. § 243 (2000).

[106] *Peters* v. *Kiff*, 407 U.S. 493 (1972).

[107] *Adler* v. *Upper Grosvenor Street Investment Ltd.* [1957] 1 W.L.R. 227 at 232 (*per* Hilbery J.).

[108] "Sufficient unto the day is the evil thereof": Matt. 6:34.

courts it has been said: "Until the Supreme Court has spoken authoritatively on the question they would do best to decide the questions
posed with as little bewordling and as few reasons as possible."[109] Yet
discussion without decision may be helpful. In the well-known words of
Holt C.J.: "However that happen, I have stirred these points, which wiser
heads in time may settle."[110] An alternative may be a prayer for guidance.
As Scrutton L.J. once said,[111] "I hope the House of Lords may soon have
an opportunity of explaining how their decision in *Hall* v. *Pim (Junior)
& Co.*[112] is to be reconciled with their decision in *Williams Bros.* v.
Agius."[113]

One difficulty lies in the increasing length and complexity of
judgments. Some would add that counsel are today more prolix in
argument than they once were, and in any case the law gets no simpler.
In America, a former president of the American Bar Association has
even resorted to the desperate educational expedient of rewriting a
17-page judgment of the Supreme Court of Washington.[114] The revised
version,[115] under a page long, was less than five per cent of the length of
the authorised version. Possibly citing a little-known English example of
brevity in judgment would encourage the Bench here today:

> *Lord Hewart, C.J.*: We need not trouble you Mr. Valentine Holmes. Mr.
> Meston has put his case such as it is very clearly. It really comes to this,
> that if this case were different from what it is he might succeed, but as this
> case is what it is this appeal must be dismissed.
>
> *du Parcq, J.*: I agree.
>
> *Goddard, J.*: I agree.[116]

---

[109] *Commr. of Internal Revenue* v. *McLean*, 127 F.2d 942, 944 (5th Cir. 1942) (*per* Hutcheson J.).

[110] *Coggs* v. *Bernard* (1703) 2 Ld.Raym. 909, at 920.

[111] *James Finlay & Co. Ltd.* v. *N.V. Kwik Hoo Tong Handel Maatschappij* [1929] 1 K.B. 400 at 410; and see 1 Misc. 325.

[112] (1928) 33 Com.Cas. 324.

[113] [1914] A.C. 510.

[114] *Thilman* v. *Thilman*, 193 P. 2d 674 (Wash. 1948).

[115] Charles A. Beardsley, *Judicial Draftsmanship*, 24 Wash. L. Rev. 146, 152 (1949).

[116] *Sidcup Building Estates Ltd.* v. *Sidery* (1936) 24 Traff.Cas. 164 at 167.

Even that is not the ultimate in brevity. On one appeal, judgment was reserved, and then in due time Lord Coleridge C.J. announced that "as the Court (Keating, Brett, Grove, and Denman JJ.) were equally divided, no judgment would be given."[117] And that was all. Even when reasons for a decision are duly given, they may be terse. In one case the Queen's Bench had refused to set aside a fraudulent preference made by an insolvent debtor merely because the subsequent bankruptcy petition had been presented by the debtor instead of by a creditor. In giving his reason for concurring with the reversal of this decision, Willes J. was content with four words: "*Dolus circuitu non purgatur.*"[118]

Like much else, brevity is relative. A judgment may be long; yet within that length there may be an apt word that illuminates the whole subject. Thus it has been long settled that if a person pays money under a mistake of law, he normally cannot recover it. In *Ex parte Simmonds*[119] Lord Esher M.R. said that this "rule has been adopted by Courts of law for the purpose of putting an end to litigation. . . . But the Court has never intimated that it is a high-minded thing to keep money obtained in this way; the Court allows the party who has obtained it to do a shabby thing in order to avoid a greater evil, in order that is, to put an end to litigation."[120] Yet where the payment has been made to an officer of the court, such as a trustee in bankruptcy, the court "will direct its officer to do that which any high-minded man would do, viz., not to take advantage of the mistake of law. This rule is not confined to the Court of Bankruptcy. If money had by a mistake of law come into the hands of an officer of a Court of Common Law, the Court would order him to repay it as soon as the mistake was discovered. Of course, as between litigant parties, even a Court of Equity would not prevent a litigant from doing a shabby thing. But . . . a trustee in bankruptcy has always been treated as an officer of the Court of Bankruptcy, and the Court will order him to

---

117 *Edmonds* v. *Alsop* (1874) L.R. 9 C.P. 310.

118 *Marks* v. *Feldman* (1870) L.R. 5 Q.B. 275 at 284 (fraud is not purged by circuity). See Bacon's *Maxims,* Bacon's *Law Tracts* (2d ed. 1741), p. 37.

119 (1885) 16 Q.B.D. 308.

120 *Ibid.*, at p. 312 (*per* Lord Esher M.R.); and see *Re T.H. Knitwear (Wholesale) Ltd.* [1988] Ch. 275.

act in an honourable and high-minded way."[121] As James L.J. had put it in the leading case, the trustee in bankruptcy "ought to set an example to the world by paying [the money] to the person really entitled to it. In my opinion the Court of Bankruptcy ought to be as honest as other people."[122]

For this, it was Cardozo J. who had the *mot juste*: "What a cobweb of fine-spun casuistry is dissipated in a breath by the simple statement of Lord Esher in *Ex parte Simonds*,[123] that the court will not suffer its own officer 'to do a shabby thing.' If the word shabby had been left out, and unworthy or dishonourable substituted, I suppose the sense would have been much the same. But what a drop in emotional value would have followed. As it is, we feel the tingle of the hot blood of resentment mounting to our cheeks."[124]

---

[121] *Ex parte Simmonds, supra* note 119, at p. 312.

[122] *Ex parte James* (1879) 9 Ch.App. 609 at 614.

[123] *Sic*: the correct spelling is *Simmonds*.

[124] Cardozo, *Law and Literature: Selected Writings of Benjamin Nathan Cardozo* (M.E. Hall ed., 1947), p. 347. Cardozo's quotation is exact in spirit, though not in the letter. See also *post* pp. 354–55.

17

~

THE PAPERWORK

As LONG ago as 1937, it was said that "the institution of marriage has long been on a slippery slope. What was once a holy estate enduring for the joint lives of the spouses, is steadily assuming the characteristics of a contract for a tenancy at will."[1] Forty years later there were many who would not even mention the institution. There was a tendency "to regard and, indeed, to speak of the celebration of marriage as 'the paperwork.' The phrase used is: 'We were living together but we never got round to the paperwork.'"[2]

Yet for many, marriage still had its attractions. In Los Angeles County in 1935, a man procured an insurance policy on a woman's life in his favour, married her, bought some rattlesnakes, made them bite her foot, and then, when this failed to kill her, joined with another man in drowning her. At the trial, the rattlesnakes were identified and put in evidence; and evidence was also given showing that the accused had previously insured, married, and drowned a woman. He was convicted, and in 1939 the Supreme Court of California upheld the conviction by five votes to two.[3] On a rehearing, the result was unchanged,[4] and after the Supreme Court of the United States had dismissed both an appeal and a series of applications in 1940, 1941, and 1942,[5] the widower was executed in San Quentin, the last man to be hanged there.[6]

---

[1] *Fender* v. *St. John-Mildmay* [1938] A.C. 1 at 34–35 (*per* Lord Russell of Killowen, dissenting).

[2] *Campbell* v. *Campbell* [1976] Fam. 347 at 352 (*per* Sir George Baker P.).

[3] *People* v. *Lisenba*, 89 P.2d 39 (Cal. 1939).

[4] *People* v. *Lisenba*, 94 P.2d 569 (Cal. 1939).

[5] *Lisenba* v. *California*, 311 U.S. 617 (1940); 313 U.S. 537 (1941); 313 U.S. 597 (1941); 314 U.S. 219 (1941); 315 U.S. 826 (1942).

[6] See Clinton T. Duffy, *88 Men and 2 Women* (1962), pp. 7–15, describing Lisenba as "Major Raymond Lisemba, alias Robert S. James," popularly known as "Rattlesnake James."

Few find much difficulty in the process of getting married. The difficulties come later: "The contract of marriage is a very simple one, which does not require a high degree of intelligence to comprehend."[7] Yet for "that most important engagement, the very essence of which is consent," some degree of intelligence is essential, since "insanity vitiates all acts."[8] Difficulties arose when a widower of 78 who had partially recovered from a stroke a year earlier married a younger woman at 11 a.m. and made a new will at 3 p.m. on the same day but died 18 days later. The will had made only modest provision for the widow, and she then successfully contended that her husband had been of unsound mind when he executed the will; a jury agreed.[9] As the marriage had revoked all former wills, there was an intestacy, under which the widow would take a substantial part of the estate.

The consequence was predictable. The principal beneficiary under an earlier will contended that the widow had herself demonstrated that she took nothing, for she was no widow and there was no intestacy: a man incapable of making a valid will at 3 p.m. must also have been incapable of making a valid marriage four hours earlier, and so there was nothing to revoke the former will. The judge's approach was that "a lesser degree of capacity is required to consent to a marriage than in the making of a will,"[10] but although this proposition failed to impress the Court of Appeal, his decision that the marriage was valid was affirmed.[11] The evidence showed that the condition of the deceased had varied from day to day, and sometimes almost from hour to hour.[12] In any case, the process of marriage could hardly be equated with that of will-making in the range of comprehensibility required.

The achievements of women are many. In one case,[13] Goddard L.J.

---

[7] *Durham* v. *Durham* (1885) 10 P.D. 80 at 82 (*per* Sir James Hannen P.).

[8] *Countess of Portsmouth* v. *Earl of Portsmouth* (1828) 1 Hagg.Ecc. 355 at 359 (*per* Sir John Nicholl); and see *Browning* v. *Reane* (1812) 2 Phill.Ecc. 69 at 70.

[9] *Re Park* [1950] *The Times*, Dec. 2.

[10] *In b. Park* [1954] P. 89 at 97 (*per* Karminski J.).

[11] *In b. Park* [1954] P. 112.

[12] *In b. Park* [1954] P. 89 at 111.

[13] *Blunt* v. *Blunt* [1942] 2 All E.R. 613; *reversed*, [1943] A.C. 517.

said of a wife who petitioned for divorce but had filed a discretion statement, "Her adultery — with a married man — was shameless and prolonged. She cannot even suggest that if set free she will be enabled to marry her paramour. There are two memorable sentences in a well-known utterance of Dr. Johnson. I need only quote the first, 'My dear sir, never accustom your mind to mingle virtue and vice.'[14] The sentence that follows[15] would certainly have been his, and may well be anyone's verdict on this petitioner."[16] Selden, indeed, used women to belabour the church: "The Clergie would have us beleive them against our owne reason: as the woman would have had her husband against his owne eyes; when he tooke her with another man; which yet she stoutely denyed; what will you beleive your owne eyes, before your owne sweet wife."[17]

Sometimes, however, things are not what they seem. Not long after the Second World War, Henn Collins J. and a friend (later Sir Roy Wilson Q.C.) called to see Denning J. in his room at the Law Courts while he was a judge of the Probate, Divorce, and Admiralty Division. Denning was still in court and Henn Collins glanced at a reserved judgment on Denning's desk, awaiting delivery. When Denning came in, Henn Collins remarked: "What extraordinary things you allow in your court, Tom!" "What do you mean?" Denning replied hotly. Henn Collins pointed to a sentence in the judgment: it ran "I am satisfied not only that the respondent has committed adultery, but that she was actually committing adultery while she was denying it in the witness-box."[18]

Sometimes there is less in adultery than at first appears. He who pursues the reference to the "Adulterine Gilds in London" that were amerced in the time of Henry II[19] may be disappointed.[20] Yet it is to be

---

14 See Boswell's *Johnson*, vol. 1, p. 478.

15 "The woman's a whore, and there's an end on't."

16 *Blunt* v. *Blunt* [1942] 2 All E.R. 613 at 616.

17 Selden, *Table Talk*, p. 31.

18 See Iris Freeman, *Lord Denning* (1993), p. 151, giving Roy Wilson's account.

19 Madox, *History and Antiquities of the Exchequer* (2d ed. 1769), vol. 1, p. 562.

20 *Ibid.* The guilds "were called Adulterine, because they were set-up without Warrant [or lawful Authority]."

remembered that the stews at Southwark were the subject of legislation as early as 1162: "In a Parliament holden at Westminster, the eighth of Henry the second, it was ordained by the Commons, and confirmed by the King and Lords, That divers Constitutions for ever should be kept within that Lordship, or Franchise, according to the old Customes, that had beene there used time time [*sic*] of minde."[21] Some of these provisions were designed to protect the inmates against the proprietors of the brothels, but at least one seems to have been intended to assure the customer of his money's worth: "No single woman to take mony to lye with any man, except she lye with him all night, till the morrow."[22]

One may come forward some eight centuries in time and across the Atlantic in space for a case[23] in which a husband and wife had been operating a house of prostitution in Grand Island, Nebraska. They went on a motoring holiday to Salt Lake City, Utah, accompanied by two of the girls employed by them as prostitutes, who had asked to be taken with them. After a fortnight's absence, all four returned to Grand Island, and the girls in due course resumed their professional activities. The married couple were then charged with an offence under the aptly named Mann Act (more correctly called the White Slave Traffic Act) in respect of the return journey from Utah to Nebraska. Section 2 of the Act is "directed at those who knowingly transport in interstate commerce 'any woman or girl for the purpose of prostitution or debauchery, or for any other immoral purpose . . . or to engage in any other immoral practice.'"[24] There was no doubt that the couple had taken the girls across state boundaries knowing that they would resume their immoral callings, and on this they were convicted.

The United States Supreme Court reversed the conviction, but by a majority of 5 to 4. The vital question was whether on the return trip the girls were transported "for the purpose of prostitution or debauchery." The minority, for whom Stone C.J. spoke, found no difficulty in saying

---

[21] Stow's *Survey of London* (ed. 1633), p. 448.

[22] *Ibid.*, at p. 449.

[23] *Mortensen* v. *U.S.*, 322 U.S. 369 (1944).

[24] *Ibid.*, at pp. 373–74 (*per* Murphy J.).

that they were. But the majority took the view that just as the outward journey, taking the girls away from the brothel, was innocent, so was the return journey: for in reality there was but a single round trip, planned from the start as a whole, and not two trips. Viewed as a whole, the round trip was "a complete break or interlude in the operation of petitioners' house of ill fame"[25] rather than a means of effecting immorality. In the words of Murphy J., who spoke for the majority: "to punish those who transport inmates of a house of prostitution on an innocent vacation trip in no way related to the practice of their commercial vice is consistent neither with the purpose nor with the language of the Act."[26] Thus was established the constitutional right of employers to take prostitutes in their employ on an innocent interstate holiday.

Another statutory problem that divided the Supreme Court was whether the accused was guilty of two offences or one if on a single occasion and in the same vehicle he transported not one woman but two. Warren C.J., Minton J., and Reed J. objected that Congress surely "did not intend to make it easier if one transported females by the bus load."[27] But the majority view was that Congress had failed to indicate sufficiently clearly that the accused could not have two for the price of one: "When Congress has the will it has no difficulty in expressing it — when it has the will, that is, of defining what it desires to make the unit of prosecution and, more particularly, to make each stick in a faggot a single criminal unit. When Congress leaves to the Judiciary the task of imputing to Congress an undeclared will, the ambiguity should be resolved in favor of lenity."[28] But the Act has been applied to a member of a Mormon sect practising polygamy who crossed a state line with one of his plural wives.[29] It has also been applied to a man who, in one state, persuaded a woman, by telegram and telephone, to fly from another

[25] *Ibid.*, at p. 375 (*per* Murphy J.).
[26] *Ibid.*, at p. 377.
[27] *Bell* v. *U.S.*, 349 U.S. 81, 84 (1954) (Minton J., dissenting).
[28] *Ibid.*, at p. 83 (*per* Frankfurter J.).
[29] *Cleveland* v. *U.S.*, 329 U.S. 14 (1946).

state and enjoy an immoral holiday with him in Miami.[30] The implicit policy is clear: let every state conserve its own immorality for itself, and lose none by export. Understandably, cautious but lubricious men have sometimes even written to the Attorney-General in an attempt to discover what they could do without a risk of prosecution.[31]

In New Zealand, it has been said: "In an era when in other parts of the world Legislatures were abolishing criminal sanctions against various types of sexual activities, our Parliament, fearless in its zeal for moral purity, by s. 155[32] for the first time made it a criminal offence for a man to have sexual intercourse with his grandmother. That no one has yet been prosecuted for this new offence is clear evidence of the effectiveness of legislative prohibition in stamping out what was presumably a wide-spread activity."[33] England has yet to make this leap forward; but Parliamentary interest in the crime is illustrated by the M.P. who sought to ask the Home Secretary "how many men convicted of incest were related to their victims."[34] It is understood that the official to whom the question was handed read it through impassively, and then handed it back to the M.P., saying evenly: "I think you will want to think about this, Sir." Something of a converse train of thought moved the father of an illegitimate daughter aged 22 when, on admitting intercourse with her, his attempt at extenuation was that he had never looked on her as his daughter, she being "more like a sister to me."[35]

Halfway across the world, Henry Miller's *Tropic of Cancer* provided a contrast. When the publication and sale of this book was enjoined, the majority of the Supreme Court of Pennsylvania unenthusiastically reversed the decision as unconstitutional. But there was a dissent, and it was emphatic:

---

[30] *U.S.* v. *Reginelli*, 133 F.2d 595 (3d Cir. 1943).

[31] See F. Biddle, *In Brief Authority* (1962), p. 252.

[32] *Sic*: in fact, the section is s. 130 of the Crimes Act 1961 (No. 43). Sect. 155(1)(d) of the Crimes Act 1908 (No. 32) had been confined to "grandfather and granddaughter," whereas s. 130(1)(c) of the Act of 1961 is in terms of "grandparent and grandchild."

[33] [1971] N.Z.L.J. 484, quoting from D.F. Dugdale in *Recent Law*.

[34] *The Justices' Clerk* No. 129 (1986) p. 16.

[35] *R.* v. *Jones* (1933) 24 Cr.App.R. 55 at 56.

To say that "Cancer" is worthless trash is to pay it a compliment. "Cancer" is the sweepings of the Augean stables, the stagnant bilge of the slimiest mudscow, the putrescent corruption of the most noisome dump pile, the dreggiest filth in the deepest morass of putrefaction . . . . "Cancer" is not a book. It is a cesspool, an open sewer, a pit of putrefaction, a slimy gathering of all that is rotten in the debris of human depravity. And in the center of all this waste and stench, besmearing himself with its foulest defilement, splashes, leaps, cavorts and wallows a bifurcated specimen that responds to the name of Henry Miller. . . . From Pittsburgh to Philadelphia, from Dan to Beersheba, and from the ramparts of the Bible to Samuel Eliot Morison's *Oxford History of the American People*, I dissent![36]

Some defences have had their day. In many jurisdictions there has long been a well-settled rule that if a husband, with full knowledge of a matrimonial offence committed by his wife, has sexual intercourse with her, he thereby condones the offence: for he cannot exercise the special privileges of a husband with her and at the same time disclaim her as a wife. Various unsuccessful attempts have been made to escape the effects of this rule. In South Africa, a single act of intercourse performed by the husband as an "experiment" in order to see whether he would recover his lost affection for his wife, and conditionally upon his doing so, has been held nevertheless to be condonation.[37] In Australia, counsel propounded the theory that it was possible for the husband to enjoy intercourse with his wife on a "without prejudice" footing: but this was rejected, "in all its disgusting absurdity," as being "an insult to common sense and an outrage upon morals."[38] Nor does it make any difference that the husband performed the act under the stimulus of alcohol[39] or when affected by a "tranquilliser,"[40] a drug that in large doses produces a sense of diminished responsibility comparable to drunkenness. But, of course, to Parliament all things are possible; and so from July 1963, there

[36] *Commonwealth* v. *Robin*, 218 A.2d 546, 552, 556, 561 (Pa. 1966) (*per* Musmanno J.).

[37] *C.* v. *C.*, 1943 E.D.L. 152.

[38] *Dorn* v. *Dorn (No. 2)* (1888) 9 N.S.W.L.R. (Div.) 7 at 14 (*per* Windeyer J.).

[39] *C.* v. *C.*, *supra* note 37.

[40] *Benton* v. *Benton* [1958] P. 12.

has been a limited statutory authority to insult common sense and outrage morality.[41]

Dower once offered a rich field for argument. In the sixteenth century one Thomas Gray, "of the age of eleven years, ten months, and twenty days,"[42] and Elizabeth, aged sixteen years, were joined in marriage. The parties "in some way consummated it, the man being put into the bed with her,"[43] but he died before he had attained the age of fourteen years, the minimum age for the marriage of a male. Nevertheless, it was held that Elizabeth was indeed a widow who was entitled to dower out of her husband's lands.[44] Three and a half centuries earlier, when there was a dispute whether Mabel had been married to William, a parson, the jury was instructed to determine whether "she held him as her husband and if she was levant and couchant with him as his wife."[45] No doubt it seemed natural enough in those days to borrow the test of the number of beasts that could be turned out to graze under a common of pasture appendant.[46] So too an aged conveyancer who, centuries ago, was unexpectedly assailed by Cupid. Unversed in the art of poetry, he fell back on the language of his craft for the Ode to his Beloved that was customary in those days:

> Fee simple and conditional fee,
> And all the fees in tail,
> Are nothing when compar'd to thee,
> Thou best of fees — female.[47]

In a case in the reign of Edward II, the issue was whether Agnes, the daughter of Simon de Punde, or Matilda, who was said to be Simon's wife and the mother of Agnes, was entitled to certain land; and the jury

---

[41] See Matrimonial Causes Act 1963, ss. 1, 2, replaced by Matrimonial Causes Act 1973, s. 2(1), (2).

[42] *Gray's Case* (1572) 3 Dy. 313a.

[43] *Gray's Case* (1580) 3 Dy. 368b at 369a.

[44] *Ibid.*

[45] *Acton* v. *Williams* (1221) 59 S.S. 493 at 494.

[46] See Megarry & Wade's *Real Property* (6th ed. 2000), p. 1098.

[47] See John Crisp, *The Conveyancer's Guide* (3d ed. 1832), p. xxii.

gave a special verdict, saying that Agnes was the daughter of Simon, and that Matilda was his wife and the mother of Agnes, but not saying that Agnes was his heir or that Matilda was generally reputed among the neighbours to be his wife. The jury was then required to amplify the verdict, and this was done by finding that Simon kept Matilda as his wife, and never married her. But, it was said, "captus fuit per amicos Matildae in camera fornicando cum ipsa per quod compellabatur unum de tribus facere, vel ipsam affidare, vel vitam suam amittere, vel ipsam Retro[48] Osculare." The jury, said a commentator, "mended their verdict, by finding that Simon . . . was taken in her chamber by some of her friends, in the very act of love, for which he was enjoined to do one of the three things mentioned in the record; and 'tis to be wish'd we had been told which of them he chose to do; it is plain he did not chuse the first, which was to marry the woman (for in that sense *affidare mulierem* is mentioned in Bracton) and I believe he was not hanged for his incontinency, therefore he must do the third thing."[49] Some options are fundamentally softer than others.

The consequences of marriage are no longer what they once were: "A woman guardian of the Fleet marries her prisoner in execution, he is immediately out of execution, for the husband cannot be prisoner to his wife, it being repugnant, that she, as jaylor, should have the custody of him, and he, as husband, the custody of her."[50] Again, in the nineteenth century a destitute pregnant spinster had a poor-law settlement in the parish of Chatteris. Some of the parishioners persuaded a poor bachelor who was chargeable to the parish of St. Ives to marry the woman, so that Chatteris would shift its burden, actual and prospective, to St. Ives. For this conspiracy the parishioners were indicted and convicted; but the Court of King's Bench held that in the absence of any evidence of force, threat, or fraud, no crime had been committed.[51]

---

[48] The Latin seems canine enough to have treated this adverb as a noun.

[49] John Lilly, *Reports and Pleadings of Cases in Assize* (1719), pp. xii, xiii.

[50] *Harrison* v. *Burwell* (1668) Vaugh. 206 at 243 (*per* Vaughan C.J., citing "Platt's case in the Com.").

[51] *R.* v. *Seward* (1834) 1 A. & E. 706.

Even statute did not at once cure all. The result of enabling a married woman to sue her husband for the protection and security of her property (but not otherwise)[52] was, as Maxwell J. pointed out in 1950, that "her husband may break her leg with civil impunity but not her watch."[53] This was a true prophecy. Next year there was a car accident in which a husband did both, and it was held that Maxwell J. had been right.[54]

Today, little is heard of wife-selling,[55] though there are some strange transactions. Wife-selling was not always so sordid a process as modern imaginations suppose. In 1832 Joseph Thornton had been married for some three years to a "spruce lively damsel, apparently not exceeding 22 years of age." They had mutually agreed to part, and so in Carlisle the bellman gave notice that she was to be sold one day at 12 noon. She stood on a large chair, and her husband made a speech to the crowd about her defects and her virtues, ending by offering her "With all her perfections and imperfections, for the sum of 50s." The offer was not at once accepted; but "after an hour or two she was purchased by Henry Mears, a pensioner, for the sum of 20s. and a Newfoundland dog. The happy couple immediately left town together."[56]

---

[52] See Married Women's Property Act 1882, s. 12; Law Reform (Married Women and Tortfeasors) Act 1935, s. 1. But the Law Reform (Husband and Wife) Act, 1962, s. 1, enabled either party to a marriage to sue the other in tort as if they were not married.

[53] *Waugh* v. *Waugh* (1950) 50 S.R.(N.S.W.) 210 at 213.

[54] *McKinnon* v. *McKinnon* [1956] V.L.R. 81. The watch is explicit (see p. 82), and the "serious personal injuries" (*ibid.*) are believed to have included a broken leg: see 29 Austr.L.J. 449.

[55] For this, see 2 Misc. 218–20.

[56] *Annual Register, 1832*, Chronicle, pp. 58, 59.

18

~

EVERY PROSPECT PLEASES

LIFE seems unpredictable in its variety. The improbable may be possible, probable, or certain. To be sure, "the improbable — by definition not being impossible — sometimes does occur."[1] Counsel who is absent when his case is called on unexpectedly may expect the judicial comment: "It is always probable that something improbable will happen."[2] Indeed, "there is nothing so certain as that something extraordinary will happen now and then."[3] This principle has been extended from the improbable to the impossible: "The advances in the exact sciences and the achievements in invention remind us that the seemingly impossible sometimes happens."[4] There have even been further local advances: for Ireland is "a country in which the impossible always happens and the inevitable never."[5]

With the aid of playing cards, possibilities have been explored in relation to breach of contract. There is a real difference between a loss that is likely to occur and one that is a serious possibility:

> In the ordinary use of language there is a wide gulf between saying that some
> event is not unlikely or quite likely to happen and saying merely that it is a

---

[1] *Old Colony Bondholders* v. *N.Y., N.H. & H.R. Co.*, 161 F.2d 413, 443 (2d Cir. 1947) (Frank J., dissenting).

[2] *Warren* v. *Purtell,* 63 Ga. 428, 430 (1879) (*per* Bleckley J.).

[3] *Ruck* v. *Williams* (1858) 3 H. & N. 308 at 319 (*per* Bramwell B.).

[4] *New St. Ice Co.* v. *Liebmann,* 285 U.S. 262, 310 (1932) (Brandeis J., dissenting).

[5] *Per* Lord Fitzalan: Earl of Oxford and Asquith, *Memories and Reflections 1852–1927* (Boston, 1928), vol. 1, p. 323. Cp. "Ireland is a country in which the probable never happens and the impossible always does": *per* J.P. Mahaffy (1839–1919), cited in Bentley & Esar, *Treasury of Humorous Quotations* (1962), p. 132.

serious possibility, a real danger, or on the cards. Suppose one takes a well-shuffled pack of cards, it is quite likely or not unlikely that the top card will prove to be a diamond: the odds are only 3 to 1 against. But most people would not say that it is quite likely to be the nine of diamonds for the odds are then 51 to 1 against. On the other hand I think that most people would say that there is a serious possibility or a real danger of its being turned up first and of course it is on the cards.[6]

If not inevitable, strife is at least probable. In 1823, in a debate in the House of Commons upon the Roman Catholic question, Brougham referred to George Canning as having "exhibited a specimen, the most incredible specimen, of monstrous truckling, for the purpose of obtaining office, that the whole history of political tergiversation could furnish —," whereat Canning said: "I rise to say, that that is false."[7] Canning firmly refused to retract, and ultimately, upon a motion to commit both Brougham and Canning, Brougham gave a labyrinthine explanation of his views, distinguishing between Canning's "highest honour" as a private individual, and his "public and political life" and "conduct as a statesman," which he (Brougham) deplored.[8] And there the incident closed — in Parliament. Yet "this scene laid the foundation for one of Charles Dickens's most amusing scenes in *Pickwick*, where a similar quarrel was adjusted among the Pickwickians by a declaration that certain offensive expressions had not been used in their *usual* and *natural*, but in their *Pickwickian* sense."[9] "Vile," "calumnious," "false," "scurrilous" and "humbug" were the words that Mr. Blotton and Mr. Pickwick had used Pickwickianly.[10] True, "a great political character, who held a high situation, in this country some years ago, but who is now dead, used to say that ministers were the better for being now and then a little peppered and salted."[11] But Brougham could have found little support in this.

---

[6] *C. Czarnikow Ltd.* v. *Koufos* [1969] 1 A.C. 350 at 390 (*per* Lord Reid).

[7] 8 Hansard (2d ser. 1823), col. 1091.

[8] *Ibid.*, at cols. 1099–1102.

[9] Camp. L. & B. 341, 342.

[10] Charles Dickens, *The Pickwick Papers*, c. 1.

[11] *R.* v. *Holt* (1793) 22 St.Tr. 1189 at 1234 (*per* Lord Kenyon C.J.).

It is to Lord Eldon that we are indebted for a characteristic story of Dr. Johnson. At Oxford, Eldon was walking "in New Inn Hall Garden with Dr. Johnson, Sir Robert Chambers, and some other Gentlemen. Sir Robert was gathering Snails, and throwing them over the Wall into his Neighbours Garden. The Doctor reproached him very roughly, and stated to him that this was unmannerly and unneighbourly. Sir, said Sir Robert, my neighbour is a Dissenter — oh, said the Doctor, if so, Chambers throw away, throw away, as hard as ever you can."[12] In the next century, there was some discussion of the relationship between the colleges and the university at Oxford. It was said: "We have been accustomed to think each essential to the perfect working of the other. The domestic discipline and paternal rule of the College, its maintenance of order, its closer inspection and catechetical instruction by tutors, being the corrective, it is thought, of the greater liberty of the University, its excitements and conflicts, with the perhaps too general and superficial teaching by professors."[13] What the professors thought of this does not appear. It is in the universities, too, that committees flourish in abundance without observing the view of Jackson J. that "the ideal committee consists of three, of whom two are unable to be present."[14]

The causes of strife are many:

- "Zeal and indignation are fervent passions."[15]

- "Persecution is a very easy form of virtue."[16]

- "We are all too prone, perhaps, to impute either weakness of intellect or corrupt motives to those who differ with us in opinion."[17]

---

[12] Lord Eldon's *Anecdote Book* (1960), p. 17.

[13] *The Case of the Oxford Poor Rate* (1857) 8 E. & B. 184 at 211 (*per* Coleridge J.).

[14] G.D. Roberts Q.C., *Without My Wig* (1957), p. 203; and see *post* pp. 318–19.

[15] *Lord Sheffeild* v. *Ratcliffe* (1621) Hob. 334 at 335 (*per* Hobart C.J.).

[16] *R.* v. *Ramsey* (1883) Cab. & El. 126 at 145 (*per* Lord Coleridge C.J.).

[17] *Burchell* v. *Marsh*, 58 U.S. 344, 350 (1854) (*per* Grier J.).

Yet "men are more often bribed by their loyalties and ambitions than by money."[18] The influence of others may be felt in different ways: "It is true that I cannot argue a man into a desire . . . . But although desire cannot be imparted by argument, it can be by contagion. Feeling begets feeling, and great feeling begets great feeling."[19] In America, it has been said: "One does not have to be an easy generalizer of national characteristics to believe that litigiousness is one of our besetting sins."[20] Whatever the country, a grievance too often carries with it blindness to the reciprocal:

> Life would indeed be unendurable if people always enforced their rights to the ultimate: and I should be slow to regard a man who fails to dispute every possible point with his neighbour as thereby admitting or representing that what his neighbour does he does as of right. The law ought not to encourage people to be aggressive about their rights by the fear that in granting any indulgence they will be treated as having yielded up their rights.[21]

The tale of human imperfections is long, and the law is tolerant: "The law has respect to human infirmity";[22] indeed, the law "would be an unwise law, if it did not make allowance for human infirmities."[23] Thus "Mistakes are the inevitable lot of mankind":[24] "I know but of one Being to whom error may not be imputed."[25] It is human, in seeking concessions, to proffer soothing assurances that there will be no repetition; but in refusing such a plea, Asquith once pointed out that "it is easy to rise superior to the temptations of tomorrow."[26] Some human qualities are occupational: "That barbers talk cannot be disputed. Some talk

---

[18] *U.S.* v. *Wunderlich*, 342 U.S. 98, 103 (1951) (Jackson J., dissenting).

[19] Holmes J., *The Occasional Speeches of Justice Oliver Wendell Holmes* (1962), p. 7.

[20] *NLRB* v. *Mexia Textile Mills, Inc.*, 339 U.S. 563, 573 (1950) (Frankfurter J., dissenting).

[21] *Neilson* v. *Poole* (1969) 20 P. & C.R. 909 at 922; and see 2 Misc. 250.

[22] *Robertson* v. *M'Dougall* (1828) 4 Bing. 670 at 679 (*per* Best C.J.).

[23] *Fraser* v. *Berkeley* (1836) 7 C. & P. 621 at 624 (*per* Lord Abinger, C.B.).

[24] *Re Taylor's Estate* (1882) 22 Ch.D. 495 at 503 (*per* Jessel M.R.).

[25] *R.* v. *Lambert* (1810) 2 Camp. 398 at 402 (*per* Lord Ellenborough C.J.).

[26] I.C. Rand J., *Rt. Hon. Sir Lyman Poore Duff, G.C.M.G. 1865–1955*, (1955) 33 Can. B.R. 1117.

more, some less, some humorously, some not, but talk they do. It is traditional and hereditary with them."[27]

Economic pressures account for much:

- "If women require a minimum wage to preserve their morals men require it to preserve their honesty."[28]

- Yet "poverty and immorality are not synonymous."[29]

- "The law does not stand upon punctilios if there is a starving wife at home."[30]

- "Miserable and disreputable housing conditions may do more than spread disease and crime and immorality. They may also suffocate the spirit by reducing the people who live there to the status of cattle. They may indeed make living an almost insufferable burden. They may also be an ugly sore, a blight on the community which robs it of charm, which makes it a place from which men turn. The misery of housing may despoil a community as an open sewer may ruin a river."[31]

- "The lowest species of receptacle for human beings is a dwelling-house . . . ."[32]

Within that species, however, there were gradations. In deciding whether a proposed house was intended for an agent of a large estate or for a farm bailiff, it was said that "the description of the house itself leads one to the conclusion that a farm bailiff is not intended, but some very superior person to that, because you find that the house is to contain two sitting-rooms, five bed-rooms, and a bath-room."[33] The

---

[27] *Vann* v. *Ionta*, 284 N.Y.S. 278, 282 (N.Y. Mun. Ct. 1935) (Pette J., in a judgment containing a long historical account of barbers).

[28] *Adkins* v. *Children's Hosp.*, 261 U.S. 525, 556 (1923) (*per* Sutherland J.).

[29] *Edwards* v. *California*, 314 U.S. 160, 177 (1941) (*per* Byrnes J.).

[30] *Coler* v. *Corn Exchange Bank*, 164 N.E. 882, 885 (N.Y. 1928) (*per* Cardozo C.J.).

[31] *Berman* v. *Parker*, 348 U.S. 26, 32 (1954) (*per* Douglas J.).

[32] *Attorney-General* v. *Hodgson* (1846) 15 L.J.Ch. 290 at 292 (*per* Shadwell V.-C.).

[33] *Re Lord Gerard's Settled Estate* [1893] 3 Ch. 252 at 263 (*per* Lopes L.J.).

ratio? "I do not think that you would supply a bath-room for a farm bailiff."[34] At the lowest financial rung of all, when bankruptcy looms, the debtor must check any impulse to divert what remains to his friends and family; for "It is the policy of the law that the debtor be just before he be generous,"[35] a policy that is distinct from the "just and generous" rule into which *ejusdem generis* was once transmuted.[36] But perhaps there is consolation in knowing that a man may be too poor to be made bankrupt, though the burden of proof is heavy.[37]

Drink may contribute; but some drinks contribute more than others. In the 1860s some merchants in Leith who traded with West Africa bought and despatched some whisky that had been coloured to suit the taste of the natives. But the colouring matter, instead of being burnt sugar, turned out to be logwood. This made the whisky unsaleable, "the natives, not unreasonably, fancying it to be poisoned";[38] and a Scottish jury's award of £3,000 damages to the merchants against the distillers was upheld on appeal. As Lord Westbury pointed out, the "logwood colouring produced effects on the body of the consumer which, to say the least, were very disagreeable and alarming; it had an astringent effect; it affected the saliva and the secretions from the kidneys, giving them the colour of blood; and it changed the colour of the skin down to the fingers and nails. I cannot conceive a more alarming picture to be presented to an *Edinburgh* or *Glasgow* jury, where toddy is supposed to be in great esteem."[39]

In California in 1854, statutes precluded any "Indian or Negro" from giving evidence in civil proceedings to which "a White person is a party,"[40] and similarly as to any "Black, or Mulatto person, or Indian" in criminal proceedings against "a White man."[41] A white man was

---

[34] *Ibid.*

[35] *Hearn 45 St. Corp.* v. *Jano*, 27 N.E.2d 814, 816 (N.Y. 1940) (*per* Finch J.).

[36] See 2 Misc. 160.

[37] *Re Field* [1978] Ch. 371 at 375.

[38] *Macfarlane & Co.* v. *Taylor & Co.* (1868) L.R. 1 Sc. & D. 245.

[39] *Ibid.*, at p. 257.

[40] Civil Practice Act, s. 394.

[41] Criminal Act, s. 14.

convicted of murder on the evidence of Chinese witnesses, and appealed on the ground that the evidence was inadmissible. After an excursion into history and ethnology, the State Supreme Court, by a majority, allowed the appeal:

> The word "White" has a distinct signification, which *ex vi termini*, excludes black, yellow, and all other colors. . . . We are of the opinion that the words "White," "Negro," "Mulatto," "Indian," and "Black person," wherever they occur in our Constitution and laws, must be taken in their generic sense, and that, even admitting the Indian of this Continent is not of the Mongolian type, that the words "Black person," in the 14th section, must be taken as contradistinguished from White, and necessarily excludes all races other than the Caucasian.[42]

In California the Chinese, it seems, were Indians. But that was a long time ago, as was the case in which it was said: "Mr. Serjeant Maynard's case was cited, who recovered in debt contracted here against the executor of an owner of a plantation in Barbadoes, and by his advice an action of trover was brought, and judgment obtained for the fourth part of a negro."[43] Such a judgment, it may be added, would be enforced not corporeally but by an order for sale and division of the proceeds.

Eccentricity takes many variant forms. The entire report of *Sir Charles Sydlyes Case*[44] is as follows: "He was fined 2000 mark, committed without bail for a week, and bound to his good behaviour for a year, on his confession of information against him, for shewing himself naked in a balkony, and throwing down bottles (pist in) vi & armis among the people in Convent Garden, contrà pacem, and to the scandal of the Government." In the words of another report, he was charged with "several misdemeanours encounter le peace del Roy & que fueront al grand scandal de Christianity, et le cause fuit quia il monstre son nude corps in un balcony in Covent Garden al grand multitude de people."[45]

---

[42] *People* v. *Hall*, 4 Cal. 399, 404 (1854) (*per* Murray C.J.).

[43] *Noel* v. *Robinson* (1687) 1 Vern. 453.

[44] (1663) 1 Keb. 620. The surname is given in other accounts as Sidley or Sedley or Sidney.

[45] *R.* v. *Sidley* (1663) 1 Sid. 168, which states that he was bound over for three years, not one.

Some years later the court was a little puzzled as to the *ratio decidendi* of this case. Fortescue J. at first attached some weight to the "force in throwing out bottles upon the people's heads."[46] Indeed, Powell J. had earlier explained that "there was something more in that case, than shewing his naked body in the balcony, for that case was quod vi et armis he piss'd down upon the peoples heads."[47] Ultimately, however, it was agreed that the force "was but a small ingredient in the judgment of the Court."[48] It was left to Pepys[49] to give further and better particulars. On the balcony, Sedley had acted "all the postures of lust and buggery that could be imagined," as well as abusing the scriptures and preaching a mountebank sermon. He had then washed his virile member in a glass of wine and swallowed the wine, before drinking the King's health.

Seventy years later *Sidley's Case* was cited in a case[50] that Victorian England would have found surprising. The facts were stated concisely: "Indictment *contra bonos mores*, for running in the common way naked down to the waist, the defendant being a woman." The defence moved to quash the indictment on the ground that "the fact is not indictable," and in opposition the prosecution cited certain authorities, including "Sir Charles Sidney's Case. 1 Keb. 620. *Quia immodeste & irreverenter* behaved himself in church." This seems a somewhat charitable view to take of Sir Charles's performance. "'*Sed per Cur,*' The indictment must be quashed, for nothing appears immodest or unlawful." Although somewhat unexpected as to the word "immodest," that seems clear enough. With no claim to the title "The Streaker's Friend," the case could at least be seen as a Charter of Liberty for the Topless.

---

[46] *R.* v. *Curl* (1727) 2 Str. 788 at 791.

[47] *R.* v. *Read* (1707) Fort. 98 at 99. In argument for the accused, Raymond referred to a case in which the indictment was for procuring men and women to come together to commit fornication, and said "this is only having a good opinion of the thing, but no libel": see p. 99.

[48] *R.* v. *Curl, supra* note 46, at p. 792.

[49] *The Diary of Samuel Pepys* (R. Latham & W. Matthews eds.), vol. 4 (1971), p. 209 (entry for July 1, 1663).

[50] *R.* v. *Gallard* (1733) Kel.W. 162. The case was in the King's Bench, which then consisted of Lord Hardwicke C.J., and Probyn, Page, and Lee JJ.

Yet clarity is not all; for a more ample report[51] of what is manifestly[52] the same case is significantly different: *vive la différence*. This report states that the defendant was indicted at Norwich Sessions "that he being a person above the age of nineteen years, and of disorderly behaviour and ill fame," assisted one Thomas Hacon "to run naked, except garters and stockings," in a public place, "with force and arms, of his own free will immodestly, openly, and publickly did appear and shew himself running with the said T.H. for the space of one hour, with his body naked, and without any covering from his neck to the waste, to and amongst a great number of the King's good subjects of both sexes," to their "great scandal, disturbance and offence," and "contrary to all morality, decency and good order," and against the peace. The defence advanced a number of arguments for quashing the indictment, including a contention that "if the defendant had run naked, it might be considered within the meaning of *Sir Charles Sedley's case*, but the defendant only ran stript from the neck to the waste." On this, the court made a rule to show cause, and afterwards made the rule absolute, thereby dismissing the case.

With sex the only vital discrepancy, the latter report must regretfully be accepted as being the more credible. Two and a half centuries later, one may question the assertion in a modern book on criminal law that although a driver may not sound his horn while his car is at rest, "he may relieve frustration by flashing";[53] for what of the Vagrancy Act 1824?[54]

Across the Atlantic, the subject still lives on. Some women who had bared their breasts in a public park in Rochester were prosecuted under a New York law[55] that prohibited women (but not men) from exposing in a public place "that portion of the breast which is below the top of the areola." The Court of Appeals unanimously upheld an acquittal on the

[51] *R. v. Gallard* (1733) Sess.Cas. K.B. 67.
[52] Same name, same date, same judges, similar facts.
[53] Glanville Williams, *Textbook of Criminal Law* (1978), p. 9; cp. 2d ed. (1983), p. 19.
[54] Sect. 4 (cited on p. 190 of the book, 1st ed.), making indecent exposure an offence. The vulgarism in full is "flashing his bishop."
[55] Penal Law No. 245.01.

amiable ground that the law had been directed against topless waitresses and their promoters and did not apply to an exposure that was not "commercial" or "lewd."[56] This made it unnecessary to decide any constitutional questions, though two[57] of the six judges would have held the law invalid as being discriminatory under the equal-protection clauses of the federal and state constitutions.

In New York, topless streetwalkers have their rights. So too in Ontario, where a woman who simply walked along city streets in very hot weather with bare breasts was held not to have been guilty of "an indecent act"; for she had not exceeded the "community standard of tolerance,"[58] and so her claim to this form of equality with men prevailed. As a result, it seems, during a heat wave many bare-breasted women were to be seen in streets and parks, on beaches and at work; and those who cleaned car windscreens in city streets received notably increased "donations" for their efforts.[59]

Questions of domicil often lead to an examination of life-style:

Errol Flynn was a film actor whose performances gave pleasure to many millions. On June 20, 1909, he was born in Hobart, Tasmania; and on October 14, 1959, he died in Vancouver . . . . When he was seventeen he was expelled from school in Sydney; and in the next thirty-three years he lived a life which was full, lusty, restless and colourful. In his career, in his three marriages, in his friendships, in his quarrels, and in bed with the many women he took there, he lived with zest and irregularity. The lives of film stars are not cast in the ordinary mould; and in some respects Errol Flynn's was more stellar than most. When he died, he posed the only question that I have to decide: Where was he domiciled at the date of his death?[60]

At one time he had undoubtedly been domiciled in California: "Holly-wood has never been deficient in what was then, as always, one of Errol's

---

[56] *People* v. *Santorelli*, 600 N.E.2d 232 (N.Y. 1992), citing *People* v. *Price* 307 N.E.2d 46 (N.Y. 1973) (walking in a street wearing a fish-net, see-through, pull-over blouse).

[57] Titone and Simons JJ.

[58] *R.* v. *Jacob* (1996) 142 D.L.R. (4th) 411, construing the Canadian Criminal Code, s. 173(1).

[59] See *The Times*, June 13, 1997, p. 17.

[60] *Re Flynn* [1968] 1 All E.R. 49 at 50.

great interests in life, namely, a generous pool of available pulchritude."[61] Yet even though "as a sexual athlete Errol may in truth have achieved Olympic standards,"[62] time brings its changes to all. Many pages later, after much geographical and personal biography, the answer to the question came: when he died, Errol was domiciled in Jamaica.[63]

It was Asquith who said that some people "can only think talking: just as some people can only think writing. Only the salt of the earth can think inside, and the bulk of mankind cannot think at all."[64] To the precept "Think before you speak," an apt reply lies in the expostulation variously attributed to a little girl and an old lady: "How can I know what I think before I hear what I say?" Indeed, the qualities of "the 'common man,' whose ancestors may be supposed to include both the man on the Clapham omnibus and the officious bystander",[65] must, it seems, include unthinkingness. Maitland was certainly no common man; yet those who revere him may not realise that he was "not a lawyer at all, but a poet."[66]

Finally, there are the rewards of those who serve the nation. Of a payment of a bonus to ex-servicemen, "some may think the service so far beyond requital that the attempt should be surrendered for mere futility. Others may think that high and unselfish sacrifice is cheapened when repaid in money."[67] Yet what can be said of M.P.s, with the high standards that they must attain? Every member of Parliament, said Coke, "should have three properties of the elephant; first, that he hath no gall: secondly, that he is inflexible, and cannot bow: thirdly, that he is of a most ripe and perfect memory." Being without gall, Coke explained, meant being "without malice, rancor, heat, and envy, *in elephante*

---

[61] *Ibid.*, at p. 53.

[62] *Ibid.*, at p. 50.

[63] *Ibid.*, at p. 62.

[64] Earl of Oxford and Asquith, *Memories and Reflections 1852–1927* (Boston, 1928), vol. 2, p. 76.

[65] *Indyka* v. *Indyka* [1967] P. 233 at 264 (*per* Russell L.J., dissenting).

[66] *Per* Macnaghten J., speaking extrajudicially: 2 *Holmes–Laski Letters* 1412.

[67] *People* v. *Westchester County Natl. Bank*, 132 N.E. 241, 250 (N.Y. 1921) (Cardozo J., dissenting).

melancholia transit in nutrimentum corporis,"[68] while being bowed meant being "turned from the right, either for fear, reward, or favour." He then added two other desirable qualities of the elephant, "the one, that though they be *maximae virtutis, et maximi intellectus*, of greatest strength, and understanding, *tamen gregatim semper incedunt*, yet they are sociable, and goe in companies; for *animalia gregalia non sunt nociva, sed animalia solivaga sunt nociva*. Sociable creatures that goe in flocks or heards are not hurtfull, as deer, sheep, &c. but beasts that walk solely, or singularly, as bears, foxes, &c. are dangerous and hurtfull. [Doubtless Coke never faced a pack of wolves; but did he never caress a cat or a rabbit?] The other, that the elephant is *philanthropos, homini erranti viam ostendit*,[69] and these properties ought every parliament man to have."[70]

---

[68] "In the elephant, melancholy is transformed into nourishment of the body".
[69] "A lover of mankind, he points out the way to the man who strays."
[70] 4 Co.Inst. 3. For elephants as analogues, see *post* pp. 303–04.

19

~

WINTER'D ONE WHOLE SUMMER

ANIMALS have long held a prominent place in the law, not least in the law
of tort. Some litigation has been strong in optimism, and in little else.
One landowner even sued for damages for trespass when a dog, "without
the consent of its master," had jumped into a field and was "trampling
down" the grass. Few but he could have been surprised when this was
held to be no trespass.[1] Over a century later a dog-owner in Missouri
was equally valiant. He counterclaimed under an insurance policy for
$7,500 damages for the "total loss" of a carpet and damage to other
furnishings caused by the failure of André, his French poodle, to
appreciate that there was a time and place for everything. The evidence
showed that the carpet had suffered on some 75 to 80 occasions, and so
it was held that the owner's reckless disregard of his property barred his
claim. Weber J. would have gone beyond the principle of allowing every
dog his first bite, and would have held two or three lapses no bar; but
two or three could not cover 75 or 80.[2] Yet some blessings come in the
name of dogs. In 1919, power was given to increase the salaries of clerks
of petty sessions in Ireland. The manna was provided under an Act, a
mere five sections long, unexpectedly called the Dogs Regulation
(Ireland) Act 1919.[3]

The bounds of judicial notice are ample. Fuld J. of the New York
Court of Appeals once spoke in delicate extrajudicial tones of the —

---

[1] *Brown Esq.* v. *Giles* (1823) 1 C. & P. 118.
[2] *Aetna Ins. Co.* v. *Sachs*, 186 F.Supp. 105 (E.D. Mo. 1960).
[3] See s. 4.

anonymous canine who in 1939 precipitated a case in 290 N.Y.[4] The plaintiff was a professional dancer whose routine on the defendant's stage followed an animal act featuring six or eight performing dogs. According to the plaintiff, as he was dancing sideways off the stage at the close of his act, his foot struck a wet spot on the floor. He slipped and fell. The puddle, about six inches in diameter, was one of those mysterious phenomena of nature about whose origin and cause man can only speculate. It was the plaintiff's theory that one of the furry thespians who preceded him had been responsible; that the defendant theater had not used reasonable care to guard against the risk of such a disaster and that therefore it was negligent. The defense was that it was just as probable that the water came from a drinking cup in the hands of a vaudeville performer or of someone in the wings. I need hardly say that we affirmed the judgment in the plaintiff's favor. We knew — dogs will be dogs.[5]

So too for the female:

We think that we may take judicial notice of the fact that the term "bitch" may imply some feeling of endearment when applied to a female of the canine species but that it is seldom, if ever, so used when applied to a female of the human race.[6] Coming as it did, reasonably close on the heels of the two revolver shots directed at the person of whom it was probably used, we think it carries every reasonable implication of ill-will towards that person.[7]

In Scotland, more than a century ago, Lord Cockburn held decided views on the liability of a man for his dog's delinquencies:

I have always thought that if a dog worries sheep his master is liable. I do not attach any weight to the law of England. I am told that knowledge on the part of the owner is requisite to make him liable. This is absurd; he cannot know it until it is done . . . .[8] The essence of the principle seems just to be,

---

[4] *Martell* v. *Harlou Inc.*, 49 N.E.2d 634 (N.Y. 1943), *aff'g* 37 N.Y.S.2d 754 (N.Y. App. Div. 1942) without opinion (Lehman C.J., dissenting).

[5] *N.Y.L.J.*, 1 Feb., 1949, p. 1. I have slightly revised the text.

[6] Cp. 2 Misc. 351 ("mere meaningless abuse"). And see *French (Elizabeth)* v. *Smith* (1922) 53 O.L.R. 31 at 33 (*per* Riddell J., stating that "bugger," as "whore," once was, as a term of "unmeaning abuse, even affectionate at times").

[7] *Smith* v. *Moran*, 193 N.E.2d 466, 469 (Ill. App. Ct. 1963) (*per* Smith J.).

[8] *Orr* v. *Fleming* (1853) 1 W.R. 339.

that every dog is to have one worry, and every bull one thrust, with absolute impunity, — that is to say, without its master being liable. If this be the law of England, they appear to have an undue toleration for a first offence. I believe my coachman to be a sober and respectable man, and a good and steady driver; would it be any defence for me against his having ridden over an old woman, that he never had done so before? The law applies to quadrupeds as well as to bipeds.[9]

But the House of Lords put matters right,[10] and England was given a "very cumbrously worded" statutory regime.[11]

The House of Lords itself has shown a proper appreciation of canine sensibilities. A pedestrian claimed damages for an eye injury caused by a splinter of glass driven from the window of a stationary car by an excited dog that had been left alone in it. Neither the Court of Appeal nor the House of Lords considered that the owner of the car had been negligent in failing to guard against so unlikely an injury. Viscount Dunedin engaged in some understanding speculation about the cause of the dog's excitement:

> There was a suggestion made that the dog might have got into an excited state because of carbon monoxide. I think that was a foolish suggestion. I do not think there is any difficulty in supposing that the dog might get into an excited state. Dogs get bored just as human beings do, and the bark is the dog's ordinary expletive. Besides that, the dog might wish to get out for purposes of his own, and if he was a well-bred dog he would intimate his desire by barking. And, last of all, he might have been irritated by some passer-by who in some way spoke to him and, as the dog considered, insulted him.[12]

There is a certain charm (and some puzzlement) in the report of a case in 1658.[13] The side-note runs: "Action sur le case pur le morder dun

---

[9] S.C., *sub nom. Fleeming* v. *Orr*, 15 D. 486 at 487.

[10] S.C. (1855) 2 Macq. 14.

[11] See Animals Act 1971, s. 2(2); *Curtis* v. *Betts* [1990] 1 W.L.R. 459 at 462. For Scotland, see Animals (Scotland) Act 1987, imposing strict liability in certain cases.

[12] *Fardon* v. *Harcourt-Rivington* (1930) 146 L.T. 391 at 392. The concept of the "reasonable dog" appears in *R.* v. *Soper* [1971] 1 O.R. 506 at 507.

[13] *Cropper* v. *Matthews* (1658) 2 Sid. 127.

bitch," and the report begins as follows: "En action sur le case le plaintiff declare pur ceo que defendant, a certain bitch accustomed to bite men al parish de . . . en Londres did knowingly retain and keep le jury trove pur plaintiff & 100 l. dammages. Et esteant move in arrest de judgment le darrein term mesme exception fuit ore move arer & ceo fuit que plaintiff nad mostre que defendant scavoit que le bitch fuit accustomed de worry ou bite homes, car knowingly refer solement al retainer . . . ."[14] But this argument convinced none of the judges, and the plaintiff held his verdict.

The transition to cats is a transition from liability to achievement. One unemployed couple carried their cat round with them in the streets of Augusta, Georgia, soliciting contributions from members of the public who wished to hear the cat speak. When the City Council contended that this made the couple liable to pay a local tax, they challenged the claim.[15] Not long before the trial, the judge,[16] in a casual encounter in the street, had met the cat. It was draped over the man's shoulder, and the judge heard it say: "I love you," and "I want my Mama."[17] At that, he gave the man a dollar. This did not deter the judge from hearing the case and holding that the tax was payable, though he said that he had excluded the encounter from consideration. Among his comments was: "The ailurophobes contend that anthropomorphosis abounds, and that it is the work of ailurophiles."[18] So far as appears, the cat, although a veteran of radio and television, let this pass unanswered.

Then there are less domestic animals. In 1957 a runaway cow had knocked down a man who was on a pedestrian crossing in Guildford. The man sued the owner of the cow for damages, but counsel for the defendant argued before Stable J. that since the owner of a tame animal was not liable for any damage done by it that was "foreign to its species",

[14] *Ibid.* A comma after "Londres," a full stop after "keep," and quotation marks round the second "knowingly" would have helped.

[15] *Miles* v. *City Council of Augusta,* 551 F.Supp. 349 (S.D. Ga. 1982), *aff'd,* 710 F.2d 1542 (11th Cir. 1983).

[16] Judge Dudley H. Bowen Jr.

[17] *Miles,* 551 F. Supp. at 350 n.1.

[18] *Ibid.,* at p. 351 n.2.

and a cow was undoubtedly tame, he would seek to prove that "the cow attacked the plaintiff; if that were so, there was no liability."

> *His Lordship* — Is one to abandon every vestige of common sense in approaching this matter?
>
> *Counsel* — Yes, my Lord.
>
> The hearing was adjourned.[19]

In his judgment, Stable J. said that

> after running from the market the cow turned into a cul-de-sac where, if people had only acted with half as much intelligence as the average cow in circumstances of this kind it could have been safely retrieved. But a number of people stood on a wall shouting and waving their arms with the object of creating as much disturbance in the cow's mind as they could. The cow, accustomed to the tranquillity of the farm, became more and more frightened. It turned into the High Street, where it trotted along in a staid manner. The cow, however unacquainted with the regulations relating to zebra crossings, did seem to recognize a policeman when it saw one. He held out his hand and gave it the appropriate signal whereupon it turned into a car park. Hearing a motor horn, the cow broke through a cordon and out of the car park. Before it was shot it went over the zebra crossing and knocked down the plaintiff. His Lordship was satisfied that the cow had never shown any vice. By the time it knocked down the plaintiff it had been driven frantic by the misguided efforts of human beings and had become dangerous. Its collision with the plaintiff was not a vicious attack: he happened to be in its way.[20]

Acquitted of any negligence, the defendant prevailed.

From cows to bulls. What is the measure of damages if a trespassing bull responds to the allure of a cow or heifer that he finds in residence? In an English case the result was a cross-bred calf that had little value compared with the thoroughbred that might otherwise have been: but the court, emphasising the "might," awarded very modest damages.[21] In

---

19 *Thorp* v. *King Bros. (Dorking) Ltd.* [1957] *The Times*, Feb. 22.

20 *Ibid.*, Feb. 23.

21 *Bracey* v. *Osborne* (1944) 144 E.G. 207 (Yeovil County Court: £5.5.0 damages and costs); and see 1945 Conv.Y.B. 267.

an earlier American decision it was held that the correct measure of damages was the difference in the value of the heifer to her owner before the trespass and after; and in computing this a relevant factor was the difference in value between the calf that had been born and the thoroughbred that the owner had intended the heifer to bear.[22] Yet nothing was said about the uncertainties of parenthood and the problems of evaluating them.

The traditional bull in a china shop does not appear to figure in any reported case. An unsuccessful claim for £1 damages was once made for the ravages of an ox in an ironmonger's shop.[23] There was also the "gate-crashing, stair-climbing, floor-bursting, tap-turning cow" of Inverness.[24] There was indeed a case concerning a china-shop, but the claim for £2.8s.1d was in respect of the activities not of a bull, but of a game-cock. The cock, it seems, had "walked into the shop, and knocked some articles off a shelf, causing great breakage in the plates and dishes on the counter." But when the judge asked the plaintiff whether he could show that the cock had a habit of breaking crockery, he could only reply, "I did not ask it"; and he was very properly non-suited.[25]

Horses and donkeys, though tame, have also posed many questions. In 1963 the Jamaica Court of Appeal had to consider a case in which the plaintiff had been riding a jenny (a female donkey) on the highway. The defendant's jackass had galloped up to the jenny and jumped on her in an attempt to serve her. The plaintiff was thrown off, and the jenny was so injured that she had to be shot. The plaintiff's claim for damages nevertheless failed, for donkeys are *mansuetae naturae*, and the jack had merely been indulging a natural propensity: jacks will be jacks. There was, indeed, evidence that the jack had previously attempted to serve this particular jenny when she was lying down, but that was far removed from being evidence that the defendant knew that the jack had any

---

[22] *Kopplin* v. *Quade*, 130 N.W. 511 (Wis. 1911).

[23] *Tillett* v. *Ward* (1882) 10 Q.B.D. 17.

[24] See 1 Misc. 287.

[25] *Marshall* v. *Dellamore* (1861) G. Pitt-Lewis, *Commissioner Kerr — An Individuality* (1903), p. 195.

propensity to serve a jenny while she was being ridden.[26] The only consolation for the plaintiff was that his mortification had been less than that of Dr. Price, Dean of Hereford, some three centuries earlier. Dr. Price was "a mighty Pontificall proud man" who went in procession to the cathedral not on foot, as was usual, but riding a mare. One day a stallion "happend to breake loose, and smelt the mare, and ran and leapt her, and held the Reverend Deane all the time so hard in his Embraces, that he could not gett off till the horse had done his bussinesse. But he would never ride in procession afterwards."[27]

The courts have shown a proper reluctance to permit any human interference with the course of nature in horses. At one time the drivers of vehicles drawn by horses or mules on the streets of the City of Charleston were required by a city ordinance to ensure that the animals were "equipped with diapers or similar devices to prevent manure and droppings from falling on city streets." But the Municipal Court was vigilant and declared the ordinance invalid as being unreasonable and imposing unnecessary suffering: "A horse was not designed by God to wear a diaper."[28] Yet, for that matter, who, or what, was?

Wild animals are another matter. The age-old rule is that he who keeps such an animal does so at his peril, so that if it escapes and causes damage he will be liable. This rule depends not upon whether the individual beast caused the damage through malevolence or innocent panic, but upon whether the animal is of a species recognised as wild: the distinction is between animals *ferae naturae* and those *mansuetae naturae*. Tigers are unquestionably wild, and so — "If a person wakes up in the middle of the night and finds an escaping tiger on top of his bed and suffers a heart attack, it would be nothing to the point that the intentions of the tiger were quite amiable."[29] (It may be interposed that "most parents probably consider their own children *mansuetae naturae* and those of their neighbours *ferae naturae*."[30])

---

26 *McIntosh* v. *McIntosh* (1963) 5 W.I.R. 398.

27 John Aubrey's *Brief Lives* (O. Lawson Dick ed., 1962), p. 168.

28 *City of Charleston* v. *Fuller*, 44 U.S.L.W. 2344 (1975) (*per* Hugo N. Spitz J.).

29 *Behrens* v. *Bertram Mills Circus Ltd.* [1957] 2 Q.B. 1 at 17–18 (*per* Devlin J.).

30 *Corby* v. *Foster* (1913) 13 D.L.R. 664 at 674 (*per* Riddell J.).

In one South African case the issue was whether certain wildebeeste which had lived in a large enclosure were *ferae naturae*. McGregor J. observed that "the exact place occupied by the wildebeest in the social economy is a matter of some interest — if not to the wildebeest himself, at least to his owner or captor." He referred to the fact that the wildebeeste "grazed with the plaintiff's cattle, that they lived (without exhibiting any marked signs of insubordination or even disaffection) in an enclosed camp, and that they only sought for opportunities to escape when pressed by the forcible arguments supplied by beater, dog and gun." Yet in this large enclosure, the wildebeeste did not "call up the same sylvan picture as the placid and unharried fallow deer leading a sleek and comfortable (though perhaps slightly inglorious) existence in the ancestral park"; and so in the end the wildebeeste were held to be wild.[31]

There have also been difficulties about what today would be called mini-horns. A Louisiana statute provided that no person should "take any fawn (a deer with horns less than three inches long) or any doe (a female wild deer), at any time." A hunter shot a deer that turned out to be a fully developed buck, except that by some quirk of nature he had no horns but only stubs less than an inch long. Under federal legislation a prosecution was launched, only to be dismissed by Dawkins C.J. He refused to hold that the buck was a fawn, despite the words of the statute, and said that the case was "a tiny tempest in a tinier teapot."[32] The judge had little patience with the legislative draftsman's poor definition of *fawn*: "All this — requiring the services of five game agents, two biologists, the opposing attorneys, the United States Marshal and three Deputies, the Clerk, Court Reporter, and a Federal Judge who is a little tired of such matters — stems at least partly from the failure of the Louisiana Legislature to reckon wisely with the exceptional or unusual."[33]

Over three centuries earlier, there had been an action on the case "of trover and conversion of three munkeys and divers musk-cats"; and

---

[31] *Richter* v. *Du Plooy* 1921 O.P.D. 117 at 118, 119.

[32] *U.S.* v. *Dowden*, 139 F. Supp. 781 (W.D. La. 1956).

[33] *Ibid.*, at p. 782.

"upon a not guilty pleaded a verdict was given for the plaint. it was moved in arrest of judgment, that the declaration was not good, because he doth not therein alledge that the munkeys were reclaimed. Flem. Chief Justice,[34] If the action had been for 60 musk-cats taken, and a parret, the action would well lye: in case of hawks, there he ought to alledge in his declaration, that they were reclaimed, but not so here in his case of munkies, the Court all clear of opinion that the declaration here is good without shewing that they were reclaimed, and so by the rule of the Court judgment was entred for the plaintiff."[35]

Mink-shooting, too, has provoked litigation. One plaintiff claimed damages against his neighbour for the shooting of four of the plaintiff's minks.[36] The defence was that the minks had been in pursuit of the defendant's geese on his geese pond, and that the defendant had shot the minks to protect his geese. To this, the plaintiff answered that just as a man must retreat so far as he can before slaying his assailant, so the defendant should have driven his geese away from the minks, rather than shooting the minks. What seems surprising is not that the contention failed,[37] but that it was explored at such an elaborate and ponderous length.[38]

The contention, said Doe J., amounted to this:

> it being impracticable to permanently eject the assailants, he must banish the assailed; and the raising of geese being impossible, the raising of minks is compulsory. A freeholder, permitted to fire blank cartridges only to cover the endless retreat of his poultry before these marauders, and obliged to suffer such an enemy to ravage his lands and waters with boldness generated by impunity, is a result of turning the fact of the reasonable necessity of retreating to the wall before a human assailant into a universal rule of law. This rule practically compels the defendant to bring his poultry to the block prematurely, and to abandon an important branch of agricultural industry. His right of protecting his fowls is merely his right of exterminating them . . . .

[34] Fleming C.J.

[35] *Anon.* (1610) 1 Bulstr. 95.

[36] *Aldrich* v. *Wright*, 53 N.H. 398 (1873).

[37] See also 2 Misc. 200.

[38] Contrast the brevity of Holmes C.J. in *Nesbett* v. *Wilbur*, 58 N.E. 586 (Mass. 1900).

To hold, in this case, that the geese should have been driven away from their home, would be equivalent to holding that they should have been killed. The doctrine of retreat would leave them a right to nothing but life in some place inaccessible to minks, where life might be unremunerative and burdensome. But that doctrine being irrelevant when the aggressor is not shielded by the inviolability of the human form and the sacred quality of human life, the geese were not bound to retreat. As against the minks, they had a right not only to live, but to live where the defendant chose, on his soil and pond, and to enjoy such food, drink, and sanitary privileges as they found there, unmolested by these vermin, in a state of tranquillity conducive to their profitable nurture. And it was for the jury to say, not whether he could have driven them away from the minks, but whether his shot was reasonably necessary for the protection of his property, considering what adequate and economical means of permanent protection were available, the legal valuation of vermin life, and the disturbance and mischief likely to be wrought upon his real and personal estate if any other than a sanguinary defence were adopted.

The plaintiff's claim, if upheld, would reach far beyond an unjust judgment taking from this defendant the sum of forty dollars and costs. It would establish a principle of law, novel in theory and practice, subversive of the authorities, extensive in its operation, and pernicious in its effect. If the defendant's geese were bound to retreat before these vermin, it follows that horses, cattle, sheep, swine, and poultry are bound, at common law, to retreat and to be driven by their owners from their own land, if retreat is possible, regardless of course or distance, before every dog that chooses to attack them: if A's dog besets B's house, and exhibits an inclination to attack the occupants when they come out, they must remain shut up till he sees fit to raise the siege; friends who would come to their relief can do nothing but retreat; and, the law of retreat not being limited to any particular lines, every person, on his own land or in the highway, menaced by another's dog, is bound not to use a deadly weapon, if he can escape by taking refuge in a tree and remaining there an indefinite period; and, in many ways, the human industries and liberties of the country are subject to interruptions, hindrances, and restrictions not heretofore judicially established or practically acknowledged. In a practical view, the perils, inconveniences, and damages caused by perverse and unruly animals, under such a system of brutish dominion, assume a serious aspect. In a legal view, the expansion of the duty of retreat is a contraction of the natural and constitutional right of defending person and property.[39]

[39] *Aldrich* v. *Wright*, 53 N.H. at 421, 423.

It was this judgment that was understandably said to have cost Doe J. a seat in the United States Supreme Court.[40]

Animals — or at least some animals — are increasingly the object of charities established for their protection. The court once had to consider a decision by Chitty J.[41] that a society established for the purpose of securing the total abolition of the vivisection of animals was in law charitable, as conducing to the promotion of kindness to animals. MacKinnon L.J. said:

> I readily assume that the motive which leads old women to make bequests to this society is concern for the welfare of the dear dogs. As one who has more than once experienced the grief of losing a beloved spaniel, I can respect and applaud that motive: though I do not think my respect and applause can be expected when it becomes a matter of the dear guinea-pigs and the dear rats. . . . On the reasoning and assumption of Chitty J., I conceive that a society, whose object was to secure legislation making illegal the manufacture and sale of rat-traps and rat poisons, would have to be held established for charitable purposes, and that the more readily if the tribunal insisted on "standing neutral" on the question whether rats are, or are not, vermin that are a menace to mankind. Indeed, if it be true, as some may think, that
>
>> "the poor beetle, that we tread upon,
>> In corporeal sufferance finds a pang as great
>> As when a giant dies,"[42]
>
> a society to promote legislation to prohibit the manufacture and sale of all insecticides would seem to have good ground for a like claim."[43]

In tort, there are difficulties in determining a farmer's liability for spraying his flowering crops with insecticides that are fatal to his neighbour's bees. But happily the courts have firmly rejected the

---

[40] See J.P. Reid, *Chief Justice: The Judicial World of Charles Doe* (1967), pp. 165, 372.

[41] *Re Foveaux* [1895] 2 Ch. 501.

[42] *Measure for Measure*, Act 3, sc. 1, ll. 78–80.

[43] *Commissioners of Inland Revenue* v. *National Anti-Vivisection Society* [1946] K.B. 185 at 211 (*affirmed* [1948] A.C. 31) (holding that the total suppression of vivisection was not a charitable purpose).

differential contention that it depends on whether the crops are of a type that require pollination by insects, and so whether the bees should be classified as being invitees, licensees, or trespassers.[44]

At times, the animal world provides convenient judicial analogues. On an application for the variation of the terms of a trust, the trustees are usually required to assume the functions of a watch-dog on behalf of unborn or unascertained persons whose interests might be adversely affected by the variation.[45] That raises the question of the standard of vigilance required, e.g., when there is a possibility that a fraud on a power may be involved. The test appears to be whether there is a real and not merely tenuous suspicion of fraud; for however alert and persistent a watch-dog should be, he ought not to be required to discharge the functions of a bloodhound or a ferret.[46]

Again, it is ancient law that if a trustee sells trust property to himself, any beneficiary is entitled to have the sale set aside. That is a simple case. But

> equity looks beneath the surface, and applies its doctrines to cases where, although in form a trustee has not sold to himself, in substance he has. Again one must regard the realities. If the question is asked: 'Will a sale of trust property by the trustee to his wife be set aside?', nobody can answer it without being told more; for the question is asked in a conceptual form, and manifestly there are wives and wives. In one case the trustee may have sold privately to his wife with whom he was living in perfect amity; in another the property may have been knocked down at auction to the trustee's wife from whom he has been living separate and in enmity for a dozen years. So here one must look at the realities.[47]

For "equity is astute to prevent a trustee from abusing his position or profiting from his trust: the shepherd must not become a wolf."[48]

---

[44] *Tutton* v. *A.D. Walter Ltd.* [1986] Q.B. 61 (see at pp. 75, 76). Instead, there was a straight-forward application of *Donoghue* v. *Stevenson* [1932] A.C. 562.

[45] *Re Druce's Settlement Trusts* [1962] 1 W.L.R. 363 at 370; *Re Munro's Settlement Trusts* [1963] 1 W.L.R. 145 at 149.

[46] *Re Wallace's Settlements* [1968] 1 W.L.R. 711 at 719.

[47] *Tito* v. *Waddell (No. 2)* [1977] Ch. 106 at 240.

[48] *Ibid.*, at p. 241.

In the end, there are some curiosities. Lawyers have not always been at their best in dealing with animals. In the first half of the seventeenth century, there was an action at Bury Assizes before Trevor B. concerning the proper charge for the wintering (i.e., winter pasturing) of cattle. The judge considered the charge excessive. "'Why, Friend,' says he, 'this is most unreasonable; I wonder thou art not asham'd, for I myself have knowne a beast winter'd one whole summer for a noble' [i.e. 6s.8d.]. 'That was a Bull, my Lord, I believe,' sayes the fellow; at which ridiculous expression of the judge, and slye retorted jeere of the countryman, the whole court fell into a most profuse laughter."[49]

It was Curran who, in order to shame an English party discussing cock-fighting, told the wondrous and far-famed story of the two Sligo cats.[50] (Later they moved south and became better-known as the Kilkenny cats.[51]) Curran explained that in Ireland cats were matched against each other as mastiffs were in England, and that one day the company at Sligo, departing for dinner, left the two cats in battle in a locked room. Whey they returned, they found that "the cats had actually eaten each other up, save some little bits of tails which were scattered round the room." To this may be added Lord Campbell's assertion that it is an "undoubted fact that, in Scotland, the crows, who take such good care to keep out of gunshot on every 'lawful day,' on the Sabbath come close up to the houses, and seek their food within a few yards of the farmer and his men, — discovering the occurrence of the sacred day from the ringing of the bells and the discontinuance of labour in the fields, — and knowing that while it lasts they are safe."[52]

Fairness and honesty have both invoked the bestiary. From time to time lawyers and judges have "tried to define what constitutes fairness.

[49] Camden Society, vol. 5, *Anecdotes and Traditions* (W.J. Thomas ed., 1839), p. 79.

[50] W. O'Regan, *Memoirs of John Philpot Curran* (1817), p. 37; and see L. Hale, *John Philpot Curran* (1958), p. 262.

[51] See *The Bench and the Bar* (1837), vol. 1, p. 42. For Kilkenny, the earliest date given by the *O.E.D.* is 1822: vol. 8, p. 427. See also the fictitious case of *Catt* v. *Arkansas*, 691 S.W.2d 120 (1985), discussed in George Rose Smith J., *A Critique of Judicial Humor*, 43 Ark. L. Rev. 1, 23–25 (1990).

[52] 10 Camp.L.CC. 297.

Like defining an elephant, it is not easy to do, although fairness in practice has the elephantine quality of being easy to recognise."[53] So too for honesty: "Of course there is the old saying that it may be difficult to define an elephant but you will know one when you see one; and perhaps a number of people seeing an elephant may all agree that it is an elephant, but a number of people looking for honesty easily find quite different things, and yet all may be perfectly honest and high-minded in differing in their views of morality upon a particular transaction."[54] Even so, it is "sometimes possible to say what a thing is not, although it may be extremely difficult to define what that thing is."[55]

Other analogies are less complimentary. Thus it has been said[56] of the writ *coram nobis*, a form of writ of error that in recent years has been living a vigorous life in America, that the writ "appears to be the wild ass of the law which the courts cannot control. It was hoary with age and even obsolete in England before the time of Blackstone, and courts who attempt to deal with it 'become lost in the mist and fog of the ancient common law.'"[57] There is also fable. When the record of a decision excludes all details of the evidence and the reasoning, it is no longer a "speaking order," but becomes, in Lord Sumner's classic phrase, "the inscrutable face of a sphinx."[58] To this, Lord Tucker afterwards added a gloss: "Is there a difference when the order speaks but speaks with the ambiguous voice of the oracle?"[59]

---

[53] *Maxwell* v. *Department of Trade & Industry* [1974] 1 Q.B. 523 at 539 (*per* Lawton L.J.). For Coke's views on elephants, see *ante* pp. 289–90.

[54] *Re Wigzell, ex parte Hart* [1921] 2 K.B. 835 at 859 (*per* Scrutton L.J.).

[55] *Edwards* v. *Tuck* (1853) 3 De G.M. & G. 40 at 57 (*per* Lord Cranworth L.C.).

[56] *Anderson* v. *Buchanan*, 168 S.W.2d 48, 55 (Ky. Ct. App. 1943) (Sims J., dissenting).

[57] *Ibid.* (quoting *Mitchell* v. *State*, 176 So. 743, 747 (Miss. 1937) (Smith C.J., dissenting)). For a modern attempt to obtain the writ in Canada, see *Bouchard* v. *R* (1980) 17 C.R. (3d) 82.

[58] See 1 Misc. 281.

[59] *Baldwin & Francis Ltd.* v. *Patent Appeal Tribunal* [1959] A.C. 663 at 687.

20

~

FUSTUM FUNNIDOS TANTARABOO

DISPUTES on the construction of wills are numberless. As every lawyer knows, no answer lies in saying that all that the court has to do is to find out the intention of the testator. Brett L.J. once said: "It sometimes amuses me when we are asked to say what was the actual intention of a foolish, thoughtless, and inaccurate testator. That is not what the Court has to determine: all the Court can do is construe, according to settled rules, the terms of a will, just as it construes the terms of any other written document."[1] The classic statement is by Parke J.: "In expounding a will, the Court is to ascertain not what the testator actually intended, as contradistinguished from what his words express, but what is the meaning of the words he has used."[2] A quarter of a century later, as Lord Wensleydale, he reiterated his views: "The first duty of the Court expounding the will is to ascertain what is the meaning of the words used by the testator. It is very often said that the intention of the testator is to be the guide, but that expression is capable of being misunderstood, and may lead to a speculation as to what the testator may be supposed to have intended to write, whereas the only and proper inquiry is, what is the meaning of that which he has actually written."[3]

In former days the rule seems to have been even stricter, and rich with moral overtones. In 1555 Brook C.J. said that a man

---

[1] *Ralph* v. *Carrick* (1879) 11 Ch.D. 873 at 876.

[2] *Doe d. Gwillim* v. *Gwillim* (1833) 5 B. & Ad. 122 at 129.

[3] *Roddy* v. *Fitzgerald* (1858) 6 H.L.C. 823 at 876; and see 1 Misc. 264.

ought to direct his meaning according to the law, and not the law according to his meaning, for if a man should bend the law to the intent of the party, rather than the intent of the party to the law, this would be the way to introduce barbarousness and ignorance, and to destroy all learning and diligence. For if a man was assured that whatever words he made use of his meaning only should be considered, he would be very careless about the choice of his words, and it would be the source of infinite confusion and incertainty to explain what was his meaning.[4]

It would, said Le Blanc J., be a "very dangerous rule to go by, because it would be to say that the same words should vary in their construction according to the quantity of the property or the situation of the party disposing of it."[5] Today, some would say "Why not?"

At times the courts show little enthusiasm for the task of construing wills: "I do not know of any more unsatisfactory duty for a Judge than that of being called upon to put a construction on an instrument with respect to which, it may be presumed, the framer of the instrument had himself no very definite notion. It is a duty, however, of necessity imposed on the Judges of this Court, who, as Lord Mansfield[6] has observed, must sometimes feel that they are the only authorised interpreters of nonsense."[7] Yet authority is not always duty. Arden M.R. (later Lord Alvanley C.J.) once exclaimed: "My duty, sir, to find out [the testator's] meaning! Suppose the will had contained only these words '*Fustum funnidos tantaraboo.*' Am I to find out the meaning of his gibberish?"[8] There are, indeed, testators who in their wills, "speak as if the office of language were to conceal their thoughts,"[9] harking back to Oliver Goldsmith's assertion that "the true use of speech is not so much to express our wants, as to conceal them."[10]

---

[4] *Throckmerton* v. *Tracy* (1555) 1 Plowd. 145 at 162.

[5] *Doe d. Hick* v. *Dring* (1814) 2 M. & S. 448 at 455.

[6] And Lord Henley L.C. before him: *Le Rousseau* v. *Rede* (1761) 2 Eden 1 at 4.

[7] *Cookson* v. *Bingham* (1853) 3 De G.M. & G. 668 at 674 (*per* Lord Cranworth L.C.).

[8] W.C. Townsend, *Lives of Twelve Eminent Judges* (1846), vol. 1, p. 149, pressed into town planning service, *arguendo*, in *Fawcett Properties Ltd.* v. *Buckingham County Council* [1961] A.C. 636 at 647; and see 2 *Law and Lawyers* (1840), at p. 74 ("fustun").

[9] *Lowe* v. *Thomas* (1854) 5 De G.M. & G. 315 at 317 (*per* Knight Bruce L.J.).

[10] *The Bee*, Oct. 20, 1759, para. 2.

Difficulties sometimes arise in unexpected places. The will of George Bernard Shaw set up elaborate trusts designed to encourage the replacement of the conventional alphabet of 26 letters by a more ample alphabet of at least 40 letters that would allow each sound to be represented by a letter of its own instead of requiring groups of letters. Unfortunately these trusts ran into legal difficulties, and in due course they came before Harman J.:

> The testator, whatever his other qualifications, was the master of a pellucid style, and the reader embarks on his will confident of finding no difficulty in understanding the objects which the testator had in mind. This document, moreover, was evidently originally the work of a skilled equity draftsman. As such, I doubt not, it was easily to be understood, if not of the vulgar, at any rate by the initiate. Unfortunately the will bears ample internal evidence of being in part the testator's own work. The two styles, as ever, make an unfortunate mixture. It is always a marriage of incompatibles: the delicate testamentary machinery devised by the conveyancer can but suffer when subjected to the cacoethes scribendi[11] of the author, even though the latter's language, if it stood alone, might be a literary masterpiece.
>
> This will is a long and complicated document made on June 12, 1950, when the testator was already 94 years old, though it is fair to say that it is rather youthful exuberance than the circumspection of old age that mars its symmetry."[12]

The judge then examined the relevant clauses of the will, including one that provided for the destination of the trust funds if the trusts "shall fail through judicial decision," and then discussed the objections to the validity of the trusts. These he found insuperable: "The result is that the alphabet trusts are, in my judgment, invalid, and must fail. It seems that their begetter suspected as much, hence his jibe about failure by judicial decision. I answer that it is not the fault of the law, but of the testator, who failed almost for the first time in his life to grasp the legal problem or to make up his mind what he wanted."[13]

---

[11] Itch for writing.

[12] *Re Shaw decd.* [1957] 1 W.L.R. 729 at 731; [1957] 1 All E.R. 745 at 747–48. Minor differences in wording and punctuation have been resolved in favour of the more Harmanian.

[13] *Ibid.*, 1 All E.R. at 759.

Sometimes there is misplaced ingenuity. Father O'Flaherty, of Glenflesk, Co. Kerry, once wished to provide certain sums for the saying of Masses and for making repairs to the church. With the aid of a bank manager he hit on the device of depositing money at a bank and receiving deposit receipts made out in favour of "the Parish Priest of Glenflesk," and naming those purposes. When he died the question was whether his successor in office took these moneys subject to trusts imposed by the receipts, or whether the moneys formed part of Father O'Flaherty's estate.

In the King's Bench Division in Ireland it was held that Father O'Flaherty's successor held the moneys in trust for the stated purposes. Lord O'Brien C.J. observed that —

> the argument that the money for Masses was lodged for Father O'Flaherty himself, involved this rather fantastic suggestion — that the Rev. Maurice O'Flaherty might, by some extraordinary resurrectionary process, rise from the dead, and at the Chapel of Barraduff, in the County of Kerry, say in the flesh Masses for the repose of his soul, which was, for the time being, in another world in a state of purgation for the sins — the venial transgressions — committed in this world. That, in fact, the reverend gentleman might arise in the flesh and leave his soul behind him. There is no warrant for this suggested segregation of animated body and suffering soul in any book of authority from the Year Books to the present day.[14]

The contentions of Mr. Daniel Browne, "who brought to the argument of the case much spiritual warmth,"[15] accordingly succeeded. But the Court of Appeal disagreed. FitzGibbon L.J. stigmatised the decision of the King's Bench as involving, not a resurrectionary process, but "the prenatal ownership of a hypothetical depositor — of a successor who may never be appointed";[16] and that was that.

One may turn to a Scunthorpe solicitor whose will, made in 1930, achieved the ultimate in providing for every eventuality. The final clause ran: "Lastly I declare that in the event of the Second Coming of Our

---

[14] *O'Flaherty* v. *Browne* [1907] 2 I.R. 416 at 421.
[15] *Ibid.*
[16] *Ibid.*, at p. 433.

Lord and Saviour Jesus Christ my Will shall (so far as may be legally permissible) come into operation and take effect as though I were dead."[17] But a retired school teacher put the Second Coming first, though with prudent precautions. He left his whole estate of over £26,000 in trust to be paid to the Lord Jesus Christ in the event of a Second Coming. The estate was to be invested for 80 years, and "if during those 80 years the Lord Jesus Christ shall come to reign on Earth, then the Public Trustee, upon obtaining proof which shall satisfy them of his identity, shall pay to the Lord Jesus Christ all the property which they hold on his behalf." If Christ did not appear within the 80 years, the whole estate was to go to the Crown; and the income was to be accumulated for 21 years and then paid to the Crown.[18]

One will looked innocent enough. Subject to a life interest to his widow, the testator left a specified part of his lands to each of his seven sons, George, Richard, Thomas, Henry, John, Becher, and William, save that to Thomas, who had already received some land, he gave one shilling. The will then directed that if any son died before he was thirty, his share should go "to his next eldest brother, and so on, respectively"; and there was a similar provision if any son died "without issue" after he was thirty. All the sons had attained the age of thirty, four had no issue, and one had no issue still living; and the question was how the will would work if one of the sons died without issue. Suppose John (No. 5) died without issue: was it Henry (No. 4) or Becher (No. 6) who was John's "next eldest brother"? Was it the youngest of the older brothers, or the oldest of the younger brothers, who was the "next eldest"? In short, upwards or downwards?

This question was argued in Ireland before three King's Bench judges; and each gave a different answer. In effect, Gibson J. said "Downwards," Wright J. said "Upwards," and Boyd J. held the provision to be void for uncertainty.[19] The natural result was an appeal, though

---

[17] From the will of R.A.C. Symes, *ob.* April 29, 1933; *ex rel.* Plowman J. The will was before the court on another point.

[18] *Re Digweed* [1977] *The Times* Jan. 21.

[19] *Crofts* v. *Beamish* [1905] 2 I.R. 349.

from indecision rather than decision.[20] All three members of the Court of Appeal said "Downwards."[21] FitzGibbon L.J. reached his conclusion by notionally resurrecting the testator for questioning. To do this would be "the fair test" of the meaning of the words: "If I asked him, 'Who is your eldest son?' he would answer, 'George.' 'Who is the next eldest?' 'Richard.' 'Who is the next eldest?' 'Thomas.' 'And so on, respectively,' until he had come to the youngest, 'William.'"[22] Yet this examination in chief was balanced by no cross-examination; and the probable course of question and answer springs readily to mind. The question would begin with the youngest, and would at least have the merit of being framed in terms of the word "brother," as used in the will, and not "son." "Who is William's next eldest brother?" "Becher." "Who is Becher's next eldest brother?" "John"; and so on, upwards. This would at least avoid equating "next eldest" with "next youngest," as proceeding downwards appears to do. The Court of Appeal did indeed succeed in distilling certainty from the obscure; yet was the appellate process even-handed throughout? Nobody, alas, pursued a further appeal. In contrast, it is hardly surprising that a will that had been "written upon three sides of a sheet of paper," and executed "at the bottom of the third side" should travel the whole way from the Vice-Chancellor's court in Ireland to the House of Lords.[23]

Opinions often differ about the advisability of particular testamentary dispositions. But "the testator is a despot, within limits, over his property."[24] Even so, despotism does not always triumph. One Canadian testator provided in his will: "It pleased the Lord to give me two sons equally dear to my heart; to give them equal justice I leave all my land to the first great grandson descending from them by lawful ordinary generation in the masculine line. . . ." The testator may have prided

---

[20] Without a decision there can usually be no appeal.

[21] See *Crofts* v. *Beamish*, *supra* note 19, at 353.

[22] S.C. at p. 364; and see *per* Walker and Holmes L.JJ. at pp. 365, 367.

[23] *Watson* v. *Arundel* (1876) 10 I.R.Eq. 299 (see p. 301), *reversed sub nom. Watson* v. *Arundell* (1876) 11 I.R.Eq. 53, *affirmed sub nom. Singleton* v. *Tomlinson* (1878) 3 App.Cas. 404 (see at p. 405).

[24] O.W. Holmes Jr., *The Theory of Legal Interpretation*, 12 Harv. L. Rev. 417, 420 (1899).

himself on the aptness of his language; but be had forgotten the rule against perpetuities, which invalidated the whole devise and so left the land to descend as on an intestacy to the testator's elder son and those claiming under him.[25] Nor are the circumstances of will-making always the best. Coke's advice was that men should provide for their wives and children by settlements made in their lifetime "by sound advice of learned counsel," rather than leaving their property "to stand wholly upon their last will, which many times is made when they lie upon their death-bed (and few men pinched with the messengers of death have a disposing memory) sometimes in haste, and commonly by slender advice."[26]

Most wills, of course, are made long before the death-bed. In Ireland Porter M.R. was once giving judgment in a case on the construction of a will: "In those circumstances," he said, "I am perfectly certain that the testator intended his farm to go to his nephew James." "Indeed he did not, me Lord," said a voice at the back of the court. "Bring forward that man," ordered Porter; and an attendant brought the culprit to the front of the court. "Who are you, Sir?" demanded Porter. "Me Lord, I'm the testator, and I never meant James to have the farm." He had left Ireland some years before, and had never written home; and so had been presumed to be dead.[27] In such circumstances, probate or letters of administration to the estate may be granted. Yet, statute apart,[28] everything done under the authority of the probate or letters of administration is in law a nullity if in fact the "deceased" is still alive.[29] It may be added that in days gone by those wishing to resort to the Prerogative Office in order to examine wills proved in the Province of Canterbury had to time their visits; for as the *Law List* 1779[30] helpfully

---

[25] *Ferguson* v. *Ferguson* (1878) 2 S.C.R. 497.

[26] 10 Co.Rep. xiv; cp. Co.Litt. 111b (where the pinch is "by" the messengers of death).

[27] A version of this appears in A.M. Sullivan, *Old Ireland* (1927), p. 66.

[28] See, e.g., Law of Property Act 1925, s. 204; Administration of Estates Act 1925, ss. 27, 37. See also *Cunnius* v. *Reading Sch. Dist.*, 56 A. 16 (Pa. 1903).

[29] *Allen* v. *Dundas* (1789) 3 T.R. 125 at 129, 130; *Devlin* v. *Commonwealth*, 101 Pa. 273 (1882); *Scott* v. *McNeal*, 154 U.S. 34 (1894).

[30] p. 94.

revealed: "Hours from 9 till 2, and 3 till 6, if light so long, as no Candles are lighted in this Office."

In considering the date on which a "provision" has been "made" by will or codicil, a question once arose about the effect of a codicil that confirmed a provision made by the will. Was the date on which the provision was "made" the date of execution of the will or that of the confirmatory codicil? Luxmoore L.J. decided in favour of the will; and he cited venerable authority on the relationship between will and codicil:[31] "Whereupon the writers conferring a testament and a codicil together and perceiving the odds betwixt the one and the other, they call a testament a great will, and a codicil a little will. And do compare the testament to a ship, and the codicil to a boat, tied most commonly to the ship."[32] To take the date of the codicil would be "to transform the codicil from the boat commonly tied to the ship into the ship itself and then to scuttle the ship."[33] But soon the House of Lords swept away these sophistries by holding that no provision was "made" until the testator died, and both will and codicil took effect together.[34]

Sometimes a will is used to settle old scores; and the jurisdiction of the court to exclude defamatory words from probate of a will is exercised sparingly. In one case,[35] the entire will was in these words:

> I leave all property of every kind to my sister Mary, in consequence of the cruel and murderous conduct of my wife, in this illness, as well as in past instances.
> 13th December, 1823.   James Curtis.

The court, however, refused to expunge any of these words. The decision was to the same effect in another case,[36] where the will concluded with the following words:

---

[31] *Re Sebag-Montefiore* [1944] Ch. 331 at p. 342.
[32] *Swinburne on Testaments* (7th ed. 1803), vol. 1, p. 29.
[33] *Re Sebag-Montefiore, supra* note 31, at p. 343.
[34] *Berkeley* v. *Berkeley* [1946] A.C. 555.
[35] *Curtis* v. *Curtis* (1825) 3 Add. 33.
[36] *In b. Honywood* (1871) L.R. 2 P. & D. 251.

Lastly, it is my most sacred wish that the brief "Honywood v. Honywood," 1859, should be kept in the family, and handed down to all ages as a witness of the terrible iniquity which has robbed me of my birthright, and blotted out the Essex branch of Honywood for ever, and by which F.E.H. did most deliberately and designedly defraud me and my heirs of our patrimony and inheritance for ever. I hereby record my most solemn conviction that my poor brother, the late W.P. Honywood, was perfectly unconscious and innocent of what was done, and that he was simply an instrument in the hands of his wicked and remorseless wife. This is my last will and testament.

An old problem may be presented in a modern dress. The case of the Seventeen Residuary Elephants can be stated thus:[37] A circus proprietor died in 1966, domiciled in England, and survived only by his three sons, A, B, and C. After his debts and funeral and testamentary expenses had been paid, the only assets of his estate consisted of seventeen elephants, each of about the same value and none of them enceinte. By his will, the deceased gave half his entire estate to A, one-third to B, and one-ninth to C. Uncertain about how to divide the elephants, and not wanting to sell any of them, the sons asked their friend X, also a circus proprietor, to advise them. X rode over on one of his elephants, and, after some thought, put his elephant among the seventeen. He then directed A to take nine of the elephants (excluding X's), and similarly directed B to take six, and C to take two, drawing lots for the order of choice. Having thus distributed all seventeen of the testator's elephants, X then mounted his own elephant and rode home. The question then was how far this division was unsatisfactory, and for whom.

The answer is not simple. It is best taken by stages.

(1) Under the will, A was entitled to eight and a half elephants, B to five and two-thirds, and C to one and eight-ninths. Expressed in fifty-fourths, these fractions (excluding the integers) amount to 27 for A, 36 for B and 48 for C; and the total of the integers and fractions is 16 and 3 fifty fourths. Thus 51 fifty-fourths of an elephant were undisposed of, and passed as on an intestacy.

---

[37] See (1959) 103 S.J. 760, 800.

(2) Under the partial intestacy the sons *prima facie* take equally on the statutory trusts. Each son is therefore *prima facie* entitled to 17 fifty-fourths in addition to his share under the will.

(3) The shares that each ought to receive under the will and the partial intestacy, taken together, are thus — A: 8 and 27 fifty-fourths, plus 17 fifty-fourths: total 8 and 44 fifty-fourths. B: 5 and 36 fifty-fourths, plus 17 fifty-fourths: total, 5 and 53 fifty-fourths. C: 1 and 48 fifty-fourths, plus 17 fifty-fourths: total, 2 and 11 fifty-fourths.

(4) Under X's distribution, A in fact received 9 elephants, which was 10 fifty-fourths too much; B received 6 elephants, which was 1 fifty-fourth too much; and C received 2 elephants, which was 11 fifty-fourths too little. C was thus the only son to whom X's division was unsatisfactory, to the extent of 11 fifty-fourths; and A and B must make up the deficiency by contributing their excess fifty-fourths.

(5) That is the *prima facie* view; but it will probably be displaced by the rule as to hotchpot. For, subject to any contrary intention, on a partial intestacy there is hotchpot of the benefits under the will among issue of the testator.[38] Neither A nor B could therefore claim under the intestacy until under the will and intestacy taken together C had received as much as they were each given by the will.

(6) From this it follows that C was entitled to the whole of the 51 fifty-fourths that passed as on intestacy. He had already had 6 of these fifty-fourths, for although the will had given him only one and 48 fifty-fourths of an elephant, X's distribution had given him two entire beasts. The remaining 45 fifty-fourths should be provided by A and B disgorging the fifty-fourths that they received in excess of their rights under the will. A must therefore give C 27 fifty-fourths, and so reduce his 9 elephants to 8 and 27 fifty-fourths, and B must correspondingly give C 18 fifty-fourths and so reduce his 6 elephants to 5 and 36 fifty-fourths.

---

[38] Administration of Estates Act 1925, ss. 47, 49.

(7) On the footing that there is nothing to exclude hotchpot, the answer to the question is thus that X's division of the elephants was unsatisfactory only to C, to the extent that although he was entitled to 2 and 45 fifty-fourths of an elephant (or 2 and five-sixths), he received only 2 elephants. The deficit of five-sixths must be made good by A as to three-sixths and by B as to the other two-sixths.

Animal lovers distressed by the prospect of dividing living elephants into fractions will take comfort from the thought that orders for the recovery of fractions of a man are enforced by sale of the undivided entirety and division of the proceeds in the appropriate fractions.[39]

At least the future George III's problems on fractions were not bedevilled by statute. While he was in his teens his mathematical tutor set him a question on a childless man who made a will during his wife's pregnancy. The will gave her one-third of his estate if she bore him a son, but two-thirds if she bore him a daughter, with the residue in each case to the child. He died, leaving an estate worth £6,300, and his widow then had twins, a boy and a girl.[40] No record of the royal answer appears to have survived.

To the problem of fractional elephants and posthumous twins may be added the problem of fractional states. To be elected President of Nigeria, a candidate must not only obtain the highest number of votes cast at the election, but also obtain "not less than one-quarter of the votes cast at the election in each of at least two-thirds of all the States in the Federation."[41] In default of any such majority, there is provision for election by an electoral college instead.[42] In an election in 1979, the candidate with the highest number of votes duly obtained over one-quarter of the votes in 12 of Nigeria's 19 states. His difficulty was that the highest vote that he could muster in any other state was 243,423 out of the 1,220,763 votes cast in the State of Kano, and that was only

[39] See *ante* p. 285.
[40] J. Brooke, *King George III* (1972), p. 88.
[41] Electoral Decree 1977 (as amended by Electoral (Amendment) Decree, 1978, s. 7), s. 34A(1)(c).
[42] *Ibid.*, s. 34A(3).

19.95 per cent. Two-thirds of 19 states is, of course, 12 2/3 states, and as there was no practicable way of dividing Kano into geographical thirds, one view was that the phrase "at least two-thirds of all the States" must mean 13 states. On that view, the candidate had failed to satisfy the statute.

The majority view, however, was that the phrase meant 12 2/3 states, and that Kano fell to be fractioned not geographically but numerically. Two-thirds of the 1,220,763 votes cast in Kano came to 813,842, and it was held that all that the statute required was that the candidate should obtain at least one-quarter of this number of votes, namely, 203,460.5. His 243,423 Kano votes duly satisfied this requirement, and so he had been validly elected.[43] This process, of course, compared the undivided total number of votes cast for the candidate with a mere fraction of the total number of votes cast for all candidates: 100 per cent of the candidate's votes was compared with 66.6 per cent of the total votes.

This abandonment of the principle that like should be compared with like is capable of producing interesting results. If, for example, 1.2 million votes had been cast in the state, and the six candidates had each obtained exactly 200,000 of these, then for these purposes each of the six would have obtained "one-quarter of the votes cast at the election" in that state, thereby showing that Nigerian votes in bulk had the remarkable quality of being divisible into six quarters.[44] Nearly ten years passed before Nigerian constitutional arithmetic was restored to orthodoxy. The expedient was simple. The number of states was increased by two, and forthwith a sweetly divisible 21[45] stood in place of the original (and equally divisible) dozen; the tyranny of the usurping prime number was no more.

---

[43] *Awolowo v. Shagari* [1979] 2 F.N.R. 60 (Sup. Ct. Nigeria), Obaseki J., concurring on different grounds, and Eso J., dissenting.

[44] Twelve quarters, if there had been 20 states; for then the fraction for the fractional state would have been one-third. For other criticisms, see B. Obinna Okere (1987) 36 I.C.L.Q. 788 at 801–03.

[45] See, e.g., G. Fawehinmi, *Bench and Bar in Nigeria* (1988), p. xiv. At p. 374 is a "List of Female Legal Practitioners Who Indicated Their Sex at the Time of Call." The *modus significandi* was doubtless at large.

21

~

A CERTAIN AMOUNT OF SOBRIETY

FOR MANY years now limited companies have been at the centre of commercial life, and incorporation is simple:

A proprietary company, controlled by one man, has to-day taken the place of John Doe, William Roe[1] and others who at an earlier time came out of ink-wells in attorneys' offices to do acts in the law of which law-abiding citizens might have the benefit while avoiding disadvantageous consequences. By incantations by typewriter, the obtaining of two signatures, payment of fees and compliance with formalities for registration, a company emerges. It is a new legal entity, a person in the eyes of the law. Perhaps it were better in some cases to say a legal *persona*, for the Latin word in one of its senses means a mask: *Eripitur persona, manet res.*[2]

Like any other legal *persona*, a company may change its name by taking the appropriate steps; and many companies do this, doubtless for good reason. Yet some changes provoke curiosity. Thus in 1978 it was solemnly announced that "Robbs Fish and Chips Consultants Ltd." had become "Carlill and Carbolic Smoke Ball Corporation."[3] Incidentally, Lord Somervell was one of those who carried into their latter years a

---

[1] Doubtless Richard's brother; and see W.J.V. Windeyer, *Lectures on Legal History* (1938), p. 155 ("'The casual ejector' was usually Richard Roe or William Styles.") See also Sir Victor Windeyer (1973) 11 Alberta Law Review 123 at 127.

[2] *Peate* v. *Commissioner of Taxation of the Commonwealth of Australia* (1964) 111 C.L.R. 443 at 478 (*per* Windeyer J.: "The mask is snatched off, yet the substance remains").

[3] *The British Columbia Gazette*, March 9, 1978, p. 337. For a century *Carlill* v. *Carbolic Smoke Ball Co.* [1893] 1 Q.B. 256 endeared itself to every student of the law of contract.

strong recollection of being made in their youth to inhale the fumes from a carbolic smoke ball in a vain attempt to ward off influenza; and he spoke with feeling of the valuable consideration that moved from any who had suffered as he.[4]

The reason for *Robbs'* change to *Carlill* seems to be that *Robbs* was formed and named for a venture that did not proceed, and so the company, thus destined to become a "shelf company," needed a new name. Instead of inventing meaningless names, a practice had grown up of using the names of well-known English cases, such as *Wagon Mound No. 2*[5] *Welders Ltd.*, a company carrying out land development; and so *Robbs* became *Carlill*. When taken off the shelf for thrifty citizens wishing to acquire and operate a trailer park, simple economy left its name unchanged;[6] and in that name was it promptly sued.[7]

Meetings are the life of companies; and there are even circumstances when one person by himself can be a "meeting." Usually he cannot; for unless there are at least two persons, one cannot meet another and so constitute a "meeting." Thus in 1874 a meeting of a company had been duly called, but only one shareholder attended. He took the chair and passed a number of resolutions, including a vote of thanks to himself for presiding; but all was in vain, for the Court of Appeal held that there had been no "meeting," and so the proceedings were void.[8] It would have made no difference if the solitary attendant had held proxies for other shareholders:[9] "A meeting at which only one member is present to play multiple parts may be thought to be nothing other than a pantomime."[10] One swallow does not make a summer, even if endowed with authority to act for other birds. Even if two shareholders attend, either may bring

[4] Personal communication.

[5] *Overseas Tankship (U.K.) Ltd.* v. *Miller Steamship Co. Pty.: The Wagon Mound (No.2)* [1967] 1 A.C. 617.

[6] I am grateful to Cecil O.D. Branson Q.C. of Vancouver for this information. The trailer park is the Lombardie Trailer Park, Fort Langley B.C.

[7] *Walker* v. *Carlill & Carbolic Smoke Ball Corporation* (1979) 11 B.C.L.R. 199.

[8] *Sharp* v. *Dawes* (1876) 2 Q.B.D. 26. Contrast *Re Fireproof Doors Ltd.* [1916] 2 Ch. 142; and see now Companies Act 1985, ss. 367(2), 371(2), replacing earlier provisions.

[9] *Re Sanitary Carbon Co.* [1877] W.N. 223.

[10] *James Prain & Sons Ltd.* 1947 S.C. 325 at 329 (*per* Lord Moncrieff).

the meeting to an end merely by departing.[11] Nevertheless, where all the preference shares in a company were vested in one person, and the memorandum of association provided that no further preference shares could be issued without the sanction of the preference shareholders at a separate "meeting" of such shareholders specially summoned for the purpose, it was held that the lone preference shareholder could, by communing with himself and signing a document consenting to the issue of more preference shares, sufficiently hold a "meeting" and pass a resolution for the purpose.[12] And, of course, one person may constitute a committee,[13] even if he is unable, as such, to hold a committee meeting.

Insurance policies have few judicial admirers: "The policy is made up of a jumble of ill-assorted documents expressed in that distinctive style which insurance companies have made their own."[14] Further, "Although as a matter of ordinary English one would not speak of a hole in the ground as 'works erected,' this is an insurance policy";[15] and of course that explains all. Yet insurance has no monopoly. It was an Australian bank guarantee in which clause 1(i) consisted of "one unpunctuated sentence of over 450 words of small print which is presented to the reader in twenty-five closely set lines, each of excessive length. There the resolute and persevering may find, in the midst of much else, the phrase 'and whether contingently or otherwise.'"[16] In the United States, the language of a Departmental letter reducing the amount that would be paid out under Medicare insurance was stigmatised as being "bureaucratic gobbledegook, jargon, double talk, a form of officialese, federalese and insurancese, and doublespeak. It does not qualify as English."[17]

Even simple language may be far from easy to apply. For insurance purposes, it has been solemnly adjudged that a person riding a bicycle is

---

[11] See *Re London Flats Ltd.* [1969] 1 W.L.R. 711.

[12] *East* v. *Bennett Bros. Ltd.* [1911] 1 Ch. 163.

[13] See *ante* p. 281 for the desirability of this.

[14] *Guardian Assurance Co. Ltd.* v. *Underwood Construction Pty. Ltd.* (1974) 48 A.L.J.R. 307 at 308 (*per* Mason J.).

[15] *Ibid.*, at p. 309 (*per* Mason J.).

[16] *National Bank of Australasia Ltd.* v. *Mason* (1975) 133 C.L.R. 191 at 203 (*per* Stephen J.).

[17] *David* v. *Heckler*, 591 F. Supp. 1033, 1043 (E.D.N.Y. 1984) (*per* Weinstein C.J.).

not travelling as an ordinary passenger in a vehicle,[18] and that he does
not become a pedestrian merely because he wheels his bicycle up a hill,[19]
though he is then "in charge of" a "vehicle,"[20] and, indeed, a "carriage."[21]
But after faltering in the Court of Appeal, a ship — which is neither an
"aircraft" nor, probably, a "vehicle" — has finally emerged (a trifle
mysteriously) as being capable of constituting "equipment" provided by
an employer for the purposes of the employer's business within a
provision stating that the word includes "any plant and machinery,
vehicle, aircraft and clothing."[22] There have also been difficulties with
floods. A house's ground-floor lavatory that has three inches of water
standing in it may indeed be said to be "flooded"; but is that water a
"flood" within the words "storm, tempest or flood" in an insurance
policy if the water has accumulated slowly from an unknown source?
After some wavering, the Court of Appeal answered No, though without
venturing on any definition; for the water lacked the qualities of
violence, abnormality, suddenness, and substantiality that a "flood," in
that context, usually bears.[23] And in Scotland, successive heavy snowfalls
may constitute a "storm."[24]

There has been much criticism of the time taken in arguing patent
cases. Lord Esher M.R. was characteristically forthright:

> It used to be said that there was something catching in a horse case: that it
> made the witnesses perjure themselves as a matter of course. It seems to me
> that there is something catching in a patent case, which is that it makes
> everybody argue, and ask questions to an interminable extent — a patent
> case with no more difficult question to try than any other case instead of
> lasting six hours is invariably made to last at least six days, if not twelve. I am

---

[18] McMillan v. Sun Life Insurance Co. of India, 1896, 4 S.L.T. 66.

[19] Harper v. Associated Newspapers, Ltd. (1927) 43 T.L.R. 331.

[20] Ibid.; Hansford v. London Express Newspaper, Ltd. (1928) 44 T.L.R. 349.

[21] See 1 Misc. 35.

[22] Coltman v. Bibby Tankers Ltd. [1988] A.C. 276, reversing the majority decision at [1987]
2 W.L.R. 1098, [1988] A.C. 280, and restoring [1986] 1 W.L.R. 751, on the construction of
the Employers' Liability (Defective Equipment) Act 1969, s. 1.

[23] Young v. Sun Alliance & London Insurance Ltd. [1977] 1 W.L.R. 104 at 106–08.

[24] Glasgow Training Group (Motor Trade) Ltd. v. Lombard Continental plc 1989 S.L.T. 375.

sure that there ought to be some remedy for it. . . . The moment there is a patent case one can see it before the case is opened, or called in the list. How can we see it? We can see it by a pile of books as high as this [holding up the papers] invariably, one set for each counsel, one set for each judge, of course, and by the voluminous shorthand notes: we know "Here is a patent case."

Now what is the result of all this? Why, that a man had better have his patent infringed, or have anything happen to him in this world, short of losing all his family by influenza, than have a dispute about a patent. His patent is swallowed up, and he is ruined. Whose fault is it? It is really not the fault of the law; it is the fault of the mode of conducting the law in a patent case. That is what causes all this mischief.[25]

It was clear, of course, where to put the blame:

I cannot help thinking that some counsel who are in the habit of arguing patent cases consider that they have a patent which obliges them to consider that no patent case can be tried under a whole day's talk. Those are the patent counsel, as they are called, of the present day. I am not sure they have not been anticipated, and that their patent is not a bad one, but, at all events, the sooner they give up the idea the better for us. . . . There is not one shadow of ground for this long argument which has taken place the whole of this day; and there is nothing in it but this — that two eminent counsel[26] in the habit of conducting patent cases have thought it right to read every bit of the evidence, whether material or immaterial, when, I venture to say, if they had been called on to advise, they must have said to those who asked them, "It is of no use; what you are asking us to do is of no use, and is a mere waste of time," and if they had said that I should have entirely agreed with them.[27]

In addition to reading too much evidence, counsel also sinned by raising too many points: "I think if the real and substantial point of the appeal had been put to us simply, and that point only, this appeal at the outside would have occupied the court for about two hours; but by bringing in a mass of absolutely hopeless points, we have had the pleasure of hearing this case argued for two days and a half. All the points but one

[25] *Ungar* v. *Sugg* (1892) 9 R.P.C. 113 at 116 (*per* Lord Esher M.R.).
[26] Fletcher Moulton Q.C. and Bousfield Q.C.
[27] *Haggenmacher* v. *Watson, Todd & Co.* (1897) 14 R.P.C. 631 at 634, 637 (*per* Lord Esher M.R.).

seem to me to be really empty points, and not to have anything in them; but I think that one point taken on behalf of the defendants is fatal to the plaintiffs."[28] Thus, "it was said that 'El Destino' was a geographical expression, and the learned counsel[29] wanted to give us, as I said, a dissertation upon geography. 'El Destino' a geographical expression! You might as well say that 'my grandmother' is a geographical expression. Therefore, all the points, as I say, which were laboured for hours were all hopeless points, and why anybody should go into a mass of hopeless points when they have a really good point under their hands, which they could bring forward in an hour and half, I never can understand."[30]

One of the habitual sinners was the indestructible Mr. Fletcher Moulton.[31] Lord Esher was firm but urbane: "I have the greatest respect for Mr. Moulton's arguments generally; they are most instructive, they are most useful to the court; but I have sometimes, perhaps not infrequently, when they are pressed to the fineness to which he does press them, often, though I respect them, differed from them. I differ from his arguments in this case; they were a great deal too refined for me."[32] Again,

> I asked Mr. Moulton to tell us where, in this patent, he found any claim for mineral oils, and where he found any other proportions than those which are thus grammatically fixed. His answer always was, "Everybody must have known that the other things were in." Now, what is the meaning of such an answer? It means, if anything, this, that there is nothing in the patent which says so, but everybody must have known that it does say so. That is very skilful; and, when it is manipulated and talked over, and turned round and round, you make a very plausible argument. But by those who have to look into arguments to see whether they are sound or not, it is an absolutely futile argument.[33]

---

[28] *Pinto* v. *Badman* (1891) 8 R.P.C. 181 at p. 188 (*per* Lord Esher M.R.).

[29] Fletcher Moulton Q.C.

[30] *Pinto* v. *Badman, supra* note 28, at p. 191 (*per* Lord Esher M.R.).

[31] Afterwards Lord Justice and then a Lord of Appeal in Ordinary.

[32] *Nobel's Explosives Co. Ltd.* v. *Anderson* (1894) 11 R.P.C. 519 at 526 (*per* Lord Esher M.R.).

[33] *The Maxim-Nordenfelt Guns & Ammunition Co. Ltd.* v. *Anderson* (1897) 14 R.P.C. 671 at 680 (*per* Lord Esher M.R.).

Mr. Fletcher Moulton was not alone. Of another counsel, Lord Esher said:

> The argument really is this: Mr. Bousfield has invented a new term, for which he shall have a patent if he can get it, and his new term is this — he calls discretion "chaos." Why is discretion "chaos"? I do not know exactly what his views of "chaos" are, but you cannot alter the law by finding out a new name, which, after all, is an inaccurate name. The old name I like better than the new one, and, therefore, I shall leave it alone, and say that a judge is entitled not to exercise "chaos," which I do not know how he is to do, but that he is to exercise his discretion, which I do think I know how he is to do. I say again, as we said before, that we will not have any cast-iron rule for the exercise of discretion; we will lay down no rule *a priori* as to the exercise of a discretion at all in any case; all that we can do is this — that after discretion has been exercised, it is our duty to consider whether we agree with the mode in which the discretion has been exercised.[34]

Yet although not chaos, discretion poses many problems, not least when the judge enters "the realm of pure discretion, where it is hardest to condense in words the dialogue of the intracranial jury room."[35]

Sometimes there were bouquets from Lord Esher: "This case has been remarkably well argued, and not only remarkably well argued in point of argument, but I may say delightfully well argued in point of temper; for we have tormented the counsel[36] a good deal (although not more than I think we ought), and he has taken it so well that it was indeed quite a pleasure."[37] Still, there were limits, and these sometimes took colour from the title of the case being argued: "We have had an admirable argument for three days nearly; and for my part I would very nearly as soon have been burnt alive as to have to listen to the whole of it. But it

[34] *Lang* v. *The Whitecross Wire & Iron Co. Ltd.* (1889) 6 R.P.C. 570 at 574 (*per* Lord Esher M.R.).

[35] *O'May* v. *City of London Real Property Co. Ltd.* [1983] 2 A.C. 726 at 742 (*per* Lord Hailsham of St. Marylebone L.C., quoting Goulding J.).

[36] One Jenkins: the report gives no initials. The probables include H.C. (1881), L.H. (1883), and C.E.E. (1885).

[37] *Crampton* v. *Patents Investment Co.* (1889) 6 R.P.C. 287 at 292 (*per* Lord Esher M.R.).

has come down, as usual, after all the elaboration and all the multitude of words, to a very simple point."[38]

Praise was not confined to the Bar. The Bench got its share:

> I never saw a judgment which was more clearly right than that of my brother Huddleston in this case. . . . If anybody had held *these* two things up before a jury of Birmingham men, this case having been tried in Birmingham, there is not a single one of the whole of the jury who would ever have looked at the defendants' counsel[39] again. They would have turned their backs upon him and looked the other way, and said, "The gentleman may talk until he is black in the face, but he can never make us believe that those two things are not substantially the one like the other." That is what they would have said. Whereupon, these parties, knowing that that would be likely to be so, try the case before my brother Huddleston in Birmingham, and think that perhaps they could puzzle a judge when they could not puzzle a single Birmingham man. But they could not puzzle him. Anything more clear than his judgment cannot be.[40]

Again:

> This case[41] was tried before Mr. Justice Kennedy without a jury. I have his judgment before me, and I am prepared to say that I never have seen a judgment to my mind more admirably written. He seems to me to have gone through the whole case consecutively step by step; to have stated each step in perfect language without any superabundant words; to have carefully considered each point, to have decided each point clearly, and then to have come to his conclusion. The judgment is, to my mind, so admirably written that I do not know how to add a word to it, and my judgment in this case may be taken really to be the judgment of Mr. Justice Kennedy to be given in the exact words which he has used, from beginning to end, because I do not know how to differ from any one of them. But I must, I suppose, refer to some points in the judgment.
>
> Now, from that judgment so distinct, so clear, so wanting in any superfluity, I have not from the beginning been able to draw my mind by all

---

[38] *The Incandescent Gas Light Co. Ltd.* v. *De Mare Incandescent Gas Light System Ltd.* (1896) 13 R.P.C. 559 at 570 (*per* Lord Esher M.R.).

[39] R.T. Lawrence.

[40] *Hinde* v. *Osborne* (1885) 2 R.P.C. 64 at 66 (*per* Sir Baliol Brett M.R.).

[41] *Muirhead* v. *The Commercial Cable Co.* (1894) 11 R.P.C. 317.

the volumes of words that were poured upon us in argument for days. It seemed to me that I preferred clear and plain and simple language to all that cloud.[42]

Praise was not confined to the trial judges: "I have been inclined not to express any judgment in this case, because I know I shall be followed by my brother Holker, who has been, to my knowledge, engaged in very nearly every patent case which has arisen in the north of England for the last twenty years — the north of England being the great nursery of patent inventions — and am fully aware, therefore, that he knows a good deal more about this subject than I do . . . ."[43] The approach of Lord Esher's predecessor at the Rolls, Sir George Jessel, was a little different: "Probably there is no one on the Bench or at the Bar who is more familiar with trade-marks than I am . . . ."[44] Nor has Lord Esher's robust approach always worn well. In one somewhat florid and rhetorical extempore judgment, he forcefully propounded the view that a man had an absolute right to trade under his own name even if that deceived the public into thinking that his goods were the goods of another trader who, under the same or similar name, had acquired a public reputation for similar goods. To assert the contrary meant that to carry on business the man "must discard his own name and take a false name. The proposition seems to me so monstrous, that the statement of it carries its own refutation."[45] Nearly a century later a long quotation from this judgment evoked the comment: "Remarkable passages these are, full of passionate intensity, rich in little else. To criticise them is not difficult. To know where to start is."[46]

The proprietors of the trademark "First Love," registered in respect of dolls, once sought to restrain a manufacturer of dolls from using the name "Baby Love" for its products. But they failed:

---

[42] *Ibid.*, (1894) 12 R.P.C. 39 at 54 (*per* Lord Esher M.R.).

[43] *Otto v. Linford* (1882) 46 L.T. 35 at 43 (*per* Brett L.J.).

[44] *Re Worthington & Co.'s Trade-Mark* (1879) 14 Ch. D. 8 at 9 (*per* Sir George Jessel M.R.).

[45] *Turton v. Turton* (1889) 42 Ch. D. 128 at 136 (*per* Lord Esher M.R.).

[46] *Boswell-Wilkie Circus (Pty.) Ltd.* v. *Brian Boswell Circus (Pty.) Ltd.* 1984(1) S.A. 734 at 746 (*per* Didcott J.): *affirmed*, 1985(4) S.A. 466.

It would be stating the obvious to say that "First" and "Baby" are strikingly dissimilar in appearance and sound. "First Love" and "Baby Love" are even more dissimilar. The former is bisyllabic and a spondee, the latter trisyllabic and dactyl rather than a cretic. And whether or not "First Love" is likely to be truncated to "Love" . . . — a question I come to later — it is in my view unlikely that a dactyl would lose its head in common parlance.

The next question is whether there is a conceptual similarity between the two names likely to deceive or confuse. I do not think so. "First Love" has little to do with infants and is a name that is not in fact as appropriately descriptive of the object sold as "Baby Love" is. Normally "First Love" connotes the first romantic affection youths of either sex feel for a member of the opposite sex: "First love is only a little foolishness and a lot of curiosity" (G. B. Shaw): "The magic of first love is our ignorance that it can ever end" (Benjamin Disraeli). It is an emotion felt by pre-adults, not primarily or ordinarily descriptive of the feeling a young girl would experience towards her baby doll, or (by analogy) any mother would feel towards a baby, save perhaps were "First" to be interpreted as meaning "first in order of strength" rather than "first chronologically." "Baby Love" cannot be intended to refer to the emotion the owner would feel towards this doll. Babies are not given dolls of this kind. This is not only a common sense inference, but appears clearly from Tri-ang's advertising material. The owner of this kind of doll when represented is always portrayed as a young girl, not an infant. "Baby Love" is descriptive of the doll itself: it is a baby as opposed to a straight-legged more "grown-up" doll, that is the object of affection. In short, I do not agree with [counsel's] contention that both names connote an early *love* or young *love* and are therefore conceptually similar. First love connotes an emotion felt, baby love as applied to a doll describes the object of affection.[47]

Copyright, it has been held,[48] cannot exist in an invented name such as "Exxon," since such a word cannot be described as being an "original literary . . . work."[49] This seems to extinguish for England the faint hope that was kept alive in America where the owners of a song called "Supercalafajalistickespeealadojus" sued the owners of a song called

---

[47] *Rovex Ltd.* v. *Prima Toys (Pty.) Ltd.* 1981(2) S.A. 447 at 451 (*per* van den Heever J.).
[48] *Exxon Corporation* v. *Exxon Insurance Consultants International Ltd.* [1982] Ch. 119.
[49] Copyright Act 1956, s. 2(1).

"Supercalifragilisticexpialidocious."[50] Certainly the differences between the two versions of what the judge prudently called "the word"[51] were small. The second word is one letter longer than the first, and there are some ten spelling differences; but in speech there is little more than the differences between "fajal" and "fragil," "espeeal" and "expial," and "dojus" and "docious." There may also be a part for the doctrine of *idem sonantia*[52] to play.

Lists may be different. Thus copyright was held to exist in the programmes of future wireless broadcasts as published in the *Radio Times*, despite a valiant argument to the contrary. Counsel contended that there was no such copyright, for if there were, then by statute[53] the author could stop the performance of the items, "which is absurd."

Judge: How can you perform a programme?

Counsel: By a performance of the items therein.

Judge: Are we performing the Daily Cause List?

Counsel: Yes, and if there were any conceivable copyright in it the Crown or the actual author could stop the hearing.[54]

This may be contrasted with a claim to copyright in race cards for greyhound racing. These cards showed the order in which the dogs would be placed in their stations or traps, as determined by drawing their names from a hat. Eve J. felt little doubt: "It cannot, of course, be suggested that there is any literary merit or literary skill in arranging the names of half a dozen or even a dozen dogs in the order in which they have been withdrawn from . . . a hat. . . . Well, then, is there any labour? Not, I should have thought, for the able-bodied gentlemen who constitute the officials of the Greyhound Racing Association. It seems to me

---

[50] *Life Music, Inc.* v. *Wonderland Music Co.*, 241 F. Supp. 653 (S.D.N.Y. 1965). For the hope, see page 656 of the case.

[51] *Ibid.*, at p. 654 (*per* Feinberg J.).

[52] See *ante* p. 224.

[53] Copyright Act 1911, s. 1(2).

[54] *British Broadcasting Co.* v. *Wireless League Gazette Publishing Co.* [1926] Ch. 433 at 438 (*per* Astbury J., and Macgillivray for the defendants).

that this is a result for the production of which neither literary ability, nor skill, nor labour, nor anything else, is required, but a certain amount of sobriety."[55]

Copyright apart, common courtesy and judicial comity alike demand that when quoting from the judgments of others a judge will duly acknowledge his sources. Rarely is this demand not met. Yet in Georgia in 1852, Nisbet J. proclaimed the rule that counsel must not comment on facts that had not been proved, and in four pages of eloquent prose he ranged wide over the forensic liberty accorded to counsel, and its boundaries.[56] In New Hampshire, in 1860, Fowler J. laid down the same rule in nearly four equally eloquent pages, so equal that most of the language was identical.[57] New Hampshire omitted two passages of Georgia's citation of some English authorities, but otherwise these pages of the two judgments are virtually interchangeable, as may be seen by setting them out in parallel columns.[58]

One example may be given. Georgia states that counsel's "illustrations may be as various as are the resources of his genius; his argumentation as full and profound as his learning can make it; and he may, if he will, give play to his wit, or wing to his imagination."[59] Apart from omitting "are" and pluralizing "wing," New Hampshire is identical, down to the last comma.[60] Its debt to Georgia is indisputable, yet the only visible trace of Georgia is its inclusion in New Hampshire's list of twelve authorities cited at the end. The name of Nisbet J. is nowhere to be seen, and the words emerge as being the words of Fowler J. alone. Curiosity prompts the question whether Fowler J. ever sat judicially in a case of plagiarism.

---

[55] *Greyhound Racing Association Ltd. v. Shallis* (1928) [1923–1928] Macg.C.C. 370 at 373.

[56] *Mitchum v. State,* 11 Ga. 615, 630–34 (1852).

[57] *Tucker v. Henniker,* 41 N.H. 317, 323–26 (1860).

[58] As they were in (1892) 4 *Green Bag* 18 at 23.

[59] *Mitchum,* 11 Ga. at 631.

[60] *Tucker,* 41 N.H. at 323.

22

~

NARROWED TO A FILAMENT

IT HAS not always been realised what a debt remarried widows and second wives owed to Edward VI for nearly three centuries. Until 1547, whether a man convicted of felony suffered death or escaped with his life, and often without any substantial punishment, might depend on whether his first (and only) wife had been a widow or a spinster when he married her. This was because if his wife was a widow, or if he had married more than once, he could not claim benefit of clergy.

If a prisoner convicted of a felony "pleaded his clergy," he was set at liberty, subject only (after 1487) to branding "upon the Braun of his left thumb" with an "M" if he was a murderer and a "T" (for "thief": this was the "Tyburn T") for any other felony.[1] This branding provided evidence for the future: for on a second occasion the plea of clergy was more strictly administered than on the first. None save those actually in holy orders could succeed on a second plea, whereas a first plea of clergy could be claimed by anybody capable of reading. In mediaeval days literacy was indeed a badge of the church; but as time passed it became less and less specific an indication, and this process was aided by the tolerant test of literacy adopted by the courts.

By the end of the fifteenth century, the test had become stabilised at the first three words of verse 1 of Psalm 51 in the Vulgate, known as the "Neck Verse." The ability to recite the words *Miserere mei, Deus* ought to

---

[1] 4 Hen. 7, c. 13, 1487. For benefit of clergy generally, see 1 Pollock & Maitland's *History of English Law* (2d ed. 1898), pp. 441–57; 2 *Encyclopaedia of the Laws of England* (3d ed. 1938), pp. 228–30: 4 Bl.Comm. 365–74: 3 H.E.L. 294–302.

have been beyond the capabilities of few; yet thousands paid for their ignorance with their lives. Women were excluded from the privilege unless they were professed nuns. So too were *bigami*, a term with a very different meaning from that of the modern term *bigamist*. A *bigamus* was a man who had married either two spinsters or one widow;[2] and such a man could not take holy orders. This rule seems, somewhat obscurely, to have been based on the words of St. Paul that "A bishop must be blameless, the husband of one wife . . .";[3] and the Council of Lyons in 1274 denied all clerical privileges to *bigami*.[4] Not until 1547 were *bigami* enabled by statute to plead their clergy.[5] One type of felon had always been outside the plea,[6] and in the course of time statute excluded most of the more serious felonies. Finally, the plea was abolished for commoners and clergy in 1827,[7] and for peers in 1841.[8]

The plea of clergy was said[9] to have been based upon the biblical text, "Touch not mine anointed, and do my prophets no harm."[10] In 1516 an unnamed advocate argued that the "exemption des Clerkes fuit fait per le expresse commaundement de nostre savior Jesus Christ en ceux parols, Nolite tangere Christos meos, A quel commaundement ascun usage ewe a le contrarie ne poit faire resistence, car si ascun ley soit fait ou use le quel ne poit estoier ovesque le ley de dieu, cest ley est dampnable en luy mesme."[11] But Standish, his adversary, crushingly pointed out that the words quoted —

> fueront parles per le Prophet David en son Psalter le quel fuit fait pluis que 1000 ans devant lincarnation de nostre Saviour: mes jeo vous assertain que

---

[2] 4 Edw. 1, St. 3, c. 5, 1276; 18 Edw. 3, St. 3, c. 2, 1344.

[3] 1 Tim. 3:2.

[4] See Tomlins, *Law Dictionary* (4th ed. 1835), vol. 1, s.v. Bigamy; 4 Edw. 1, St. 3, c. 5, 1276.

[5] 1 Edw. 6, c. 12, 1547, s. 16.

[6] The *felo de se*: see Camden Society, vol. 5, *Anecdotes and Traditions* (W.J. Thoms ed., 1839), p. 43 (*per* Sir Edward Peyton, at Cambridgeshire Assizes).

[7] Criminal Law Act 1827, s. 6.

[8] Felony Act 1841.

[9] 4 Bl.Comm. 366 n.

[10] 1 Chron. 16:22; Psalms 105:15.

[11] *Anon.* (1516) Keil. 180 at 181: (ascun: some; ewe: had; estoier ovesque: stand with).

vous ne trovastes jammes en vostre vie, nec jammes trovers en ascun liver, que ceux parols fueront motes ou parles per le vouche de nostre Saviour Jesus: Et le cause que movoit le roy David de mitter ceux parols en le Psalter fuit tiel, le greinder part del people al cest temps fueront miscreants, & il ny aver forsque petit number queux adonques fueront de son sect, cestassavoir, de ceux queux croyerent en le ley de Moyses, & en le auncient Testament; Et ceux queux fueront de son sect il nosma ceux Christes, & pur cest cause il commaunda le residue queux fueront miscreants que ils ne duist toucher ne noier ses Christes.

To this there was no answer.[12]

Kelyng J. once recorded a deplorable incident at Winchester Assizes in 1666:

The clerk appointed by the bishop to give clergy to the prisoners, being to give it to an old thief; I directed him to deal clearly with me, and not to say *legit* in case he could not read; and thereupon he delivered the book to him, and I perceived the prisoner never looked upon the book at all, and yet the bishop's clerk, upon the demand of *legit* or *non legit*, answered *legit*; and thereupon I wished him to consider, and told him I doubted he was mistaken, and bid the clerk of the Assizes ask him again, *legit* or *non legit*, and he answered again something angrily, *legit*: then I bid the clerk of the Assizes not to record it, and I told the parson he was not the judge whether he read or no, but a ministerial officer to make a true report to the Court. And so I caused the prisoner to be brought near, and delivered him the book, and then the prisoner confessed he could not read; whereupon I told the parson he had reproached his function, and unpreached more that day than he could preach up again in many daies; and because it was his personal offence and misdemeanour, I fined him 5 *marks* and did not fine the bishop, as in case he had failed to provide an Ordinary.[13]

To the modern eye, the position of a prisoner accused of a felony in the seventeenth century was indeed parlous; and there were contemporary critics. Yet not everyone would guess which judge uttered the following words to counsel during a trial: "I think it is a hard case, that a

---

12 *Ibid.* (Ne . . . jammes: never; motes: expressed; vouche (bouche): mouth; greinder: greater; forsque: only; adonques: then; cestassavoir: to wit; duist: ought; noier: to harm).

13 Kel. 51.

man should have counsel to defend himself for a two-penny-trespass, and his witnesses examined upon oath; but if he steal, commit murder or felony, nay, high-treason, where life, estate, honour, and all are concerned, he shall neither have counsel, nor his witnesses examined upon oath: But yet you know as well as I, that the practice of the law is so; and the practice is the law."[14] These very proper sentiments were in fact uttered by the notorious Jeffreys,[15] when Chief Justice.

It was not long before statute brought partial relief; but its first appearance was in deplorable circumstances. The Treason Act 1695[16] provided, *inter alia*, that a prisoner accused of high treason should be entitled to counsel to argue his case for him. The Act was to come into force "from and after" March 25, 1696;[17] and on March 24, 1696, Sir William Parkyns was arraigned for high treason before Holt C.J., and Treby and Rokeby JJ. He applied for counsel, but to his eternal discredit Holt C.J. not only refused the application on the ground that the Act was not yet in force, even though it lacked but a day, but also refused an application for a day's adjournment in order to allow the Act to come into force.[18] The trial proceeded, and Sir William was convicted and executed.

There was a happier outcome in the trial of Lilburne for treason against Oliver Cromwell. The accused repeatedly sought an adjournment, first of a week, then of a day, and lastly of an hour, to enable him to meet the case made against him. But the judge refused these requests, whereupon the case proceeded as follows:

---

[14] *R.* v. *Rosewell* (1684) 10 St.Tr. 147 at 267.

[15] George Jeffreys (1648–1689), who in 1685 became Baron Jeffreys of Wem, was infamous for his judicial cruelty and corruption. He presided over the Bloody Assizes in 1685 after the failure of the Duke of Monmouth's rebellion; he was responsible for the hangings of about 200 prisoners and for hundreds of others who were transported, imprisoned, or whipped. Meanwhile, he extorted money from the victims. Charles II made him Lord Chancellor. See 10 *D.N.B.* 714–21; G.W. Keeton, *Lord Chancellor Jeffreys* (1965).

[16] Sect. 1.

[17] *Ibid.*

[18] *R.* v. *Parkyns* (1696) 13 St.Tr. 63 at 72, 73. But see *R.* v. *Walsall Justices, ex parte W.* [1990] 1 Q.B. 253.

Lilburne.   Well, then, if it must be so, that you will have my blood, right or wrong; and if I shall not have one hour's time to refresh me, after my strength is spent, and to consider that which hath been alledged against me, then I appeal [which he uttered with a mighty voice] to the righteous God of heaven and earth, against you, when I am sure I shall be heard, and find access; and the Lord God Omnipotent, and a mighty judge betwixt you and me, require and requite my blood upon the heads of you and your posterity, to the third and fourth generations! [Immediately after the uttering of which the scaffold fell down which was on the left hand, which occasioned a great noise and some confusion, by reason of the people's tumbling; but silence being made, the prisoner was busy at his papers and books, being invited by Sheriff Pack to come out of the bar, for fear he should have fallen with the rest, and so he might have lost his prisoner.]

Lord Keble.   How came the prisoner there?

Lilburne.   I went not thither of my own accord, but by Mr. Sheriff's invitation; and if I am in a place where I ought not to be, blame Mr. Sheriff and not me.

Lord Keble.   Dispatch, Sir.

Lilburne.   Sir, if you will be so cruel as not to give me leave to withdraw to ease and refresh my body, I pray you let me do it in the Court. Officer, I entreat you to help me to a chamber-pot. [Whilst it was fetching, Mr. Lilburne followeth his papers and books close; and when the pot came, he made water, and gave it to the foreman.[19]]

Lord Keble.   Proceed, Mr. Lilburne. [But he pressed for a little respite, which was granted him with much ado, as also a chair to sit down upon; but within a very little space the Lord Keble said,]

Lord Keble.   The Court cannot stay for you, proceed on to answer.

Lilburne.   Good Sir, would you have me answer to impossibilities? Will you not give me breath? If you thirst after my blood, and nothing else will satisfy you, take it presently, without any more to do. [But the prisoner struggled out a little respite.]

Lord Keble.   The Court can stay no longer; take away his chair, for I cannot see the bar, and plead what you have to say, for it grows very late.[20]

---

[19] Presumably not the foreman of the jury.
[20] *Trial of Lt. Col. John Lilburne* (1649) 4 St.Tr. 1269 at 1378–79.

Lilburne then proceeded. His first proposition had scant appeal to the Bench:

> *Lilburne.*　　The jury by law are not only judges of fact, but of law also: and you that call yourselves judges of the law, are no more but Norman intruders; and in deed and in truth, if the jury please, are no more but cyphers, to pronounce their verdict. . . .
>
> *Judge Jermin.*　　Was there ever such a damnable blasphemous heresy as this, to call the judges of the law, cyphers?[21]

Yet, as always, the last word lay with the jury; and they acquitted Lilburne.[22]

Once, indeed, in courts of ancient demesne, there had been jurors with comprehensive powers. It was "a strange wild jurisdiction; where the jurors are judges both of law and of fact, and ignorant country fellows are to determine the nicest points of law."[23] Today, the jury's tradition lives on across the globe, guarded and tended by the Bench: "You are to determine this matter as a British jury, guided by your intelligence, and not overwhelmed by your sympathy, but I should be sorry, gentlemen, if the day should ever come when the angel of mercy cannot stand by the throne of justice, and with outstretched wings, shelter it from the bitterest winds of inhumanity."[24]

At least in legal theory the accused has much on his side. Timidity should be no disadvantage: "Probable cause cannot be found from submissiveness, and the presumption of innocence is not lost or impaired by neglect to argue with a policeman."[25] Further, "An accused man should have the benefit of the presumption of integrity which arises from the virtue of a lifetime."[26] At times the courts sound a little grudging: "As to his reputation, it is possible he might have been an

---

[21] *Ibid.*, at cols. 1379, 1380. Richard Keeble was one of the Lords Commissioner of the Great Seal; and Jermyn J. was a judge of the Upper Bench.

[22] S.C. at col. 1405.

[23] *Doe d. Rust* v. *Roe* (1760) 2 Burr. 1046 at 1047 (*per* Wilmot J.).

[24] *R.* v. *Jacob* [1932] S.A.S.R. 456 at 461 (*per* Angas Parsons J.). Verdict: Not Guilty.

[25] *U.S.* v. *Di Re*, 332 U.S. 581, 595 (1948) (*per* Jackson J.).

[26] *Symington* v. *Symington* (1875) L.R. 2 Sc. & D. 415 at 425 (*per* Lord O'Hagan).

honest man: a man is not born a knave, there must be time to make him so, nor is he presently discovered after he becomes one."[27] Yet the inconspicuous get credit: "In my opinion, the best character is that which is the least talked of."[28] The lost, too, may be restored. Thus in the United States it has been said: "A pardon strips from a convict the striped apparel of infamy and shame and clothes him in the suit of innocence and integrity."[29] In England, however, the pardon, though removing all the penalties and punishments of the conviction, does not eliminate the conviction itself.[30] The pardon "affirms the verdict, and dis-affirms it not . . . . So that to take it for both is to imply contra-dictories."[31] Yet after pardon or punishment a felon was a "felon" no more.[32]

Other immunities come earlier: "Under our system of government, police cannot compel people to furnish the evidence necessary to send them to prison."[33] Yet the firmly established immunity from compulsory self-incrimination has not remained unquestioned: "Today as in the past there are students of our penal system who look upon the immunity as a mischief rather than a benefit, and who would limit its scope, or destroy it altogether. . . . Justice . . . would not perish if the accused were subject to a duty to respond to orderly inquiry."[34] Furthermore, "The Constitution safeguards the right of the defendant to remain silent; it does not assure him that he may remain silent and still enjoy the advantages that might have resulted from testifying."[35] Bentham's comment on the so-called right to silence still awaits a convincing answer: "If all the criminals of every class had assembled, and framed a system after their

27 *R. v. Swendsen* (1702) 14 St.Tr. 425 at 596 (*per* Holt C.J., trial for forcibly taking away and marrying Pleasant Rawlings, an heiress under 18).
28 *R. v. Rowton* (1865) Le. & Ca. 520 at 535 (*per* Erle C.J., dissenting).
29 *Commonwealth* v. *Cannon*, 123 A.2d 675, 683 (Pa. 1956) (Musmanno J., dissenting).
30 *R. v. Foster* [1985] Q.B. 115.
31 *Searle* v. *Williams* (1620) Hob. 288 at 293 (*per* Hobart C.J.).
32 *Leyman* v. *Latimer* (1878) 3 Ex.D. 352.
33 *Breithaupt* v. *Abram*, 352 U.S. 432, 443 (1957) (Douglas J., dissenting).
34 *Palko* v. *Connecticut*, 302 U.S. 319, 325–26 (1937) (*per* Cardozo J.).
35 *Stein* v. *N.Y.*, 346 U.S. 156, 177 (1953) (*per* Jackson J.).

own wishes, is not this rule the very first which they would have established for their security? Innocence never takes advantage of it; innocence claims the right of speaking, as guilt invokes the privilege of silence."[36]

"If any fundamental assumption underlies our system, it is that guilt is personal and not inheritable."[37] "'Guilt by association' is an epithet frequently used and little explained, except that it is generally accompanied by another slogan, 'guilt is personal.' Of course it is; but personal guilt may be incurred by joining a conspiracy."[38] Yet "many join associations, societies, and fraternities with less than full endorsement of all their aims."[39] It is not difficult to understand why the count of conspiracy should have been described as the "darling of the modern prosecutor's nursery."[40] Nor should it be forgotten that "a man can be known by the ideas he spreads as well as by the company he keeps."[41]

Although the right to a fair trial is paramount, "a defendant is entitled to a fair trial but not a perfect one":[42]

- "In a criminal proceeding the question is not alone whether substantial justice has been done, but whether justice has been done according to law. . . . [A judge] cannot set himself above the law which he has to administer, or make or mould it to suit the exigencies of a particular occasion."[43]
- "The constitutional guarantee of due process is meaningful enough, and sufficiently adaptable, to protect soldiers — as well as civilians — from the crude injustices of a trial so conducted that it becomes bent on fixing guilt by dispensing with rudimentary fairness rather than

---

[36] Bentham, *A Treatise on Judicial Evidence* (1825), p. 241.

[37] *Korematsu* v. *U.S.*, 323 U.S. 214, 243 (1944) (Jackson J., dissenting).

[38] *Am. Commun. Assn., C.I.O.* v. *Douds*, 339 U.S. 382, 433 (1950) (Jackson J., dissenting in part).

[39] *Beilan* v. *Bd. of Public Educ., Sch. Dist. of Philadelphia*, 357 U.S. 399, 415 (1958) (Douglas J., dissenting).

[40] *Harrison* v. *U.S.*, 7 F.2d 259, 263 (2d Cir. 1925) (*per* Learned Hand J.).

[41] *Schneiderman* v. *U.S.*, 320 U.S. 118, 197 (1943) (Stone C.J., dissenting).

[42] *Lutwak* v. *U.S.*, 344 U.S. 604, 619 (1953) (*per* Minton J.).

[43] *Martin* v. *Mackonochie* (1878) 3 Q.B.D. 730 at 775 (*per* Cockburn C.J.).

finding truth through adherence to those basic guarantees which have long been recognized and honored by the military courts as well as the civil courts."[44]

- "A hearing is not a hearing in the American sense if faceless informers or confidential information may be used to deprive a man of his liberty."[45]
- "There can be no equal justice where the kind of trial a man gets depends on the amount of money he has."[46]

Much depends on the judge: "A criminal trial is not a game where one side is entitled to claim the benefit of any omission or mistake made by the other side, and a judge's position in a criminal trial is not merely that of an umpire to see that the rules of the game are observed by both sides. A judge is an administrator of justice, he is not merely a figurehead, he has not only to direct and control the proceedings, according to recognised rules of procedure but to see that justice is done."[47] Nearly thirty years later, Denning L.J. put it in much the same way in a civil case: "Even in England . . . a judge is not a mere umpire to answer the question 'How's that?' His object, above all, is to find out the truth, and to do justice according to law."[48] So also in the United States: "Federal judges are not referees at prize-fights but functionaries of justice."[49] Yet "a jury trial is a fight and not an afternoon tea,"[50] and it is "not a game of blind man's buff."[51]

Over the years many miscarriages of justice have emerged. One of the worst was in 1661. Joan Perry and her two sons, John and Richard Perry, were tried for the murder of William Harrison, aged about seventy years. No body was found, but Harrison had disappeared, and in the highway

---

[44] *Burns* v. *Wilson*, 346 U.S. 137, 142–43 (1953) (*per* Vinson C.J.).

[45] *Jay* v. *Boyd*, 351 U.S. 345, 376 (1956) (Douglas J., dissenting).

[46] *Griffin* v. *Illinois*, 351 U.S. 12, 19 (1956) (*per* Black J.).

[47] *R.* v. *Hepworth*, 1928 A.D. 265 at 277 (*per* Curlewis J.A.).

[48] *Jones* v. *National Coal Board* [1957] 2 Q.B. 55 at 63 (*per curiam*).

[49] *Johnson* v. *U.S.*, 333 U.S. 46, 54 (1948) (Frankfurter J., dissenting in part).

[50] *Dale* v. *Toronto R.W. Co.* (1915) 34 Ont.L.R. 104 at 108 (*per* Riddell J.).

[51] *Johnson* v. *U.S.*, 333 U.S. at 54.

on which he had been travelling there were a hat and comb of his, hacked about, and a band that was bloody. The elder son, John, accused his mother and brother, and gave a circumstantial account of the murder. The trial was before Hyde J., and all three were convicted and hanged.[52] Two years later, William Harrison reappeared. He gave a detailed account of how he had been kidnapped, sold into slavery in Turkey, and finally had escaped and returned to England.[53]

Under a statute making it an offence if any person shall "profanely swear or curse" (with a tariff of fines according to the rank of the accused),[54] a man was once convicted on the ground that he did "profanely swear 54 oaths, and profanely curse 160 curses"; and at the rate of 2s. an expression he was fined £21.8.0. The Court of King's Bench, however, quashed the conviction. One ground for doing all this was "that the oaths and curses were not set forth; for what is a profane oath or curse is a matter of law, and ought not to be left to the judgment of the witness; . . . and it is a matter of great dispute among the learned, what are oaths, and what curses."[55]

More recently in Canada it was made an offence "to operate a motor vehicle on the highway without a windshield wiper." One defendant confessed and avoided: true, his car had no windshield wiper, but neither had it any windshield to be wiped. In the end a somewhat puzzled magistrate recorded a conviction. In doing this he recalled Thomas Reed Powell's description of a legal mind:[56] "If you think you can think of something that is attached to something else without thinking about the thing to which it is attached, you have a legal mind." It may be added that a glance at the rows of parked cars in any city street today would have astonished Lord Ellenborough C.J. in more senses than one; for it

---

[52] *R. v. Perry* (1661) 14 St.Tr. 1312.

[53] *Ibid.*, at col. 1319. See generally *The Campden Wonder* (Sir George Clark ed., 1959); J. Bennett Miller, *The Campden Wonder*, 1973 Jurid. Rev. 148.

[54] 6 & 7 Will. 3, c. 11, 1695, s. 1, later replaced by the Profane Oaths Act 1745, s. 1 (on which see 1 Misc. 225), which was repealed by the Criminal Law Act 1967, s. 13, 4th Sched., Pt. I.

[55] *R. v. Sparling* (1722) 1 Stra. 497 at 498 (*per curiam*).

[56] J.A. Corry, *Law and Policy* (1959), p. 47.

was he who laid it down that "no one can make a stable-yard of the King's highway."[57]

The paths of escape are many. Thus it may be questionable whether in law the facts disclose any offence. Lord Coleridge C.J. once had occasion to cite *R. v. Druitt*,[58] a case in which he had, while at the Bar, appeared for the defence.[59] He said that it was a case "in which, unless he is misreported, Bramwell B. said that he thought a combination to treat a man with 'black looks' was an indictable misdemeanour (a decision, if it be one, which might assuredly land us in unexpected and singular results)."[60] During the argument on appeal, however, Bowen L.J. mentioned that "Lord Bramwell, in a letter to a publication[61] which we always read but do not cite, explained the meaning of the words 'black looks' which he used in *The Queen v. Druitt*";[62] and in the House of Lords Lord Halsbury L.C., too, dissented from Lord Coleridge's criticism.[63]

Instead of looks, there may be gestures. Is "giving the finger" an offence? In Connecticut in 1978, a State trooper pulled up behind a school bus at a street junction, whereupon a high-school student in the back of the bus "gave the trooper the finger," i.e., raised his hand with his middle finger extended. The trooper boarded the bus and arrested the student. Later the student was convicted of the statutory offence of using an "obscene gesture" in a public place with intent to cause inconvenience, annoyance, or alarm, or recklessly create a risk thereof. On appeal, it was accepted that the extended middle finger, or *digitus impudicus*, was a phallic symbol; Diogenes was said to have insulted Demosthenes with it. But the gesture, it was held, was not obscene, for it

---

[57] *R. v. Cross* (1812) 3 Camp. 224 at 227.

[58] (1867) 10 Cox C.C. 592; see at p. 602.

[59] See 10 Cox C.C. at p. 598.

[60] *Mogul Steamship Co. Ltd.* v. *McGregor, Gow & Co.* (1888) 21 Q.B.D. 544 at 551; *affirmed* 23 Q.B.D. 598; [1892] A.C. 25.

[61] *The Times*, Aug. 17, 1888, p. 6, col. 2.

[62] *Mogul Steamship Co. Ltd.* v. *McGregor, Gow & Co.*, *supra* note 60, as reported 58 L.J.Q.B. 465 at 471 (omitted from 23 Q.B.D. 598).

[63] *Ibid.*, [1892] A.C. 25 at 38.

was not erotic in any significant way; it would be likely to arouse anger rather than sexual desire, as, indeed, it seems to have done. The conviction was therefore quashed.[64] Yet what if the student had borrowed not from ancient Greece but from modern Britain, and had given his *digitus impudicus* the companionship of his index finger? Would this have altered the result? One day we may know.

In South Africa a man was convicted of a breach of a prison regulation because "he committed an act with an intention of endangering his life or injuring his health or interfering with his work, to wit: by contracting a venereal disease — gonorrhoea." On appeal, van den Heever J. quashed the conviction.[65] The particulars, he said,

> cannot sustain the charge, unless they allege the commission of an act by the accused. Now the expression "to contract a disease" is active and even transitive in form, but it conveys a purely passive notion. Surely a prisoner cannot be guilty of an offence every time he catches a cold. "To age" is active in form and is undoubtedly dangerous to life but it is not a crime. I do not suggest that an act within the contemplation of the prohibition cannot be committed *omittendo*: not to eat would under the circumstances be such an act. It is clear, however, that no conduct can be an act within the meaning of the statute unless it be voluntary. It seems to me therefore that the charge is bad and does not disclose an offence.[66]

Even apart from this, and on the assumption that all concerned knew the implication was that the accused had committed an act of sexual intercourse, and that this was the act complained of, still the conviction was bad:

> In this case there was no direct evidence of the accused's intention; as will in general be the case, therefore, the court had to infer this from the circumstances. Is it at all likely that the accused had sexual intercourse with the object of contracting a venereal disease? To draw this inference seems to me to be as sound as the suggestion would be that murderers kill in order that

---

[64] *State* v. *Anon.*, 377 A.2d 1342, 1343 (Conn. Super. 1977).

[65] *R.* v. *Frank* 1942 O.P.D. 89.

[66] *Ibid.*, at p. 89.

they themselves may hang: that murder is therefore a form of deferred suicide. Our criminal law recognises constructive intention in certain circumstances — for example, if, without aiming, I discharge a rifle down a street thronged with people, reckless whether I hit anyone or not. But there must be such a high degree of probability of the result following the act that it may be regarded as an intended result. Sexual intercourse, however, is not an act of self-immolation; the accused is a human being, not a mantis.[67]

Prosecutors must look to themselves as well as to the accused: "To declare that in the administration of the criminal law the end justifies the means — to declare that the Government may commit crimes in order to secure the conviction of a private criminal — would bring terrible retribution. Against that pernicious doctrine this court should resolutely set its face."[68] For "The endeavor to put a stop to illicit practices must not itself become illicit."[69] Indeed, "Disinterested zeal for the public good does not assure either wisdom or right in the methods it pursues."[70] Similarly, "zeal in tracking down crime is not in itself an assurance of soberness of judgment."[71] There must be no confessions procured by any form of coercion; and "coercion might be the product of subtlety as well as of violence."[72] Again, "Means unlawful in their inception do not become lawful by relation when suspicion ripens into discovery."[73] Difficulties also flow from notoriety: "Cases of notorious criminals — like cases of small, miserable ones — are apt to make bad law. When guilt permeates a record, even judges sometimes relax and let the police take shortcuts not sanctioned by constitutional procedures."[74]

Some short-cuts are elaborate. In 1970, an experienced Canadian police sergeant not only pretended to be a bail bondsman but also arranged for a fellow police officer to impersonate a Justice of the Peace and hear an

---

[67] *Ibid.*, at p. 90.

[68] *Olmstead* v. *U.S.*, 277 U.S. 438, 485 (1928) (Brandeis J., dissenting).

[69] *Sugar Institute Inc.* v. *U.S.*, 297 U.S. 553, 599 (1936) (*per* Hughes C.J.).

[70] *Haley* v. *Ohio*, 332 U.S. 596, 605 (1948) (*per* Frankfurter J.).

[71] *McNabb* v. *U.S.*, 318 U.S. 332, 343 (1943) (*per* Frankfurter J.).

[72] *Breithaupt* v. *Abram*, 352 U.S. 432, 443 (1957) (Douglas J., dissenting).

[73] *People* v. *Defore*, 150 N.E. 585, 586 (N.Y. 1926) (*per* Cardozo J.).

[74] *Abel* v. *U.S.*, 362 U.S. 217, 241–42 (1960) (Douglas J., dissenting).

application by the accused for bail. At the hearing a recognizance for bail was drawn up, and the accused was released into the custody of the "bondsman." Not surprisingly, incriminating statements then made by the accused to the bondsman were held to be inadmissible. The case presented "a new concept in police trickery," and what had been done was "the action of irresponsible policemen totally bankrupt of all ideas of fair play."[75]

Yet the courts do not allow themselves to be blinded by such gross misconduct. Criminal justice must not become one-sided: "A miscarriage of justice may arise from the acquittal of the guilty no less than from the conviction of the innocent."[76] Again: "Justice, though done to the accused, is due to the accuser also. The concept of fairness must not be strained till it is narrowed to a filament. We are to keep the balance true."[77]

The criminal process normally involves the Deity, if only in the oaths that are taken in court; but sometimes there is more than that — much more. A man suspected of being involved in starting a forest fire in British Columbia voluntarily agreed to take a polygraph ("lie-detector") test, and went to an R.C.M.P. subdivisional headquarters for the purpose. He was shown into the room housing the apparatus and given a lengthy card explaining how it worked. After he had been left alone in the room to read the card, he sank to his knees, and with upraised arms said: "Oh, God, let me get away with it just this once"; and he continued to address God, "promising future obedience in return for present deliverance."[78] Unknown to him, the room also contained a concealed microphone and closed-circuit television, and the police both saw and heard the prayer, and recorded it. The question was whether this evidence was admissible against the accused.

---

75 *R.* v. *Pettipiece* (1972) 7 C.C.C.(2d) 133 at 148 (*per* Branca J.A.). The conviction was quashed, and a new trial ordered. It does not appear whether the policemen were prosecuted.

76 *Stirland* v. *Director of Public Prosecutions* [1944] A.C. 315 at 324 (*per* Viscount Simon L.C.).

77 *Snyder* v. *Massachusetts*, 291 U.S. 97, 122 (1934) (*per* Cardozo J.).

78 *R.* v. *Davie* (1980) 54 C.C.C.(2d) 216 at 218 (*per* Nemetz C.J.B.C.).

Statute excluded evidence of a "private communication" that without lawful authority had been "intercepted," a term that included merely listening to it; and a "private communication" was defined as being a communication made in circumstances in which it was reasonable for the originator to expect it not to be intercepted by "any person other than the person intended by the originator thereof to receive it."[79] Plainly the accused intended God alone to hear his prayer: but was God a "person" within the statute?

It was this momentous question that on May 30, 1979, fell for decision in Cariboo County Court. The prosecution contended that the answer was No, despite the part that His Name played in the oath taken in court: but Judge Lander, in an extempore judgment, held that this argument was absurd, and so rejected the evidence. There seems to have been no argument based on God being not one person but three, no doubt because theologically He was both, and at law the singular is presumed to include the plural.

On appeal, the majority in the British Columbia Court of Appeal disagreed, and held that what the judge had thought absurd was indeed the law. In the statutes of Canada the word "person" was used "to describe someone to whom rights are granted and upon whom obligations are placed," and there was no earthly authority that could grant rights to God, or impose duties upon Him.[80] The question whether God was a person did not arise; the true question was whether He was a person *for the purposes of the Canadian Criminal Code*; and to that there could be only one answer. Ask the wrong question and you get the wrong answer. It also appeared that the statutory language contemplated no protection being given where there was no living human recipient of the information, as where a person spoke to his deceased mother or a family pet,[81] so that if utterances to them were overheard, they would be as unprotected as prayers to God.[82]

---

[79] Criminal Code (Canada), ss. 178.1, 178.16(1).

[80] *R. v. Davie* (1980) 54 C.C.C.(2d) 216 at 223 (*per* Hutcheon J.A., Seaton J.A. concurring).

[81] *Ibid.*, citing *R. v. Horvath* (1979) 93 D.L.R. (3d) 1.

[82] *R. v. Davie* (1980) 54 C.C.C.(2d) 216, setting aside the acquittal and ordering a new trial.

Other admissions have their problems. Prisoners often assert that they have been "verballed," meaning that evidence of admissions that they are said to have made is false. Yet caution is needed. One defending counsel was imprudent enough to ask an experienced police sergeant the meaning of the term, only to be met by a reply that was as discordant as it was prompt: "A 'verbal' is that spontaneous and genuine expression of guilt and remorse that a criminal makes in the shock of arrest but later retracts on the advice of his solicitor."[83]

An Atlantic crossing may be unsettling. A serious study of some 550 pages, entitled *The Lawyers* and published in New York in 1967, states:

> Despite the general maxim that people cannot be punished for violating laws that have not been announced and defined, the British courts probably retain some marginal power to create new crimes. In 1927 a London magistrate was confronted with a man who had jumped off Westminster Bridge on a bet, whose defense was that there was no law against it. The magistrate convicted and fined him anyway, and the conviction was upheld on appeal.
>
> "It is a principle of English law," said the Court of Criminal Appeal, "that a person who appears in a police court has done something undesirable, and citizens who take it upon themselves to do unusual actions which attract the attention of the police should be careful to bring those actions into one of the recognized categories of crimes and offenses, for it is intolerable that the police should be put to the pains of inventing reasons for finding them undesirable. . . . It is not for me to say what offense the appellant has committed, but I am satisfied that he has committed some offense, for which he has been most properly punished."
>
> No such opinion could be written by an American court.[84]

Nor, it should be added, by an English court. Those who seek to verify the quotation by referring to the notes, some 400 pages on, will find the citation "*Rex* v. *Haddock*, CCA Miscellaneous Cases, *Criminal Law* 31 (1927)." A case of this name, and containing this quotation does indeed appear in A.P. Herbert's *Misleading Cases in the Common Law*, published

---

[83] A variant of this appears in P. Molloy, *Operation Seal Bay* (1986), p. 57.
[84] Martin Mayer, *The Lawyers* (N.Y.: Harper & Row 1967), p. 167.

in 1927, at page 31. It is but a guess; yet may not the link be some abbreviation such as "Mis. Cases C. Law," uncomprehendingly expanded? At least the author deserves castigation for not telling his readers that the judgment from which he quoted was delivered by Frog L.J., that Mudd J. said that in his opinion "the appellant had done his trousers no good and the offence was damage to property,"[85] and that Adder J. merely concurred.[86] But in another report of what is plainly the same case, by the same reporter, the leading judgment is ascribed to Lord Light L.C.J., and the judgment of Mudd J. was that in his opinion "the appellant had polluted a water-course under the Public Health Act 1875,"[87] with not a word about trousers. Adder J., instead of merely concurring, is reported as saying that he thought that "the appellant had attempted to pull down a bridge, under the Malicious Damage Act, 1861."[88] But whether the leading judgment was delivered by Frog L.J. or by Lord Light L.C.J., the passage quoted from it appears verbatim in both reports, well worthy of its transatlantic translation from fiction to fact, a translation that would have enchanted A.P.H.

Fact, of course, may rival fiction, and even outstrip it. One example[89] began on a moonlit July night in 1971, when a youth of 19 found himself inflamed by drink and lust. Not long after 3 a.m. he went to the house where a girl of 18 whom he knew slightly lived with her mother. The girl had spent the evening with her boyfriend, and at about 2 a.m., having drink taken, she had gone to bed. As was her habit, she slept without any night apparel in a bed close to an open window. When the youth reached the house, he found a stepladder, put it against the house, climbed it,

---

[85] *R.* v. *Haddock* (1927) Herb. Misl. Cas. Com. Law 31 at 37. Perhaps it is unduly technical to mention that in 1927 appeals from a magistrates' court went not to the Court of Criminal Appeal but to a King's Bench Divisional Court, and that normally no Lord Justice sat in either court.

[86] *Ibid.*

[87] *R.* v. *Haddock*, Herbert's *Uncommon Law* (1935) 24 at 28. In the District Court of Appeal of Florida, Second District, in *Ashmore* v. *Ashmore*, 241 So. 2d 424, 425 (Fla. 2d Dist. App. 1970), Mann J. achieved a notable conflation of titles by referring to A.P. Herbert's *Some Misleading Cases in the Uncommon Law*. And see Elmer M. Million, Book Review, 27 Okla. L. Rev. 574, 580 (1974).

[88] *R.* v. *Haddock*, Herbert's *Uncommon Law* (1935) 24 at 29.

[89] *R.* v. *Collins* [1973] Q.B. 100.

and looked in at the girl's window, where she lay naked and asleep. He descended, removed all his clothes save his socks, ascended the step-ladder again, and pulled himself up onto the window-sill, on which he knelt in order to get in. At that point, the girl woke up and saw at the window in the moonlight a blond male, naked and with an erection. She assumed him to be her boyfriend, with whom she was on terms of intimacy, and promptly sat up in bed. The youth descended from the window and joined the girl in bed; and after a while they had sexual intercourse. But the girl began to think that things were not as they usually were between her and her boyfriend: from the length of her bedfellow's hair, his voice, and other features, she felt that somehow something was different. She turned on a light, saw that her bedfellow was indeed not her boyfriend, slapped his face, and then, when he took hold of her arm, bit him and told him to go. Thereupon she went to the bathroom and he disappeared. His attachment to his socks is a curious feature of a remarkable case, but he seems to have had a theory that in some way they would speed his escape if he was surprised by the girl's mother.[90]

The result of this affair was that the youth, doubtless much to his astonishment, was charged with burglary, and convicted.[91] That crime is committed if a person "enters" a building "as a trespasser" with intent to commit various offences, including rape.[92] On the youth's appeal against conviction, which succeeded,[93] the crucial question was whether he had entered the house as a trespasser. When the girl first manifested her mistaken welcome, was the youth still kneeling on the outer sill, so that he then entered at her invitation, or had he already reached the inner sill, so that he had entered uninvited, knowing that he would not be welcome, or not caring? The replacement of the common-law concept of breaking and entering by the statutory concept of entering as a trespasser has necessarily jettisoned the ancient learning on "breaking";

---

[90] *Ibid.*: see at pp. 102, 103.
[91] There was no charge of rape.
[92] Theft Act 1968, s. 9.
[93] The summing up was held to be defective.

but what of "entering"? There is old authority for saying that for this purpose there was a sufficient entry if only a hand of the accused,[94] or even "the forepart of the prisoner's finger,"[95] went inside the line of the glass in a window. But in the 1971 case, the evidence was understandably lacking in precision on what might indeed have been a delicate point. In any case, the Court of Appeal, to which no authorities were cited, held that for the conviction to be supported there must have been "an effective and substantial entry into the bedroom" before the girl had done anything to cause the youth to believe that she was consenting to his entry.[96] Yet the days of anatomical particularity have not passed; for it still suffices if the only entry is by a hand.[97]

Fact and fiction sometimes combine to produce great richness.[98] In 1889 there was a remarkable case in Jersey; and one author gives an even more remarkable account of it.[99] He refers to

> some costly litigation before the Judicial Committee of the Privy Council during the last decade of the nineteenth century, in the course of which Lord Haldane, as Counsel for the Island of Jersey, obtained £1,000 damages from Great Britain for trespass and violation of the laws of Rollo, Duke of Normandy.[100]
>
> What might have been a serious international affair started with a collective decision of the jurats in St. Helier to carry into execution the laws of Rollo by publicly burning at the stake a Frenchwoman and a dog who had transgressed against these laws. She appealed to the French Consul, who in vain expounded to the jurats the more progressive doctrines of the *Code Napoléon*, which were denounced in St. Helier as pagan and immoral. Consequently the French Foreign Office appealed to the English Foreign Office, who in turn appealed to the Home Office, which deals with the affairs of the Channel Islands.

[94] *R.* v. *William Bailey* (1818) Russ. & Ry. 341.

[95] *R.* v. *John Davis* (1823) Russ. & Ry. 499.

[96] *R.* v. *Collins, supra* note 89, at p. 106.

[97] *R.* v. *Brown* [1985] *The Times* Jan. 31.

[98] See also *ante* pp. 68–71. With minor variations, this account appeared at (1984) 100 L.Q.R. 41.

[99] E.S.P. Haynes, *Pages from a Lawyer's Notebook* (1939), pp. 148, 149.

[100] Rollo was recognised as Duke of Normandy in 911.

The protests of the British Civil Servant against the laws of Rollo were, however, equally unavailing, and finally the Admiralty had to send without delay a gun-boat to Jersey. A force of marines released the Frenchwoman from her dungeon and restored her to her native land in order to prevent any danger of war with France, although considering French enthusiasm for women and British enthusiasm for dogs, the medieval ceremony might more probably have resulted in a joint bombardment of St. Helier by the navies of the two great powers.[101]

After commenting that this exploit had never received the praise that it deserved from "our patriotic newspapers," the account observes that "the facts are fully recorded in the Law Reports."

This is indeed a striking story, and none the less so because of the inadequate attention that the press is said to have accorded to it. What really happened, though remarkable in a different way, was less dramatic. On 1 November 1889, Marie Françoise Daniel was tried in the Royal Court of Jersey on a charge of committing bestiality on 23 August 1899, or alternatively of attempting it. The verdict of the jury (which was 24 in number) was that the accused had "tenté d'avoir un commerce charnel et contre nature avec un chien, mais qu'au moment òu elle a commis cette tentative, elle ne jouissait pas de ses facultés intellectuelles." On this verdict of guilty of the attempt but insane, the court ordered the prisoner to be detained during Her Majesty's pleasure, and ordered the Greffier (the clerk of the court) to ascertain through the Privy Council an expression of that pleasure.

On 18 December 1889, a Royal Warrant was issued, directing that the prisoner should be discharged and sent to France. Nine days later the Vicomte (the executive officer of the court) informed the gaoler that a "pardon" had been received for the prisoner, and that she was to be sent to France on 30 December 1889 at 3 a.m. At this, the gaoler consulted the bailiff, who was the president of the legislative assembly and the chief magistrate and judge. He directed the gaoler not to release the prisoner until the "pardon" had been presented to the Royal Court and registered.

---

[101] Haynes, *supra* note 99, at 149.

After some discussion and a vigorous correspondence, the Vicomte made a second attempt, this time on Sunday, 26 January 1890. He again visited the gaoler, and this time he produced a certified copy of the Royal Warrant. Again the gaoler consulted the bailiff, and again the bailiff directed him not to release the prisoner until the Royal Warrant had been registered in the Royal Court. At this, the bailiff and the jurats presented a petition to the Queen, seeking a direction to the Lieutenant-Governor to present the Royal Warrant to the Royal Court for registration. The petition was forthwith transmitted to the Privy Council, but before it could be acted on, the Vicomte had made his third attempt, on 31 January 1890. This time he had reinforcements; for he was one of a party that included the Lieutenant-Governor and the Attorney-General. The opposition was weakened by the absence of the gaoler, who had left the turnkey in charge. The Lieutenant-Governor ordered the turnkey to bring the prisoner to the boardroom; and when she was there the Vicomte read a warrant from the Secretary of State ordering her to be set at liberty at once. The turnkey then said that he had instructions from the gaoler not to liberate the prisoner in his absence; and at that the Lieutenant-Governor ordered him to deliver his key into the hands of the Vicomte. In fear of the consequence of disobedience, the turnkey complied with the order. The Vicomte thereupon opened the door for the prisoner, and she left the prison, 13 weeks after her conviction and just over a month after she should have been released under the first attempt. She was lodged for the night in the police station, and placed next day on a steamer leaving the island. The petition of the bailiff and jurats was considered promptly by the Committee of the Privy Council for the Affairs of Jersey and Guernsey; but it was too late. On 6 February 1890, the committee understandably reported that as the warrant had been executed, it was not considered that any directions need be given. Two days later this report was approved by Order in Council.[102]

The action of the bailiff in directing the gaoler not to comply with the Royal Warrant until it had been registered in the Royal Court was based

[102] The Order in Council is reprinted in F. de L. Bois, *A Constitutional History of Jersey* (1972), p. 229.

on a passage in a code of laws drawn up in 1771;[103] this was founded upon an Order in Council of Charles II made on 21 May 1679. The Order provided that "no Orders, Warrants, or Letters, of what Nature soever"[104] were to be put into execution in Jersey until they had first been presented to the Royal Court in order to be registered and published. If they were found to be contrary to the Island's charters and privileges, and burdensome to the Island, the Order provided that their operation could be suspended until the Crown's further pleasure was known. The code of laws, however, seems to have been defective, since the Order in Council that it relied on in this respect had promptly been recalled and replaced by another Order in Council, dated 17 December 1679. This later Order had restricted the requirement of registration to "all Orders, Warrants, or Letters relating to the Publicq Justice of the said Island"; other orders, warrants, and letters were to require no registration.[105] Nevertheless, the code had been ratified and confirmed by an Order in Council made on 28 March 1771.[106]

The defeat of the bailiff by the Lieutenant-Governor led the bailiff and the jurats to seek redress in a petition to the Privy Council dated 5 April 1890, in a case that is usually called *Re Daniel*.[107] This was heard by the Committee of the Privy Council for the Affairs of Jersey and Guernsey on 7 and 8 July 1890; and Haldane appeared for the States of Jersey.[108] On 12 January 1891, an Order in Council was made at Osborne to give effect to the advice of the Committee.[109] This was that even if the Order in Council of 21 May 1679, was still in force, a Royal Warrant exercising the royal prerogative of mercy did not fall within the phrase "Orders,

---

[103] Set out in *Re Jersey Prison Board* (1894), unrep., App. Pt. II, pp. 520, 521. The material for this case is to be found in 10 volumes: Lincoln's Inn Library 269[1]F. There is the Case for the States of Jersey, with four appendices and the Order in Council of 27th June, 1894 ("Case"); 6 volumes of Appendices ("App."); two volumes of Memoranda ("Memo."); and an index.

[104] The version in *Case* p. 72 seems preferable to that in *Memo.* p. 43.

[105] *Case*, p. 87.

[106] *Case*, p. 101.

[107] See n. 110, *infra*.

[108] App. Pt. I, pp. 86–89; App. Pt. II, pp. 864–69.

[109] App. Pt. II, pp. 864–70.

Warrants, or Letters, of what Nature soever" within the intent and meaning of that order. The challenge to the Lieutenant-Governor's action
therefore failed.[110]

That seems to have been the end of the matter. So far as appears, there
were no £1,000 damages for trespass and violation of the laws of Rollo or
anything else,[111] no decision of the jurats that a Frenchwoman and a dog
should be publicly burned at the stake, no gun-boat, and no release of
the Frenchwoman by the marines after a failure by the French consul to
persuade the jurats, and abortive diplomatic and civil service activity.
Instead, the Frenchwoman simply walked out of prison when, rather
tardily, the Vicomte opened the door for her. Nor, for that matter, were
the facts fully recorded in the Law Reports; for, not surprisingly, the Law
Reports do not appear even to mention the case.[112]

Some four years later there was a sequel to *Re Daniel*, concerning the
Jersey Prison Board;[113] and in this case, too, Haldane appeared for Jersey
before the Committee of the Privy Council for the Affairs of Jersey and
Guernsey.[114] In this, Jersey succeeded in procuring the recall of an Order
in Council affecting the presidency of the Board; and in the end a
legislative compromise in Jersey's favour was effected.[115] Yet remarkable
though *Re Daniel* itself was, Haldane's account of it in his *Autobiography*
was hardly less remarkable. The documents on which he had argued
both cases made it abundantly clear that the facts were as stated above,

---

[110] *Re Daniel* (1891) unrep. This account is mainly based on the documents in *Re Jersey Prison Board, supra* note 103, esp. App. Pt. II, at 864–70, together with material kindly supplied to me by Mr. R. Arthur from documents in Jersey. See also H.R.S. Pocock, *The Memoirs of Lord Coutanche* (1975), pp. 208–11.

[111] The "damages" were possibly a distorted version of the costs of £1,050 that Jersey had to bear: App. Pt. I, pp. 67, 75; and see C.R. Balleine, *A History of the Island of Jersey* (1950), p. 308.

[112] The editorial reference to the case in a note to the report of *Re the States of Jersey* (1853) 8 St.Tr. (N.S.) 285 at 314 n.(a) is very brief.

[113] *Re Jersey Prison Board* (1894) unrep.; heard on 23rd and 24th May 1894. For the material, see footnote 103.

[114] Pocock, *supra* note 110, at p. 212, calls it a Special Committee; but the Order in Council of 27th June 1894 is explicit on the point.

[115] See Order in Council of June 23, 1891, recalled by Order in Council of June 27, 1894; and Law of March 25, 1895, confirmed by Order in Council of May 11, 1895. The case is summarised in Pocock, *supra* note 110, at pp. 211–13.

and in particular that the verdict on the Frenchwoman had been Guilty but Insane, and that she had been released by the Vicomte and sent away from Jersey on a steamer.[116] Yet Haldane related that she had been "sentenced to death" and that she had been rescued from prison in Jersey by a gunboat party of the British Navy.[117] One can only say that Haldane was writing in the last two years of his life, when he was over 70, about events that had occurred nearly 40 years earlier. Many and great are the curiosities of human memory.

---

[116] And see *The Times* [1890] Mar. 12, p. 12a (" . . . with respect to the recent act of the Lieutenant-Governor in liberating a prisoner in defiance of the local authorities . . . .). A 37-page typescript of Haldane's proposed argument on the constitutional aspects of the case is in Lincoln's Inn Library: 269[1]F.

[117] *Richard Burdon Haldane, An Autobiography* (1929), pp. 59, 60. There are other questions about his account. Other biographies (Sir Frederick Maurice, *Haldane: 1856–1915* (1937); D. Sommer, *Haldane of Cloan* (1960)) do not appear to mention the case, possibly from an attack of prudence.

23

~

THE EVIL OF EVILS

FRAUD stands in a class of its own. English comments are short and downright: "By the law of England fraud cuts down everything."[1] "Fraud vitiates every thing."[2] "Fraud unravels everything."[3] America has been more expansive: "Fraud is a corrosive acid which destroys whatever it touches. Fraud is the evil of evils. It embraces hypocrisy, deception, corruption, deceit. It is the match in the hayloft, the serpent in the garden, the weasel in the chicken yard, the spider in the web, the false bottom to the pool."[4] To one litigant in person the word "fraudulantly" [sic] appeared to be "some kind of legal lubricant which made the words of his statement of claim read better."[5] He was suing his counsel for negligence in defending him on a charge (inter alia) for biting off part of a man's ear. He accepted that his bite "sounds difficult to understand in cold blood but I can demonstrate it"; but, said Lord Denning M.R., "We did not accept the offer."[6]

Perhaps there never has been a time, and never will be, when judges have not said, in one form or another, what Coke C.J. said in 1601:

---

[1] *Rogers* v. *Hadley* (1863) 32 L.J.Ex. 241 at 248 (*per* Pollock C.B.).

[2] *Master* v. *Miller* (1791) 4 T.R. 320 at 337 (*per* Buller J.).

[3] *Lazarus Estates Ltd.* v. *Beasley* [1956] 1 Q.B. 702 at 712 (*per* Denning L.J.); *May* v. *Platt* [1900] 1 Ch. 616 at 623 (*per* Farwell L.J.); and see *Campbell* v. *Edwards* [1976] 1 W.L.R. 403 at 407 (*per* Lord Denning M.R.) ("Fraud or collusion unravels everything").

[4] *In re Contest of Election for the Off. of Sch. Dir. from the Seventh Legis. Dist. of Luzerne County*, 162 A.2d 363, 368 (Pa. 1960) (Musmanno J., dissenting).

[5] *Rondel* v. *Worsley* [1967] 1 Q.B. 443 at 453 (*per* Lawton J.).

[6] *Ibid.*, at pp. 492, 494.

"Fraud and deceit abound in these days more than in former times."[7] Further, "The strongest mind cannot always contend with deceit and falsehood";[8] and as is well known, "fraud may consist as well in the suppression of what is true, as in the representation of what is false."[9] Yet "Truth and falsehood, it has been well said, are not always opposed to each other like black and white, but oftentimes and by design are made to resemble each other so as to be hardly distinguishable; just as the counterfeit thing is counterfeit because it resembles the genuine thing."[10] Still, "there is in many, if not in all men a constant inward struggle between the principles of good and evil; and because a man has grossly fallen, and, at the time of his fall added the guilt of hypocrisy to another sort of immorality, it is not necessary, therefore, to believe that his whole life has been false, or that all the good which he ever professed was insincere or unreal."[11] Nor are all charges true: "It is not uncommon for ignorant and corrupt men to falsely charge others with doing what they imagine that they themselves, in their narrow minds and experience, would have done under the circumstances of a given case."[12]

Attempts to escape the consequences of fraud are many and various. In one case an investor who had been induced to take shares in a company by an ambiguous sentence in a prospectus sued those responsible in deceit. In the House of Lords, Lord Blackburn said:

> The motive of the person saying that which he knows not to be true to another with the intention to lead him to act on the faith of the statement is immaterial. The defendants might honestly believe that the shares were a capital investment, and that they were doing the plaintiff a kindness by tricking him into buying them. I do not say this is proved, but if it were, if they did trick him into doing so, they are civilly responsible as for a deceit. And if with intent to lead the plaintiff to act upon it, they put forth a statement which they know may have two meanings, one of which is false to

---

[7] *Twyne's Case* (1601) 3 Co.Rep. 80b at 82a.

[8] *Blachford* v. *Christian* (1829) 1 Knapp 73 at 77 (*per* Lord Wynford).

[9] *Tapp* v. *Lee* (1803) 3 B. & P. 367 at 371 (*per* Chambre J.).

[10] *Johnson* v. *Emerson* (1871) L.R. 6 Exch. 329 at 357 (*per* Cleasby B.).

[11] *Symington* v. *Symington* (1875) L.R. 2 Sc. & D. 415 at 428 (*per* Lord Selborne).

[12] *Valdez* v. *U.S.*, 244 U.S. 432, 450 (1917) (Clarke J., dissenting).

their knowledge, and thereby the plaintiff putting that meaning on it is misled, I do not think they can escape by saying he ought to have put the other. If they palter with him in a double sense, it may be that they lie *like* truth; but I think they lie, and it is a fraud. Indeed, as a question of casuistry, I am inclined to think the fraud is aggravated by a shabby[13] attempt to get the benefit of a fraud, without incurring the responsibility.[14]

As was said by Lord Mansfield C.J., "Nothing is so silly as cunning."[15]

Silence is another matter. A purchaser who knows a fact that might influence the price need not disclose it to the vendor: "Simple reticence does not amount to legal fraud, however it may be viewed by moralists."[16] Yet equity will not enforce a contract if the purchaser has done anything intended to induce a belief in a non-existent fact that might influence the price; it may be only "a single word, or (I may add) a nod or a wink, or a shake of the head, or a smile."[17] There is a place in the law for —

> "Quips and cranks, and wanton wiles,
> Nods, and becks, and wreathed smiles."[18]

Knowledge is not a prerequisite: "Fraud includes the pretense of knowledge when knowledge there is none."[19] There is even authority for the proposition that *expressio veri* may be *suggestio falsi*. Alderson B. once said:

> I consider that if a person makes a representation, or takes an oath, of that which is true, if he intend that the party to whom the representation is made should not believe it to be true, that is a false representation; and so he who takes an oath in one sense, knowing it to be administered to him in another, takes it falsely. This may be illustrated by an anecdote of a very eminent ambassador, Sir Henry Wotton[20] who, when he was asked what advice he

13 On this adjective, see the views of Cardozo J., *ante* p. 268.

14 *Smith* v. *Chadwick* (1884) 9 A.C. 187 at 201.

15 *Anon.* (1772) Lofft 53 (reported in *oratio obliqua*).

16 *Walters* v. *Morgan* (1861) 3 De G.F. & J. 718 at 723 (*per* Lord Campbell L.C.).

17 *Ibid.*, at p. 724 (*per* Lord Campbell L.C.).

18 Milton's *L'Allegro*, ll. 27–28; also "oomphies" (1 Misc. 88) and "humph" (*Powell* v. *M'Glynn* [1902] 2 I.R. 154).

19 *Ultramares Corp.* v. *Touche*, 174 N.E. 441, 444 (N.Y. 1931) (*per* Cardozo C.J.).

20 1568–1639.

would give to a young diplomatist going to a foreign court, said — "I have found it best always to tell the truth, as they will never believe any thing an ambassador says, so you are sure to take them in." Now Sir Henry Wotton meant that he should tell a lie. This, no doubt, was only said as a witticism, but it illustrates my meaning.[21]

It has also been said that "when suspicion is suggested, it is easily entertained."[22] Yet there are many gradations between transparent honesty and arrant swindling, so that at times "it is a question of how strong an infusion of fraud is necessary to turn a flavor into a poison."[23] But fraud there must be, and not mere mistake: "An honest blunder in the use of language is not dishonest. What is honest is not dishonest."[24]

In one case the issue was whether an allegation of fraud in the pleadings in an earlier action was made maliciously, and so, under Scots law, was not protected by the plea of privilege in an action for slander. The majority of the court held that in determining this, the strength of the language used in alleging fraud in the pleadings was relevant; but Lord Sands dissented. In his view, "the fact that a charge is strongly expressed founds no presumption that the person making it knew it to be false. Faith may be as vocal as unbelief. Moreover, there is no reason to take it that the defender adjusted his own pleadings. The lurid language of the adjuster of pleadings is no key to the state of mind of his client. A litigant may be responsible for statements made on his behalf by his professional advisers, but it seems to be quite a different matter to draw inferences as to the state of his knowledge from forms of expression used by them in adjusting his pleadings."[25]

One problem of the law, mooted from time to time, arises when fraud is alleged against a person who employed an agent. If one of them innocently made an untrue statement but the other had knowledge of facts showing the falsity of that statement, will an action for fraud lie? It

---

[21] *Moens* v. *Heyworth* (1842) 10 M. & W. 147 at 158.

[22] *U.S.* v. *Clark*, 200 U.S. 601, 609 (1906) (*per* Holmes J.).

[23] *Intl. News Serv.* v. *Associated Press*, 248 U.S. 215, 247 (1918) (*per* Holmes J., dissenting, discussing unfair trading).

[24] *Angus* v. *Clifford* [1891] 2 Ch. 449 at 472 (*per* Bowen L.J.).

[25] *Mitchell* v. *Smith*, 1919 S.C. 664 at 676.

seems at last to be established that "you cannot add an innocent state of mind to an innocent state of mind and get as a result a dishonest state of mind."[26] Yet the case from which this doctrine stems[27] has its difficulties. In 1907 Lord Halsbury said of it: "If it was supposed to decide that the principals and agent could be so divided in responsibility that — like the schoolboy's game 'I did not take it, I have not got it' — the united principal and agent might commit fraud with impunity, it would be quite new to our jurisprudence."[28] Lord Halsbury was 84 at the time, and if he was speaking of the games of his own schooldays, his recollections were carrying him back to about the time of Queen Victoria's accession. Today, the nature of the game has faded into history and conjecture.

Deceivers sometimes escape. Youth is not enough: "Infants have no Privilege to cheat Men."[29] But there are other grounds. In the seventeenth century, an action on the case was brought by a man against a husband and wife on the ground that the woman had asserted to the plaintiff that she was "sole & unmarry," and did "importune & strenue requisivit" the plaintiff to marry her. The plaintiff yielded; but when he discovered that his "wife" was already the wife of another, he "fuit mult trouble in minde, et mis al grand charges et damnify diu son reputacion." He duly got the verdict, but then failed to hold it; for Twisden J. held that the action did not lie "quia le chose icy fait est felony." A melancholy note adds that "le feme ad obtain pardon del felony," but that this did not appear on the record.[30] Still, these were the days of fine distinctions: "Action sur case pur ceux parols, — Thou art a buggering rogue, and I could hang thee — et fuit move in arrest de judgment, et tenus que sont actionable issint pur ceux parols — Thou art a thieving rogue — pur ceo que in ambideux cases ils imply un act fait, mes est auterment de ceux parols . . . Thou art a thievish rogue . . . que imply solement un inclination."[31] Again, the words "Thou art a

---

26 *Armstrong* v. *Strain* [1951] 1 T.L.R. 856 at 872 (*per* Devlin J.); *affirmed*, [1952] 1 K.B. 232.

27 *Cornfoot* v. *Fowke* (1840) 6 M. & W. 358.

28 *S. Pearson & Son Ltd.* v. *Lord Mayor &c. of Dublin* [1907] A.C. 351 at 357.

29 *Evroy* v. *Nicholas* (1733) 2 Eq. Ca. Abr. 488 at 489 (*per* Lord King L.C.).

30 *Cooper* v. *Witham* (1668) 1 Sid. 375.

31 *Collier* v. *Burrel* (1668) 1 Sid. 373 ("thieving" implies an act done, "thievish" merely an inclination).

thief, and hast stollen my appletrees out of my orchard" were held to be actionable, though it would have been otherwise if "for thou" had replaced "and."[32] Yet the insertion of an inept causal connection was not permitted to become a licence to defame with impunity.[33] Further, "Cestuy que laugh quant il oye un auter a lier le libel n'est un publisher sil ne fait pluis."[34] Those were days when some defendants seem to have been strangely slow to take an easy way out of litigation. One action on the case for words alleging that the plaintiff was forsworn was compromised for "3 juggs of beer." But the beer was not tendered, the action was fought, and the plaintiff won.[35]

Like fraud, negligence has become almost infinite in its scope: "Our law has grown out of its primitive myopy in the recognition of harmful causes. The manager of a crowded theatre who, without having reasonable ground for it, shouts 'fire!' during a performance,[36] cannot be heard to say that he aimed a word, not blows, at the audience."[37] Negligence remains obscure in its boundaries: "To apply the concepts of 'negligence' and 'proximate cause' to the infinite complexities of modern industry is like catching butterflies without a net."[38] Some cases need little explanation, and may be summarised with a combination of meiosis and bathos: "We can imagine no reason why, with ordinary care, human toes could not be left out of chewing tobacco, and if toes are found in chewing tobacco, it seems to us that somebody has been very careless."[39] Sometime judicial moderation is indeed immoderate; "$13.44 is not enough compensation for a broken neck."[40]

---

[32] *Ayres* v. *Oswall* (1609) Noy 135: trees growing on land were not the subject of larceny. See also *Normans Case* (1587) Gould. 56 (words "spoken absolutely by themselves").

[33] See *Anon.* (1591) Sav. 126.

[34] *Lambes Case de Libells* (1610) Moo.K.B. 813; 9 Co.Rep. 59b (oye: hears; lier: read).

[35] *Trevanian* v. *Penhollow* (1655) Sty. 452.

[36] See also 2 Misc. 205.

[37] *Herschel* v. *Mrupe*, 1954 (3) S.A. 464 at 490 (*per* van den Heever J.A.) (no liability on motorist who negligently gives the name of the wrong insurance company and so leads to wasted expenditure in negotiations).

[38] *Carter* v. *Atlanta & St. Andrews Bay Ry. Co.*, 338 U.S. 430, 437–38 (1949) (*per* Frankfurter J.).

[39] *Pillars* v. *R.J. Reynolds Tobacco Co.*, 78 So. 365, 366 (Miss. 1918) (*per* Cook P.J.).

[40] *Stacey* v. *State Indus. Accident Commn.*, 26 P.2d 1092, 1094 (Or. 1933) (*per* Kelly J.).

There may be dangers in placing undue reliance on the principle *de minimis non curat lex*:

> There once was a camel which carried loads across the desert for his master. Although no one knew it this camel had a weaker back than other camels, but as his master had never loaded him too heavily he had been able to do his job well and was his master's favorite. At the beginning of one trip the camel was loaded as usual but while his master's back was turned a prankster wrongfully put a straw atop the load. The weight of this straw was just enough so that the camel's weak back collapsed. From the point of view of legal cause the prankster is liable to the camel's master for all damages the master suffers because of the camel's broken back.[41]

Some judges have expected much. In speaking of strictness in relation to negligence, Harcourt J. once referred to an unnamed English judge "of whom it was said that he required of the litigants the foresight of a Hebrew prophet and the agility of an acrobat."[42] (The judge it seems, was Lord Bramwell; the phrase was Sir Percy Winfield's.[43]) Certainly he who undertakes must perform. One action for negligence before Maule J. was brought by a Mrs. Joy Smith against a doctor. Her complaint was that she had engaged the defendant to deliver the child that she was expecting, but that when in her hour of need he had been summoned, he had refused to leave the ball that he was attending. As might be expected, the plaintiff's counsel cross-examined the defendant with some severity, and not least about the attitude of "studied indifference" that he had adopted. "His attitude," observed the judge "seems to have been 'On with the dance! Let Joy be unconfined.'"[44] Even a self-imposed duty may suffice: "The hand once set to a task may not always be withdrawn with impunity though liability would fail if it had never been applied at all."[45]

---

[41] *Tatman* v. *Provincial Homes*, 382 P.2d 573, 576 (Ariz. 1963) (*per* Bernstein C.J.). See also *ante* p. 223.

[42] *Broom* v. *The Administrator, Natal* 1966(3) S.A. 505 at 516.

[43] See *Winfield on Tort* (6th ed. 1954), p. 491.

[44] *Ex rel.* Trovato B. The quotation is from Byron's *Childe Harold*, c. III, xxii.

[45] *H.R. Moch Co.* v. *Rensselaer Water Co.*, 159 N.E. 896, 898 (N.Y. 1928) (*per* Cardozo C.J.). But contrast, e.g., *East Suffolk Rivers Catchment Board* v. *Kent* [1941] A.C. 74.

Contributory negligence comes in all forms. In one case, in a jurisdiction in which there was no provision for apportionment of liability, a
girl of seventeen was injured when the car in which she was a passenger
struck a steel bridge abutment; and she sued the boy who had been
driving. The defence was contributory negligence. The girl had removed
some of her clothes, and for twenty miles before the accident she had
lain with her head on the defendant's lap, her body naked above the
waist and exposed to the defendant's sight and touch. This, it was
contended, had so aroused and distracted the defendant that at the time
of the accident he hardly knew what he was doing. The girl met this
contention by saying that as the defendant had removed his hand from
her body about a minute before the accident and had lit a cigarette, her
conduct had not been the proximate cause of the accident, since the
defendant had had time to regain his composure. On this the defendant
joined issue, and added that the girl had been guilty of further contributory negligence in reaching for the cigarette that he had tried to
hand her under the steering wheel. He had done this when he had seen
another car containing friends of his father, as his father did not know
that he smoked. Both the trial judge and the Court of Appeals accepted
the defendant's contentions and rejected the girl's.[46]

Similar approaches have appeared in the sphere of employment. In
one case in 1891, the House of Lords reversed the decision of the Court
of Appeal and held that a workman who had been injured by a stone
falling from a crane in his employer's quarry had not disabled himself
from recovering damages from his employers merely because he knew of
the danger when he undertook and continued in the employment. Lord
Bramwell vigorously dissented: "I have no objection to 'res ipsa loquitur.'
I believe I was one of the first, if not the first, to use it in some cases
about fifteen years ago; but it does not apply here. At least I cannot use
it."[47]

This intimation of paternity is suspect. The principle (without the

[46] *Claiborne* v. *McLean*, 1966-2 Auto. L. Rep. (CCH) ¶ ¶ 12,001, 12,228 (Tenn. App. June
29, 1966).
[47] *Smith* v. *Baker & Sons* [1891] A.C. 325 at 340.

Latin) appeared at least as early as 1809.[48] The Latin may be traced back to Cicero: "Res loquitur, judices, ipsa; quae semper valet plurimum."[49] And in 1863, nearly thirty years before Lord Bramwell's statement, Pollock C.B. had put together both the principle and the Latin: "There are certain cases of which it may be said res ipsa loquitur, and this seems one of them. In some cases the Courts have held that the mere fact of the accident having occurred is evidence of negligence, as, for instance, in the case of railway collisions."[50] Over the years there has been much disputation on the subject: "one thing can certainly be said of the phrase *res ipsa loquitur.* That is that it has not been allowed to speak for itself."[51]

After staking his claim to *res ipsa loquitur,* Lord Bramwell continued his speech by explaining why the term did not apply: "I know that bales and barrels do not move and fall of their own accord. I do not know that stones slung carefully will not come apart and fall. My notion is that they will. I think I have often lifted up a piece of coal and found that the part I had hold of remained in the tongs and the rest broke away. I should think there might be some cleavage, I think it is called, which would prevent the parts holding together. This may be ignorance on my part. But if it is, it should have been removed by evidence, and there is none."[52] He then turned to the questions left to the jury. The last was:

> Did the plaintiff voluntarily undertake a risky employment with knowledge of its risks? The jury say, 'No.' I wonder what they meant. Indeed, the question is wonderful. The answer, to make it favourable to the plaintiff, is necessarily negative, a negative pregnant of one affirmative and another negative — twins. It might mean that the plaintiff did not voluntarily undertake the employment, or that it was not risky, or that he had not a knowledge of its risks. In any and every sense it is untrue, and, I think, not to the credit of the jury who gave it.[53]

48 *Christie* v. *Griggs* (1809) 2 Camp. 79.

49 Cicero, *Pro Milone* XX, 53, as cited in Broom's *Legal Maxims* (10th ed. 1939), p. 204. ("The matter speaks for itself, members of the jury; and this always carries the greatest weight").

50 *Byrne* v. *Boadle* (1863) 2 H. & C. 722 at 725.

51 *Anchor Products Ltd.* v. *Hedges* (1966) 115 C.L.R. 493 at 496 (*per* Windeyer J.).

52 *Smith* v. *Baker & Sons, supra* note 47, at p. 340.

53 *Ibid.,* at p. 342.

Next he considered *volenti non fit injuria*, and said:

> If this is a maxim, is it any the worse? What are maxims but the expression of
> that which good sense has made a rule? It is a rule of good sense that if a
> man voluntarily undertakes a risk for a reward which is adequate to induce
> him, he shall not, if he suffers from the risk, have a compensation for which
> he did not stipulate. He can, if he chooses, say, "I will undertake the risk for
> so much, and if hurt, you must give me so much more, or an equivalent for
> the hurt." But drop the maxim. Treat it as a question of bargain. The plaintiff
> here thought the pay worth the risk, and did not bargain for a compensation
> if hurt: in effect, he undertook the work, with its risks, for his wages and no
> more. He says so. Suppose he had said, "If I am to run this risk, you must
> give me 6s. a day and not 5s.," and the master agreed, would he in reason
> have a claim if he got hurt? Clearly not. What difference is there if the master
> says, "No; I will only give the 5s."? None. I am ashamed to argue it.[54]

Lord Bramwell then turned to the consequences:

> It is said that to hold the plaintiff is not to recover is to hold that a master
> may carry on his work in a dangerous way and damage his servant. I do so
> hold, if the servant is foolish enough to agree to it. This sounds very cruel.
> But do not people go to see dangerous sports? Acrobats daily incur fearful
> dangers, lion-tamers and the like. Let us hold to the law. If we want to be
> charitable, gratify ourselves out of our own pockets."[55]

Finally, he dealt with the contention that the defendants had not taken
the point about *volenti non fit injuria*:

> Whether taken or not it should be open to the defendants. Error is caput
> lupinum.[56] Up to the last moment, if there is irremediable error, it may be
> objected to. That was here. On this ground also the defendants should
> succeed. Something ought to be done, a new trial granted, if necessary, to
> prevent the defendants being made liable to pay damages which, in the
> opinion of many judges, there was no ground for claiming against them, and

---

[54] *Ibid.*, at p. 344.

[55] *Ibid.*, at p. 346.

[56] "The head of a wolf", and as such lawfully subject to being attacked.

which never would have been claimed but in the hope of an unjust verdict from a jury.[57]

But Lord Halsbury L.C., Lord Watson, Lord Herschell, and Lord Morris thought otherwise.

There have been a number of dissents from the modern tendency of legislatures to impose liability on employers for accidents to their employees, regardless of any fault in the employer. McKenna J. was one of the dissentients: "It seems to me to be of the very foundation of right — of the essence of liberty as it is of morals — to be free from liability if one is free from fault. It has heretofore been the sense of the law and the sense of the world, pervading the regulations of both, that there can be no punishment where there is no blame."[58]

Extravagant arguments receive short shrift. Viscount Simonds's view was to "deprecate any tendency to treat the relation of employer and skilled workman as equivalent to that of nurse and imbecile child."[59] Further, "To argue that an occupation is hazardous because someone engaged therein has received personal injuries is not helpful. Many have suffered fatal accidents while eating, but eating could hardly be called hazardous."[60] So too with drinking. Some years ago in a Pennsylvania bar a male customer "made some passes" at a female customer. At this, the bartender objected, and then, pulling out a pistol from under the bar, shot the man in his hand and neck. The victim thereupon sued the proprietor of the bar, and the jury awarded him $8,800; but both the trial judge and the State Supreme Court held that the proprietor was not liable, despite the verdict. The duties and responsibilities of a bartender are many and varied, but even in Pennsylvania the scope of a bartender's employment does not embrace shooting the amorous and importunate.[61]

There are many ways of constituting a nuisance: "A nuisance may be merely a right thing in the wrong place, like a pig in the parlor instead of

---

57 *Smith* v. *Baker & Sons, supra* note 47, at p. 347.

58 *Arizona Copper Co.* v. *Hammer*, 250 U.S. 400, 436 (1919) (McKenna J., dissenting). The majority held that the statute was not unconstitutional.

59 *Smith* v. *Austin Lifts Ltd.* [1959] 1 W.L.R. 100 at 105.

60 *Ward & Gow* v. *Krinsky*, 259 U.S. 503, 528–29 (1922) (McReynolds J., dissenting).

61 *Howard* v. *Zaney Bar*, 85 A.2d 401 (Pa. 1952).

the barnyard."[62] Many years ago it was indeed argued that "one ought not to have so delicate a nose, that he cannot bear the smell of hogs";[63] but the argument failed.

Although in popular speech it is said that two rights cannot make a wrong, two rights can make a tort. Thus if one man makes a noise that, by itself, would not amount to an actionable nuisance, he may nevertheless be liable in tort if his noise, when added to a similar noise made by another, passes the bounds of toleration.[64] In one case an injunction was granted to restrain the incumbent of a church in a residential suburb from ringing his church bell in the early morning on Sundays and saints' days. A'Beckett J. said: "I think it is a plain, sober, and simple notion[65] to object to being roused from sleep by your neighbour's bell when you are lying in bed at half-past 7 on Sunday morning, unless lying there at that hour is an exceptional indulgence to which only sluggards or invalids are addicted."[66]

One account of *Trimmer* v. *Lord Huntingtower* was that the plaintiff, a clergyman, ran a boys' school near Grantham. The defendant established a bull pound opposite the school and brought women of bad character from Leicester, "who would when almost in a state of nudity rush out and run before the boys, so that the parents were obliged to take their children away, as the school became demoralized." The jury, it was said, awarded the plaintiff £10,000 damages, but as a mere £2,000 had been claimed, judgment had to be entered for only that sum, although the judge had said that he would have endorsed an award of £10,000.[67]

This brief account whets the appetite for further details of so engaging a case. Yet as is so often the case, the tale seems to have grown in the telling, and truth is less bold than fiction. What seems to have happened

---

[62] *Village of Euclid* v. *Ambler Realty Co.*, 272 U.S. 365, 388 (1926) (*per* Sutherland J.).

[63] *William Aldred's Case* (1610) 9 Co.Rep. 57b at 58a. Compare sea-coal: *ante* pp. 171–72.

[64] *Lambton* v. *Mellis* [1894] 3 Ch. 163.

[65] This refers to the test laid down by Knight Bruce V.-C. in *Walters* v. *Selfe* (1851) 4 De G. & Sm. 315 at 322.

[66] *Haddon* v. *Lynch* [1911] V.L.R. 5 at 9 (*affirmed. ibid.*, at p. 230).

[67] R. Walton, *Random Recollections of the Midland Circuit, Second Series* (1878), p. 53, assigning no date to the case.

was that the plaintiff, who had been appointed to a living at Buckminster in Leicestershire, came to live in the vicarage with two of his pupils. The defendant strongly objected to this, and promptly erected a pinfold some thirty feet from the vicarage. The bull was supplied with cows daily, and there was also a male ass, to whom she-asses were led "even on Sundays, about the time when the afternoon service was over."[68] But there is no trace of nude women from Leicester or anywhere else, or a multiple withdrawal of children. There was, however, a statement by the defendant to a male pupil 17 or 18 years old that a woman had a girl for him who would invite him to drink tea and sleep with her. This had been followed by an anonymous letter to the pupil's mother, apparently written by the defendant, alleging that the pupil had made a local girl pregnant; and as a result of this the mother withdrew her son from the school. The defendant was guilty of other odd and offensive conduct as well. Heredity may well have played a part in the deplorable matrimonial conduct of his son, as later laid bare to the world.[69]

As for the damages in the *Trimmer* case, no trace of the alleged £10,000 appears; all that was said was that "the jury returned a verdict for the plaintiff for the full sum laid in the declaration, — namely £2,000 damages."[70] Possibly the £10,000 crept in as being the sum that the defendant had said he "would willingly spend" on a lawsuit with the plaintiff. The case had a sequel: for the defendant, as part of a campaign to induce the plaintiff to forgo his damages, later prosecuted the pupil for taking part in a riot. But the pupil was acquitted, and on suing Lord Huntingtower for malicious prosecution, was awarded £1,000 damages.[71]

Assaults range from the trivial to the outrageous; yet the trivial may itself be outrageous. Heath J. once observed: "I remember a case where a jury gave £500 damages for merely knocking a man's hat off; and the

---

[68] *Trimmer* v. *Lord Huntingtower* [1829] *Annual Register* 324 at 325; [1829] *The Times*, Aug. 19; *cor.* Alexander C.B. at Leicester Assizes. The action was for nuisance.

[69] *Countess of Dysart* v. *Earl of Dysart* (1847) 1 Rob.Ecc. 470, reversing *Earl of Dysart* v. *Countess of Dysart* (1844) 1 Rob.Ecc. 106. The son had succeeded to the earldom of Dysart on the death of his grandmother in 1840: see *The Complete Peerage* (1916), vol. 4, p. 566.

[70] *Trimmer* v. *Lord Huntingtower* [1829] *Annual Register* 324 at 328.

[71] *Langdon* v. *Lord Huntingtower* [1830] *Annual Register* 128.

Court refused a new trial." As he pointed out, the power of the jury to give exemplary damages for insulting assaults "goes to prevent the practice of duelling."[72] In this field *Booth* v. *Hanley*[73] is not as well known as it deserves to be. The head-note is brief and pointed (or some would say oblique): "If a party be turning towards the wall in a street at night for a particular occasion, a watchman is not justified in collaring him, to prevent him so doing." The "party" recovered £20 damages for assault and false imprisonment in proceedings in which Abbott C.J. gave the jury robust instructions. "The watchman," he said, "had no right to go up to a man and collar him for that which the plaintiff appears to have been doing. He might have gone up to him and remonstrated with him, or have asked him to go somewhere else; but he clearly had no right to assault him for that."[74]

In a similar action against an Australian policeman (though in respect of different acts), the main issue was whether the defendant had acted in the honest execution of his statutory powers, or whether he had abused them. The claim succeeded, with general damages of £500. One of the determining factors was the policeman's rejection of a request by two witnesses of the incident that they might accompany him and the plaintiff to the police station. In the words of Fullagar J., "the defendant's refusal was conveyed by the words: 'We're not interested in bloody witnesses.' A man who was anxious merely to do his duty would have been very interested in witnesses, whether bloody or not."[75]

In the seventeenth century a sheriff once hanged a man in chains on private land, and the owner sued the sheriff in trespass. The jury found for the defendant, and the court refused a new trial, "it being done for convenience of place, and not to affront the owner."[76] The sidenote is no more than — "New trial rarely granted in hard actions." The only

---

[72] *Merest, Esq.* v. *Harvey* (1814) 5 Taunt. 442 at 444.

[73] (1826) 2 C. & P. 288.

[74] *Ibid.* See also *R.* v. *Barnsley Metropolitan Borough Council, ex parte Hook* [1976] 1 W.L.R. 1052 at 1055.

[75] *Trobridge* v. *Hardy* (1955) 94 C.L.R. 147 at 159.

[76] *Sparks* v. *Spicer* (1698) 2 Salk. 648.

recompense for the landowner seems to have been grim, trifling, and somewhat strange. For Holt C.J. said: "If a man be hung in chains upon my land; after the body is consumed, I shall have the gibbet and chain."[77] *Quicquid plantatur solo, solo cedit*[78] could well account for the gibbet, but hardly for the chains.

As Lord Shaw of Dunfermline has pointed out, in the assessment of damages there is one underlying principle, that of restoration. In the case of financial loss, damages are "capable of correct appreciation in stated figures." But in cases of loss of life, faculty, or limb, restoration is difficult or impossible, and so the assessment must be accomplished to a large extent "by the exercise of a sound imagination and the practice of the broad axe."[79] Some axes indeed need to be broad: "The plaintiff . . . has, I am told, been accepted in Ceylon as a Buddhist nun. She also practices yoga. This requires her to assume certain ceremonial positions for the purpose of meditation. Her injury renders the assumption of some of these positions difficult or impossible. . . . I do not find it easy to assess such an element of damages, but I shall do my best."[80] After all, "Even the loss to a chartered accountant of the ability to earn his living as a pearl diver deserves some damages, however small."[81]

---

[77] *Spark* v. *Spicer* (1698) 1 Ld. Raym. 738.

[78] "Whatever is attached to land becomes part of the land."

[79] *Pott* v. *Watson, Laidlaw & Co. Ltd.* (1914) 31 R.P.C. 104 at 118. For *rusticum judicium*, see *ante* p. 200.

[80] *Burian* v. *Sullivan*, Feb. 25, 1969, B.C., unrep. [1969] *Canadian Current Law*, Sept., p. iii (*per* Wilson C.J.S.C.).

[81] *Mann* v. *Ellbourn* (1974) 8 S.A.S.R. 298 at 302 (*per* Bray C.J.).

24

~

POWAFUCHSWOWITCHAHAVAGGANEABBA

(CHICAGO)

IN LINCOLN'S INN, it has long been the custom to toll the chapel bell at midday when news of a bencher's death is received.[1] Thereupon many a barrister has asked a clerk to find out who it is that has gone to a just reward. It may well be that a former barrister who from 1616 to 1622 was Preacher to the Inn, and then Dean of St. Paul's,[2] had this practice in mind when he wrote the well-known words: "No man is an Iland, intire of it selfe; every man is a peece of the Continent, a part of the maine; if a Clod bee washed away by the Sea, Europe is the lesse, as well as if a Promontorie were, as well as if a Mannor of thy friends or of thine own were; any mans death diminishes me, because I am involved in Mankinde; And therefore never send to know for whom the bell tolls; It tolls for thee."[3]

Close though the association between law and religion has sometimes been, at times they run ill in harness. The jurisdiction of the Judicial Committee of the Privy Council in matters ecclesiastical was long a bone of contention. In one famous eschatological case the Committee[4]

---

[1] Sir Gerald Hurst, *A Short History of Lincoln's Inn* (1946), p. 46. More recently the bell has been tolled from 12.45 to 1.15.

[2] *Ibid.*, at p. 71.

[3] John Donne, *Devotions upon Emergent Occasions* (1624), XVIII (*Complete Poetry and Selected Prose* (J. Haywood ed., 1929), p. 538).

[4] *Williams* v. *Bishop of Salisbury* (1864) 2 Moo.P.C. (N.S.) 375.

by a majority[5] reversed the decision of the Court of Arches, which had suspended Dr. Rowland Williams and Rev. H.B. Wilson for a year on the ground (*inter alia*) that they had denied the plenary inspiration of the Holy Scriptures, and that the latter had also denied the doctrine of everlasting life or death. Lord Westbury L.C. delivered the majority judgment, and so earned for himself Sir Philip Rose's mock epitaph, with the finest line contributed by the future Lord Bowen:[6]

RICHARD, BARON WESTBURY.

Lord High Chancellor of England.[7]
He was an eminent Christian,
An energetic and merciful statesman,
And a still more eminent and merciful Judge.
During his three years' tenure of office
He abolished the ancient method of conveying land,
The time-honoured institution of the Insolvents' Court,
And
The Eternity of Punishment.
Towards the close of his earthly career
In the Judicial Committee of the Privy Council
He dismissed Hell with costs,
And took away from orthodox members of the Church of England
Their last hope of everlasting damnation.[8]

According to Hawkins J., at about this time a churchwarden brought proceedings against his vicar for refusing to administer the sacrament to him on the ground that the churchwarden did not believe in the personality of the devil; and ultimately the House of Lords held that the vicar was wrong. When it was said that the House of Lords had abolished hell with costs, Westbury demurred: "What I did say was that the poor churchwarden who did not at one time believe in the personality of the

---

[5] The two Archbishops dissenting. *Ibid.*, at p. 434.

[6] See, however, the inferior version attributed to James L.J.: Manson, at p. 171; contrast *ibid.*, at p. 156.

[7] *Sic*: he was Lord High Chancellor of Great Britain; see *ante* p. 9.

[8] 2 Atlay 264.

devil returned to the true orthodox Christian faith when he received his attorney's bill."[9] It was reputedly Bowen, too, who, without questioning Divine impartiality, pointed to the part played by man. It is the Almighty who "sendeth rain on the just and on the unjust";[10] yet delivery does not always follow despatch. For —

> The rain it raineth on the just,
> And also on the unjust fella;
> But chiefly on the just, because
> The unjust filches his umbrella.

In times past, the bonds of law and religion were closer than they are today. Until 1859,[11] an Act of 1605[12] required November 5th of each year to be celebrated as a day of thanksgiving, and enacted that all citizens should attend the services to be held in every church to celebrate "this joyful day of deliverance." The Act, which was to be read at the end of the services, paid due tribute to royal percipience, for it recited that the gunpowder plot would have succeeded "had it not pleased Almighty God, by inspiring the King's most excellent Majesty with a Divine Spirit, to interpret some dark Phrases of a Letter shewed to his Majesty, above and beyond all ordinary Construction, thereby miraculously discovering this hidden Treason not many Hours before the appointed Time for the Execution thereof."[13]

More recently, religion has felt the revising hand of the law. At a multi-denominational service to commemorate the centenary of the Law Society of New South Wales,[14] the printed service sheet duly set out the psalms, hymns, and prayers in the usual way. But there was an exception. The Lord's Prayer was shown as including the lines —

---

[9] R. Harris, *The Reminiscences of Sir Henry Hawkins* (1904), p. 326.

[10] Matt. 5:45.

[11] 22 Vict., c. 2.

[12] 3 Jac. 1, c. 1.

[13] See generally Antonia Fraser, *The Gunpowder Plot* (1996).

[14] Monday, September 17, 1984, at the Parish Church of St. James, King Street, Sydney. I was there: the Prayer was *spoken* impeccably by all.

> "Lead us to into temptation.
> but deliver us from evil."

The first line, though a little clumsy, was plainly intended to be emphatic: the suppliant is to be led not only "to" the temptation but also "into" it. (The idea that "to" may be a misprint for "two" will at once be spurned). The devout may well object; yet is not this wording an improvement? To attain purity of life in the total absence of any temptation demands little effort; the achievement, surely, is to face manifold temptations and yet to be delivered from evil. The conjunction, too ("but" and not "and") seems more apt for the old than the new.

Selden cast a sardonic eye on the Church of his day: "For a preist to turne a man when hee lyes a dying, is just like one that has a long time sollicited a Woman & cannott obteine his End, at length makes her drunke & so lyes with her."[15] Again: "Preachers will bring any thing into the Text, the younger Masters of Art preach'd against Non Residency in the University — whereupon the heads made an order, that no man should meddle with any thing, but what was in his Text. The next day one preach'd upon these words (Abraham begatt Issac); when hee had gone on a good way att last hee observed, That Abraham was Resident, for if hee had been non Resident, hee could never have begatt Isaac, & so fell foule upon the Non Residents."[16]

Once Parliament even adjudicated upon the title to the Papacy. In 1378 there was the Great Schism. Urban VI was elected Pope, and hard on the heels of his election came the rival election of Clement VII to be Pope at Avignon. Each had powerful adherents, but England's rivalry with France was unlikely to favour Avignon, and the question was promptly resolved by legislation. By an Act of 1378,[17] "Urban was proclaimed Pope and Chief of Holy Church. Opposition to the award of Parliament was discouraged by a provision subjecting the benefices and possessions of the cardinals and others who supported Urban's rival to

---

[15] Selden, *Table Talk*, p. 115.
[16] *Ibid.*, at p. 105.
[17] 2 Ric. 2, stat. 1, c. 7, 1378.

seizure by the Crown. Further, those who were obedient to any Pope other than Urban were put out of the King's protection, and their goods and chattels were made liable to forfeiture to the Crown. The word "pape" in the original statute was afterwards translated as "Bishop of Rome,"[18] which indicates that the translation was made after Henry VIII had abolished the papal supremacy.

Selden's comment was that "the papists call our Religion a Parliamentary Religion, but there was once, I am sure, a Parliamentary pope."[19] He added that the Act was "not in the booke of Statutes, either because hee that compiled the Booke would not have the name of the pope there, or els hee would not lett it appear that they medled with any such thing but 'tis upon the Rolles."[20] In fact, a summary of the statute, as appropriate to an expired Act, did appear in at least one edition of the statutes current in Selden's time,[21] and it duly appeared in later collections of statutes.[22] Not until 1863 was it removed from the statute-book.[23]

At one time the British Army Estimates included entries for scalping-knives and crucifixes. These seem to have been part of the British policy pursued in the American War of Independence, a policy that Lord Camden bitterly described in the House of Lords as "letting loose the savages to scalp and murder the aged, the innocent and the impotent."[24] It was the Bishop of Peterborough[25] who had referred to the entries in the Estimates. As he said, "If such is the Christianity which we are henceforth to propagate among the Indians, it is better for their teachers, better for themselves, that they should live and die in ignorance."[26] If this is coupled with some of the extremities of religious beliefs that have

[18] Statutes of the Realm, vol. 2 (1816), p. 11 n.

[19] Selden, *Table Talk*, p. 98.

[20] *Ibid.*, at p. 99.

[21] Pulton (1618), p. 205, under cap. VI ("Urban was duely chosen Pope, and so ought to be accepted and obeyed"). Rastell, vol. 1 (1618), however, omits all mention of it: see at p. 133.

[22] E.g., Ruffhead, vol. 1 (1769), p. 343; Statutes of the Realm, vol. 2 (1816), p. 11.

[23] Statute Law Revision Act 1863.

[24] (1778) 20 Parl.Hist. 43.

[25] John Hinchcliffe.

[26] (1778) 20 Parl.Hist. 11.

flourished in recent decades, it becomes difficult to accept to the full the proposition that "as between . . . different religions the law stands neutral, but it assumes that any religion is at least likely to be better than none."[27] People always like their own brands of theology: "We must not forget that in our country are evangelists and zealots of many different political, economic, and religious persuasions whose fanatical conviction is that all thought is divinely classified into two kinds — that which is their own and that which is false and dangerous."[28] Atheism, too, has its claims: "The day that this country ceases to be free for irreligion it will cease to be free for religion."[29]

An old link between religion and the armed forces emerged in a case where the liability for rates of Serjeants Inn, Chancery Lane, was being contested. Part of the evidence produced by the parish was a book that "contained entries of 6s. 8d., paid by Sir Julius Caesar, Master of the Rolls, Mr. Justice Croke, and Mr. Serjent Glanville, for licences to eat flesh."[30] These licences, the reporter considerately explained in a footnote,[31] were granted under the statute 5 Eliz. I, c. 5, 1562, "which was an Act for maintaining and increasing the navy. By that statute it was enacted, that every person eating flesh on a Wednesday, or other fish day, should forfeit three pounds, or suffer three months' imprisonment.[32] But these penalties were not to extend to persons licensed;[33] and for a licence lords of Parliament and their wives were to pay 26s. 8d.; knights and their wives 13s. 4d.; other persons 6s. 8d. to the poor's box of their parish;[34] and persons sick were to be licensed by the rector, vicar, or curate of their parish, and if there was none, by the curate of the adjoining parish;[35] but no licence was to extend to the eating of beef:[36] and any

[27] *Neville Estates Ltd.* v. *Madden* [1962] Ch. 832 at 853 (*per* Cross J.).

[28] *Am. Commun. Assn., C.I.O.* v. *Douds,* 339 U.S. 382, 438 (1950) (Jackson J., concurring in part and dissenting in part).

[29] *Zorach* v. *Clauson,* 343 U.S. 306, 325 (1952) (Jackson J., dissenting).

[30] *Lens* v. *Brown* (1824) 1 C. & P. 224 at 228.

[31] *Ibid.,* at n.(c).

[32] S. 15; but see ss. 36, 37. The penalties were reduced by 35 Eliz. 1, c. 7, 1593, s. 22.

[33] S. 17.

[34] S. 18. These were annual sums.

[35] S. 20.

[36] S. 19, applying also to veal from Michaelmas to May 1.

person preaching, writing, or saying, that eating fish is of any necessity to the saving of the soul of man, should be punished as a spreader of false news.[37] This may seem rather a singular method of manning the British navy; but I take this apparently absurd Act to have been passed, because the sudden abolition of *maigre* days by the change of religion, must have nearly ruined the fishermen, and therefore it was feared that they would join the Catholic party in disturbing the Government, as a Catholic Government would be more favourable to their vocation."[38]

Today, it is to the United States that one must turn for most of the contacts between law and religion. Constitutional protection for religious freedom is a fruitful source of dispute: "No single principle can answer all of life's complexities."[39] Zeal thwarts empathy: "People with a consuming belief that their religious convictions must be forced on others rarely ever believe that the unorthodox have any rights which should or can be rightfully respected."[40] Jackson J. criticized a statute that compelled public-school children released from classes during the day to attend off-campus religious instruction: "It is possible to hold a faith with enough confidence to believe that what should be rendered to God does not need to be decided and collected by Caesar."[41] But there are limits: "We cannot conceive that cursing a public officer is the exercise of religion in any sense of the term."[42] Nor is the reach of the Constitution unlimited. At one stage of proceedings in the United States Tax Court, the taxpayer was moved to say: "As God is my judge, I do not owe this tax," whereat Murdock C.J. replied: "He's not. I am. You do."[43] There are many other attributions of this exchange. Faulks J. ascribed it to Judge Cluer, who added "With costs."[44]

---

[37] S. 40.

[38] *Lens* v. *Brown, supra* note 30, at p. 228. By sect. 51 the Act was to continue in force for ten years, but later statutes extended its life (see note to s. 51 in Ruffhead). The Sea Fisheries Act 1868, s. 71, 2d Sched., repealed the whole Act.

[39] *Minersville Sch. Dist.* v. *Gobitis,* 310 U.S. 586, 594 (1940) (*per* Frankfurter J.).

[40] *Adamson* v. *California,* 332 U.S. 46, 88 (1947) (Black J., dissenting).

[41] *Zorach,* 343 U.S. at 324–25 (1952) (Jackson J., dissenting).

[42] *Chaplinsky* v. *New Hampshire,* 315 U.S. 568, 571 (1942) (*per* Murphy J.).

[43] *Per* Biggs C.J., as quoted by Henry Weihofen, *Legal Writing Style* (1961), p. iv.

[44] Sir Neville Faulks, *No Mitigating Circumstances* (1977), p. 52.

The Constitution apart, there is much material for the law in the luxuriant variety of religions that flourish in the United States. One of the oddest actions for deceit was that brought in *Ellis* v. *Newbrough*,[45] decided by the Supreme Court of New Mexico in 1891. The plaintiff's case was that he and his two children had been induced by the defendants to join with them in setting up a community of "Faithists," incorporated under the name and style of the "First Church of the Tae." The defendants, Ellis said, had fraudulently represented that the community's property would be held in common, and that the community would be conducted on principles of brotherly love and morality. In fact, he alleged, all the property was vested in one of the defendants, who was guilty of tyrannical and immoral acts, and the defendants refused to pay Ellis for the work and labour of himself and his children during the 18 months that they lived in the community: and he claimed $10,000 damages. The trial court awarded the plaintiff $1,500, and overruled a demurrer based on a variety of grounds. But on appeal this decision was reversed.

The judgment of the New Mexico Supreme Court was delivered by Freeman J.[46] He described the action as being "a most extraordinary proceeding," and as being "without precedent."[47] After stating the issues and referring to the demurrer, he said:

> We think the court erred in overruling this demurrer. The most that can be gathered from the declaration is that the defendants had conceived some Utopian scheme for the amelioration of all the ills, both temporal and spiritual, to which human flesh and soul are heir; had located their new Arcadia near the shores of the Rio Grande, in the county of Dona Ana, in the valley of the Mesilla; had christened this new-found Vale of Tempe the "Land of Shalam"; had sent forth their siren notes, which, sweeter and more seductive than the music that led the intrepid Odysseus to the Isle of

[45] 6 N.M. 181, 27 P. 490 (N.M. Terr. 1891). All the quotations are from the official New Mexico reports. The font and punctuation vary from that of the unofficial *Pacific Reporter*, but the texts are otherwise identical.

[46] 27 P. at 490 (O'Brien C.J., and Lee & Seeds JJ., concurring). McFie J., who had been of counsel in the court below, took no part in the case: *ibid.*, at p. 494.

[47] *Ibid.*, at p. 490.

Calypso, reached the ears of the plaintiff at his far-off home in Georgia, and induced him to "consecrate his life and labors, and all his worldly effects," etc., to this new gospel of Oahspe. This much is gathered from the pleadings.[48]

The core of the plaintiff's case was that he was the victim of "a deceit practiced upon him; that he was misled by the Oahspe and other writings of the society."[49] Freeman J. opened the court's review: "The evidence adduced in support of the plaintiff's demand is as startling as the declaration is unique. What the declaration leaves as uncertain, the proof makes incomprehensible." It also led to some novel declarations in *dicta* by the court, whose opinion gives the reader as many difficulties as the declaration and the proof gave the court.

The plaintiff offered the Faithist Bible, Oahspe,[50] as evidence of the Faithists' doctrines. Freeman J. summarized the first several hundred pages of the book, which "endeavor[ed] to demonstrate that Christianity had its origin in fraud" by proving that Christ ("Looeamong") had been a man of war and was improperly named God in a hotly contested celestial election to which he had brought an army of angels. The court commented: "We think this part of the exhibit ought to have been excluded from the jury, because it is an attack in a collateral way on the title of this man Looeamong, who is not a party to this proceeding, showing that he had not only packed the convention (council) with his friends, but had surrounded the place of meeting with his hosts, 'a thousand angels deep on every side,' thus violating that principle of our laws which forbids the use of troops at the polls."[51]

The court then explained the first of several reasons why the plaintiff could not prevail on his claim of deceit. Ellis apparently argued that he

[48] *Ibid.*, at p. 491.

[49] *Ibid.*, at p. 493.

[50] The full, florid title was "Oahspe: A New Bible in the words of Jehovih and his Angel Embassadors. A sacred history of the dominions of the higher and lower heavens on the earth for the past twenty-four thousand years, together with a synopsis of the cosmogony of the universe; the creation of planets; the creation of man; the unseen worlds; the labor and glory of gods and goddesses in the ethereal heavens. With the new commandments of Jehovih to man of the present day. With revelations from the second resurrection, formed in words in the thirty-third year of the Kosmon era." *Ibid.*, at p. 491.

[51] *Ibid.*, at p. 492.

had been led to commit an overt act of disloyalty against the United States by singing the tune (though not the words) of *Dixie*[52] when, as a member of the community's choir, he joined in singing:

> For all things are held in common
> Hooray! Hooray!
> Thus everything belongs to all,
> And peace abounds in Shalam;
> Away, away, away out west in Shalam![53]

After rhapsodizing about how the memory of similar lines of poetry carried "him back to the days of his boyhood, and to the land of the 'magnolia and the mocking bird,'" Freeman J. said that the court rejected the plaintiff's argument on the unique ground that "it matters not whether they kept step to the martial strains of Dixie, or declined their voices to the softer melody of Little Annie Rooney, the appellee became forever estopped from setting up a claim for work and labor done; nor can he be heard to say that 'he has suffered great anguish of mind in consequence of the dishonor and humiliation brought on himself and children by reason of his connection with said defendants' community.' His joining in the exercises aforesaid constitutes a clear case of estoppel in Tae."[54] More rationally, the court added: "There is another reason, however, why this act of disloyalty on the part of the appellants should not prejudice them; and that is that the plaintiff himself joined in the chorus when the 'tune of Dixie' was sung. . . . the parties were in pari delicto, and, therefore, neither can avail himself of the other's wrong."[55]

The plaintiff insisted that he had "a right to recover for a deceit

---

[52] *Ibid.*, at pp. 492–93. *Dixie* was one of the most popular songs in the short-lived Confederate States of America. The court does not explain why singing *Dixie* or its tune was apparently a badge of disloyalty to the United States after the American Civil War (1861–1865), but it presumably grated on lingering wounds and hostilities. In a letter to the Richmond *Dispatch*, published on March 19, 1893 (two years after this case), the writer declared that "'Dixie' became to the South what the 'Marseillaise' is to France."

[53] *Ibid.*, at p. 492.

[54] *Ibid.*

[55] *Ibid.*, at p. 492–93.

practiced upon him; that he was misled by the Oahspe and other writings of the society." But the court rejected this view, for

> the defendants maintain that the appellee is a man who can read, and who has ordinary intelligence, and this the appellee admits. This admission precludes any inquiry as to whether appellee's connection with the Faithists, their inner and outer circles, their music and other mystic ceremonies, their general warehouse and co-operative store, and other communistic theories and practices, gave evidence of such imbecility as would entitle him to maintain the suit. Admitting, therefore, that the appellee was a man of ordinary intelligence, we find nothing in the exhibits which in our opinion was calculated to mislead him.[56]

True, the Oahspe, "like other inspired writings, such as the Koran, Bunyan's Pilgrim's Progress, and other works of like character, deals largely in figures and tropes and allegories. But, read in the light of modern sciences, they are beautiful in their very simplicity."[57]

The judgment includes some passages from the Oahspe that describe not only the Land of Shalam but also its neighbours. Next in the south, there was the

> kingdom of Himalawowoaganapapa, rich in legends of the people who lived here before the flood; a kingdom of seventy cities and six great canals, coursing east and west, and north and south, from the Ghiee mountain in the east, to the West mountain, the Yublahahcolaesavaganawakka, the place of the king of bears, the EEughehabakax (grizzly). And to the south, to the middle kingdom, on the deserts of Geobiathhaganeganewohwoh, where the rivers empty not into the sea, but sink into the sand, the Sonogallakaxkax, creating prickly Thuazhoogallakhoomma, shaped like a pear.

Then:

> "In the high north lay the kingdom of Olegalla, the land of giants, the place of yellow rocks and high spouting waters. Olegalla it was who gave away his kingdom, the great city of Powafuchswowitchahavagganeabba, with the

---

[56] *Ibid.*, at p. 493.
[57] *Ibid.*

four and twenty tributary cities spread along the valley of Anemoosagoo-chakakfuela. Gave his kingdom to his queen, Minneganewashaka, with the yellow hair, long hanging down." This unquestionably refers to Chicago.[58]

Even if Ellis had been entitled to recover, he could not. Before he joined the Faithists, he had "read their books thoroughly" and had also

> entered into the Holy Covenant. That covenant is found in chapter 5 of the Book of Jehovih's Kingdom on Earth. The twenty-fourth verse of the covenant is as follows: "I covenant unto Thee, Jehovih, that, since all things are thine, I will not own nor possess, exclusively unto myself, anything under the sun, which may be intrusted to me, which any other person or persons may covet or desire, or stand in need of." Under the terms of the covenant, he can not maintain his suit, for the defendants insist, and the proof is clear, that they "covet or desire or stand in need of" the $10,000 for which the plaintiff sues. This is a complete answer to so much of plaintiff's cause of action as is laid in assumpsit, just as his participation in the church exercises, music, etc., was an estoppel to his right to set up "anguish of mind" and ruined reputation and other matters founded in tort.[59]

In the end the court held that no proper claim had been set out in the declaration, and that there was no evidence to sustain the award of damages. As Freeman J. said: "If the court below had been invested with spiritual jurisdiction, it might have been enabled, through an inspired interpreter, to submit to a mortal jury the precise character of plaintiff's demand."[60] A similar process might explain why the court embarked on its exhaustive geographical essay in democratic theology. Yet the temptation to speculate remains minimal.

---

[58] *Ibid.*
[59] *Ibid.* (internal citations removed).
[60] *Ibid.*, at p. 491.

TABLE OF CASES

~

TABLE OF STATUTES

~

1. Acts of English and United Kingdom Parliament

2. Other Statutes

Statutory Instruments

2. Other Jurisdictions
Australia

California

Hawaii

INDEX

~

Abbott C.J., 366
Abbott C.J.K.B., Sir Charles, 101
Abbott J., 70
A'Beckett J., 364
Abinger C.B., Lord (James Scarlett), 123, 282
    disrespectful to benchers, 83
    guidance to offended author, 91
    very wide divaricating dictum, 254
Abraham, Isaac's father, logically resident in university, 372
Abridgement (Rolle's), 171
abstention, 264, 265
Abstracts, 91
accusation, penalty for false, 65
acquittal,
    eloquence and saintly appearance leading to, 97
    miscarriage of justice, 342
    offences included, 168
    without leaving jury box, 69
Acts of Sederunt, 1553–1790, 48
adage, feudal, 167
adhaesit pavimento, 102
adjectives,
    applied to witnesses, 236–37
    insufficient for comprehensive principle, 150
adjournment, application for, 62, 104, 332
administration of estate. *See* will.
Admiral of the Fleet, judgment delivered by, 43
admissions. *See* evidence.
Adulterine Gild, 271
adultery,
    attempt to repudiate condonation, 275
    committing while in witness-box, 271
    comparing wife to whore, 271
    denying though caught in act, 271
advocacy,
    by counsel, 99–101, 109
    coherent expression, 103
    good and bad, examples of, 108

judicial dissatisfaction, 114
judicial interruptions, 113–15
legal skills, 93, 94, 102, 103
length of speeches,
    aquam dare, 109
    aquam perdere, 109
    counsel exonerated, 161
    water clock (clepsydra), use of, 109
persuasion, 103, 105, 106
receptiveness, 106
styles, 99–101
witness, preventing perjury of, 233–34
    See also argument.
Advocate's Devil, The, 138
affidare mulierem, 277
affidavits, criticism of, 242
agent, 220
    as word, abused, 197
    definition, 197
    donkey as, 197
    fraud involving, 356, 357
    superior to bailiff, 283
    untrue statements, 356, 357
Albert, Prince. *See* Prince Albert.
Alderney, 151, 152
Alderson B., 83, 84, 127, 229
    expressio veri may be *suggestio falsi*, 355–56
    particular inconvenience, 259
Alexander the Great, 106
alphabet, replacement encouraged by George Bernard Shaw, 307
Alvanley C.J., Lord. *See* Arden M.R., Sir Richard.
Alverstone C.J., Lord, 36
America. *See* United States.
American Bar Association, 266
American Civil War, 378
American War of Independence, British policy in, 373
Amicus Humoriae: An Anthology of Legal Humor, 179

omitted word in Lord's Prayer, 371–72
verdict given under, 124
See also error.
mistress,
Lord Thurlow's living with, 10
Sir Edward Sugden L.C., marriage to,
10–11
visit to, as defence against driving under
influence charge, 125
misuse of power, 146
Molloy, P., 344
Monboddo, Lord, 59
money,
argument against contractual payability
of, 106–07
champions hired for, 64
deposited for safekeeping, 93, 94
executor's former right to retain for debt
owed, 221
paid under mistake of law, 267–68
prostitutes' customers assured of
worth, 272
recovered by trickery, 94
monkeys ("munkeys"), 298, 299
Monmouth, Duke of, 43, 332
Moody J., 212
mop, causing panic in court, 60
More, Sir Thomas,
as Lord Chancellor, 1
averia de withernam, 6
student in Flanders, 7
withernam, 6, 7
Morison, Samuel Eliot, 275
Morris, Lord, 363
Morris K.C., Sir Harold, 97
mortgage bill of sale, invalidity, 162
Morton, G.A., 96
Morton J., 173
Moses, first law reporter, 175
most important person in a court-
room, 111
motorway, common law not a, 143
Moulton (Q.C., L.J., and Lord), Fletcher,
245, 321, 323
arguments too refined, 322
cases argued by junior counsel, 86
mules, diapers required for, 297
Multitude of Counsellours, 27
Munster Circuit, The, 199

murder, 172
acquittal, 68–70
appeal of, 63, 66, 67
autrefois acquit, 68, 70, 71
drowning, 269
imprisoning with a small-pox victim, by,
67
insurance proceeds as motive, 269
judges, of, 37–38, 39–42
rattlesnakes as means of, 269
report of, in Law French, 172
sentence of burning for poisoning, 67
term of art, 197
Murder Trial of Judge Peel, The, 41
Murdock C.J., 375
murmuring a judge, 56
Murphy J., 273
Murray, David, 107
musk-cat, 298, 299
Musmannodicts, 206–09
joys of the ear, 209
powers of darkness metaphors, 208
sea-going, 206–07
transport by land or air, 207
water-related, 206–07
Musmanno J., Michael Angelo, 205, 209
attempting to compel publication of
judgment, 177–78
geographically and literarily diverse
adamant dissent, 275
"Tropic of Cancer" worthless trash, 275
My Own Way, 39, 77

name,
changed to "Carbolic Smoke Ball", 317,
318
company, 317, 318
invented, 326
medicines, commercial, inventive,
199–200
own, right to use, 325
similar, restraint on, 325–26
trade, 326, 327
well-known English cases, 318
"narrowed to a filament", 342
natural justice, 113
"Neck Verse", 329
negligence,
boundaries obscure, 358